LANDSCAPE GARDENING
AND
RURAL ARCHITECTURE

LANDSCAPE GARDENING
AND
RURAL ARCHITECTURE

A. J. DOWNING

With a New Introduction by
GEORGE B. TATUM

DOVER PUBLICATIONS, INC.
NEW YORK

Introduction copyright © 1991 by George B. Tatum.
Published in Canada by General Publishing Company, Ltd., 30 Lesmill Road,
Don Mills, Toronto, Ontario.
Published in the United Kingdom by Constable and Company, Ltd., 3 The
Lanchesters, 162–164 Fulham Palace Road, London W6 9ER.

This Dover edition, first published in 1991, is an unabridged and unaltered
republication (except for the correction of errors in the numbering of illustrations, and the modification of the pagination of the frontmatter) of the seventh
edition of *A Treatise on the Theory and Practice of Landscape Gardening,
Adapted to North America; With a View to the Improvement of Country
Residences*, originally published by Orange Judd Agricultural Book Publisher,
New York, in 1865.
The Dover edition also contains a new introduction prepared especially for
this reprint by George B. Tatum.

Manufactured in the United States of America
Dover Publications, Inc., 31 East 2nd Street, Mineola, N.Y. 11501

Library of Congress Cataloging-in-Publication Data

Downing, A. J. (Andrew Jackson), 1815–1852.
    [Treatise on the theory and practice of landscape gardening]
    Landscape gardening and rural architecture / A.J. Downing : with a new
introduction by George B. Tatum.
        p.   cm.
    "Unabridged and (except for the correction of errors in the numbering of
illustrations . . .) unaltered republication of the seventh edition of a treatise on
the theory and practice of landscape gardening, adapted to North America,
with a view to the improvement of country residences, originally published by
Orange Judd Agricultural Book Publisher, New York, in 1865"—T.p. verso.
    Includes index.
    ISBN 0-488-26737-7
    1. Landscape gardening. 2. Landscape architecture. 3. Landscape
gardening—United States. 4. landscape architecture—United
States. 5. Ornamental trees. 6. Ornamental trees—United States.
    I. Title.
SB471.D7   1991
    712—dc20   91-2629
                                                                        CIP

INTRODUCTION TO THE DOVER EDITION

THE PUBLICATION in 1841 of Andrew Jackson Downing's *A Treatise on the Theory and Practice of Landscape Gardening, Adapted to North America; with a View to the Improvement of Country Residences* established its author as the undisputed arbiter of American taste in matters relating to rural architecture and garden design. In fact, so well received was the *Treatise* that Downing promptly turned his attention to additional publishing ventures in the same or related fields: new and considerably expanded editions of the *Treatise* were called for in 1844 and again in 1849, while its author's views on architecture, which had been largely limited to a single chapter in his first book, were given fuller and more specific treatment in *Cottage Residences* (1842, 1847 and 1852) and in *The Architecture of Country Houses* (1850).[1]

Nor did the potential for profit implicit in the newly discovered interests of the emerging middle class go unnoticed by others. Largely to capitalize on Downing's growing popularity, in July 1846 Luther Tucker, the Albany publisher of agricultural periodicals, brought out a new magazine popularly known simply as *The Horticulturist* but more accurately identified in its full title as a *Journal of Rural Art and Rural Taste*.[2] This Downing was persuaded to edit, and to it he contributed a leading article each month, beginning with the first number and continuing until his tragic death in the burning of the Hudson River steamer *Henry Clay*, July 28, 1852, just three months short of his thirty-seventh birthday.[3]

In great part as a result of the success of the *Treatise on Landscape Gardening*, Downing was enabled to develop a thriving practice as a designer of gardens, but his association with architecture was at first limited to the advice contained in his writings and to a very few projects for which he served as consultant. Not until 1850 did he attempt to take a more direct

hand in architectural design and then it was with the assistance
of several English associates, of whom Calvert Vaux and
Frederick Clarke Withers were most notable.

Of the major commissions received by the new firm Downing
had set up in an office wing of his Newburgh residence, the most
important came in the form of an invitation from President
Millard Fillmore to supervise the landscaping of the L-shaped
area between the Capitol and the White House, known then as
the Public Grounds. This was in 1851 and may fairly be considered to have afforded an opportunity to design the first public
park in America, apart from the colonial square or common, and
an amenity that Downing had earlier urged be adopted for New
York City.[4] Its author's untimely death prevented his design for
the Public Grounds from being executed as planned, and much
of the Victorian park that eventually came to occupy the site
was later replaced by the present Mall, beginning in 1901. So it
was that Downing's principal influence on the American scene
continued to be exerted through his writings, an influence that
proved so pervasive that later historians would find "scarcely a
city park . . . or a [rural or suburban] building still standing
from the 1850s and 60s in which his ideas, sometimes distorted
almost beyond recognition, cannot be detected."[5]

As "father" of the public park in America and the first of their
countrymen to practice successfully their profession, Downing
retained the respect and admiration of subsequent generations
of landscape architects.[6] As late as 1915 Bailey's *Standard Cyclopedia of Horticulture* was still claiming that "by many . . .
Downing is considered the greatest single figure in the history
of American horticulture and one of the few persons who can be
said to have had real genius."[7] But the emphasis he came to place
on rural architecture during the latter part of his career inevitably meant that Downing would share in the scorn the early
twentieth century heaped upon its Victorian predecessors.
Writing in the 1920s, a contributor to the popular magazine
House and Garden characterized Downing's architectural designs as having "absolutely no esthetic or architectural merit"
and any of its readers who thought otherwise as clearly "mis-
guided."[8] One who may well have concurred in this opinion was
Frank Albert Waugh, the prominent author and practitioner
who founded the Department of Landscape Architecture at

what is now the University of Massachusetts. At least, when he came to edit the tenth edition of Downing's *Treatise on Landscape Gardening* in 1921, Waugh omitted the section on "Landscape or Rural Architecture" while substituting for it and other portions of the original text a number of the essays Downing had contributed to *The Horticulturist*.

Fortunately, the history of taste suggests that what was once admired is likely to find favor again; the reappraisal of the whole Victorian era that took place following the Second World War inevitably brought new interest in Downing and a reexamination of many aspects of his career. Even details of his early life and training, once accepted as fact, have proved on closer examination to be less than completely accurate. Especially in need of revision—or at least of modification—is the romantic concept of Downing as an "obscure nurseryman,"[9] too poor to obtain the education he desired,[10] who, having "leapt the social barriers"[11] imposed by his "lowly birth," found himself famous almost overnight by reason of the publication of his first book.

Although it was unquestionably the *Treatise on Landscape Gardening* that first established Downing's international reputation, as early as 1832, when he would have been only 17 years old, he had begun publishing notices in agricultural and horticultural periodicals. These, together with his activities as a nurseryman, apparently made him sufficiently well known that by 1838 he could appropriately join with Jesse Buel, publisher of the influential *Cultivator*, and John Torrey, professor of chemistry at Princeton and at the University of the City of New York, in an effort to found the Horticultural Society of the Valley of the Hudson. In this undertaking Downing and his associates were unsuccessful, but the following year when Charles Hovey sought to attract subscribers for his *Magazine of Horticulture* by publishing the names of future contributors, he placed Downing's at the head of a lengthy list.[12] Moreover, even before the *Treatise* had appeared in print, Downing had become associated with Asa Gray, the distinguished Harvard professor of botany, in editing John Lindley's *Theory of Horticulture* as part of an effort by a small group of Americans to advance the study of botany and horticulture in the United States to a level more nearly approaching that in Europe. When the *Treatise* was published in 1841 the United States was still an agricultural nation; if Downing, then in his twenty-sixth year, was not yet widely known outside horticultural and botanical circles, neither could he be accurately described as "obscure." And a similar objection might be made to the view that Downing failed to obtain a college education for lack of funds. To be sure, Downing's father was a wheelwright, who, together with his new wife, about 1800 left Lexington, Massachusetts, for Newburgh, New York, and there a decade later established a successful nursery, which he bequeathed to Andrew and his older brother Charles. Because Andrew was considerably younger than the three other Downing children who lived to maturity, his father was at some pains to provide for his education in a will made a few months before his own death in 1822. Free public education was not available in Newburgh until after the middle of the century, but young Andrew must have attended one or more of the village schools before completing his education at nearby Montgomery Academy, then among the earliest and best institutions of its kind in the state. When Downing left school at the age of sixteen, he was probably motivated not so much by a lack of funds for further education as by impatience to join his older brother in the management of the nursery in which he had a half-interest. During the 1830s few Americans attended college; by the standards of that day, Downing was comparatively well educated, as his writings clearly attest.

When it comes to a more precise estimate of the profitability of the Downing nursery or of Andrew's financial arrangements with his older brother, we can do little more than speculate. What is certain is that in 1837, several years after his own marriage and a year before Andrew's, Charles Downing moved to the outskirts of Newburgh. There on a thirteen-acre site, he built a handsome residence in the popular Greek Revival style. Then, about a year later and on a site adjacent to the nursery and near the small cottage where he was born, Andrew, in turn, began the Tudor villa he illustrated (Fig. 49)* in all editions of his *Treatise on Landscape Gardening*. True, it now appears that the material of Andrew's new house was not cut stone, as once thought, but nonetheless its substantial size and solid

---

*All numbered illustrations referred to are those of the seventh edition that follows.

construction must have set it apart from a majority of its neighbors.[13] Even if some allowance be made for possible dowries from their respective wives, surely there is nothing here to indicate that by the late 1830s either brother was greatly hampered by financial considerations.

Nor can his social standing have proved much of a handicap to young Andrew, as some have suggested. When he dedicated the *Treatise on Landscape Gardening* to "his friend" John Quincy Adams, Downing was, in fact, referring to his wife's greatuncle. Through her mother, Caroline De Wint (De Windt) was the great-granddaughter of John Adams, second president of the United States, and therefore the grandniece of his son, John Quincy Adams, the sixth president. And if Andrew's own background could not be said to quite equal in distinction that of his wife, both his parents came of solid Yankee stock. The Downings had been in New England since the early 1640s, and John Bridge, from whom Eunice Bridge Downing was descended, had had a part in the founding of Harvard College. There is no evidence to suggest that the large De Wint family was anything but pleased when Andrew and Caroline were married on June 7, 1838, at Cedar Grove, the bride's home in Fishkill Landing (now Beacon), directly across the Hudson River from the Downing nursery.

Andrew's practice of wearing his dark hair a trifle long, even for ante-bellum America, doubtless helped confirm the view of those later historians who came to think of him as essentially a "kind, gentle," but perhaps not very effective, young man about whom "we can feel just a little . . . sad."[14] Like many interested in the arts, he may not have had much of a head for business, it is true. But to think of him simply as a "Hudson River aesthete"[15] ignores his development of one of the most extensive nurseries of the period, his success as editor of a popular monthly magazine, and especially his scientific achievements as a leading pomologist with an international reputation. By the time of his death, his *Fruits and Fruit Trees of America*, first published in 1845, had gone through thirteen editions and had sold nearly fifteen thousand copies.[16] By helping to standardize the nomenclature of fruits, it played a significant part in the emergence of New York State—and later of the far West—as major fruit-growing regions of the world. It is therefore not altogether

inappropriate that *Downingia pulchella*, a low bedding plant
having blue, purple or white flowers, is grown principally in the
western states, especially California.

With the advantage of hindsight, several reasons for the
success of Downing's *Treatise on Landscape Gardening* are
easily identified. It was the first book on the subject published
in the United States by an American. Its text was graceful,
even felicitous, while most of its numerous illustrations were
drawn on the woodblock by the New York architect Alexander J.
Davis, arguably the most talented architectural delineator then
practicing, and were engraved by Alexander Anderson, the
first American wood engraver of importance. In combination,
these factors held such attraction that each merits an additional
word of explanation.

In the Historical Sketches (or Notices) that serve as an introduction to his *Treatise on Landscape Gardening*, Downing recognizes as his predecessors in the United States only two men:
Bernard McMahon (M'Mahon), the first American author to
have "treated directly" the English or Modern style of gardening, and André Parmentier, the only "practitioner of . . . note"
to employ the new styles in designs for American clients. With
this assessment modern historians would essentially agree.
Today McMahon is chiefly remembered as the Philadelphia nurseryman to whom Jefferson consigned much of the horticultural
material brought back from the Lewis and Clark Expedition.
But however important his contributions for American horticulture, McMahon was not a talented writer, and the short section
on "The Pleasure, or Flower Garden" he inserted in his *American Gardener's Calendar* (first published in 1806 and numerous
times thereafter) was illustrated with only one plan and cast
in so involved a style that its influence cannot have been
very great.[17]

André-Joseph Ghislain Parmentier, for his part, had come to
New York City from Belgium in 1824 and the following year
established a nursery on 25 acres at the juncture of the Jamaica
and Flatbush roads in Brooklyn. Part of the nursery was laid
out in the English or Natural style, and in a brief, unillustrated
essay inserted in the nursery catalog and revised for publication
in Thomas Fessenden's *New American Gardener* (1828 and
later) Parmentier noted with satisfaction that gardens in Ａ ner-

ica were now beginning to be "treated like natural landscapes, the charms of which are generally injured by any interference of art." Parmentier is said to have received a number of important commissions in the United States and Canada, including that for Dr. David Hosack's 700-acre estate called Hyde Park, which Downing singled out for illustration (Fig. 1) in his *Treatise* and there praised "as one of the finest specimens of the modern style of Landscape Gardening in America" (p. 29). Parmentier's death in 1830 ended his brief career in the United States, leaving it to Downing to publish there the first book devoted to rural architecture and garden design and through it, and his own widespread practice, to lay the foundation for the emergence in his country of the profession that has come to be known as landscape architecture.[18]

In 1839, while still at work on his first book, Downing found in A. J. Davis just the illustrator he needed.[19] Their introduction came through Robert Donaldson, a friend and client of Davis and the owner of Blithewood, which Downing described for his readers as "one of the most charming villa residences in the Union" (p. 30). Although an engraving of Blithewood serves as the frontispiece for the *Treatise on Landscape Gardening*, and *Cottage Residences* is dedicated to its owner in his role as *arbiter elegantiarum*, there is no evidence that Downing had any substantial part in the design of Donaldson's Hudson River estate, as has sometimes been suggested. More certain is that the informal partnership that developed between Downing and Davis over the next decade proved one of those fortunate and mutually beneficial relationships with which the history of art abounds; neither would have been as successful without the other. In the end, so closely attuned did the two men become that it proved possible for Downing to send the roughest of sketches for Davis to redraw for the engraver. And because this assistance was provided at a modest fee, Downing, in return, lost no opportunity to praise the professional qualifications of his friend or to recommend his services to prospective clients. When compared to those of Davis, Downing's drawings are clearly the work of an amateur, but those are mistaken who suppose he was entirely without ability in this regard. Some of the early drawings he sent Davis are competent beyond the ordinary; the artist of a few of the engravings in his books is identified by his own initials; and although, save for the plan of the Washington park, none appear to survive, Downing promised drawings to clients who applied to him for garden designs.

Because he worked with the engraver's tool, or burin—as opposed to the knife employed by the maker of woodcuts—Alexander Anderson is usually identified as a wood engraver, and prints pulled from the blocks he cut by following the drawings Davis had made on their whitened surfaces are customarily referred to as "wood engravings." This is something of a misnomer, however, because, unlike the true engraving, which is an intaglio process by which images are created from lines *incised* on a metal plate, in the wood engraving the printed lines are produced from the *raised* surface. In this they resemble woodcuts and therefore printers' type, a significant advantage in that text and illustrations could now be printed together, instead of separately, as in the case of earlier books that relied on illustrations produced by lithography (for example, Davis' own *Rural Residences* of 1838) or on metal engraving (as in the case of Asher Benjamin's popular architectural books). Moreover, Downing's *Treatise* was probably printed on the steam press then coming into widespread use and, instead of the traditional and expensive leather, was bound in cloth with gilt lettering and decoration, the so-called "publishers' binding."[20] The result was a moderately priced book produced in relatively large editions and well suited to the growing numbers of middle-class Americans whom Downing had succeeded in interesting in the appearance of their homes and gardens. In this way the *Treatise* had a substantial impact on the publishing trade and did much to form Americans' concept of what a book on architecture and gardening ought to be. But, however important, priority in its field, an innovative format, a graceful style and unusually effective illustrations are not in themselves likely to have been sufficient to inspire the continuing demand the *Treatise on Landscape Gardening* has enjoyed. For this, we must look to Downing's text and its two revisions, noted earlier.

Despite suggestions to the contrary, attempts to show that the substantial changes made in the editions of 1844 and 1849 are indicative of any significant evolution in the author's thought are likely to prove unsuccessful. Not only was the time between editions comparatively short, but even more important, most of the basic principles Downing advocated had become established over the course of many years and by the early nineteenth century were widely accepted throughout much of Europe. Downing's achievement lay not so much in the originality of his thought as in his ability to weld abstruse English theory from a variety of sources into a comprehensive program that proved intelligible and attractive to practical Americans, hitherto largely unfamiliar with the subject. In a way, this estimate of its author's contribution finds expression in the full title of the *Treatise on Landscape Gardening*; if the words "theory and practice" deliberately borrow from the titles of two books by Humphry Repton,[21] Downing was careful to assure prospective readers that what he was offering had been especially "adapted to North America."

Anyone who pursues the numerous references to English theorists such as William Shenstone, Archibald Alison, Richard Payne Knight or Thomas Whateley, in which the *Treatise* abounds, should gain a very respectable understanding of the origins and development of eighteenth-century esthetic theory. But for more practical advice Downing turned to the books of the late Humphry Repton, who at the time of his death in 1818 was the leading landscape gardener in England, and to those of his own older contemporary John Claudius Loudon, who, by Downing's time, had largely given up active practice in order to devote his full attention to writing about landscape gardening and related subjects. In the Preface common to all editions of the *Treatise*, Loudon is referred to as "the most distinguished gardening author of the age" (p. 10); a number of the illustrations in later sections of the book are based more or less directly on those in Loudon's publications; and the lengthy description of an English suburban cottage that appears as Appendix II in the early editions of the *Treatise* is taken, with permission, from Loudon's *Gardener's Magazine*.[22] Although it was the summer of 1850 before Downing was able to make his first trip abroad and to see for himself the principal English gardens, his admiration for things British seems, if anything, to have increased as his career progressed. The English architects he chose to assist him were mentioned earlier, and English architectural designs appear in *The Horticulturist* with increasing regularity.[23]

Only a few weeks after the publication of the first edition of the *Treatise*, Downing wrote his friend John Jay Smith in Philadelphia that he was hard at work on a revision that he hoped by "copious additions and improvements" to make "the standard work on the subject for [the] country."[24] To that end, he completely recast and greatly expanded the first, or historical section, which serves as a kind of introduction in all editions, and there introduced ten engravings of houses and grounds he considered worthy of special notice.[25] As was to be expected, Downing is at his best when discussing those aspects of landscape gardening that were grounded in his practical experience as a nurseryman and gardener. Accordingly, the sections dealing with deciduous trees (IV), evergreens (V), vines and climbing plants (VI) and "embellishments" (X)—which here include garden ornaments, flower beds, seats, arbors, bridges, rockworks and the like—are well-written, practical expositions of the subject that are repeated, essentially unchanged, in both revisions of the *Treatise* made during the author's lifetime.

When he comes to deal with the "beauties and principles of the art" (Section II) and to apply these, in turn, to plant materials (Section III), to the treatment and the formation of walks (Section VII) and to the handling of water (Section VIII), Downing is clearly much less comfortable. Throughout the more or less extensive revisions of these sections, he appears to be trying for a synthesis with which he is satisfied and that he can readily justify to others. To help clarify for his readers (and perhaps for himself) the all-important difference between the Beautiful (characterized by smoothness, regularity and gradual variation) and the Picturesque (marked by roughness, irregularity and sudden variation), with the second edition Downing introduces into Section II the comparative views (Figs. 13 and 14) often reproduced in discussions of his work and perhaps the most original and imaginative of the numerous illustrations in the *Treatise*.[26]

Recognizing that architectural components are an important part of most landscape designs, Downing devoted Section IX of the *Treatise* to the subject of rural architecture. While admitting that classical styles might do well enough for public buildings in urban settings, he considered them generally unsuited for domestic structures, especially the rural ones with which he was exclusively concerned. Depending on the character of the site, the styles considered most appropriate for rural architecture turn out to be the modern Italian, the Castellated, the Tudor, the Elizabethan and the rural Gothic. To this roster, the second edition adds the Swiss and the Bracketed, the latter reputedly derived in part from the Swiss but probably owing most to designs of Davis and as near as Downing ever came to developing anything that could be considered an original American style.[27] By way of making clear the characteristics of the various styles and their proper relationship to rural scenery, Downing illustrated about a dozen houses, most of them owned by prominent Americans, and including his own Tudor residence in Newburgh, noted earlier.

In writing of the various editions of the *Treatise on Landscape Gardening* published during Downing's lifetime, it is possible to speak only of the first, second and fourth. No copies of a third edition are known, and it has long been accepted that none was published. Why this should be so has never been satisfactorily explained. It might be noted, however, that about 1846 or 1847, when Downing could have been expected to be busy preparing a third edition, he was experiencing serious personal and financial problems about which few details have come to light but which may have had a bearing on his decision to sell the Newburgh nursery late in 1846. Whatever the reason, when at last the second revision of the *Treatise* appeared in 1849, it was designated the "fourth" edition. This, in turn, was reprinted in 1850 and again thereafter, with no major changes, every year for six years, beginning in 1852. The last five of these reprintings the publisher labeled a "fifth" edition, but all bear the 1849 copyright and are essentially unaltered in form and content. Only with the sixth edition of 1859 do we encounter important changes in the *Treatise* as Downing had last revised it three years before his death.

The editor of the sixth edition of the *Treatise on Landscape Gardening*, here republished for at least the fourth time,[28] was Henry Winthrop Sargent, whom Downing once referred to as "the best friend I have in the world"[29] and to whom he dedicated his last book, *The Architecture of Country Houses*. As his name perhaps suggests, Sargent was born in New England. A native of Boston, where he continued to spend most of his winters, his personal fortune proved sufficient to enable him to purchase as

his summer home an estate of 22 acres on the east bank of the
Hudson in what is now Beacon, New York, and to retire there in
1841, when he would have been but 31 years old. For the remainder
of his life, Sargent devoted himself to making Wodenethe
not only a model rural retreat but also a kind of horticultural
station where he could experiment with unusual varieties of
trees imported from all over the world.[30]

Much earlier in England, both Humphry Repton and J. C.
Loudon had differed from some of their contemporaries—and
most particularly from their predecessor Lancelot (nicknamed
"Capability") Brown—in favoring the introduction of exotic
plant materials and a more formal garden design near the
house, an approach Loudon came to think of as a distinctive
style he proposed to call "Gardenesque." After the first edition
of the *Treatise*, Downing does not discuss the Gardenesque by
name, but a number of his designs include elements of the style,
which was also gaining favor with many well-to-do Americans,
including Sargent. In time, Wodenethe became famous not only
for vistas that terminated in spectacular views of the Hudson
River, but also for its formal walks and gardens.

In editing the *Treatise on Landscape Gardening* Sargent
followed fairly closely the 1849 edition. He did, however, drop
some dozen plates and added about half that number. His own
increasing regard for the formal garden perhaps encouraged
him to omit descriptions—not always complimentary—of the
gardens of the ancient world as well as many of Downing's
references to English authors, a total of perhaps a thousand
lines or about thirty pages. Of the five appendices in the earlier
editions, Sargent retains only two: those dealing with the transplanting
of trees and the treatment of lawns.

Shortening Downing's text also made it easier for Sargent to
add his own Supplement of about forty-five pages. Many fine
country seats had been created since Downing's day, and Sargent
lists over two dozen of these, including his own Wodenethe
and the estate of his kinsman Horatio Hollis Hunnewell at
Wellesley, Massachusetts. Perhaps even more than Wodenethe,
which is usually considered to have inspired it, Hunnewell's
terraced garden clearly illustrates the growing popularity of
Loudon's Gardenesque style. Both it and Wodenethe are described
by Sargent in some detail and pictured in handsome
engravings. Still other sections of the Supplement are appro-

priately devoted to New York's Central Park and to Llewellyn Park at West Orange, New Jersey, one of the earliest American suburbs.[31] Although Downing had been killed just prior to the creation of both park and suburb, both followed the general principles he advocated. Indeed, together with Frederick Law Olmsted, the designer of Central Park was Downing's former partner, Calvert Vaux, and while Llewellyn Park was laid out by Eugene Baumann, a recent emigrant from Europe, both he and the developer had the advice of Downing's long-time associate, A. J. Davis, who designed many of the Park's first houses and other architectural features.

Except for adding several full-page engravings, Sargent leaves the sections of the *Treatise* dealing with deciduous and evergreen trees much as Downing had written them. This permits him to reserve for the Supplement his discussion of some of the newer trees and shrubs, both deciduous and evergreen, which is, of course, his overriding interest. In addition to helpful descriptions of each variety, the reader is provided with an elaborate table showing which evergreens could be expected to be hardy in a variety of different areas.

Sargent's son is said to have always denied that Downing had any direct hand in the design of the grounds at Wodenethe, but there can be no doubt that it was he who inspired the elder Sargent's interest in arboriculture. Predictably, most of the exotic trees planted at Wodenethe failed to survive for long, a lesson that was not lost on the owner's cousin, Charles Sprague Sargent, when he came to apply what he had learned at Wodenethe in the establishment of the Arnold Arboretum, today considered by many the finest tree museum in the world.

In 1921 what remained of Wodenethe was purchased for use as a sanitarium, but Hunnewell's garden at Wellesley continues to look much as pictured by Sargent. Today its admirers, like all Americans who live in an attractive suburb, visit an arboretum, or spend the afternoon in a large urban park, are the beneficiaries of a landscape tradition begun a century and a half ago with Andrew Jackson Downing and fostered by the first book of its kind, *A Treatise on the Theory and Practice of Landscape Gardening, Adapted to North America.*

GEORGE B. TATUM

Old Lyme, Conn.
Sept. 1, 1990

NOTES

1. The editions noted here are only those that contain substantial revisions and that appeared during Downing's lifetime; for a more complete list, including reprintings, *see* Henry-Russel Hitchcock, *American Architectural Books*, Minneapolis, 1962.
2. Copies of *The Horticulturist* are now comparatively rare, but the year following Downing's death George P. Putnam & Company republished the most important of Downing's editorials in a volume entitled *Rural Essays*, which was reprinted at least half a dozen times thereafter, most recently by the Da Capo Press in 1974. The "Memoir" of Downing by the writer and editor George William Curtis (1824–1892) that serves as an introduction to *Rural Essays* is the source for much of the information found in later biographical notices, including a number of minor, but troublesome, errors.
3. Downing was born Oct. 31, 1815. For a fuller discussion of his life and work than is possible in a brief introductory essay, *see* the nine papers that comprise *Prophet with Honor: The Career of Andrew Jackson Downing, 1815–1852*, Washington, D.C., 1989, edited by E. B. MacDougall and G. B. Tatum.
4. *See* David Schuyler, "The Washington Park and Downing's Legacy to Public Landscape Design," *Prophet with Honor*, 291–311. Some ten architectural designs provided by Downing and his English collaborators during 1851 and 1852 were illustrated and discussed in *Villas and Cottages*, the "pattern book" published by Calvert Vaux (1824–1895) in 1857, enlarged in a second edition in 1864 and reissued several times thereafter, including a modern reprint of the first edition by Da Capo in 1968 and of the second by Dover in 1970. Like Vaux, with whom he practiced architecture from time to time, Frederick Clarke Withers (1828–1901) remained in the United States, where he designed a number of important buildings in the late Victorian and Gothic

Revival styles; *see* Francis R. Kowsky, *The Architecture of Frederick Clarke Withers*, Middletown, Conn., 1980.

5. Russell Lynes, "The Smiling Lawns and Tasteful Cottages of Andrew Jackson Downing," *Harper's Bazaar*, Sept. 1954, 200.

6. "Andrew Jackson Downing, Father of American Parks," *The Park International*, July 1920, 42–48. *See also* Richard Schermerhorn, Jr., "Andrew Jackson Downing, the First American Landscape Architect," *House and Garden*, Aug. 1909, 43ff. In his own time Downing would have been known as a "landscape gardener," or possibly as a "rural architect," a title he appears to have chosen for himself. Not until the 1860s does "landscape architect" begin to be used to describe those who create designs in open space, and then the designation seems to have originated with Downing's sometime partner, Calvert Vaux.

7. Wilhelm Miller in L. H. Bailey, *Standard Cyclopedia of Horticulture*, New York, 1915, III, 1572–1573.

8. Richard Pratt, "In the Days of Downing," *House and Garden*, Dec. 1927, 102, 103.

9. Sarah Lewis Pattee, "Andrew Jackson Downing and His Influence on Landscape Architecture in America," *Landscape Architecture*, 19 (1928–29), 79.

10. Russell Lynes, *The Tastemakers*, New York, 1954, 22.

11. Carl Carmer, "The Lordly Hudson," *American Heritage*, Dec. 1958, 105. *See also* Carmer, *The Hudson*, New York, 1939, 240.

12. *The Magazine of Horticulture*, 5 (1839), iii.

13. A decade after its completion, the Downings' Newburgh residence was described by a visitor as being constructed of "sepia-colored sandstone" (Fredrika Bremer, *Homes of the New World*, New York, 1853, I, 19), a description that has generally been accepted uncritically by modern historians. In 1989, however, Mills Lane published a hitherto overlooked letter in which Downing suggests that the New York plasterer George Gill be engaged to stucco the exterior of the Alabama capitol, adding, by way of recommendation, that it was Gill who had "stuccoed the exterior of [his] own house" (*Architecture of the Old South: Mississippi & Alabama*, New York, 1989, 89). Much altered, the house built by Charles Downing (1802–1885) still stands at 3 Beech

Street in the section of greater Newburgh known as Balmville, but Andrew's Tudor villa was demolished about 1920.

14. Pratt, *House and Garden*, 102, 136.
15. Carl Carmer so titles Chapter 21 in *The Hudson*, New York, 1939.
16. Don C. Seitz, "Best Sellers of the Fifties," *The Publishers' Weekly*, Jan. 28, 1922, 183.
17. About 1796 Bernard McMahon (c.1775–1816) had emigrated from Ireland to Philadelphia and there established a thriving commercial garden and seed business.
18. Nothing remains of the nursery André Parmentier (1780–1830) established in Brooklyn, while time and later changes have obscured much of his work at Hyde Park. For brief, but helpful, discussions of Parmentier's career, *see* the *Brooklyn Botanic Garden Record*, Jan. 1926, 10–15, and Ann Leighton, *American Gardens of the Nineteenth Century*, Amherst, 1987, 124–132.
19. For the definitive discussion of Downing's relationship to Davis, *see* Jane B. Davies, "Davis and Downing: Collaborators in the Picturesque," *Prophet with Honor*, 81–123.
20. In the first edition of the *Treatise on Landscape Gardening* all the illustrations are printed with the text. However, in order to assure a better impression, later editions have many of the most important wood engravings printed separately on heavier stock. The place of Downing's books in the history of American publishing is more fully discussed by Charles B. Wood III, "The New 'Pattern Books' and the Role of the Agricultural Press," *Prophet with Honor*, 183–186.
21. *Observations on the Theory and Practice of Landscape Gardening* (1803) and *Fragments on the Theory and Practice of Landscape Gardening* (1816).
22. Downing has been called "the American Loudon," and much like Downing, J. C. Loudon (1783–1843) was largely ignored by modern historians until comparatively late in the twentieth century; *see* Melanie Louise Simo, *Loudon and the Landscape*, New Haven, 1988.
23. In addition to serving as one of the editors of the American edition of John Lindley's *Theory of Horticulture*, noted earlier, Downing edited the American editions of two other English publications: Jane (Mrs. J. C.) Loudon's *Gardening*

for Ladies (1846) and George Wightwick's *Hints to Young Architects* (1847 and later).

24. Letter of Dec. 3, 1841, J. Jay Smith papers, The Library Company of Philadelphia, on deposit at The Historical Society of Pennsylvania.

25. Section I in the first edition of the *Treatise* is unillustrated. To the ten engravings added in the second edition, the edition of 1849 adds five more.

26. Although Downing does not appear to be familiar with it, the classic definition of the Beautiful is found in Edmund Burke's *A Philosophical Enquiry into the Origin of our Ideas of the Sublime and Beautiful*, first published in 1757 and revised in 1759. A number of writers contributed to the concept of the Picturesque, but the clearest statement of its distinctive qualities, and one quoted by Downing, was that of Uvedale Price, *An Essay on the Picturesque*, first published in 1794 and later revised and expanded.

27. To illustrate his Bracketed mode, in the second edition of the *Treatise* Downing borrowed a design for a house that serves as Figure 40 in the 1842 edition of his *Cottage Residences*. Later editions of the *Treatise* substitute for this the engraving of a garden seat that originally appeared as Figure 14 in Appendix II, and which continues to be repeated there in all editions that retain this portion of the original.

28. The addition of another plate hardly justified calling the reprinting of 1865 a "seventh" edition. In subsequent reprintings of the *Treatise* the date appears to be omitted and editions are simply labeled "new." That of about 1875 contains a short second supplement, also by Sargent, which describes briefly new trees introduced between 1859 and 1875.

29. In a letter to John Jay Smith dated Oct. 1, 1847, collection of The Library Company of Philadelphia, now on deposit in The Historical Society of Pennsylvania. Downing was asking for a letter introducing Sargent to the Queen's ranger at Windsor Park.

30. J. E. Spingarn, "Henry Winthrop Sargent and the Early History of Landscape Gardening and Ornamental Horticulture in Dutchess County, New York," *Year Book*, Dutchess County Historical Society, 1937; reprinted in

slightly abbreviated form and with additional illustrations as "Henry Winthrop Sargent and the Landscape Tradition at Wodenethe," *Landscape Architecture*, Oct. 1938, 24–39. Sargent should be especially remembered by the residents of American suburbs, for it was he who introduced from England the modern lawnmower.

31. Jane B. Davies, "Llewellyn Park in West Orange, New Jersey," *Antiques*, Jan. 1975, 142–157.

A TREATISE

ON THE

THEORY AND PRACTICE

OF

LANDSCAPE GARDENING,

ADAPTED TO

North America;

WITH A VIEW TO THE

IMPROVEMENT OF COUNTRY RESIDENCES.

COMPRISING

HISTORICAL NOTICES AND GENERAL PRINCIPLES OF THE ART,
DIRECTIONS FOR LAYING OUT GROUNDS AND ARRANGING PLANTATIONS, THE
DESCRIPTION AND CULTIVATION OF HARDY TREES, DECORATIVE
ACCOMPANIMENTS OF THE HOUSE AND GROUNDS,
THE FORMATION OF
PIECES OF ARTIFICIAL WATER, FLOWER GARDENS, ETC.

WITH

REMARKS ON RURAL ARCHITECTURE.

BY THE LATE A. J. DOWNING, ESQ.

SEVENTH EDITION,

ENLARGED, REVISED, AND NEWLY ILLUSTRATED.

WITH A SUPPLEMENT,

CONTAINING SOME REMARKS ABOUT COUNTRY PLACES, AND THE BEST METHODS OF MAKING
THEM; ALSO, AN ACCOUNT OF THE NEWER DECIDUOUS AND EVERGREEN PLANTS,
LATELY INTRODUCED INTO CULTIVATION, BOTH HARDY AND HALF-HARDY.

BY

HENRY WINTHROP SARGENT.

————— • ◆ • —————

New-York:

ORANGE JUDD AGRICULTURAL BOOK PUBLISHER,
41 PARK ROW.

—

1865.

[original title page]

TO

JOHN QUINCY ADAMS, LL.D.,

EX-PRESIDENT OF THE UNITED STATES;

THE LOVER OF RURAL PURSUITS,

AS WELL AS

THE DISTINGUISHED PATRIOT, STATESMAN,

AND SAGE;

THIS VOLUME

BY PERMISSION,

IS RESPECTFULLY AND AFFECTIONATELY

DEDICATED,

BY HIS FRIEND,

THE AUTHOR.

PREFACE

TO THE FOURTH EDITION.

IT is even more gratifying to the author of this work to know, from actual observation, that the public taste in Rural Embellishment has, within a few years past, made the most rapid progress in this country, than to feel assured by the call for a fourth edition, that his own imperfect labors for the accomplishment of that end have been most kindly appreciated.

In the present edition considerable alterations and amendments have been made in some portions—especially in that section relating to the nature of the Beautiful and the Picturesque. The difference among critics regarding natural expression and its reproduction in Landscape Gardening, has led him more carefully to examine this part of the subject, in order, if possible, to present it in the clearest and most definite manner.

The whole work has also been revised, and more copiously illustrated, and is now offered in a more complete form than in any previous edition.

A. J. D.

Newburgh, New York, Jan. 1849.

PREFACE.

A TASTE for rural improvements of every description is advancing silently, but with great rapidity in this country. While yet in the far west the pioneer constructs his rude hut of logs for a dwelling, and sweeps away with his axe the lofty forest trees that encumber the ground, in the older portions of the Union, bordering the Atlantic, we are surrounded by all the luxuries and refinements that belong to an old and long cultivated country. Within the last ten years, especially, the evidences of the growing wealth and prosperity of our citizens have become apparent in the great increase of elegant cottage and villa residences on the banks of our noble rivers, along our rich valleys, and wherever nature seems to invite us by her rich and varied charms.

In all the expenditure of means in these improvements, amounting in the aggregate to an immense sum, professional talent is seldom employed in Architecture or Landscape Gardening, but almost every man fancies himself an amateur, and endeavors to plan and arrange his own residence. With but little practical knowledge, and few correct principles for his guidance, it is not surprising that we witness much incongruity and great waste of time and money. Even those who are familiar with foreign works on the subject in question labor under many obstacles in practice, which grow out of the difference in our soil and climate, or our social and political position.

These views have so often presented themselves to me of late, and have been so frequently urged by persons desiring advice, that I have ventured to prepare the present volume, in the hope of supplying, in some degree, the desideratum so much felt at present. While we have treatises, in abundance, on the various departments of the arts and sciences, there has not appeared even a single essay on the elegant art of Landscape Gardening. Hundreds of individuals who wish to ornament their grounds and embellish their places, are at a loss how to proceed, from the want of some *leading principles*, with the knowledge of which they would find it comparatively easy to produce delightful and satisfactory results.

In the following pages I have attempted to trace out such principles, and to suggest practicable methods of embellishing our Rural Residences, on a scale commensurate to the views and means of our proprietors. While I have availed myself of the works of European authors, and especially those of Britain, where Landscape Gardening was first raised to the rank of a fine art, I have also endeavored to adapt my suggestions especially to this country and to the peculiar wants of its inhabitants.

As a people descended from the English stock, we inherit much of the ardent love of rural life and its pursuits which belongs to that nation ; but our peculiar position, in a new world that required a population full of enterprise and energy to subdue and improve its vast territory, has, until lately, left but little time to cultivate a taste for Rural Embellishment. But in the older states, as wealth has accumulated, the country become populous, and society more fixed in its character, a return to those simple and fascinating enjoyments to be found in country life and rural pursuits, is witnessed on every side. And to this innate feeling, out of which grows a strong attachment to natal soil, we must look for a counterpoise to the great tendency towards constant change, and the restless spirit of emigration, which form part of our national character ; and which, though to a certain extent highly necessary to our national prosperity, are, on the other hand, opposed to social and domestic happiness. " In the midst of the continual movement which agitates a democratic community," says the most philosophical writer who has yet discussed our institutions, " the tie which unites one generation to another is relaxed or broken ; every man

PREFACE. 9

readily loses the trace of the ideas of his forefathers, or takes no care about them."

The love of country is inseparably connected with the *love of home.* Whatever, therefore, leads man to assemble the comforts and elegancies of life around his habitation, tends to increase local attachments, and render domestic life more delightful; thus not only augmenting his own enjoyment, but strengthening his patriotism, and making him a better citizen. And there is no employment or recreation which affords the mind greater or more permanent satisfaction, than that of cultivating the earth and adorning our own property. "God Almighty first planted a garden; and, indeed, it is the purest of human pleasures," says Lord Bacon. And as the first man was shut out from the *garden,* in the cultivation of which no alloy was mixed with his happiness, the desire to return to it seems to be implanted by nature, more or less strongly, in every heart.

In Landscape Gardening the country gentleman of leisure finds a resource of the most agreeable nature. While there is no more rational pleasure than that derived from its practice by him, who

" Plucks life's roses in his quiet fields,"

the enjoyment drawn from it (unlike many other amusements) is unembittered by the after recollection of pain or injury inflicted on others, or the loss of moral rectitude. In rendering his home more beautiful, he not only contributes to the happiness of his own family, but improves the taste, and adds loveliness to the country at large. There is, perhaps, something exclusive in the taste for some of the fine arts. A collection of pictures, for example, is comparatively shut up from the world, in the private gallery. But the sylvan and floral collections,— the groves and gardens, which surround the country residence of the man of taste,—are confined by no barriers narrower than the blue heaven above and around them. The taste and the treasures, gradually, but certainly, creep beyond the nominal boundaries of the estate, and re-appear in the pot of flowers in the window, or the luxuriant, blossoming vines which clamber over the porch of the humblest cottage by the way side.

In the present volume I have sought, by rendering familiar to the reader most of the beautiful sylvan materials of the art, and by describing their peculiar effects in Landscape Gardening, to encourage a taste among general readers. And I have also endeavored to place before the amateur such directions and guiding principles as, it is hoped, will assist him materially in laying out his grounds and arranging the general scenery of his residence.

The lively interest of late manifested in Rural Architecture, and its close connexion with Landscape Gardening, have induced me to devote a portion of this work to the consideration of buildings in rural scenery.

I take pleasure in acknowledging my obligations and returning thanks to my valued correspondent, J. C. Loudon, Esq., F. L. S., etc., of London, the most distinguished gardening author of the age, for the illustrations and description of the English Suburban Cottage in the Appendix; to the several gentlemen in this country who have kindly furnished me with plans or drawings of their residences ; and to A. J. Davis, Esq., of New York, and J Notman, Esq., of Philadelphia, architects, for architectural drawings and descriptions.

PREFACE TO SIXTH EDITION.

ALTHOUGH our advance in rural life has not attained, and may never reach, the extent mentioned by Mr. DOWNING, in his account of his visit to Woburn Abbey, where he says, " there are 20,000 country houses in England, each larger than the President's house at Washington;" yet our progress has been very great—partly, perhaps, from the increasing discomfort and expense of our large cities, and the great facilities which our numerous railways and steamers offer to business persons to reside permanently in the country ; but more, let us hope, from an improving taste, and love for rural life, which is always one of the agreeable and graceful accompaniments of increasing civilization.

As a country advances in age, she improves in a taste for all the elegant and artistic pursuits of life, which naturally follow in the train of wealth and refinement. The sword is turned into the pruning-hook, while " *arma cedunt togæ.*"

If one could compare the extremely crude condition of our rural knowledge, upon the first appearance of this book, with the vast progress since made, both in the useful and ornamental cultivation of the soil, it would seem difficult to realize that a nation could move with such giant strides. Still, though much has been done, much yet remains to do. Those who have already put their hand to the plough, do not desire to turn back, they wish only to know how to go on ; want of further information, like the cry of Ajax,

" Give me to see—"

pervades the whole land.

" What shall I plant?" seems one of the great in-
quiries, in attempting to answer which, the Editor of this
New Edition has endeavored to give a list of such of the
newer trees and shrubs as have come into notice within
the past ten years, with such descriptions of their habits
and character as his own information, together with the
experience of others (both, he regrets to say, very meagre), will enable him to give.

With regard to the acclimatizing of Evergreens, he
would have preferred to have had the experience of
another year, in order to test still further certain varieties, as yet comparatively untried ; but perhaps some
future edition may enable him to do this.

In conclusion, he would beg to acknowledge the assistance he has derived, in the identification and classification
of new and doubtful varieties, from Mr. Gordon's excellent work on "The Pinetum," and also from the very
complete and thorough "Traite Général des Conifères,"
par M. Carrière.

To those gentlemen, in this country, who have given
him the result of their experience in acclimatizing Evergreens, he desires also to make his acknowledgments.

H. W. S.

WODENETHE, FISHKILL LANDING, DUCHESS CO., }
  New York, January, 1859.   }

CONTENTS.

SECTION I.

HISTORICAL SKETCHES.

OBJECTS of the art. Origin of the modern and natural style. Influence of the English poets and writers. Examples of the art abroad. Landscape Gardening in North America, and examples now existing.

SECTION II.

BEAUTIES OF LANDSCAPE GARDENING.

Capacities of the art. The beauties of the ancient style. The Beautiful and the Picturesque. Nature and principles of Landscape Gardening as an imitative art. The Production of Beautiful Landscape. Of Picturesque do. Simple beauty of the art. The principles of Unity, Harmony, and Variety.

SECTION III.

WOOD AND PLANTATIONS.

The beauty of trees in rural embellishments. Pleasure resulting from their cultivation. Plantations in the ancient style. In the modern style. Grouping trees. Arrangement and grouping in the Graceful school. In the Picturesque school. Illustrations in planting villa, ferme ornée, and cottage grounds. General classification of trees as to forms, with leading characteristics of each class.

SECTION IV.

DECIDUOUS ORNAMENTAL TREES.

The history and description of all the finest hardy deciduous trees. Remarks on their effects in Landscape Gardening, individually and in composition ; their cultivation, etc.

SECTION V.

EVERGREEN ORNAMENTAL TREES.

The history and description of all the finest hardy evergreen trees. Remarks on their effects in Landscape Gardening, individually and in composition. Their cultivation, etc.

APPENDIX.

NOTES on transplanting trees. Reasons for frequent failures in removing large trees. Directions for performing this operation. Preparing trees for removal. Transplanting evergreens.

On the treatment of Lawns. Use of machines for mowing the Lawn.

SUPPLEMENT.

INDEX.

LIST OF ILLUSTRATIONS.

Drawn by A.J.Davis.

Engraved by R.Jordan.

VIEW IN THE GROUNDS AT BLITHEWOOD, DUTCHESS CO. N.Y.

THE RESIDENCE OF ROBERT DONALDSON, ESQ.

ESSAY ON LANDSCAPE GARDENING.

SECTION I.

HISTORICAL SKETCHES.

Objects of the Art. Sketch of the rise and progress of the Modern style. Influence of the English poets and writers. Examples of the Art abroad. Landscape Gardening in North America, and examples now existing.

> " L'un à nos yeux présente
> D'un dessein régulier l'ordonnance imposante,
> Prête aux champs des beautés qu'ils ne connaissaient pas,
> D'une pompe étrangère embellit leur appas,
> Donne aux arbres des lois, aux ondes des entraves,
> Et, despote orgueilleux, brille entouré d'esclaves ;
> Son air est moins riant et plus majestueux
> *L'autre*, de la nature amant respectueux,
> L'orne sans la farder, traite avec indulgence
> Ses caprices charmants, sa noble négligence,
> Sa marche irrégulière, et fait naître avec art
> Des beautés du désordre, et même du hasard."
>
> DELILLE.

U R first, most endearing, and most sacred associations," says the amiable Mrs. Hofland, "are connected with gardens ; our most simple and most

refined perceptions of beauty are combined with them.'
And we may add to this, that Landscape Gardening, which
is an artistical combination of the beautiful in nature and
art—an union of natural expression and harmonious cultivation—is capable of affording us the highest and most intellectual enjoyment to be found in any cares or pleasures
belonging to the soil.

The development of the Beautiful is the end and aim of
Landscape Gardening, as it is of all other fine arts. The
ancients sought to attain this by a studied and elegant
regularity of design in their gardens ; the moderns, by the
creation or improvement of grounds which, though of limited extent, exhibit a highly graceful or picturesque epitome
of natural beauty. Landscape Gardening differs from gardening in its common sense, in embracing the whole scene
immediately about a country house, which it softens and
refines, or renders more spirited and striking by the aid of
art. In it we seek to embody our *ideal* of a rural home ;
not through plots of fruit trees, and beds of choice flowers,
though these have their place, but by collecting and combining beautiful forms in trees, surfaces of ground, buildings,
and walks, in the landscape surrounding us. It is, in short,
the Beautiful, embodied in a home scene. And we attain
it by the removal or concealment of everything uncouth
and discordant, and by the introduction and preservation of
forms pleasing in their expression, their outlines, and their
fitness for the abode of man. In the orchard, we hope to
gratify the palate ; in the flower garden, the eye and the
smell ; but in the landscape garden we appeal to that sense
of the Beautiful and the Perfect, which is one of the highest attributes of our nature.

This embellishment of nature, which we call **Landscape**

Gardening, springs naturally from a love of country life, an attachment to a certain spot, and a desire to render that place attractive—a feeling which seems more or less strongly fixed in the minds of all men. But we should convey a false impression, were we to state that it may be applied with equal success to residences of every class and size, in the country. Lawn and trees, being its two essential elements, some of the beauties of Landscape Gardening may, indeed, be shown wherever a rood of grass surface, and half a dozen trees are within our reach; we may, even with such scanty space, have tasteful grouping, varied surface, and agreeably curved walks; but our art, to appear to advantage, requires some extent of surface—its lines should lose themselves indefinitely, and unite agreeably and gradually with those of the surrounding country.

In the case of large landed estates, its capabilities may be displayed to their full extent, as from fifty to five hundred acres may be devoted to a park or pleasure grounds. Most of its beauty, and all its charms, may, however, be enjoyed in ten or twenty acres, fortunately situated, and well treated; and Landscape Gardening, in America, combined and working in harmony as it is with our fine scenery, is already beginning to give us results scarcely less beautiful than those produced by its finest efforts abroad. The lovely villa residences of our noble river and lake margins, when well treated—even in a few acres of tasteful fore-ground,—seem so entirely to appropriate the whole adjacent landscape, and to mingle so sweetly in their outlines with the woods, the valleys, and shores around them, that the effects are often truly enchanting.

But if Landscape Gardening, in its proper sense, cannot be applied to the embellishment of the smallest cottage residences in the country, its principles may be studied with advantage, even by him who has only three trees to plant for ornament; and we hope no one will think his grounds too small, to feel willing to add something to the general amount of beauty in the country. If the possessor of the cottage acre would embellish in accordance with propriety, he must not, as we have sometimes seen, render the whole ridiculous by aiming at ambitious and costly embellishments; but he will rather seek to delight us by the good taste evinced in the *tasteful simplicity* of the whole arrangement. And if the proprietors of our country villas, in their improvements, are more likely to run into any one error than another, we fear it will be that of too great a desire for display—too many vases, temples, and seats,—and too little purity and simplicity of general effect.

The inquiring reader will perhaps be glad to have a glance at the history and progress of the art of tasteful gardening; a recurrence to which, as well as to the history of the fine arts, will afford abundant proof that, in the first stage or infancy of all these arts, while the perception of their ultimate capabilities is yet crude and imperfect, mankind has, in every instance, been completely satisfied with the mere exhibition of *design* or *art*. Thus in Sculpture the first statues were only attempts to imitate rudely the *form* of a human figure, or in painting, to represent that of a tree : the skill of the artist, in effecting an imitation successfully, being sufficient to excite the astonishment and admiration of those who had not yet made such advances as to enable them to appreciate the superior beauty of *expression*.

Landscape Gardening is, indeed, only a modern word first coined, we believe, by Shenstone.

The most distinguished English Landscape Gardeners of recent date, are the late Humphrey Repton, who died in 1818; and since him John Claudius Loudon better known in this country, as the celebrated gardening author. Repton's taste in Landscape gardening was cultivated and elegant, and many of the finest parks and pleasure grounds of England, at the present day, bear witness to the skill and harmony of his designs. His published works are full of instructive hints, and at Cobham Hall, one of the finest seats in Britain, is an inscription to his memory, by Lord Darnley.

Mr. Loudon's* writings and labors in tasteful gardening, are too well known, to render it necessary that we should do more than allude to them here. Much of what is known of the art in this country undoubtedly is, more or less directly, to be referred to the influence of his published works. Although he is, as it seems to us, somewhat deficient as an artist in imagination, no previous author ever deduced, so clearly, sound artistical principles in Landscape Gardening and Rural Architecture ; and fitness, good sense, and beauty, are combined with much unity of feeling in all his works.

As the modern style owes its origin mainly to the English, so it has also been developed and carried to its greatest perfection in the British Islands. The law of primogeniture, which has there so long existed, in itself, contributes greatly to the continual improvement and embellishment of those vast landed estates, that remain perpetually in the hands of the same family. Magnificent

* While we are revising the second edition, we regret deeply to learn the death of Mr. Loudon. His herculean labors as an author have at last destroyed him ; and in his death we lose one who has done more than any other person that ever lived, to popularize, and render universal, a taste for Gardening and Domestic Architecture.

buildings, added to by each succeeding generation, who often preserve also the older portions with the most scrupulous care ; wide spread parks, clothed with a thick velvet turf, which, amid their moist atmosphere, preserves during great part of the year an emerald greenness— studded with noble oaks and other forest trees which number centuries of growth and maturity ; these advantages, in the hands of the most intelligent and the wealthiest aristocracy in the world, have indeed made almost an entire landscape garden of "merry England." Among a multitude of splendid examples of these noble residences, we will only refer the reader to the celebrated Blenheim, the seat of the Duke of Marlborough, where the lake alone (probably the largest piece of artificial water in the world) covers a surface of two hundred acres : Chatsworth, the varied and magnificent seat of the Duke of Devonshire, where there are scenes illustrative of almost every style of the art : and Woburn Abbey, the grounds of which are full of the choicest specimens ·of trees and plants, and where the park, like that of Ashbridge, Arundel Castle, and several other private residences in England, is only embraced within a circumference of from ten to twenty miles.

On the continent of Europe, though there are a multitude of examples of the modern style of landscape gardening, which is there called the *English* or *natural* style, yet in the neighborhood of many of the capitals, especially those of the south of Europe, the taste for the geometric or ancient style of gardening still prevails to a considerable extent ; partially, no doubt, because that style admits, with more facility, of those classical and architectural accompaniments of vases, statues, busts, etc.

the passion for which pervades a people rich in ancient and
modern sculptural works of art. Indeed many of the
gardens on the continent are more striking from their
numerous sculpturesque ornaments, interspersed with
fountains and jets-d'eau, than from the beauty or rarity
of their vegetation, or from their arrangement.

In the United States, it is highly improbable that we
shall ever witness such splendid examples of landscape
gardens as those abroad, to which we have alluded. Here
the rights of man are held to be equal ; and if there are
no enormous parks, and no class of men whose wealth is
hereditary, there is, at least, what is more gratifying to
the feelings of the philanthropist, the almost entire absence
of a very poor class in the country ; while we have, on
the other hand, a large class of independent landholders,
who are able to assemble around them, not only the useful
and convenient, but the agreeable and beautiful, in country
life.

The number of individuals among us who possess wealth
and refinement sufficient to enable them to enjoy the
pleasures of a country life, and who desire in their private
residences so much of the beauties of landscape gardening
and rural embellishment as may be had without any
enormous expenditure of means, is every day increasing.
And although, until lately, a very meagre plan of laying
out the grounds of a residence, was all that we could lay
claim to, yet the taste for elegant rural improvements is
advancing now so rapidly, that we have no hesitation in
predicting that in half a century more, there will exist a
greater number of beautiful villas and country seats of
moderate extent, in the Atlantic States, than in any
country in Europe, England alone excepted. With us, a

feeling, a taste, or an improvement, is contagious ; and once fairly appreciated and established in one portion of the country, it is disseminated with a celerity that is indeed wonderful, to every other portion. And though it is necessarily the case where amateurs of any art are more numerous than its professors, that there will be, in devising and carrying plans into execution, many specimens of bad taste, and perhaps a sufficient number of efforts to improve without any real taste whatever, still we are convinced the effect of our rural embellishments will in the end be highly agreeable, as a false taste is not likely to be a permanent one in a community where everything is so much the subject of criticism.

With regard to the literature and practice of Landscape Gardening as an art, in North America, almost everything is yet before us, comparatively little having yet been done. Almost all the improvements of the grounds of our finest country residences, have been carried on under the direction of the proprietors themselves, suggested by their own good taste, in many instances improved by the study of European authors, or by a personal inspection of the finest places abroad. The only American work previously published which treats directly of Landscape Gardening, is the *American Gardener's Calendar*, by Bernard McMahon of Philadelphia. The only practitioner of the art, of any note, was the late M. Parmentier of Brooklyn, Long Island.

M. André Parmentier was the brother of that celebrated horticulturist, the Chevalier Parmentier, Mayor of Enghien, Holland. He emigrated to this country about the year 1824, and in the Horticultural Nurseries which he established at Brooklyn, he gave a specimen of the natural style of laying out grounds, combined with a scientific arrangement of plants, which excited public curiosity, and contributed not a little to the dissemination of a taste for the natural mode of landscape gardening.

During M. Parmentier's residence on Long Island, he was almost constantly applied to for plans for laying out the grounds of country seats, by persons in various parts of the Union, as well as in the immediate proximity of New York. In many cases he not only surveyed the demesne to be improved, but furnished the plants and trees necessary to carry out his designs. Several plans were prepared by him for residences of note in the Southern States ; and two or three places in Upper Canada, especially near Montreal, were, we believe, laid out by his own hands and stocked from his nursery grounds. In his periodical catalogue, he arranged the hardy trees and shrubs that flourish in this latitude in classes, according to their height, etc., and published a short treatise on the superior claims of the natural, over the formal or geometric style of laying out grounds. In short, we consider M Parmentier's labors and examples as having effected, directly, far more for landscape gardening in America, than those of any other individual whatever.

The introduction of tasteful gardening in this country is, of course, of a very recent date. But so long ago as from 25 to 50 years, there were several country residences highly remarkable for extent, elegance of arrangement, and the highest order and keeping. Among these, we desire especially to record here the celebrated seats of Chancellor Livingston, Wm. Hamilton, Esq., Theodore Lyman, Esq., and Judge Peters.

Woodlands, the seat of the Hamilton family, near

Philadelphia, was, so long ago as 1805, highly celebrated
for its gardening beauties. The refined taste and the
wealth of its accomplished owner, were freely lavished in
its improvement and embellishment; and at a time when
the introduction of rare exotics was attended with a vast
deal of risk and trouble, the extensive green-houses and
orangeries of this seat contained all the richest treasures
of the exotic flora, and among other excellent gardeners
employed, was the distinguished botanist Pursh, whose
enthusiastic taste in his favorite science was promoted and
aided by Mr. Hamilton. The extensive pleasure grounds
were judiciously planted, singly and in groups, with a
great variety of the finest species of trees. The attention
of the visitor to this place is now arrested by two very
large specimens of that curious tree, the Japanese Ginko
(*Salisburia*), 60 or 70 feet high, perhaps the finest in
Europe or America, by the noble magnolias, and the rich
park-like appearance of some of the plantations of the
finest native and foreign oaks. From the recent un-
healthiness of this portion of the Schuylkill, Woodlands
has fallen into decay, but there can be no question that it
was, for a long time, the most tasteful and beautiful
residence in America.

The seat of the late Judge Peters, about five miles from
Philadelphia, was, 30 years ago, a noted specimen of the
ancient school of landscape gardening. Its proprietor had
a most extended reputation as a scientific agriculturist,
and his place was also no less remarkable for the design
and culture of its pleasure-grounds, than for the excellence
of its farm. Long and stately avenues, with vistas
terminated by obelisks, a garden adorned with marble
vases, busts, and statues, and pleasure grounds filled with

the rarest trees and shrubs, were conspicuous features here. Some of the latter are now so remarkable as to attract strongly the attention of the visitor. Among them, is the chestnut planted by Washington, which produces the largest and finest fruit; very large hollies; and a curious old box-tree much higher than the mansion near which it stands. But the most striking feature now, is the still remaining grand old avenue of hemlocks (*Abies canadensis*). Many of these trees, which were planted 100 years ago, are now venerable specimens, ninety feet high, whose huge trunks and wide spread branches are in many cases densely wreathed and draped with masses of English Ivy, forming the most picturesque sylvan objects we ever beheld.

Lemon Hill, half a mile above the Fairmount water-works of Philadelphia, was, 20 years ago, the most perfect specimen of the geometric mode in America, and since its destruction by the extension of the city, a few years since, there is nothing comparable with it, in that style, among us. All the symmetry, uniformity, and high art of the old school, were displayed here in artificial plantations, formal gardens with trellises, grottoes, spring-houses, temples, statues, and vases, with numerous ponds of water, jets-d'eau, and other water-works, parterres and an extensive range of hothouses. The effect of this garden was brilliant and striking; its position, on the lovely banks of the Schuylkill, admirable; and its liberal proprietor, Mr. Pratt, by opening it freely to the public, greatly increased the popular taste in the neighborhood of that city.

On the Hudson, the show place of the last age was the still interesting *Clermont*, then the residence of Chancellor Livingston. Its level or gently undulating lawn, four or

five miles in length, the rich native woods, and the long
vistas of planted avenues, added to its fine water view,
rendered this a noble place. The mansion, the green-
houses, and the gardens, show something of the French
taste in design, which Mr. Livingston's residence abroad,
at the time when that mode was popular, no doubt, led
him to adopt. The finest yellow locusts in America are
now standing in the pleasure-grounds here, and the
gardens contain many specimens of fruit trees, the first of
their sorts introduced into the Union.

Waltham House, about nine miles from Boston, was, 25
years ago, one of the oldest and finest places, as regards
Landscape Gardening. Its owner, the late Hon. T.
Lyman, was a highly-accomplished man, and the grounds
at Waltham House bear witness to a refined and elegant
taste in rural improvement. A fine level park, a mile in
length, enriched with groups of English limes, elms, and
oaks, and rich masses of native wood, watered by a fine
stream and stocked with deer, were the leading features
of the place at that time; and this, and Woodlands, were
the two best specimens of the modern style, as Judge
Peters' seat, Lemon Hill, and Clermont, were of the ancient style, in the earliest period of the history of Landscape Gardening among us.

There is no part of the Union where the taste in Landscape Gardening is so far advanced, as on the middle portion of the Hudson. The natural scenery is of the finest
character, and places but a mile or two apart often
possess, from the constantly varying forms of the water,
shores, and distant hills, widely different kinds of home
landscape and distant view. Standing in the grounds of
some of the finest of these seats, the eye beholds only the

FIG. 1.—View in the Grounds at Hyde Park

FIG. 2.—The Manor of Livingston.

soft foreground of smooth lawn, the rich groups of trees
shutting out all neighboring tracts, the lake-like expanse
of water, and, closing the distance, a fine range of wooded
mountain. A residence here of but a hundred acres, so
fortunately are these disposed by nature, seems to appropriate the whole scenery round, and to be a thousand in
extent.

At the present time, our handsome villa residences are
becoming every day more numerous, and it would require
much more space than our present limits, to enumerate
all the tasteful rural country places within our knowledge,
many of which have been newly laid out, or greatly improved within a few years. But we consider it so important and instructive to the novice in the art of Landscape Gardening to examine, personally, country seats of
a highly tasteful character, that we shall venture to refer
the reader to a few of those which have now a reputation
among us as elegant country residences.

Hyde Park, on the Hudson, formerly the seat of the late
Dr. Hosack, now of W. Langdon, Esq., has been justly
celebrated as one of the finest specimens of the modern
style of Landscape Gardening in America. Nature has,
indeed, done much for this place, as the grounds are finely
varied, beautifully watered by a lively stream, and the
views are inexpressibly striking from the neighborhood of
the house itself, including, as they do, the noble Hudson
for sixty miles in its course, through rich valleys and bold
mountains. (See Fig. 1.) But the efforts of art are not
unworthy so rare a locality; and while the native woods,
and beautifully undulating surface, are preserved in their
original state, the pleasure-grounds, roads, walks, drives
and new plantations, have been laid out in such a judi-

cious manner as to heighten the charms of nature.   Large
and costly hot-houses were erected by Dr. Hosack, with
also entrance lodges at two points on the estate, a fine
bridge over the stream, and numerous pavilions and seats
commanding extensive prospects ; in short, nothing was
spared to render this a complete residence.   The park,
which at one time contained some fine deer, afforded a delightful drive within itself, as the whole estate numbered
about seven hundred acres.   The plans for laying out the
grounds were furnished by Parmentier, and architects from
New York were employed in designing and erecting the
buildings.   For a long time, this was the finest seat in
America, but there are now many rivals to this claim.

The Manor of Livingston, lately the seat of Mrs. Mary
Livingston (but now of Jacob Le Roy, Esq.), is seven
miles east of the city of Hudson.   The mansion stands
in the midst of a fine park, rising gradually from the
level of a rich inland country, and commanding prospects
for sixty miles around.   The park is, perhaps, the most
remarkable in America, for the noble simplicity of its
character, and the perfect order in which it is kept.   The
turf is, everywhere, short and velvet-like, the gravel-roads
scrupulously firm and smooth, and near the house are the
largest and most superb evergreens.   The mansion is one
of the chastest specimens of the Grecian style, and there
is an air of great dignity about the whole demesne.

Blithewood, formerly the seat of R. Donaldson, Esq.,
(now John Bard, Esq.), near Barrytown, on the Hudson,
is one of the most charming villa residences in the
Union.   The natural scenery here, is nowhere surpassed in its enchanting union of softness and dignity
—the river being four miles wide, its placid bosom
broken only by islands and gleaming sails, and the horizon

FIG. 8.—Montgomery Place, Seat of Mrs. Edward Livingston.

grandly closing in with the tall blue summits of tne distant Kaatskills. The smiling, gently varied lawn is studded with groups and masses of fine forest and ornamental trees, beneath which are walks leading in easy curves to rustic seats, and summer houses placed in secluded spots, or to openings affording most lovely prospects. (See Frontispiece.) In various situations near the house and upon the lawn, sculptured vases of Maltese stone are also disposed in such a manner as to give a refined and classic air to the grounds.

As a *pendant* to this graceful landscape, there is within the grounds scenery of an opposite character, equally wild and picturesque—a fine, bold stream, fringed with woody banks, and dashing over several rocky cascades, thirty or forty feet in height, and falling altogether a hundred feet in a distance of half a mile. There are also, within the grounds, a pretty gardener's lodge, in the rural cottage style, and a new entrance lodge by the gate, in the bracketed mode; in short, we can recall no place of moderate extent, where nature and tasteful art are both so harmoniously combined to express grace and elegance.

Montgomery Place, the residence of Mrs. Edward Livingston, which is also situated on the Hudson, near Barrytown, deserves a more extended notice than our present limits allow, for it is, as a whole, nowhere surpassed in America, in point of location, natural beauty, or the landscape gardening charms which it exhibits.

It is one of our oldest improved country seats, having been originally the residence of Gen. Montgomery, the hero of Quebec. On the death of his widow it passed into the hands of her brother, Edward Livingston, Esq., the late minister to France, and up to the present moment has

always received the most tasteful and judicious **treat**
ment.

The lover of the expressive in nature, or the beautiful in
art, will find here innumerable subjects for his study.
The natural scenery in many portions approaches the character of grandeur, and the foreground of rich woods and
lawns, stretching out on all sides of the mountain, completes
a home landscape of dignified and elegant seclusion, rarely
surpassed in any country.

Among the fine features of this estate are the *wilderness*, a richly wooded and highly picturesque valley, filled
with the richest growth of trees, and threaded with dark,
intricate, and mazy walks, along which are placed a

variety of rustic
seats (Fig. 4).
This valley is
musical with the
sound of water-
falls, of which
there are several
fine ones in the
bold impetuous
stream which
finds its course
through the low-

[Fig. 4. One of the Rustic Seats at Montgomery Place.]   er part of the
wilderness. Near the further end of the valley is a beautiful lake (Fig. 5), half of which lies cool and dark under the
shadow of tall trees, while the other half gleams in the
open sunlight.

In a part of the lawn, near the house, yet so surrounded
by a dark setting of trees and shrubs as to form **a rich**

picture by itself, is one of the most perfect flower gardens in the country, laid out in the arabesque manner, and glowing with masses of the gayest colors—each bed being composed wholly of a single hue. A large conservatory, an exotic garden, an arboretum, etc., are among the features of interest in this admirable residence. Including a *drive* through a fine bit of natural wood, south of the mansion, there are five miles of highly varied and picturesque private roads and walks, through the pleasure-grounds of Montgomery Place.

[Fig. 5. The Lake at Montgomery Place.]

Ellerslie is the seat of William Kelly, Esq. It is three miles below Rhinebeck. It comprises over six hundred acres, and is one of our finest examples of high keeping and good management, both in an ornamental and an agricultural point of view. The house is conspicuously placed on a commanding natural terrace, with a fair foreground of park surface below it, studded with beautiful groups of elms and oaks, and a very fine reach of river and

distant hills.   This is one of the most celebrated places on
the Hudson, and there are few that so well pay the lover
of improved landscape for a visit.

Just below Ellerslie are the fine mansion and pleasing
grounds of Wm. Emmet, Esq.,—the former a stone edifice,
in the castellated style, and the latter forming a most
agreeable point on the margin of the river.

The seat of Mrs. Gardiner Howland, near New Hamburgh, is not only beautiful in situation, but is laid out
with great care, and is especially remarkable for the
many rare trees and shrubs collected in its grounds.

Wodenethe, near Fishkill landing, is the seat of H. W.
Sargent, Esq., and is a bijou full of interest for the lover
of rural beauty ; abounding in rare trees, shrubs, and
plants, as well as vases, and objects of rural embellishment of all kinds.

Kenwood, formerly the residence of J. Rathbone, Esq.,
is one mile south of Albany. Ten years ago this spot was a
wild and densely wooded hill, almost inaccessible.   With
great taste and industry Mr. Rathbone has converted it
into a country residence of much picturesque beauty,
erected in the Tudor style, one of the best villas in the
country, with a gate-lodge in the same mode, and laid out
the grounds with remarkable skill and good taste.   There
are about 1200 acres in this estate, and pleasure grounds,
forcing houses, and gardens, are now flourishing where all
was so lately in the rudest state of nature ; while, by the
judicious preservation of natural wood, the effect of a long
cultivated demesne has been given to the whole.

The Manor House of the "*Patroon*" (as the eldest son
of the Van Rensselaer family is called) is in the northern
suburbs of the city of Albany.   The mansion, greatly

Fig. 6.—Beaverwyck, the Seat of Wm. P. Van Rensselaer, Esq.

Fig. 7.—Cottage Residence of Wm. H. Aspinwall, Esq.

enlarged and improved a few years since, from the designs of Upjohn, is one of the largest and most admirable in all respects, to be found in the country, and the pleasure-grounds in the rear of the house are tasteful and beautiful.

Beaverwyck, a little north of Albany, on the opposite bank of the river, was formerly the seat of Wm. P. Van Rensselaer, Esq. The whole estate is ten or twelve miles square, including the village of Bath on the river shore, and a large farming district. The home residence embraces several hundred acres, with a large level lawn, bordered by highly varied surface of hill and dale. The mansion, one of the first class, is newly erected from the plans of Mr. Diaper, and in its interior—its hall with mosaic floor of polished woods, its marble staircase, frescoed apartments, and spacious adjoining conservatory —is perhaps the most splendid in the Union. The grounds are yet newly laid out, but with much judgment; and *six or seven miles* of winding gravelled roads and walks have been formed—their boundaries now leading over level meadows, and now winding through woody dells. The drives thus afforded, are almost unrivalled in extent and variety, and give the stranger or guest, an opportunity of seeing the near and distant views to the best advantage.

At Tarrytown, is the cottage residence of Washington Irving, which is, in location and accessories, almost the beau ideal of a cottage ornée. The charming manner in which the wild foot-paths, in the neighborhood of this cottage, are conducted among the picturesque dells and banks, is precisely what one would look for here. A little below, Mr. Sheldon's cottage (now Mr. Hoag's), with its pretty lawn and its charming brook, is one of the best specimens of this kind of residence on the river. At Hastings, four or five miles south, is the agreeable seat of Robt. B. Minturn, Esq.

About twelve miles from New York, on the Sound, is *Hunter's Island,* the seat of John Hunter, Esq., a place of much simplicity and dignity of character. The whole island may be considered an extensive park carpeted with soft lawn, and studded with noble trees. The mansion is simple in its exterior, but internally, is filled with rich treasures of art. The seat of James Munroe, Esq., on the East river in this neighborhood, abounds with beautiful trees, and many other features of interest.

The Cottage residence of William H. Aspinwall, Esq., on Staten Island, is a highly picturesque specimen of Landscape Gardening. The house is in the English cottage style, and from its open lawn in front, the eye takes in a wide view of the ocean, the Narrows, and the blue hills of Neversink. In the rear of the cottage, the surface is much broken and varied, and finely wooded and planted. In improving this picturesque site, a nice sense of the charm of natural expression has been evinced; and the sudden variations from smooth open surface, to wild wooden banks, with rocky, moss-covered flights of steps, strike the stranger equally with surprise and delight. A charming greenhouse, a knotted flower-garden, and a pretty, rustic moss-house, are among the interesting points of this spirited place. (See Fig. 7.)

The seat of the Wadsworth family, at *Geneseo,* is the finest in the interior of the state of New York. Nothing, indeed, can well be more magnificent than the *meadow park* at Geneseo. It is more than a thousand acres in extent, lying on each side of the Genesee river, and is filled with thousands of the noblest oaks and elms, many of which, but

more especially the oaks, are such trees as we see in the
pictures of Claude, or our own Durand ; richly developed,
their trunks and branches grand and majestic, their heads
full of breadth and grandeur of outline.

These oaks, distributed over a nearly level surface, with
the trees disposed either singly or in the finest groups, as
if most tastefully planted centuries ago, are solely the work
of nature ; and yet so entirely is the whole like the
grandest planted park, that it is difficult to believe that
all is not the work of some master of art, and intended for
the accompaniment of a magnificent residence.   Some of
the trees are five or six hundred years old.

In Connecticut, *Monte Video*, the seat of Daniel Wadsworth, Esq., near Hartford, is worthy of commendation, as
it evinces a good deal of beauty in its grounds, and is one
of the most tasteful in the state.   The residence of James
Hillhouse, Esq., near New-Haven, is a pleasing specimen
of the simplest kind of Landscape Gardening, where graceful forms of trees, and a gently sloping surface of grass,
are the principal features.   The villa of Mr. Whitney
near New-Haven, is one of the most tastefully managed in
the state.   In Maine, the most remarkable seat, as respects
landscape gardening and architecture, is that of Mr. Gardiner, of Gardiner.

The environs of Boston are more highly cultivated than
those of any other city in North America.   There are here
whole rural neighborhoods of pretty cottages and villas, admirably cultivated, and, in many cases, tastefully laid out
and planted.   The character of even the finest of these
places is, perhaps, somewhat suburban, as compared with
those of the Hudson river, but we regard them as furnish-

ing admirable hints for a class of residence likely to become
more numerous than any other in this country—the tasteful suburban cottage. The owner of a small cottage residence may have almost every kind of beauty and enjoyment in his grounds that the largest estate will afford, so
far as regards the interest of trees and plants, tasteful arrangement, recreation, and occupation. Indeed, we have
little doubt that he, who directs personally the curve of
every walk, selects and plants every shrub and tree, and
watches with solicitude every evidence of beauty and progress, succeeds in extracting from his tasteful grounds of
half a dozen acres, a more intense degree of pleasure, than
one who is only able to direct and enjoy, in a general
sense, the arrangement of a vast estate.

Belmont, the seat of J. P. Cushing, Esq., is a residence
of more note than any other near Boston ; but this is,
chiefly, on account of the extensive ranges of glass, the
forced fruits, and the high culture of the gardens. A new
and spacious mansion has recently been erected here, and
the pleasure-grounds are agreeably varied with fine groups
and masses of trees and shrubs on a pleasing lawn
(Fig. 8.)

The seat of Col. Perkins, at Brookline, is one of the
most interesting in this neighborhood. The very beautiful
lawn here, abounds with exquisite trees, finely disposed ;
among them, some larches and Norway firs, with many
other rare trees of uncommon beauty of form. At a short
distance is the villa residence of Theodore Lyman, Esq.,
remarkable for the unusually fine avenue of Elms leading
to the house, and for the beautiful architectural taste displayed in the dwelling itself. The seat of the Hon. John

FIG. 8.—Belmont Place, near Boston, the seat of J. P. Cushing, Esq.

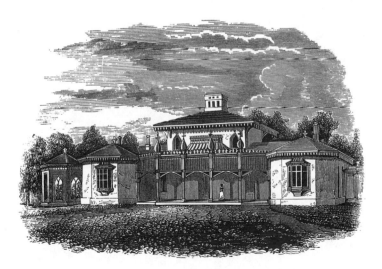

FIG. 9.—Mr. Dunn's Cottage, Mount Holly, N. J.

Lowell, at Roxbury, possesses also many interesting gardening features.*

Pine Bank, the Perkins estate, on the border of Jamaica lake, is one of the most beautiful residences near Boston. The natural surface of the ground is exceedingly flowing and graceful, and it is varied by two or three singular little *dimples*, or hollows, which add to its effect. The perfect order of the grounds; the beauty of the walks, sometimes skirting the smooth open lawn, enriched with rare plants and shrubs, and then winding by the shadowy banks of the water; the soft and quiet character of the lake itself,—its margin richly fringed with trees, which conceal here and there a pretty cottage, its firm clean beach of gravel, and its water of crystal purity; all these features make this place a little gem of natural

* We Americans are proverbially impatient of delay, and a few years in prospect appear an endless futurity. So much is this the feeling with many, that we verily believe there are hundreds of our country places, which owe their bareness and destitution of foliage to the idea, so common, that it requires "an age" for forest trees to "*grow up.*"

The middle-aged man hesitates about the good of planting what he imagines he shall never see arriving at maturity, and even many who are younger, conceive that it requires more than an ordinary lifetime to rear a fine wood of planted trees. About two years since, we had the pleasure of visiting the seat of the late Mr. Lowell, whom we found in a green old age, still enjoying, with the enthusiasm of youth, the pleasures of Horticulture and a country life. For the encouragement of those who are ever complaining of the tardy pace with which the growth of trees advances, we will here record that we accompanied Mr. L. through a belt of fine woods (skirting part of his residence), nearly half a mile in length, consisting of almost all our finer hardy trees, many of them apparently full grown, the whole of which had been planted by him when he was thirty-two years old. At that time, a solitary elm or two were almost the only trees upon his estate. We can hardly conceive a more rational source of pride or enjoyment, than to be able thus to walk, in the decline of years, beneath the shadow of umbrageous woods and groves, planted by our own hands, and whose growth has become almost identified with our own progress and existence.

and artistical harmony, and beauty.   Mr. Perkins has just
rebuilt the house, in the style of a French *maison de cam-
pagne;* and Pine Bank is now adorned with a most
complete residence in the latest continental taste, from
the designs of M. Lémoulnier.

On the other side of the lake is the *cottage of Thomas
Lee, Esq.*   Enthusiastically fond of botany, and gardening
in all its departments, Mr. Lee has here formed a residence
of as much variety and interest as we ever saw in so
moderate a compass—about 20 acres.   It is, indeed, not
only a most instructive place to the amateur of landscape
gardening, but to the naturalist and lover of plants.   Every
shrub seems placed precisely in the soil and aspect it likes
best, and native and foreign Rhododendrons, Kalmias, and
other rare shrubs, are seen here in the finest condition.
There is a great deal of variety in the surface here, and
while the lawn-front of the house has a polished and
graceful air, one or two other portions are quite picturesque.
Near the entrance gate is an English oak, only fourteen
years planted, now forty feet high.

The whole of this neighborhood of Brookline is a kind
of landscape garden, and there is nothing in America, of
the sort, so inexpressibly charming as the lanes which lead
from one cottage, or villa, to another.   No animals are
allowed to run at large, and the open gates, with tempting
vistas and glimpses under the pendent boughs, give it quite
an Arcadian air of rural freedom and enjoyment.   These
lanes are clothed with a profusion of trees and wild shrubbery, often almost to the carriage tracks, and curve and
wind about, in a manner quite bewildering to the stranger
who attempts to thread them alone ; and there are more
hints here for the lover of the picturesque in lanes, than

we ever saw assembled together in so small a compass.

In the environs of New Bedford are many beautiful residences. Among these, we desire particularly to notice the
residence of James Arnold, Esq. There is scarcely a small
place in New England, where the *pleasure-grounds* are so
full of variety, and in such perfect order and keeping, as at
this charming spot; and its winding walks, open bits of
lawn, shrubs and plants grouped on turf, shady bowers,
and rustic seats, all most agreeably combined, render this
a very interesting and instructive suburban seat. (Fig. 11.)

In New Jersey, the grounds of the Count de Survilliers,
at Bordentown, were very extensive ; and although the surface is mostly flat, it has been well varied by extensive
plantations. At Mount Holly, about twenty miles from
Camden, is Mr. Dunn's unique, semi-oriental cottage, with
a considerable extent of pleasure ground, newly planted,
after the designs of Mr. Notman. (Fig. 9.)

About Philadelphia there are several very interesting
seats on the banks of the Delaware and Schuylkill, and
the district between these two rivers.

The country seat of George Sheaff, Esq., one of the most
remarkable in Pennsylvania, in many respects, is twelve
miles north of Philadelphia. The house is a large and respectable mansion of stone, surrounded by pleasure-grounds
and plantations of fine evergreen and deciduous trees. The
conspicuous ornament of the grounds, however, is a magnificent white oak, of enormous size, whose wide stretching
branches, and grand head, give an air of dignity to the
whole place. (Fig. 10.) Among the sylvan features here,
most interesting, are also the handsome evergreens, chiefly
Balsam or Balm of Gilead firs, some of which are now

much higher than the mansion. These trees were planted by Mr. Sheaff twenty-two years ago, and were then so small, that they were brought by him from Philadelphia, at various times, in his carriage—a circumstance highly encouraging to despairing planters, when we reflect how comparatively slow growing is this tree. This whole estate is a striking example of science, skill, and taste, applied to a country seat, and there are few in the Union, taken as a whole, superior to it.*

Cottage residence of Mrs. Camac. This is one of the most agreeable places within a few miles of Philadelphia. The house is a picturesque cottage, in the rural gothic style, with very charming and appropriate pleasure grounds, comprising many groups and masses of large and finely grown trees, interspersed with a handsome collection of shrubs and plants; the whole very tastefully arranged. (Fig. 11.) The lawn is prettily varied in surface, and there is a conservatory attached to the house, in which the plants in pots are hidden in beds of soft green moss, and which, in its whole effect and management, is more tasteful and elegant than any plant house, connected with a dwelling, that we remember to have seen.

* The farm is 300 acres in extent, and, in the time of De Witt Clinton, was pronounced by him the model farm of the United States. At the present time we know nothing superior to it; and Capt. Barclay, in his agricultural tour, says it was the only instance of regular, scientific system of husbandry in the English manner, he saw in America. Indeed, the large and regular fields, filled with luxuriant crops, everywhere of an exact evenness of growth, and everywhere free from weeds of any sort; the perfect system of manuring and culture; the simple and complete fences; the fine stock; the very spacious barns, every season newly whitewashed internally and externally, paved with wood, and as clean as a gentleman's stable (with stalls to fatten 90 head of cattle); these, and the masterly way in which the whole is managed, both as regards culture and profit, render this estate one of no common interest in an agricultural, as well as ornamental point of view.

Fig. 10.—The Seat of George Sheaff, Esq.

Fig. 11.—Mrs. Camac's Residence.

Stenton, near Germantown, four miles from Philadelphia, is a fine old place, with many picturesque features. The farm consists of 700 acres, almost without division fences—admirably managed—and remarkable for its grand old avenue of the hemlock spruce, 110 years old, leading to a family cemetery of much sylvan beauty. There is a large and excellent old mansion, with paved halls, built in 1731, which is preserved in its original condition. This place was the seat of the celebrated Logan, the friend of William Penn, and is now owned by his descendant, Albanus Logan.

The villa residence of Alexander Brown, Esq., is situated on the Delaware, a few miles from Philadelphia. There is here a good deal of beauty, in the natural style, made up chiefly by lawn and forest trees. A pleasing drive through plantations of 25 years' growth, is one of the most interesting features—and there is much elegance and high keeping in the grounds.

Below Philadelphia, the lover of beautiful places will find a good deal to admire in the country seat of John R Latimer, Esq., near Wilmington, which enjoys the reputation of being the finest in Delaware. The place has all the advantages of high keeping, richly stocked gardens and conservatories, and much natural beauty, heightened by judicious planting, arrangement, and culture.

At the south are many extensive country residences remarkable for trees of unusual grandeur and beauty, among which the live oak is very conspicuous; but they are, in general, wanting in that high keeping and care, which is so essential to the charm of a landscape garden.

Of smaller villa residences, suburban chiefly, there are great numbers, springing up almost by magic, in the borders of our towns and cities. Though the possessors of these can scarcely hope to introduce anything approaching to a landscape garden style, in laying out their limited grounds, still they may be greatly benefited by an acquaintance with the beauties and the pleasures of this species of rural embellishment. When we are once master of the principles, and aware of the capabilities of an art, we are able to infuse an expression of tasteful design, or an air of more correct elegance, even into the most humble works, and with very limited means.

While we shall endeavor, in the following pages, to give such a view of modern Landscape Gardening, as will enable the improver to proceed with his fascinating operations, in embellishing the country residence, in a practical mode, based upon what are now generally received as the correct principles of the art, we would desire the novice, after making himself acquainted with all that can be acquired from written works within his reach, to strengthen his taste and add to his knowledge, by a practical inspection of the best country seats among us. In an infant state of society, in regard to the fine arts, much will be done in violation of good taste; but here, where nature has done so much for us, there is scarcely a large country residence in the Union, from which useful hints in Landscape Gardening may not be taken. And in nature, a group of trees, an accidental pond of water, or some equally simple object, may form a study more convincing to the mind of a true admirer of natural beauty, than the most carefully drawn plan, or the most elaborately written description.

SECTION II.

BEAUTIES AND PRINCIPLES OF THE ART.

Capacities of the art. The beauties of the ancient style. The modern style. The Beautiful and the Picturesque: their distinctive characteristics. Illustrations drawn from
Nature and Painting. Nature and principles of Landscape Gardening as an Imitative
art. Distinction between the Beautiful and Picturesque. The principles of Unity
Harmony, and Variety.

> " Here Nature in her unaffected dresse,
>   Plaited with vallies and imbost with hills,
>   Enchast with silver streams, and fringed with woods
> Sits lovely."—
>
> Chamberlayne.

> " Il est des soins plus doux, un art plus enchanteur.
>   C'est peu de charmer l'œil, il faut parler au cœur.
>   Avez-vous donc connu ces rapports invisibles,
>   Des corps inanimés et des êtres sensibles?
>   Avez-vous entendu des eaux, des prés, des bois,
>   La muette éloquence et la secrète voix?
>   Rendez-nous ces effets."   *Les Jardins, Book I.*

EFORE we proceed to a detailed and
more practical consideration of the subject,
let us occupy ourselves for a moment with
the consideration of the different results
which are to be sought after, or, in other
words, what kinds of beauty we may hope to
produce by Landscape Gardening. To attempt the smallest
work in any art, without knowing either the capacities of

that art, or the schools, or modes, by which it has previously been characterized, is but to be groping about in a dim
twilight, without the power of knowing, even should we be
successful in our efforts, the real excellence of our production ; or of judging its merit, comparatively, as a work of
taste and imagination.

[Fig. 12. The Geometric style, from an old print.]

The beauties elicited by the ancient style of gardening
were those of regularity, symmetry, and the display of
labored art.   These were attained in a merely mechanical
manner, and usually involved little or no theory.   The
geometrical form and lines of the buildings were only extended and carried out in the garden.   In the best classical
models, the art of the sculptor conferred dignity and elegance on the garden, by the fine forms of marble vases and
statues ; in the more intricate and labored specimens of the

Dutch school, prevalent in England in the time of William IV. (Fig. 12), the results evince a fertility of odd conceits, rather than the exercise of taste or imagination. Indeed, as, to level ground naturally uneven, or to make an avenue, by planting rows of trees on each side of a broad walk, requires only the simplest perception of the beauty of mathematical forms, so, to lay out a garden in the geometric style, became little more than a formal routine, and it was only after the superior interest of a more natural manner was enforced by men of genius, that natural beauty of expression was recognised, and Landscape Gardening was raised to the rank of a fine art.

The ancient style of gardening may, however, be introduced with good effect in certain cases. In public squares and gardens, where display, grandeur of effect, and a highly artificial character are desirable, it appears to us the most suitable; and no less so in very small gardens, in which variety and irregularity are out of the question. Where a taste for imitating an old and quaint style of residence exists, the symmetrical and knotted garden would be a proper accompaniment; and pleached alleys, and sheared trees, would be admired, like old armor or furniture, as curious specimens of antique taste and custom.*

* There has been a great revival of this kind of garden in England the past ten years—more, perhaps, inclining to the Italian school than the Dutch. Chatsworth, Woburn Abbey, Castle Howard, Bowood, Eaton Hall, and, in fact, most of the great places, have more or less adopted the Italian or Architectural school on one or more sides of the house, as a sort of connection between art and nature. Trentham (the Duke of Sutherland's) is, we believe, especially rich in architectural gardens. Both here and at the other places above-mentioned, the grade between the house and the park is let down, as it were, by a series of terraces, each divided from the other by heavy stone balustrades, surmounted, at regular intervals, with vases, planted either with Geraniums, or with Yucca, Aloe, Bonapartias, and other formal plants. Flights of broad, heavy stone or marble steps conduct from one terrace to the other, and finally

The earliest professors of modern Landscape Gardening have generally agreed upon two variations, of which the art is capable—variations no less certainly distinct, on the one hand, than they are capable of intermingling and combining, on the other. These are the *beautiful* and the *picturesque:* or, to speak more definitely, the beauty characterized by simple and flowing forms, and that expressed by striking, irregular, spirited forms.

The admirer of nature, as well as the lover of pictures and engravings, will at once call to mind examples of scenery distinctly expressive of each of these kinds of beauty. In nature, perhaps some gently undulating plain, covered with emerald turf, partially or entirely encompassed by rich, rolling outlines of forest canopy,—its wildest expanse here broken occasionally, by noble groups of round-headed trees, or there interspersed with single specimens whose trunks support heads of foliage flowing in outline, or drooping in masses to the very turf beneath them. In such a scene we often behold the azure of heaven, and its silvery clouds, as well as the deep verdure of the luxuriant and shadowy branches, reflected in the placid bosom of a silvan lake ; the shores of the latter swelling out, and receding, in gentle curved lines ; the banks, sometimes covered with soft turf sprinkled with flowers, and in other portions clothed with luxuriant masses of verdant shrubs. Here are

to the Park. The flat of the terrace, being laid out either in the most formal and precise parterre, or in extremely rich and intricate beds of arabesque patterns in scrolls, to resemble carpets. In either case, great use is made of statues and fountains, very elaborately and artistically designed and executed, and of Portugal Laurel, trimmed up to imitate orange-trees in tubs; as, also, of the Irish and Golden Yew, and other pyramidal evergreens, either planted in the ground, or in boxes, and, also, of different-colored gravel in the division of the beds, the whole producing, when seen from the windows of the house, a brilliant combination, which, with the soft, verdant park as a background, is inexpressibly gay and effective.—H. W. S.

all the elements of what is termed natural beauty,—or a landscape characterized by simple, easy, and flowing lines

For an example of the opposite character, let us take a stroll to the nearest woody glen in your neighborhood—perhaps a romantic valley, half shut in on two or more sides by steep rocky banks, partially concealed and over-hung by clustering vines, and tangled thickets of deep foliage. Against the sky outline breaks the wild and irre-gular form of some old, half decayed tree near by, or the horizontal and unique branches of the larch or the pine, with their strongly marked forms. Rough and irregular stems and trunks, rocks half covered with mosses and flowering plants, open glades of bright verdure opposed to dark masses of bold shadowy foliage, form prominent ob-jects in the foreground. If water enlivens the scene, we shall hear the murmur of the noisy brook, or the cool dash-ing of the cascade, as it leaps over the rocky barrier. Le. the stream turn the ancient and well-worn wheel of the old mill in the middle ground, and we shall have an illustration of the picturesque, not the less striking from its familiarity to every one.

To the lover of the fine arts, the name of Claude Lor-raine cannot fail to suggest examples of beauty in some of its purest and most simple forms. In the best pictures of this master, we see portrayed those graceful and flowing forms in trees, foreground, and buildings, which delight so much the lover of noble and chaste beauty,—compositions emanating from a harmonious soul, and inspired by a cli-mate and a richness of nature and art seldom surpassed.

On the other hand, where shall we find all the elements of the picturesque more graphically combined than in the vigorous landscapes of Salvator Rosa! In those rugged

scenes, even the lawless aspects of his favorite robbers and
banditti are not more spirited, than the bold rocks and wild
passes by which they are surrounded.   And in the productions of his pencil we see the influence of a romantic and
vigorous imagination, nursed amid scenes teeming with
the grand as well as the picturesque—both of which he
embodied in the most striking manner.

In giving these illustrations of beautiful and of picturesque scenes, we have not intended them to be understood
in the light of exact models for imitation in Landscape
Gardening—only as striking examples of expression in
natural scenery.   Although in nature many landscapes
partake in a certain degree of both these kinds of expression,
yet it is no doubt true that the effect is more satisfactory,
where either the one or the other character predominates.
The accomplished amateur should be able to seize at once
upon the characteristics of these two species of beauty in
all scenery.   To assist the reader in this kind of discrimi-
nation, we shall keep these expressions constantly in view,
and we hope we shall be able fully to illustrate the difference in the expression of even single trees, in this respect.
A few strongly marked objects, either picturesque or simply
beautiful, will often confer their character upon a whole
landscape ; as the destruction of a single group of bold
rocks, covered with wood, may render a scene, once picturesque, completely insipid.

The early writers on the modern style were content with
trees allowed to grow in their natural forms, and with an
easy assemblage of sylvan scenery in the pleasure-grounds,
which resembled the usual woodland features of nature.
The effect of this method will always be interesting, and an
agreeable effect will always be the result of following the

simplest hints derived from the free and luxuriant forms of nature. No residence in the country can fail to be pleasing, whose features are natural groups of forest trees, smooth lawn, and hard gravel walks.

But this is scarcely Landscape Gardening in the true sense of the word, although apparently so understood by many writers. By Landscape Gardening, we understand not only an imitation, in the grounds of a country residence, of the agreeable forms of nature, but *an expressive, harmonious, and refined imitation.** In Landscape Gardening, we should aim to separate the accidental and extraneous in nature, and to preserve only the spirit, or essence. This subtle essence lies, we believe, in the expression more or less pervading every attractive portion of nature. And it is by eliciting, preserving, or heightening this expression, that we may give our landscape gardens a higher charm, than even the polish of art can bestow.

Now, the two most forcible and complete expressions to be found in that kind of natural scenery which may be reproduced in Landscape Gardening, are the BEAUTIFUL and the PICTURESQUE. As we look upon these as quite distinct, and as success in practical embellishment must depend on our feeling and understanding these expressions beforehand, it is necessary that we should attach some definite meaning to terms which we shall be continually obliged to employ. This is, indeed, the more requisite, from

* " Thus, there is a beauty of nature and a beauty of art. To copy the beauty of nature cannot be called being an artist in the highest sense of the word, as a mechanical talent only is requisite for this. The beautiful in art depends on ideas ; and the true artist, therefore, must possess, together with the talent for technical execution, that genial power which revels freely in rich forms, and is capable of producing and animating them. It is by this, that the merit of the artist and his production is to be judged ; and these cannot be the vague and conflicting opinions of most preceding writers on this branch of the subject ; some, like Repton, insisting that they are identical; and others, like Price, that they are widely different.

Gilpin defines Picturesque objects to be " those which please from some quality capable of being illustrated in painting."

Nothing can well be more vague than such a definition We have already described the difference between the beautiful landscapes of Claude and the picturesque scenes painted by Salvator. No one can deny their being essentially distinct in character ; and no one, we imagine, will deny that they both please from "some quality capable of being illustrated in painting." The beautiful female heads of Carlo Dolce are widely different from those of the picturesque peasant girls of Gerard Douw, yet both are favorite subjects with artists. A symmetrical American elm, with its wide head drooping with garlands of graceful foliage, is very different in expression from the wild and twisted larch or pine tree, which we find on the steep sides of a mountain ; yet both are favorite subjects with the painter. It is clear, indeed, that there is a widely different idea hidden under these two distinct types, in material forms.

Beauty, in all natural objects, as we conceive, arises from their expression of those attributes of the Creator—infinity, unity, symmetry, proportion, etc.—which he has stamped more or less visibly on all his works ; and a beautiful living form is one in which the individual is a harmo-

properly estimated among those barren copyists which we find so many of our flower, landscape, and portrait painters to be. But the artist stands much higher in the scale, who, though a copyist of visible nature, is capable of seizing it with poetic feeling, and representing it in its more dignified sense ; such, for example, as Raphael, Poussin, Claude, &c."—WEINBREUNER.

nious and well balanced development of a fine type. Thus, taking the most perfect specimens of beauty in the human figure, we see in them symmetry, proportion, unity, and grace—the presence of everything that could add to the idea of perfected existence. In a beautiful tree, such as a fine American elm, we see also the most complete and perfect balance of all its parts, resulting from its growth under the most favorable influences. It realizes, then, perfectly, the finest form of a fine type or species of tree.

But all nature is not equally Beautiful. Both in living things and in inorganized matter, we see on all sides evidences of nature struggling with opposing forces. Mountains are upheaved by convulsions, valleys are broken into fearful chasms. Certain forms of animal and vegetable life instead of manifesting themselves in those more complete and perfect forms of existence where the matter and spirit are almost in perfect harmony, appear to struggle for the full expression of their character with the material form, and to express it only with difficulty at last. What is achieved with harmony, grace, dignity, almost with apparent repose, by existences whose type is the Beautiful, is done only with violence and disturbed action by the former. This kind of manifestation in nature we call the Picturesque.

More concisely, the Beautiful is nature or art obeying the universal laws of perfect existence (i. e. Beauty), easily, freely, harmoniously, and without the *display* of power. The Picturesque is nature or art obeying the same laws rudely, violently, irregularly, and often displaying power only.

Hence we find all Beautiful forms characterized by curved and flowing lines—lines expressive of infinity,* of grace, and willing obedience : and all Picturesque forms character ized by irregular and broken lines—lines expressive of violence, abrupt action, and partial disobedience, a struggling of the idea with the substance or the condition of its being. The Beautiful is an idea of beauty calmly and harmoniously expressed ; the Picturesque an idea of beauty or power strongly and irregularly expressed. As an example of the Beautiful in other arts we refer to the Apollo of the Vatican ; as an example of the Picturesque, to the Laocoon or the Dying Gladiator. In nature we would place before the reader a finely formed elm or chestnut, whose wel balanced head is supported on a trunk full of symmetry and dignity, and whose branches almost sweep the turf in their rich luxuriance ; as a picturesque contrast, some pine or larch, whose gnarled roots grasp the rocky crag on which it grows, and whose wild and irregular branches tell of the storm and tempest that it has so often struggled against.†

In pictures, too, one often hears the Beautiful confounded with the Picturesque. Yet they are quite distinct ; though in many subjects they may be found harmoniously combined. Some of Raphael's angels may be taken as perfect illustrations of the Beautiful. In their serene and heavenly

* Hogarth called the curve the line of beauty, and all artists have felt instinct-vely its power, but Mr. Ruskin (in Modern Painters) was, we believe, the first to suggest the cause of that power—that it expresses in its varying ten-dencies, the infinite.

† This also explains why trees, though they retain for the most part their characteristic forms, vary somewhat in expression according to their situation. Thus the larch, though always picturesque, is far more so in mountain ridges where it is exposed to every blast, than in sheltered lawns where it only finds soft airs and sunshine.

countenances we see only that calm and pure existence of
which perfect beauty is the outward type; on the other hand,
Murillo's beggar boys are only picturesque. What we admire in them (beyond admirable execution) is not their rags
or their mean apparel, but a certain irregular struggling
of a better feeling within, against this outward poverty of
nature and condition.

Architecture borrows, partly perhaps by association, the
same expression. We find the Beautiful in the most sym
metrical edifices, built in the finest proportions, and of the
purest materials. It is, on the other hand, in some irregu
lar castle formed for defence, some rude mill nearly as wild as
the glen where it is placed, some thatched cottage, weather
stained and moss covered, that we find the Picturesque.
The Temple of Jupiter Olympus in all its perfect proportions
was prized by the Greeks as a model of beauty; we, who
see only a few columns and broken architraves standing
with all their exquisite mouldings obliterated by the vio
lence of time and the elements, find them Picturesque.

To return to a more practical view of the subject,
we may remark, that though we consider the Beautiful and
the Picturesque quite distinct, yet it by no means follows
that they may not be combined in the same landscape.
This is often seen in nature ; and indeed there are few
landscapes of large extent where they are not thus harmoniously combined.

But it must be remembered, that while Landscape Gardening is an imitation of nature, yet it is rarely attempted
on so large a scale as to be capable of the same extended
harmony and variety of expression ; and also, that in Landscape Gardening as in the other fine arts, we shall be more
successful by directing our efforts towards the production

of a *leading* character or expression, than by endeavoring to join and harmonize several.

Our own views on this subject are simply these. When a place is small, and only permits a single phase of natural expression, always endeavor to heighten or to make that single expression predominate; it should clearly either aim only at the Beautiful or the Picturesque.

When, on the contrary, an estate of large size comes within the scope of the Landscape Gardener, he is at liberty to give to each separate scene its most fitting character; he will thus, if he is a skilful artist, be able to create great variety both of beautiful and picturesque expression, and he will also be able to give a higher proof of his power, viz. by uniting all those scenes into one whole, by bringing them all into harmony. An artist who can do this has reached the ultimatum of his art.

Again and again has it been said, that Landscape Gardening and Painting are allied. In no one point does it appear to us that they are so, more than in this—that in proportion to the limited nature of the subject should simplicity and unity of expression be remembered. In some of the finest smaller compositions of Raphael, or some of the Landscapes of Claude, so fully is this borne in mind, that every object, however small, seems to be instinct with the same expression; while in many of the great historical pictures, unity and harmony are wrought out of the most complex variety of expression.

We must not be supposed to find in nature only the Beautiful and the Picturesque. Grandeur and Sublimity are also expressions strongly marked in many of the noblest portions of natural landscape. But, except in very rare instances, they are wholly beyond the powers of the landscape gardener, at least in the comparatively limited scale

of his operations in this country.   All that he has to do, is
to respect them where they exist in natural landscape which
forms part of his work of art, and so treat the latter, as
to make it accord with, or at least not violate, the higher
and predominant expression of the whole.

There are, however, certain subordinate expressions
which may be considered as qualities of the Beautiful, and
which may originally so prevail in natural landscape, or be
so elicited or created by art, as to give a distinct character
to a small country residence, or portions of a large one.
These are simplicity, dignity, grace, elegance, gaiety,
chasteness, &c.   It is not necessary that we should go
into a labored explanation of these expressions.   They are
more or less familiar to all.   A few fine trees, scattered
and grouped over any surface of smooth lawn, will give a
character of simple beauty ; lofty trees of great age,
hills covered with rich wood, an elevation commanding a
wide country, stamp a site with dignity ; trees of full and
graceful habit or gently curving forms in the lawn, walks,
and all other objects, will convey the idea of grace ; as
finely formed and somewhat tall trees of rare species, or a
great abundance of bright climbers and gay flowering shrubs
and plants, will confer characters of elegance and gaiety.

He who would create in his pleasure grounds these more
delicate shades of expression, must become a profound stu-
dent both of nature and art ; he must be able, by his
own original powers, to seize the subtle essence, the half
disclosed idea involved in the finest parts of nature, and to
reproduce and develope it in his Landscape Garden.

Leaving such, however, to a broader range of study than
a volume like this would afford, we may offer what, perhaps, will not be unacceptable to the novice—a more de-

tailed sketch of the distinctive features of the Beautiful and
the Picturesque, as these expressions should be embodied
in Landscape Gardening.

THE BEAUTIFUL in Landscape Gardening (Fig. 13) is
produced by outlines whose curves are flowing and gradual,
surfaces of softness, and growth of richness and luxuriance.
In the shape of the ground, it is evinced by easy undulations
melting gradually into each other.   In the form of trees, by
smooth stems, full, round, or symmetrical heads of foliage,
and luxuriant branches often drooping to the ground,—which
is chiefly attained by planting and grouping, to allow free
development of form ; and by selecting trees of suitable character, as the elm, the ash, and the like.   In walks and
roads, by easy flowing curves, following natural shapes of
the surface, with no sharp angles or abrupt turns.   In water,
by the smooth lake with curved margin, embellished with
flowing outlines of trees, and full masses of flowering
shrubs—or in the easy winding curves of a brook.   The
keeping of such a scene should be of the most polished
kind,—grass mown into a softness like velvet, gravel walks
scrupulously firm, dry, and clean ; and the most perfect
order and neatness should reign throughout.   Among the
trees and shrubs should be conspicuous the finest foreign
sorts, distinguished by beauty of form, foliage, and blossom ;
and rich groups of shrubs and flowering plants should be
arranged in the more dressed portions near the house.
And finally, considering the house itself as a feature in the
scene, it should properly belong to one of the classical
modes ; and the Italian, Tuscan, or Venetian forms are
preferable, because these have both a polished and a
domestic air, and readily admit of the graceful accompaniments of vases, urns, and other harmonious
accessories.   Or, if we are to have a plainer dwelling,

FIG. 13.—Example of the Beautiful in Landscape Gardening.

FIG. 14.—Example of the Picturesque in Landscape Gardening.

it should be simple and symmetrical in its character, and
its veranda festooned with masses of the finest climbers.

THE PICTURESQUE in Landscape Gardening (Fig. 14)
aims at the production of outlines of a certain spirited
irregularity, surfaces comparatively abrupt and broken,
and growth of a somewhat wild and bold character. The
shape of the ground sought after, has its occasional
smoothness varied by sudden variations, and in parts runs
into dingles, rocky groups, and broken banks. The trees
should in many places be old and irregular, with rough
stems and bark ; and pines, larches, and other trees of
striking, irregular growth, must appear in numbers sufficient
to give character to the woody outlines. As, to produce
the Beautiful, the trees are planted singly in open groups
to allow full expansion, so for the Picturesque, the grouping
takes every variety of form ; almost every object should
group with another ; trees and shrubs are often planted
closely together ; and intricacy and variety—thickets—
glades—and underwood—as in wild nature, are indispensable. Walks and roads are more abrupt in their windings,
turning off frequently at sudden angles where the form of
the ground or some inviting object directs. In water, all
the wildness of romantic spots in nature is to be imitated
or preserved ; and the lake or stream with bold shore and
rocky, wood-fringed margin, or the cascade in the secluded
dell, are the characteristic forms. The keeping of such a
landscape will of course be less careful than in the
graceful school. Firm gravel walks near the house, and
a general air of neatness in that quarter, are indispensable
to the fitness of the scene in all modes, and indeed properly
evince the recognition of art in all Landscape Gardening.
But the lawn may be less frequently mown, the edges of

the walks less carefully trimmed, where the Picturesque
prevails; while in portions more removed from the house,
the walks may sometimes sink into a mere footpath
without gravel, and the lawn change into the forest glade
or meadow. The architecture which belongs to the
picturesque landscape, is the Gothic mansion, the old
English or the Swiss cottage, or some other striking
forms, with bold projections, deep shadows, and irregular
outlines. Rustic baskets, and similar ornaments, may
abound near the house, and in the more frequented parts
of the place.

The *recognition of art*, as Loudon justly observes, is a
first principle in Landscape Gardening, as in all other arts;
and those of its professors have erred, who supposed that
the object of this art is merely to produce a fac-simile of
nature, that could not be distinguished from a wild scene.
But we contend that this principle may be fully attained
with either expression—the picturesque cottage being as
well a work of art as the classic villa; its baskets, and
seats of rustic work, indicating the hand of man as well
as the marble vase and balustrade; and a walk, sometimes
narrow and crooked, is as certainly recognised as man's
work, as one always regular and flowing. Foreign trees
of picturesque growth are as readily obtained as those of
beautiful forms. The recognition of art is, therefore,
always apparent in both modes. The evidences are
indeed stronger and more multiplied in the careful polish
of the Beautiful landscape,* and hence many prefer this

* The *beau ideal* in Landscape Gardening, as a fine art, appears to us to be
embraced in the creation of scenery full of expression, as the beautiful or picturesque, the materials of which are, to a certain extent, different from those in
wild nature, being composed of the floral and arboricultural riches of *all climates,*
as far as possible; uniting in the same scene, a richness and a variety never to

species of landscape, not, as it deserves to be preferred, because it displays the most beautiful and perfect ideas in its outlines, the forms of its trees, and all that enters into its composition, but chiefly because it also is marked by that careful polish, and that completeness, which imply the expenditure of money, which they so well know how to value.

If we declare that the Beautiful is the more perfect expression in landscape, we shall be called upon to explain why the Picturesque is so much more attractive to many minds. This, we conceive, is owing partly to the imperfection of our natures by which most of us sympathize more with that in which the struggle between spirit and matter is most apparent, than with that in which the union is harmonious and complete; and partly because from the comparative rarity of highly picturesque landscape, it affects us more forcibly when brought into contrast with our daily life. Artists, we imagine, find somewhat of the same pleasure in studying wild landscape, where the very rocks and trees seem to struggle with the elements for foothold, that they do in contemplating the phases of the passions and instincts of human and animal life. The manifestation of power is to many minds far more captivating than that of beauty.

All who enjoy the charms of Landscape Gardening, may perhaps be divided into three classes : those who have arrived only at certain primitive ideas of beauty which are found in regular forms and straight lines; those who in the Beautiful seek for the highest and most perfect

be found in any one portion of nature ;—a scene characterized as a work of art, by the variety of the materials, as foreign trees, plants, &c., and by the polish and keeping of the grounds in the natural style, as distinctly as by the uniform and symmetrical arrangement in the ancient style.

development of the idea in the material form ; and those who in the Picturesque enjoy most a certain wild and incomplete harmony between the idea and the forms in which it is expressed.

As the two latter classes embrace the whole range of modern Landscape Gardening, we shall keep distinctly in view their two governing principles—the Beautiful and the Picturesque, in treating of the practice of the art.

There are always circumstances which must exert a controlling influence over amateurs, in this country, in choosing between the two. These are, fixed locality, ex- pense, individual preference in the style of building, and many others which readily occur to all. The great variety of attractive sites in the older parts of the country, afford an abundance of opportunity for either taste   Within the last five years, we think the Picturesque is beginning to be pre- ferred. It has, when a suitable locality offers, great advan- tages for us. The raw materials of wood, water, and sur- face, by the margin of many of our rivers and brooks, are at once appropriated with so much effect, and so little art, in the picturesque mode ; the annual tax on the purse too is so comparatively little, and the charm so great!

While, on one hand, the residences of a country of level plains usually allow only the beauty of simple and grace- ful forms ; the larger demesne, with its swelling hills and noble masses of wood (may we not, prospectively, say the rolling prairie too ?), should always, in the hands of the man of wealth, be made to display all the breadth, va- riety, and harmony of both the Beautiful and the Pictu- resque.

There is no surface of ground, however bare, which has not, naturally, more or less tendency to one or the other of these expressions. And the improver who detects the true character, and plants, builds, and embellishes, as he should constantly aiming to elicit and strengthen it—will soon arrive at a far higher and more satisfactory result, than one who, in the common manner, works at random.   The latter may succeed in producing pleasing grounds—he will **un**doubtedly add to the general beauty and tasteful appearance of the country, and we gladly accord him our thanks.   But the improver who unites with pleasing forms an expression of sentiment, will affect not only the common eye, but much more powerfully, the imagination, and the refined and delicate taste.

But there are many persons with small cottage places, of little decided character, who have neither room, time, nor income, to attempt the improvement of their grounds fully, after either of those two schools. How shall they render their places tasteful and agreeable, in the easiest manner ? We answer, *by attempting only the simple and the natural;* and the unfailing way to secure this, is by employing as leading features only trees and grass. A soft verdant lawn, a few forest or ornamental trees well grouped, walks, and a few flowers, give universal pleasure ; they contain in themselves, in fact, the basis of all our agreeable sensations in a landscape garden (natural beauty, and the recognition of art) ; and they are the most enduring sources of enjoyment in any place. There are no country seats in the United States so unsatisfactory and tasteless, as those in which, without any definite aim, everything is attempted ; and a mixed jumble of discordant forms, materials, ornaments, and decorations, is assembled—a part in one style and a bit in another, without the least feeling of unity or congruity. These rural bedlams, full of all kinds of absurdities, without a leading character or expression of any sort, cost their

owners a vast deal of trouble and money, without giving a
tasteful mind a shadow of the beauty which it feels at the
first glimpse of a neat cottage residence, with its simple,
sylvan character of well kept lawn and trees.   If the latter
does not rank high in the scale of Landscape Gardening
as an art, it embodies much of its essence as a source of
enjoyment—the production of the Beautiful in country
residences.

Besides the beauties of form and expression in the different modes of laying out grounds, there are certain universal and nherent beauties common to all styles, and, indeed,
to every composition in the fine arts.   Of these, we shall
especially point out those growing out of the principles of
UNITY, HARMONY, and VARIETY.

UNITY, or the *production of a whole*, is a leading
principle of the highest importance, in every art of taste or
design, without which no satisfactory result can be
realized   This arises from the fact, that the mind can only
attend, with pleasure and satisfaction, to one object, or one
composite sensation, at the same time.   If two distinct
objects, or classes of objects, present themselves at once to
us, we can only attend satisfactorily to one, by withdrawing our attention for the time from the other.   Hence the
necessity of a reference to this leading principle of unity.

To illustrate the subject, let us suppose a building,
partially built of wood, with square windows, and the
remainder of brick or stone, with long and narrow
windows.   However well such a building may be constructed, or however nicely the different proportions of the
edifice may be adjusted, it is evident it can never form a
satisfactory whole.   The mind can only account for such
an absurdity, by supposing it to have been built by two

individuals, or at two different times, as there is nothing indicating unity of mind in its composition.

In Landscape Gardening, violations of the principle of unity are often to be met with, and they are always indicative of the absence of correct taste in art. Looking upon a landscape from the windows of a villa residence, we sometimes see a considerable portion of the view embraced by the eye, laid out in natural groups of trees and shrubs, and upon one side, or perhaps in the middle of the same scene, a formal avenue leading directly up to the house. Such a view can never appear a satisfactory whole, because we experience a confusion of sensations in contemplating it. There is an evident incongruity in bringing two modes of arranging plantations, so totally different, under the eye at one moment, which distracts, rather than pleases the mind. In this example, the avenue, taken by itself, may be a beautiful object, and the groups and connected masses may, in themselves, be elegant; yet if the two portions are seen together, they will not form a whole, because they cannot make a composite idea. For the same reason, there is something unpleasing in the introduction of fruit trees among elegant ornamental trees on a lawn, or even in assembling together, in the same beds, flowering plants and culinary vegetables—one class of vegetation suggesting the useful and homely alone to the mind, and the other, avowedly, only the ornamental.

In the arrangement of a large extent of surface, where a great many objects are necessarily presented to the eye at once, the principle of unity will suggest that there should be some grand or leading features to which the others should be merely subordinate. Thus, in grouping trees, there should be some large and striking masses to which the others appear to belong, however distant, instead of scattered groups, all of the same size. Even in arranging walks, a whole will more readily be recognised, if there are one or two of large size, with which the others appear connected as branches, than if all are equal in breadth, and present the same appearance to the eye in passing.

In all works of art which command universal admiration we discover an unity of conception and composition, an unity of taste and execution. To assemble in a single composition forms which are discordant, and portions dissimilar in plan, can only afford pleasure for a short time to tasteless minds, or those fona of trifling and puerile conceits. The production of an accordant whole is, on the contrary, capable of affording the most permanent enjoyment to educated minds, everywhere, and at all periods of time.

After unity, the principle of VARIETY is worthy of con-sideration, as a fertile source of beauty in Landscape Gar-dening. Variety must be considered as belonging more to the details than to the production of a whole, and it may be attained by disposing trees and shrubs in numerous dif-ferent ways ; and by the introduction of a great number ot different species of vegetation, or kinds of walks, ornamental objects, buildings, and seats. By producing intricacy, it creates in scenery a thousand points of interest, and elicits new beauties, through different arrangements and combi-nations of forms and colors, light and shades.   In pleasure-grounds, while the whole should exhibit a general plan, the different scenes presented to the eye, one after the other, should possess sufficient variety in the detail to keep alive the interest of the spectator, and awaken further curiosity.

HARMONY may be considered the principle presiding over variety, and preventing it from becoming discordant. It, indeed, always supposes *contrasts*, but neither so strong nor so frequent as to produce discord ; and *variety,* but not so great as to destroy a leading expression.   In plantations, we seek it in a combination of qualities, opposite in some respects, as in the color of the foliage, and similar in others more important, as the form.   In embellishments, by a great variety of objects of interest, as sculptured vases, sun dials, or rustic seats, baskets, and arbors, of different forms, but all in accordance, or keeping with the spirit of the scene.

To illustrate the three principles, with reference to **Landscape Gardening,** we may remark, that, if unity only were consulted, a scene might be planted with but one kind of tree, the effect of which would be sameness ; on the other hand, variety might be carried so far as to have every tree of a different kind, which would produce a confused effect. Harmony, however, introduces contrast and variety, but keeps them subordinate to unity, and to the leading expression ; and is, thus, the highest principle of the three.

In this brief abstract of the nature of imitation in Landscape Gardening and the kinds of beauty which it is possible to produce by means of the art, we have endeavored to elucidate its leading principles, clearly, to the reader. These grand principles we shall here succinctly recapitulate, premising that a familiarity with them is of the very first importance in the successful practice of this elegant art, viz. :

THE IMITATION OF THE BEAUTY OF EXPRESSION, derived from a refined perception of the sentiment of nature : THE RECOGNITION OF ART, founded on the immutability of the true, as well as the beautiful : AND THE PRODUCTION OF UNITY, HARMONY, AND VARIETY, in order to render complete and continuous, our enjoyment of any artistical work.

Neither the professional Landscape Gardener, nor the amateur, can hope for much success in realizing the nobler effects of the art, unless he first make himself master of the natural character or prevailing expression of the place to be improved. In this nice perception, at a glance, of the natural expression, as well as the capabilities of a residence, lies the secret of the superior results produced even by the improver, who, to use the words of Horace Walpole, " is proud of no other art than that of softening nature's harshness, and copying her graceful touch." When we discover the *picturesque* indicated in the grounds of the residence to be treated, let us take advantage of it ; and while all harshness incompatible with scenery near the house is removed, the original expression may in most cases be heightened, in all rendered more elegant and appropriate, without lowering it in force or spirit. In like manner good taste will direct us to embellish scenery expressive of *the Beautiful*, by the addition of forms, whether in trees, buildings, or other objects, harmonious in character, as well as in color and outline.

SECTION III.

ON WOOD.

The beauty of **Trees in Rural Embellishments.** Pleasure resulting from their cultivation.
Plantations in the Ancient Style; their formality. In the Modern Style; grouping trees.
Arrangement and grouping in the Graceful school; in the Picturesque school. Illustrations in planting villa, ferme ornée, and cottage grounds. General classification of trees
as to forms, with leading characteristics of each class.

> " He gains all points, who pleasingly confounds,
> Surprises, varies, and conceals the bounds.
> Calls in the country, catches opening glades,
> Joins willing woods, and varies shades from shades ;
> Now breaks, or now directs the intending lines ;
> Paints as you plant, and, as you work, designs."
>
> POPE.

M O N G all the materials at our disposal
for the embellishment of country residences, none are at once so highly orna-
mental, so indispensable, and so easily managed, as *trees*, or
wood. We introduce them in every part of the landscape,
—in the foreground as well as in the distance, on the tops
of the hills and in the depths of the valleys. They are, indeed, like the drapery which covers a somewhat ungainly
figure, and while it conceals its defects, communicates to it
new interest and expression.

A tree, undoubtedly, is one of the most beautiful objects
in nature. Airy and delicate in its youth, luxuriant and
majestic in its prime, venerable and picturesque in its old

age, it constitutes in its various forms, sizes, and developments, the greatest charm and beauty of the earth in all
countries. The most varied outline of surface, the finest
combination of picturesque materials, the stateliest country
house would be comparatively tame and spiritless, without
the inimitable accompaniment of foliage. Let those who
have passed their whole lives in a richly wooded country,
—whose daily visions are deep leafy glens, forest clad hills,
and plains luxuriantly shaded,—transport themselves for a
moment to the desert, where but a few stunted bushes raise
their heads above the earth, or those wild steppes where
the eye wanders in vain for some "leafy garniture,"—where
the sun strikes down with parching heat, or the wind
sweeps over with unbroken fury, and they may, perhaps
estimate, by contrast, their beauty and value.

We are not now to enumerate the great usefulness of
trees,—their value in the construction of our habitations,
our navies, the various implements of labor,—in short, the
thousand associations which they suggest as ministering to
our daily wants; but let us imagine the loveliest scene, the
wildest landscape, or the most enchanting valley, despoiled
of *trees*, and we shall find nature shorn of her fair proportions, and the character and expression of these favorite
spots almost entirely destroyed.

Wood, in its many shapes, is then one of the greatest
sources of interest and character in Landscapes. Variety,
which we need scarcely allude to as a fertile source of
beauty, is created in a wonderful degree by a natural
arrangement of trees. To a pile of buildings, or even of
ruins, to a group of rocks or animals, they communicate
new life and spirit by their irregular outlines, which, by
partially concealing some portions, and throwing others

into stronger light, contribute greatly to produce intricacy and variety, and confer an expression, which, without these latter qualities, might in a great measure be wanting. By shutting out some parts, and inclosing others, they divide the extent embraced by the eye into a hundred different landscapes, instead of one tame scene bounded by the horizon.

The different seasons of the year, too, are inseparably connected in our minds with the effects produced by them on woodland scenery. Spring is joyous and enlivening to us, as nature then puts on her fresh livery of green, and the trees bud and blossom with a renewed beauty, that speaks with a mute and gentle eloquence to the heart. In summer they offer us a grateful shelter under their umbrageous arms and leafy branches, and whisper unwritten music to the passing breeze. In autumn we feel a melancholy thoughtfulness as

" We stand among the fallen leaves,"

and gaze upon their dying glories. And in winter we see in them the silent rest of nature, and behold in their leafless spray, and seemingly dead limbs, an annual type of that deeper mystery—the deathless sleep of all being.

By the judicious employment of trees in the embellishment of a country residence, we may effect the greatest alterations and improvements within the scope of Landscape Gardening. Buildings which are tame, insipid, or even mean in appearance, may be made interesting, and often picturesque, by a proper disposition of trees. Edifices, or parts of them that are unsightly, or which it is desirable partly or wholly to conceal, can readily be hidden or improved by wood; and walks and roads, which otherwise would be but simple ways of approach from one point to another, are, by an elegant arrangement of trees on their margins, or adjacent to them, made the most interesting and pleasing portions of the residence.

In Geometric gardening, trees disposed in formal lines, exhibit as strongly art or design in the contriver, as regular architectural edifices; while, in a more elevated and enlightened taste, we are able to dispose them in our pleasure-grounds and parks, around our houses, in all the variety of groups, masses, thicket, and single trees, in such a manner as to rival the most beautiful scenery of general nature; producing a portion of landscape which unites with all the comforts and conveniences of rural habitation, the superior charm of refined arrangement, and natural beauty of expression.

If it were necessary to present any other inducement to the country gentleman to form plantations of trees, than the great beauty and value which they add to his estate, we might find it in the pleasure which all derive from their cultivation. Unlike the pleasure arising from the gratification of our taste in architecture, or any other of the arts whose productions are offered to us perfect and complete, the satisfaction arising from planting and rearing trees is never weakened. "We look," says a writer, "upon our trees as our offspring; and nothing of inanimate nature can be more gratifying than to see them grow and prosper under our care and attention,— nothing more interesting than to examine their progress, and mark their several peculiarities. In their progress from plants to trees, they every year unfold new and characteristic marks of their ultimate beauty, which not only compensate for past cares and troubles, but like the returns of gratitude, raise a most delightful train of sensations in the mind; so innocent and rational, that they may justly rank with the most exquisite of human enjoyments."

> " Happy is he, who in a country life
> Shuns more perplexing toil and jarring strife;
> Who lives upon the natal soil he loves,
> And sits beneath his old ancestral groves."

To this, let us add the complacent feelings with which a man in old age may look around him and behold these leafy monarchs, planted by his boyish hands and nurtured by him in his youthful years, which have grown aged and venerable along with him;

> " A wood coeval with himself he sees,
> And loves his own contemporary trees."

PLANTATIONS IN THE ANCIENT STYLE. In the arrangement and culture of trees and plants in the ancient style of Landscape Gardening, we discover the evidences of the formal taste,—abounding with every possible variety of quaint conceits, and rife with whimsical expedients, so much in fashion during the days of Henry and Elizabeth, and until the eighteenth century in England, and which is still the reigning mode in Holland, and parts of France. In these gardens, nature was tamed and subdued, or as some critics will have it, tortured into every shape which the ingenuity of the gardener could suggest; and such kinds of vegetation as bore the shears most patiently, and when carefully trimmed, assumed gradually the appearance of verdant statues, pyramids, crowing cocks, and rampant lions, were the especial favorites of the gardeners of the old school.

It has been remarked, that the geometric style would always be preferred in a new country, or in any country where the amount of land under cultivation is much less than that covered with natural woods and forests; as the inhabitants being surrounded by scenery abounding with natural beauty, would always incline to lay out their gardens and pleasure-grounds in regular forms, because the distinct exhibition of art would give more pleasure by contrast, than the elegant imitation of beautiful nature. That this is true as regards the mass of uncultivated minds, we do not deny. But at the same time we affirm that it evinces a meagre taste, and a lower state of the art, or a lower perception of beauty in the individual who employs the geometrical style in such cases. A person, whose place is surrounded by inimitably grand or sublime scenery, would undoubtedly fail to excite our admiration, by attempting a fac-simile imitation of such scenery on the small scale of a park or garden; but he is not, therefore, obliged to resort to right-lined plantations and regular grass plots, to produce something which shall be at once sufficiently different to attract notice, and so beautiful as to command admiration. All that it would be requisite for him to do in such a case, would be to employ rare and foreign ornamental trees; as for example, the horse-chestnut and the linden, in situations where the maple and the sycamore are the principal trees,—elegant flowering shrubs and beautiful creepers, instead of sumacs and hazels,—and to have his place kept in high and polished order, instead of the tangled wildness of general nature.

On the contrary, were a person to desire a residence newly laid out and planted, in a district where all around is in a high state of polished cultivation, as in the suburbs of a city, a species of pleasure would result from the imitation of scenery of a more spirited, natural character, as the picturesque, in his grounds. His plantations are made in irregular groups, composed chiefly of picturesque trees, as the larch, &c.—his walks would lead through varied scenes, sometimes bordered with groups of rocks overrun with flowering creepers and vines; sometimes with thickets or little copses of shrubs and flowering plants; sometimes through wild and comparatively neglected portions; the whole interspersed with open glades of turf.

In the majority of instances in the United States, the modern style of Landscape Gardening, wherever it is appreciated, will, in practice, consist in arranging a demesne of from five to some hundred acres,—or rather that portion of it, say one half, one third, etc., devoted to lawn and pleasure-ground, pasture, etc.—so as to exhibit groups of forest and ornamental trees and shrubs, surrounding the dwelling of the proprietor, and extending for a greater or less distance, especially towards the place of entrance from the public highway. Near the house, good taste will dictate the assemblage of groups and masses of the rarer or more beautiful trees and shrubs; commoner native forest trees occupying the more distant portions of the grounds.*

---

* Although we love planting, and avow that there are few greater pleasures than to see a darling tree, of one's own placing, every year stretching wider its feathery head of foliage, and covering with a darker shadow the soft turf beneath it, still, we will not let the ardent and inexperienced hunter after a location for a country residence, pass without a word of advice. This is, *always to make considerable sacrifice to get a place with some existing wood, or a few ready grown trees upon it;* especially near the site for the house. It is better to yield a little in the extent of prospect, or in the direct proximity to a certain

PLANTATIONS IN THE MODERN STYLE. In the Modern Style of Landscape Gardening, it is our aim, in plantations, to produce not only what is called natural beauty, but even higher and more striking beauty of expression, and ot individual forms, than we see in nature ; to create variety and intricacy in the grounds of a residence by various modes of arrangement ; to give a highly elegant or polished air to places by introducing rare and foreign species ; and to conceal all defects of surface, disagreeable views, unsightly buildings, or other offensive objects.

As uniformity, and grandeur of single effects, were the aim of the old style of arrangement, so variety and harmony of the whole are the results for which we labor in the modern landscape. And as the *Avenue*, or the straight line, is the leading form in the geometric arrangement of plantations, so let us enforce it upon our readers, the GROUP is equally the key-note of the Modern style. The smallest place, having only three trees, may have these pleasingly connected in a group ; and the largest and finest park—the Blenheim or Chatsworth, of seven miles square, is only composed of a succession of groups, becoming masses, thickets, woods. If a demesne with the most beautiful surface and views has been for some time stiffly and

locality, than to pitcn your tent in a plain,—desert-like in its bareness—on which your leafy sensibilities must suffer for half a dozen vears at least, before you can hope for any solace. It is doubtful whether there is not almost as much interest in studying from one's window the curious ramifications, tne variety of form, and the entire harmony, to be found in a fine old tree, as .n gazing from a site where we have no interruption to a panorama of tne whole horizon ; and we have generally found tha no planters have so little courage and faith, as those who have commenced without the smallest group of large trees, as a nucleus for their plantations.

awkwardly planted, it is exceedingly difficult to give it a natural and agreeable air ; while many a tame level, with scarcely a glimpse of distance, has been rendered lovely by its charming groups of trees. How necessary, therefore, is it, in the very outset, that the novice, before he begins to plant, should know how to arrange a tasteful group!

Nothing, at first thought, would appear easier than to arrange a few trees in the form of a natural and beautiful group,—and nothing really is easier to the practised hand. Yet experience has taught us that the generality of persons, in commencing their first essays in ornamental planting, almost invariably crowd their trees into a close, regular *clump*, which has a most formal and unsightly appearance as different as possible from the easy, flowing outline of the group.

" Natural groups are full of openings and hollows, of trees advancing before, or retiring behind each other ; all productive of intricacy, of variety, of deep shadows and brilliant lights."

The chief care, then, which is necessary in the forma tion of groups, is, *not* to place them in any regular or artificial manner,—as one at each corner of a triangle, square, octagon, or other many-sided figure ; but so to dispose them, as that the whole may exhibit the variety, connexion, and intricacy seen in nature. " The greatest beauty of a group of trees," says Loudon, "as far as respects their stems, is in the varied direction these take as they grow into trees ; but as that is, for all practical purposes, beyond the influence of art, all we can do, is to vary as much as possible the ground plan of groups, or the relative positions which the stems have to each other where they spring from the earth. This is considerable,

even where a very few trees are used, of which any
person may convince himself by placing a few dots on
paper. Thus two trees (fig. 15), or a tree and shrub,
which is the smallest group (*a*), may be placed in three
different positions with reference to a spectator in a fixed
point; if he moves round them, they will first vary in form
separately, and next unite in one or two groups, according
to the position of the spectator. In like manner, three
trees may be placed in four different positions ; four trees
may be placed in eight different positions (*b*) ; five trees
may be grouped in ten different ways, as to ground plan;
six may be placed in twelve different ways (*c*), and so on."
  Encyclopædia of Gard.)

[Fig. 15. Grouping of Trees.]

In the composition of larger masses, similar rules must

be observed as in the smaller groups, in order to prevent them from growing up in heavy, clumpish forms. The outline must be flowing, here projecting out into the grass, there receding back into the plantation, in order to take off all appearance of stiffness and regularity. Trees of medium and smaller size should be so interspersed with those of larger growth, as to break up all formal sweeps in the line produced by the tops of their summits, and occasionally, low trees should be planted on the outer edge of the mass, to connect it with the humble verdure of the surrounding sward.

In many parts of the union, where new residences are being formed, or where old ones are to be improved, the grounds will often be found, partially, or to a considerable extent, clothed with belts or masses of wood, either previously planted, or preserved from the woodman's axe. How easily we may turn these to advantage in the natural style of Landscape Gardening; and by judicious trimming when too thick, or additions when too much scattered, elicit often the happiest effects, in a magical manner!

Where there are large masses of wood to regulate and arrange, much skill, taste, and judgment, are requisite, to enable the proprietors to preserve only what is really beautiful and picturesque, and to remove all that is superfluous. Most of our native woods, too, have grown so closely, and the trees are consequently so much drawn up, that should the improver thin out any portion, at once, to *single* trees, he will be greatly disappointed if he expects them to stand long; for the first severe autumnal gale will almost certainly prostrate them. The only method, therefore, is to allow them to remain in groups of considerable size at first, and to thin them out as is finally desired, when they have made stronger roots and become more inured to the influence of the sun and air.

But to return to grouping; what we have already endeavored to render familiar to the reader, may be called
grouping in its simple meaning—for general effect, and
with an eye only to the natural beauty of pleasing forms
Let us now explain, as concisely as we may, the mode of
grouping in the two schools of Landscape Gardening heretofore defined, that is to say, grouping and planting for
Beautiful effect, and for Picturesque effect; as we wish it
understood that these two different expressions, in artificial
landscape, are always to a certain extent under our control.

PLANTING AND GROUPING TO PRODUCE THE BEAUTIFUL.
The elementary features of this expression our readers
will remember to be fulness and softness of outline, and
perfectly luxuriant development.   To insure these in plantations, we must commence by choosing mainly trees of
graceful habit and flowing outlines; and of this class of
trees, hereafter more fully illustrated, the American elm
and the maple may be taken as the type.   Next, in disposing them, they must usually be planted rather distant
in the groups, and often singly.   We do not mean by this,
that close groups may not occasionally be formed, but there
should be a predominance of trees grouped at such a distance from each other, as to allow a full development of
the branches on every side.   Or, when a close group is
planted, the trees composing it should be usually of the
same or a similar kind, in order that they may grow up
together and form one finely rounded head.   Rich creepers
and blossoming vines, that grow in fine luxuriant wreaths
and masses, are fit accompaniments to occasional groups
in this manner.   Fig. 16 represents a plan of trees grouped
along a road or walk, so as to develope the Beautiful.

It is proper that we should here remark, that a distinct
species of after treatment is required for the two modes.
Trees, or groups, where the Beautiful is aimed at, should be

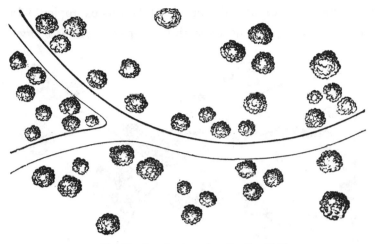

[Fig. 16. Grouping to produce the Beautiful.]

pruned with great care, and indeed scarcely at all, except
to remedy disease, or to correct a bad form.   Above all,
the full luxuriance and development of the tree should be
encouraged by good soil, and repeated manurings when
necessary ; and that most expressively elegant fall and
droop of the branches, which so completely denotes the
Beautiful in trees, should never be warred against by any
trimming of the lower branches, which must also be carefully preserved against cattle, whose *browsing line* would
soon efface this most beautiful disposition in some of our
fine lawn trees.   Clean, smooth stems, fresh and tender
bark, and a softly rounded pyramidal or drooping head,
are the characteristics of a Beautiful tree.   We need not
add that gently sloping ground, or surfaces rolling in easy
undulations, should accompany such plantations.

PLANTING AND GROUPING TO PRODUCE THE PICTURESQUE.
All trees are admissible in a picturesque place, but a predominance must be used by the planter of what are truly
called picturesque trees, of which the larch and fir tribe

and some species of oak, may be taken as examples. In Picturesque plantations everything depends on *intricacy*

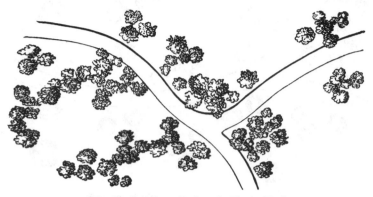

[Fig. 17 Grouping to produce the Picturesque.]

and *irregularity*, and grouping, therefore, must often be done in the most irregular manner—rarely, if ever, with single specimens, as every object should seem to connect itself with something else; but most frequently there should be irregular groups, occasionally running into thickets, and always more or less touching each other; trusting to after time for any thinning, should it be necessary. Fig. 17 may, as compared with Fig. 16, give an idea of picturesque grouping.

There should be more of the wildness of the finest and most forcible portions of natural woods or forests, in the disposition of the trees; sometimes planting them closely, even two or three in the same hole, at others more loose and scattered. These will grow up into wilder and more striking forms, the barks will be deeply furrowed and rough, the limbs twisted and irregular, and the forms and outlines distinctly varied. They should often be intermixed with smaller undergrowth of a similar character, as the hazel, hawthorn, etc., and formed into such picturesque and striking groups, as painters love to study and introduce into their pictures. Sturdy and bright vines, or such as are themselves picturesque in their festoons and hangings, should be allowed to clamber over occasional trees in a negligent manner; and the surface and grass, in parts of the scene not immediately in the neighborhood of the mansion, may be kept short by the cropping of animals, or allowed to grow in a more careless and loose state, like that of tangled dells and natural woods.

There will be the same open glades in picturesque as in beautiful plantations; but these openings, in the former, will be bounded by groups and thickets of every form, and of different degrees of intricacy, while in the latter the eye will repose on softly rounded masses of foliage, or single open groups of trees, with finely balanced and graceful heads and branches.

In order to know how a plantation in the Picturesque mode should be treated, after it is established, we should reflect a moment on what constitutes picturesqueness in any tree. This will be found to consist either in a certain natural roughness of bark, or wildness of form and outline, or in some accidental curve of a branch of striking manner of growth, or perhaps of both these conjoined. A broken or crooked limb, a leaning trunk, or several stems springing from the same base, are frequently peculiarities that at once stamp a tree as picturesque. Hence, it is easy to see that the excessive care of the cultivator of trees in the graceful school to obtain the smoothest trunks, and the most sweeping, perfect, and luxuriant heads of foliage, is quite the opposite of what is the picturesque arboriculturist's ambition. He desires to encourage a certain wildness of growth, and allows his trees to spring up occasionally in thickets

to assist this effect; he delights in occasional irregularity
of stem and outline, and he therefore suffers his trees here
and there to crowd each other; he admires a twisted limb
or a moss covered branch, and in pruning he therefore is
careful to leave precisely what it would be the aim of the
other to remove; and his pruning, where it is at all necessary, is directed rather towards increasing the naturally
striking and peculiar habit of the picturesque tree, than
assisting it in developing a form of unusual refinement and
symmetry.   From these remarks we think the amateur
will easily divine, that planting, grouping, and culture to
produce the Beautiful, require a much less artistic eye
(though much more care and attention) than performing
the same operations to elicit the Picturesque.   The charm
of a refined and polished landscape garden, as we usually
see it in the Beautiful grounds with all the richness and
beauty developed by high culture, arises from our admiration of the highest perfection, the greatest beauty of form,
to which every object can be brought; and, in trees, a
judicious selection, with high cultivation, will always produce this effect.

But in the Picturesque landscape garden there is visible
a piquancy of effect, certain bold and striking growths
and combinations, which we feel at once, if we know them
to be the result of art, to be the production of a peculiar
species of attention—not merely good, or even refined
ornamental gardening.   In short, no one can be a picturesque improver (if he has to begin with young plantations)
who is not himself something of an artist—who has not
studied nature with an artistical eye—and who is not
capable of imitating, eliciting, or heightening, in his plantations or other portions of his residence, the picturesque

in its many variations. And we may add here, that efficient and charming as is the assistance which all ornamental planters will derive from the study of the best landscape engravings and pictures of distinguished artists, they are indispensably necessary to the *picturesque* improver. In these he will often find embodied the choicest and most captivating studies from picturesque nature ; and will see at a glance the effect of certain combinations of trees, which he might otherwise puzzle himself a dozen years to know how to produce.

After all, as the picturesque improver here will most generally be found to be one who chooses a comparatively wild and wooded place, we may safely say that, if he has the true feeling for his work, he will always find it vastly easier than those who strive after the Beautiful; as the majority of the latter may be said to begin nearly anew—choosing places not for wildness and intricacy of wood, but for openness and the smiling, sunny, undulating plain, where they must of course to a good extent plant anew.

After becoming well acquainted with grouping, we should bring ourselves to regard those principles which govern our improvements as a whole. We therefore must call the attention of the improver to the two following principles, which are to be constantly in view : *the production of a whole, and the proper connexion of the parts.*

Any person who will take the trouble to reflect for a moment on the great diversity of surface, change of position, aspects, views, etc., in different country residences, will at once perceive how difficult, or, indeed, how impossible it is, to lay down any fixed or exact rules for arranging plantations in the modern style. What would be precisely adapted to a hilly rolling park, would often be found entirely unfit for adoption in a smooth, level surface, and the contrary. Indeed, the chief beauty of the modern style is the variety produced by following a few leading principles. and applying them to different and varied localities ; un like the geometric style, which proceeded to level, and arrange, and erect its avenues and squares, alike in every situation, with all the precision and certainty of mathematical demonstration.

In all grounds to be laid out, however, which are of a lawn or park-like extent, and call for the exercise of judgment and taste, the mansion or dwelling-house, being itself the chief or leading object in the scene, should form, as it were, the central point, to which it should be the object of the planter to give importance. In order to do this effectually, the large masses or groups of wood should cluster round, or form the back-ground to the main edifice ; and where the offices or out-buildings approach the same neighborhood, they also should be embraced. We do not mean by this to convey the idea, that a thick wood should be planted around and in the close neighborhood of the mansion or villa, so as to impede the free circulation of air ; but its appearance and advantages may be easily produced by a comparatively loose plantation of groups well connected by intermediate trees, so as to give all the effect of a large mass. The front, and at least that side nearest the approach road, will be left open, or nearly so ; while the plantations on the *back-ground* will give dignity and importance to the house, and at the same time effectually screen the approach to the farm buildings, and other objects which require to be kept out of view ; and here both for the purposes of shelter and richness of effect, a good proportion of evergreens should be introduced.

From this principal mass, the plantations must break off in groups of greater or less size, corresponding to the extent covered by it; if large, they will diverge into masses of considerable magnitude, if of moderate size, in groups made up of a number of trees. In the lawn front of the house, appropriate places will be found for a number of the most elegant single trees, or small groups of trees, remarkable for the beauty of their forms, foliage, or blossoms. Care must be taken, however, in disposing these, as well as many of the groups, that they are not placed so as, at some future time, to interrupt or disturb the finest points of prospect.

In more distant parts of the plantations will also appear masses of considerable extent, perhaps upon the boundary line, perhaps in particular situations on the sides, or in the interior of the whole; and the various groups which are distributed between should be so managed as, though in most cases distinct, yet to appear to be the connecting links which unite these distant shadows in the composition, with the larger masses near the house. Sometimes several small groups will be almost joined together; at others the effect may be kept up by a small group, aided by a few neighboring single trees. This, for a park-like place. Where the place is small, a pleasure-ground character is all that can be obtained. But by employing chiefly shrubs, and only a few trees, very similar and highly beautiful effects may be attained.

The grand object in all this should be to open to the eye, from the windows or front of the house, a wide surface, partially broken up and divided by groups and masses of trees into a number of pleasing lawns or openings, differing in size and appearance, and producing

a charming *variety* in the scene, either when seen from a
given point or when examined in detail.   It must not be
forgotten that, as a general rule, the grass or surface of
the lawn answers as the principal light, and the woods or
plantations as the shadows, in the same manner in nature
as in painting; and that these should be so managed as to
lead the eye to the mansion as the most important object
when seen from without, or correspond to it in grandeur
and magnitude, when looked upon from within the house.
If the surface is too much crowded with groups of foliage,
breadth of light will be found wanting; if left too bare,
there will be felt, on the other hand, an absence of the
noble effect of deep and broad shadows.

One of the loveliest charms of a fine park is, undoubtedly, variation or undulation of surface.   Everything,
accordingly, which tends to preserve and strengthen this
pleasing character, should be kept constantly in view.
Where, therefore, there are no obvious objections to such
a course, the eminences, gentle swells, or hills, should be
planted, in preference to the hollows or depressions. By
planting the elevated portions of the grounds, their
apparent height is increased ; but by planting the hollows,
all distinction is lessened and broken up.   Indeed, where
there is but a trifling and scarcely perceptible undulation
the importance of the swells of surface already existing is
surprisingly increased, when this course of planting is
adopted ; and the whole, to the eye, appears finely
varied.

Where the grounds of the residence to be planted are
level, or nearly so, and it is desirable to confine the view
on any or all sides, to the lawn or park itself, the boundary
groups and masses must be so connected together as from

the most striking part or parts of the prospect (near .he house for example) to answer this end. This should be done, not by planting a continuous, uniformly thick belt of trees round the outside of the whole ; but by so arranging the various outer groups and thickets, that when *seen from the given points* they shall appear connected in one whole In this way, there will be an agreeable variation in the margin, made by the various bays, recesses, and detached projections, which could not be so well effected if the whole were one uniformly unbroken strip of wood.

But where the house is so elevated as to command a more extensive view than is comprised in the demesne itself, another course should be adopted. The grounds planted must be made to connect themselves with the surrounding scenery, so as not to produce any violent contrast to the eye, when compared with the adjoining country. If then, as is most frequently the case, the lawn or pleasure-ground join, on either side or sides, cultivated farm lands, the proper connexion may be kept up by advancing a few groups or even scattered trees into the neighboring fields. In the middle states there are but few cultivated fields, even in ordinary farms, where there is not to be seen, here and there, a handsome cluster of saplings or a few full grown trees ; or if not these, at least some tall growing bushes along the fences, all of which, by a little exercise of this leading principle of *connexion*, can, by the planter of taste, be made to appear with few or trifling additions, to divaricate from, and ramble out of the park itself.' Where the park joins natural woods, connexion is still easier, and where it bounds upon one of our noble rivers, lakes, or other large sheets of water, of course connexion is not expected ; for

sudden contrast and transition is there both natu al **and**
beautiful.

In all cases good taste will suggest that the more polished
parts of the lawns and grounds should, whatever character
is attempted, be those nearest the house.   There the most
rare and beautiful sorts of trees are displayed, and the
entire plantations agree in elegance with the style of art
evinced in the mansion itself.   When there is much extent,
however, as the eye wanders from the neighborhood of the
residence, the whole evinces less polish; and gradually,
towards the furthest extremities, grows ruder, until it assi-
milates itself to the wildness of general nature around.
This, of course, applies to grounds of large extent, and must
not be so much enforced where the lawn embraced is but
moderate, and therefore comes more directly under the
eye.

It will be remembered that, in the foregoing section, we
stated it as one of the leading principles of the art of Landscape Gardening, that in every instance where the grounds
of a country residence have a marked natural character,
whether of beautiful or picturesque expression, the efforts
of the improver will be most successful if he contributes
by his art to aid and strengthen that expression.   This
should ever be borne in mind when we are commencing
any improvements in planting that will affect the general
expression of the scene, as there are but few country residences in the United States of any importance which have
not naturally some distinct landscape character; and the
labors of the improver will be productive of much greater
satisfaction and more lasting pleasure, when they aim at
effects in keeping with the whole scene, than if no regard
be paid to this important point.   This will be felt almost

intuitively by persons who, perhaps, would themse'ves be incapable of describing the cause of their gratification, but would perceive the contrary at once; as many are unable to analyse the pleasure derived from harmony in music, while they at once perceive the introduction of discordant notes.

We do not intend that this principle should apply so closely, that extensive grounds naturally picturesque shall have nothing of the softening touches of more perfect beauty; or that a demesne characterized by the latter expression should not be occasionally enlivened with a few " *smart touches*" of the former. This is often necessary, indeed, to prevent tame scenery from degenerating into insipidity, or picturesque into wildness, too great to be appropriate in a country residence. Picturesque trees give new spirit to groups of highly beautiful ones, and the latter sometimes heighten by contrast the value of the former. All of which, however, does not prevent the *predominance* of the leading features of either style, sufficiently strong to mark it as such ; while, occasionally, something of zest or elegance may be borrowed from the opposite character, to suit the wishes or gratify the taste of the proprietor.

GROUND PLANS OF ORNAMENTAL PLANTATIONS. To llustrate partially our ideas on the arrangement of plantations we place before the reader two or three examples, premising that the small scale to which they are reduced prevents our giving to them any character beyond that of the general one of the design. The first (Fig. 20) represents a portion, say one third or one half of a piece of property selected for a country seat, and which has hitherto been kept in tillage as ordinary farm land. The public

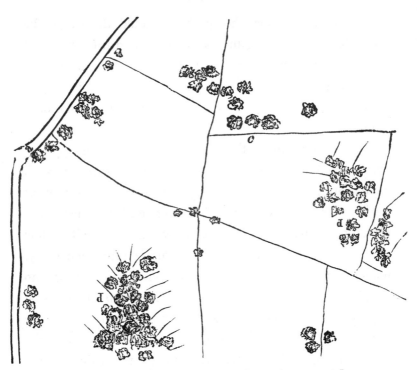

[Fig. 18. Plan of a common Farm, before any improvements.]

road, *a*, is the boundary on one side : *dd* are prettily wooded dells or hollows, which, together with a few groups near the proposed site of the house, *c*, and a few scattered single trees, make up the aggregate of the original woody embellishments of the locality.

In the next figure (Fig. 19) a ground plan of the place is given, as it would appear after having been judiciously laid out and planted, with several years' growth. At *a*, the approach road leaves the public highway and leads to the house at *c :* from whence paths of smaller size, *b*, make the circuit of the ornamental portion of the residence, taking advantage of the wooded dells, *d*, originally existing, which offer some scope for varied walks concealed from each other by the intervening masses of thicket. It will

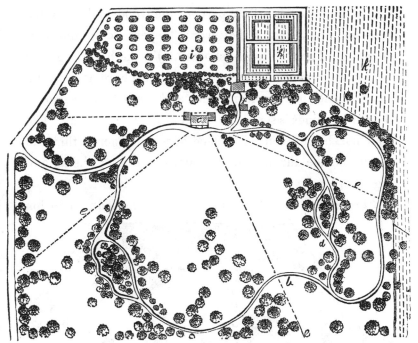

[Fig. 19.   Plan of the foregoing grounds as a Country Seat, after ten years' improvement.]

be seen here, that one of the largest masses of wood forms
a background to the house, concealing also the out-buildings ; while, from the windows of the mansion itself, the
trees are so arranged as to group in the most pleasing and
effective manner ; at the same time broad masses of turf
meet the eye, and fine distant views are had through the
vistas in the lines, e e.   In this manner the lawn appears
divided into four distinct lawns or areas bounded by groups
of trees, instead of being dotted over with an unmeaning
confusion of irregular masses of foliage.   The form of these
areas varies also with every change of position in the spectator, as seen from different portions of the grounds, or different points in the walks ; and they can be still further varied
at pleasure by adding more single trees or small groups,
which should always, to produce variety of outline, be

placed opposite the *salient* parts of the wood, and not in the recesses, which latter they would appear o diminish or clog up. The stables are shown at *f;* the barn at *g,* and the kitchen garden adjacent at *h;* the orchard at *i;* and a small portion of the farm lands at *k;* a back entrance to the out-buildings is shown in the rear of the orchard. The plan has been given for a place of seventy acres, thirty of which include the pleasure grounds, and forty the adjoining farm lands.

Figure 20 is the plan of an American mansion

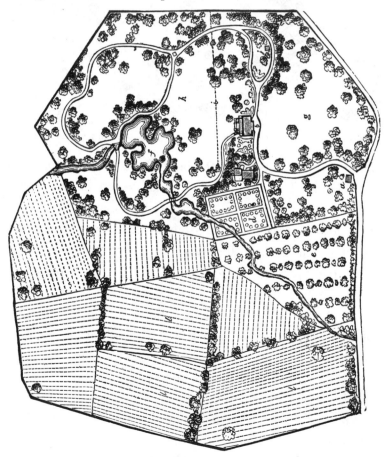

[FIg. 20. Plan of a Mansion Residence, laid out in the natural style.]

residence of considerable extent, only part of the farm
lands, *l*, being here delineated. In this residence, as there
is no extensive view worth preserving beyond the bounds
of the estate, the pleasure grounds are surrounded by an
irregular and picturesque belt of wood. A fine natural
stream or rivulet, which ran through the estate, has been
formed into a handsome pond, or small lake, *f*, which adds
much to the interest of the grounds. The approach road
breaks off from the highway at the entrance lodge, *a*,
and proceeds in easy curves to the mansion, *b ;* and the
groups of trees on the side of this approach nearest the
house, are so arranged that the visitor scarcely obtains
more than a glimpse of the latter, until he arrives at the
most favorable position for a first impression. From the
windows of the mansion, at either end, the eye ranges
over groups of flowers and shrubs ; while, on the entrance
front, the trees are arranged so as to heighten the natural
expression originally existing there. On the other front,
the broad mass of light reflected from the green turf at *h*,
is balanced by the dark shadows of the picturesque
plantations which surround the lake, and skirt the whole
boundary. At *i*, a light, inconspicuous wire fence
separates that portion of the ground, *g*, ornamented with
flowering shrubs and kept mown by the scythe, from the
remainder, of a park-like character, which is kept short by
the cropping of animals. At *c*, are shown the stables,
carriage house, etc., which, though near the approach
road, are concealed by foliage, though easily accessible by
a short curved road, *returning from* the house, so as not
to present any road leading in the same direction, to
detract from the dignity of the approach in going to it.
A prospect tower, or rustic pavilion, on a little eminence

overlooking the whole estate, is shown at *j*. The small arabesque beds near the house are filled with masses of choice flowering shrubs and plants ; the kitchen garden is shown at *d*, and the orchard at *e*.

Suburban villa residences are, every day, becoming more numerous ; and in laying out the grounds around them, and disposing the sylvan features, there is often more ingenuity, and as much taste required, as in treating a country residence of several hundred acres. In the small area of from one half an acre to ten or twelve acres, surrounding often a villa of the first class, it is desirable to assemble many of the same features, and as much as possible of the enjoyment, which are to be found in a large and elegant estate. To do this, the space allotted to various purposes, as the kitchen garden, lawn, etc., must be judiciously portioned out, and so characterized and divided by plantations, that the whole shall appear to be much larger than it really is, from the fact that the spectator is never allowed to see the whole at a single glance ; but while each portion is complete in itself, the plan shall present nothing incongruous or ill assorted.

An excellent illustration of this species of residence, is afforded the reader in the accompanying plan (Fig. 21) of the grounds of *Riverside Villa*. This pretty villa at Burlington, New Jersey (to which we shall again refer), was lately built, and the grounds, about six or eight acres in extent, laid out, from the designs of John Notman, Esq., architect, of Philadelphia ; and while the latter promise a large amount of beauty and enjoyment, scarcely anything which can be supposed necessary for the convenience or wants of the family, is lost sight of.

The house, *a*, stands quite near the bank of the river,

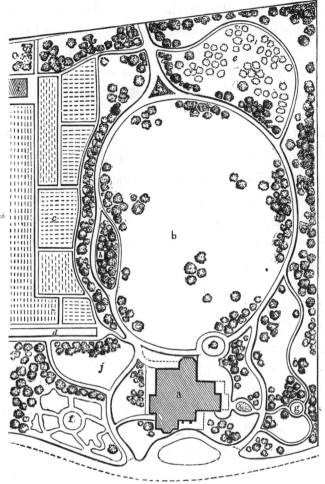

[Fig. 21. Plan of a Suburban Villa Residence.]

while one front commands fine water views, and the other looks into the lawn or pleasure grounds, *b*. On one side of the area is the kitchen garden, *c*, separated and concealed from the lawn by thick groups of evergreen and deciduous trees. At *e*, is a picturesque orchard, in which the fruit trees are planted in groups instead of straight lines, for the sake of effect. Directly under the windows of the drawing-room is the flower garden, *f;* and

at *g*, is a seat. The walk around the lawn is also a
carriage road, affording entrance and egress from the rear
of the grounds, for garden purposes, as well as from the
front of the house. At *h*, is situated the ice-house; *d*,
hot-beds; *j*, bleaching green; *i*, gardener's house, etc. In
the rear of the latter are the stables, which are not shown
on the plan.

The embellished farm (*ferme ornée*) is a pretty mode
of combining something of the beauty of the landscape
garden with the utility of the farm, and we hope to see
small country seats of this kind become more general. As
regards profit in farming, of course, all modes of arranging
or distributing land are inferior to simple square fields;
on account of the greater facility of working the land in
rectangular plots. But we suppose the owner of the small
ornamental farm to be one with whom profit is not the
first and only consideration, but who desires to unite
with it something to gratify his taste, and to give a higher
charm to his rural occupations. In Fig. 22, is shown part
of an embellished farm, treated in the picturesque style
throughout. The various trees, under grass or tillage, are
divided and bounded by winding roads, *a*, bordered by
hedges of buckthorn, cedar, and hawthorn, instead of
wooden fences; the roads being wide enough to afford
a pleasant drive or walk, so as to allow the owner or
visitor to enjoy at the same time an agreeable circuit, and
a glance at all the various crops and modes of culture.
In the plan before us, the approach from the public road
is at *b;* the dwelling at *c;* the barns and farm-buildings
at *d;* the kitchen garden at *e;* and the orchard at *f*.
About the house are distributed some groups of trees, and
here the fields, *g*, are kept in grass, and are either mown

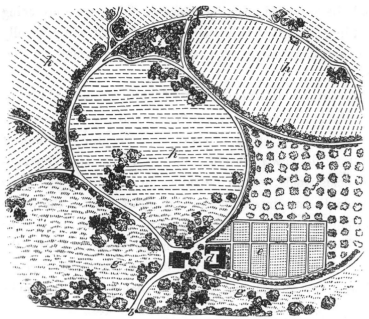

[Fig. 22. View of a Picturesque farm (*ferme ornée*).]

or pastured. The fields in crops are designated *h*, on the
plan ; and a few picturesque groups of trees are planted,
or allowed to remain, in these, to keep up the general
character of the place. A low dell, or rocky thicket, is
situated at *i*,. Exceedingly interesting and agreeable
effects may be produced, at little cost, in a picturesque
farm of this kind. The hedges may be of a great variety
of suitable shrubs, and, in addition to those that we have
named, we would introduce others of the sweet brier, the
Michigan or prairie rose (admirably adapted for the
purpose), the flowering crab, and the like—beautiful and
fragrant in their growth and blossoms. These hedges we
would cause to grow thick, rather by interlacing the
branches, than by constant shearing or trimming, which
would give them a less formal, and a more free and
natural air. The winding lanes traversing the farm need

only be gravelled near the house, in other portions being left in grass, which will need little care, as it will generally be kept short enough by the passing of men and vehicles over it.

A picturesque or ornamental farm like this would be an agreeable residence for a gentleman retiring into the country on a small farm, desirous of experimenting for himself with all the new modes of culture. The small and irregular fields would, to him, be rather an advantage, and there would be an air of novelty and interest about the whole residence. Such an arrangement as this would also be suitable for a fruit farm near one of our large towns, the fields being occupied by orchards, vines, grass, and grain. The house and all the buildings should be of a simple, though picturesque and accordant character.

The *cottage ornée* may have more or less ground attached to it. It is the ambition of some to have a great house and little land, and of others (among whom we remember the poet Cowley) to have a little house and a large garden. The latter would seem to be the more natural taste. When the grounds of a cottage are large, they will be treated by the landscape gardener nearly like those of a villa residence; when they are smaller a more quiet and simple character must be aimed at. But even where they consist of only a rood or two, something tasteful and pretty may be arranged.* In Fig. 23, is shown a small piece of ground on one side of a cottage, in which a picturesque character is attempted to be maintained. The plantations here are made mostly with shrubs instead of trees, the latter being

---

* For a variety of modes of treating the grounds of small places, see our *Designs for Cottage Residences.*

only sparingly introduced for the want of room. In the disposition of these shrubs, however, the same attention to picturesque effect is paid as we have already pointed out in our remarks on grouping ; and by connecting the thickets and groups here and there, so as to conceal one walk from the other, a surprising variety and effect will frequently be produced in an exceedingly limited spot.

[Fig. 23. Grounds of a Cottage *ornée*.]

The same limited grounds might be planted so as to produce the Beautiful ; choosing, in this case, shrubs of symmetrical growth and fine forms, planting and grouping them somewhat singly, and allowing every specimen to attain its fullest luxuriance of development.

In making these arrangements, even in the small area of a fourth of an acre, we should study the same principles and endeavor to produce the same harmony of effects, as if we were improving a mansion residence of the first class. The extent of the operations, and the sums lavished, are not by any means necessarily connected with successful and pleasing results. The man of correct taste will, by the aid of very limited means and upon a small surface, be able to afford the mind more true pleasure, than the improver who lavishes thousands without it, creating no other emotion than surprise or pity at the useless expenditure incurred ; and the Abbé Delille says nothing more true than that,

> " Ce noble emploi demand un artiste qui pense,
> Prodigue de génie, et non pas de dépense."

From the inspection of plans like these, the tyro **may** learn something of the manner of arranging plantations, and of the general effect of the natural style in particular cases and situations. But the knowledge they afford is so far below that obtained by an inspection of the effects in reality, that the latter should in all cases be preferred where it is practicable. In this style, unlike the ancient, it is almost impossible that the same plan should exactly suit any other situation than that for which it was intended, for its great excellence lies in the endless variety produced by its application to different sites, situations, and surfaces; developing the latent capacities of one place and heightening the charms of another.

But the leading principles as regards the formation of plantations, which we have here endeavored briefly to elucidate, are the same in all cases. After becoming familiar with these, should the amateur landscape gardener be at a loss how to proceed, he can hardly do better, as we have before suggested, than to study and recur often to the beautiful compositions and combinations of nature, displayed in her majestic groups, masses, and single trees, as well as open glades and deep thickets; of which, fortunately, in most parts of our country, checkered here and there as it is with beautiful and picturesque scenery, there is no dearth or scarcity. Keeping these few principles in his mind, he will be able to detect new beauties and transfer them to his own estate; for nature is truly inexhaustible in her resources of the Beautiful.

CLASSIFICATION OF TREES AS TO EXPRESSION. The amateur who wishes to dispose his plantations in the natural style of Landscape Gardening so as to produce graceful or picturesque landscape, will be greatly aided by a study of the peculiar expression of trees individually and in com-position. The effect of a certain tree singly is often ex-ceedingly different from that of a group of the same trees. To be fully aware of the effect of groups and masses requires considerable study, and the progress in this study may be greatly facilitated by a recurrence from groups in nature to groups in pictures.

As a further aid to this most desirable species of infor-mation we shall offer a few remarks on the principal vari-eties of character afforded by trees in composition.

Almost all trees, with relation to forms, may be divided into three kinds, viz. *round-headed* trees, *oblong* or *pyra-midal* trees, and *spiry-topped* trees; and so far as the expressions of the different species comprised in these dis-tinct classes are concerned, they are, especially when viewed at a distance (as much of the wood seen in a prospect of any extent necessarily must be), productive of nearly the same general effects.

Round-headed trees compose by far the largest of these divisions. The term includes all those trees which have

an irregular surface in their boughs, more or less varied in outline, but exhibiting in the whole a top or head comparatively round : [Fig. 24. Round-headed Trees.] as the oak, ash, beech, and walnut. They are generally beautiful when young, from their smoothness, and the ele-gance of their forms; but often grow picturesque when age and time have had an opportunity to produce their wonted effects upon them. In general, however, the dif-ferent round-headed trees may be considered as the most appropriate for introduction in highly-cultivated scenery, or landscapes where the character is that of graceful or polished beauty ; as they harmonize with almost all scenes, buildings, and natural or artificial objects, uniting well with other forms and doing violence to no expression of scenery From the numerous breaks in the surface of their foliage, which reflect differently the lights and produce deep shadows, there is great intricacy and variety in the heads of many round-topped trees; and therefore, as an outer surface to meet the eye in a plantation, they are much softer and more pleasing than the unbroken line exhibited by the sides of oblong or spiry-topped trees. The sky outline also, or the upper part of the head, varies greatly in round-topped trees from the irregularity in the disposition of the upper branches in different species, as the oak and ash, or even between individual specimens of the same kind of tree, as the oak, of which we rarely see two trees alike in form and outline, although they have the same characteristic expression; while on the other hand no two verdant objects can bear a greater general resemblance to each other and show more sameness of figure than two Lombardy poplars.

"In a tree," says Uvedale Price, "of which the foliage is everywhere full and unbroken, there can be but little variety of *form;* then, as the sun strikes only on the surface, neither can there be much variety of *light* and *shade;* and as the apparent color of objects changes according to the different degrees of light or shade in which they are placed, there can be as little variety of *tint;* and lastly, as there are none of these openings that excite and nourish curiosity, but the eye is everywhere opposed by one uniform leafy screen, there can be as little intricacy as variety." From these remarks, it will be perceived that even among round-headed trees there may be great difference in the comparative beauty of different sorts ; and judging from the excellent standard here laid down, it will also be seen how much in the eye of a painter a tree with a beautifully diversified surface, as the oak, surpasses in the composition of a scene one with a very regular and compact surface and outline, as the horse-chestnut. In planting large masses of wood, therefore, or even in forming large groups in park scenery, round-headed trees of the ordinary loose and varied manner of growth common in the majority of forest trees, are greatly to be preferred to all others. When they cover large tracts, as several acres, they convey an emotion of *grandeur* to the mind ; when they form vast forests of thousands of acres, they produce a feeling of *sublimity ;* in the landscape garden when they stand alone, or in fine groups, they are *graceful* or *beautiful.* While young they have an elegant appearance ; when old they generally become majestic or picturesque. Other trees may suit scenery or scenes of particular and decided characters, but *round-headed* trees are decidedly the chief adornment of general landscape.

Spiry-topped trees (Fig. 25) are distinguished by straight leading stems and horizontal branches, which are

[Fig. 25. Spiry-topped Trees.]

comparatively small, and taper gradually to a point. The foliage is generally ever-green, and in most trees of this class hangs in parallel or drooping tufts from the branches. The various evergreen trees, composing the spruce and fir families, most of the pines, the cedar, and among deciduous trees, the larch, belong to this division. Their hue is generally much darker than that of deciduous trees, and there is a strong similarity, or

almost sameness, in the different kinds of trees which
may properly be called spiry-topped.

From their sameness of form and surface this class
of trees, when planted in large tracts or masses, gives
much less pleasure than round-headed trees ; and the eye
is soon wearied with the *monotony* of appearance
presented by long rows, groups, or masses, of the same
form, outline, and appearance ; to say nothing of the effect
of the uniform dark color, unrelieved by the warmer tints
of deciduous trees.   Any one can bear testimony to this,
who has travelled through a pine, hemlock, or fir forest,
where he could not fail to be struck with its gloom,
tediousness, and monotony, especially when contrasted
with the variety and beauty in a natural wood of
deciduous, round-headed trees.

Although spiry-topped trees in large masses cannot be
generally admired for ornamental plantations, yet they
have a character of their own, which is very striking and
peculiar, and we may add, in a high degree, valuable to
the Landscape Gardener.   Their general expression when
single or scattered is extremely spirited, wild, and
picturesque ; and when judiciously introduced into
artificial scenery, they produce the most charming and
unique effects.   " The situations where they have most
effect is among rocks and in very irregular surfaces, and
especially on the steep sides of high mountains, where their
forms and the direction of their growth seem to harmonize
with the pointed rocky summits."   Fir and pine forests are
extremely dull and monotonous in sandy plains and
smooth surfaces (as in the pine barrens of the southern
states) ; but among the broken rocks, craggy precipices,

and otherwise endlessly varied surfaces (as in the Alps, abroad, and the various rocky heights in the Highlands of the Hudson and the Alleghanies, at home) they are full of variety.   It will readily be seen, therefore, that spiry-topped trees should always be planted in considerable quantities in wild, broken, and picturesque scenes, where they will appear perfectly in keeping, and add wonderfully to the peculiar beauty of the situation.   In all grounds where there are abruptly varied surfaces, steep banks, or rocky precipices, this class of trees lends its efficient aid to strengthen the prevailing beauty, and to complete the finish of the picture.   In smooth, level surfaces, though spiry-topped trees cannot be thus extensively employed they are by no means to be neglected or thought valueless, but may be so combined and mingled with other round-headed and oblong-headed trees, as to produce very rich and pleasing effects.   A tall larch or two, or a few spruces rising out of the centre of a group, give it life and spirit, and add greatly, both by contrast of form and color, to the force of round-headed trees.   A stately and regular white pine or hemlock, or a few thin groups of the same trees peeping out from amidst, or bordering a large mass of deciduous trees, have great power in adding to the interest which the same awakens in the mind of the spectator. Care must be taken, however, that the very spirited effect which is here aimed at, is not itself defeated by the over anxiety of the planter, who, in scattering too profusely these very strongly marked trees, makes them at last so plentiful, as to give the whole a mingled and confused look, in which neither the graceful and sweeping outlines of the round-headed nor the picturesque summits of the spiry-topped trees predominate ; as the former decidedly should, in all scenes where an expression of peculiarly irregular kind is not aimed at.

The larch, to which we shall hereafter recur at some length, may be considered one of the most picturesque trees of this division ; and being more rapid in its growth than most evergreens, it may be used as a substitute for, or in conjunction with them, where effect is speedily desired.

Oblong-headed trees show heads of foliage more lengthened out, more formal, and generally more tapering, than

 round-headed ones. They differ from spiry-topped trees in having upright branches instead of horizontal ones, and in forming a conical or

[Fig. 26. Oblong-headed trees.] pyramidal mass of foliage, instead of a spiry, tufted one.   They are mostly deciduous; and approaching more nearly to round-headed trees than spiry-topped ones do, they may perhaps be more frequently introduced. The Lombardy poplar may be considered the representative of this division, as the oak is of the first, and the larch and fir of the second.   Abroad, the oriental cypress, an evergreen, is used to produce similar effects in scenery.

The great use of the Lombardy poplar, and other similar trees in composition, is to relieve or break into groups, large masses of wood.   This it does very effectually, when its tall summit rises at intervals from among round-headed trees, forming pyramidal centres to groups where there was only a swelling and flowing outline.   Formal rows, or groups of oblong-headed trees, however, are tiresome and monotonous to the last degree ; a straight line of them being scarcely better in appearance than a tall, stiff, gigantic hedge.   Examples of this can be easily found in many parts of the Union where the crude and formal taste of proprietors, by leading them to plant long lines of Lombardy poplars, has had the effect of destroying the beauty of many a fine prospect and building.

Conical or oblong-headed trees, when carefully employed, are very effective for purposes of *contrast*, in conjunction with horizontal lines of buildings such as we see in Grecian or Italian architecture. Near such edifices, *sparingly introduced, and mingled in small proportion with round-headed trees*, they contrast advantageously with the long cornices, flat roofs, and horizontal lines that predominate in their exteriors. Lombardy poplars are often thus introduced in pictures of Italian scenery, where they sometimes break the formality of a long line of wall in the happiest manner. Nevertheless, if they should be indiscriminately employed, or even used in any con-siderable portion in the decoration of the ground immediately adjoining a building of any pretensions, they would inevitably defeat this purpose, and by their tall and formal growth diminish the apparent magnitude, as well as the elegance of the house.

Drooping trees, though often classed with oblong-headed trees, differ from them in so many particulars, that they deserve to be ranked under a separate head. To this class belong the weeping willow, the weeping birch, the drooping elm, etc. Their prominent charac-teristics are gracefulness and elegance ; and we consider them as unfit, therefore, to be employed *to any extent* in scenes where it is desirable to keep up the expression of a wild or highly picturesque character. As single objects, or tastefully grouped in beautiful landscape, they

are in excellent keeping, and contribute much to give value to the leading expression.

When drooping trees are mixed indiscriminately with other round-headed trees in the composition of groups or masses, much of their individual character is lost, as it depends not so much on the top (as in oblong and spiry trees) as upon the side branches, which are of course concealed by those of the adjoining trees. Drooping trees, therefore, as elms, birches, etc., are shown to the best advantage on the *borders* of groups or the *boundaries* of plantations. It must not be forgotten, but constantly kept in mind, that all strongly marked trees, like bright colors in pictures, only admit of occasional employment; and that the very object aimed at in introducing them will be defeated if they are brought into the lawn and park in masses, and distributed heedlessly on every side. An English author very justly remarks, therefore, that the poplar, the willow, and the drooping birch, are "most dangerous trees in the hands of a planter who has not considerable knowledge and good taste in the composition of a landscape." Some of them, as the native elm, from their abounding in our own woods, may appear oftener; while others which have a peculiar and exotic look, as the weeping willow, should only be seen in situations where they either do not disturb the prevailing expression, or (which is better) where they are evidently in good keeping. "The weeping willow," says Gilpin, with his usual good taste, "is not adapted to sublime objects. We wish it not to screen the broken buttress and Gothic windows of an abbey, or to overshadow the battlements of a ruined castle. These offices it resigns to the oak, whose dignity can support them. The weeping willow seeks an humble scene—some romantic footpath bridge, which it half conceals, or some grassy pool over which it hangs its streaming foliage,

————' And dips
Its pendent boughs, as if to drink.' " *

The manner in which a picturesque bit of landscape can be supported by picturesque spiry-topped trees, and its expression degraded by the injudicious employment of graceful drooping trees, will be apparent to the reader in the two accompanying little sketches. In the first (Fig.

[Fig. 27. Trees in keeping.]

27), the abrupt hill, the rapid mountain torrent, and the distant Alpine summits, are in fine keeping with the tall spiry larches and firs, which, shooting up on either side of the old bridge, occupy the foreground. In the second (Fig. 30), there is evidently something discordant in the scene which strikes the spectator at first sight; this is the misplaced introduction of the large willows, which

[Fig. 28. Trees out of keeping.]

belong to a scene very different in character. Imagine a removal of the surrounding hills, and let the rapid stream spread out into a smooth peaceful lake with gradu-ally retiring shores, and the blue summits in the distance and then the willows will harmonize admirably.

Having now described the peculiar characteristics of these different classes of round-headed, spiry-topped oblong, and drooping trees, we should consider the proper

* Forest Scenery, p. 133.

method by which a harmonious combination of the different forms composing them may be made so as not to violate correct principles of taste. An indiscriminate mixture of their different forms would, it is evident, produce anything but an agreeable effect. For example, let a person plant together in a group, three trees of totally opposite forms and expressions, viz. a weeping willow, an oak, and a poplar; and the expression of the whole would be destroyed by the confusion resulting from their discordant forms. On the other hand, the mixture of trees that exactly correspond in their forms, if these forms, as in oblong or drooping trees, are similar will infallibly create sameness. In order then to produce beautiful variety which shall neither on the one side run into confusion, nor on the other verge into monotony, it is requisite to give some little attention to the harmony of form and color in the composition of trees in artificial plantations.

The only rules which we can suggest to govern the planter are these : First, if a certain leading expression is desired in a group of trees, together with as great a variety as possible, such species must be chosen as harmonize with each other in certain leading points. And, secondly, in occasionally intermingling trees of opposite characters, discordance may be prevented, and harmonious expression promoted, by interposing other trees of an intermediate character.

In the first case, suppose it is desired to form a group of trees, in which gracefulness must be the leading expression. The willow alone would have the effect; but in groups, willows alone produce sameness : in order therefore, to give variety, we must choose other trees which, while they differ from the willow in some particulars, agree in others. The elm has mucn larger and darker foliage, while it has also a drooping spray ; the weeping birch differs in its leaves, but agrees in the pensile flow of its branches ; the common birch has few pendent boughs, but resembles in the airy lightness of its leaves ; and the three-thorned acacia, though its branches are horizontal, has delicate foliage of nearly the same hue and floating lightness as the willow. Here we have a group of five trees, which is, in the whole, full of gracefulness and variety, while there is nothing in the composition inharmonious to the practised eye.

To illustrate the second case, let us suppose a long sweeping outline of maples, birches, and other light, mellow-colored trees, which the improver wishes to vary and break into groups, by spiry-topped, evergreen trees. It is evident, that if these trees were planted in such a manner as to peer abruptly out of the light-colored foliage of the former trees, in dark or almost black masses of tapering verdure, the effect would be by no means so satisfactory and pleasing, as if there were a partial transition from the mellow, pale green of the maples, etc., to the darker hues of the oak, ash, or beech, and finally the sombre tint of the evergreens. Thus much for the coloring ; and if, in addition to this, oblong-headed trees or pyramidal trees were also placed near and partly intermingled with the spiry-topped ones, the unity of the whole composition would be still more complete.*

---

* We are persuaded that very few persons are aware of the beauty, varied and endless, that may be produced by arranging trees with regard to their *coloring.* It requires the eye and genius of a Claude or a Poussin, to develope all these hidden beauties of harmonious combination. Gilpin rightly

Contrasts, again. are often admissible in woody scenery ; and we would not wish to lose many of our most superb trees, because they could not be introduced in particular portions of landscape. Contrasts in trees may be so violent as to be displeasing ; as in the example of the groups of the three trees, the willow, poplar, and oak : or they may be such as to produce spirited and pleasing effects. This must be effected by planting the different divisions of trees, first, in small leading groups, and then by effecting a union between the groups of different character, by intermingling those of the nearest similarity into and near the groups : in this way, by easy transitions from the drooping to the round-headed, and from these to the tapering trees, the whole of the foliage and forms harmonize well.

[Fig. 29.   Example in grouping.]

" Trees," observes Mr. Whately, in his elegant treatise on this subject, " which differ in but one of these circumstances, of shape, green, or growth, though they agree in every other, are sufficiently distinguished for the

says, in speaking of the dark Scotch fir, " with regard to color in general, I think I speak the language of painting, when I assert that the picturesque eye makes little distinction in this matter.   It has no attachment to one color in preference to another, but considers the beauty of all coloring as resulting, not from the colors themselves, but almost entirely from their harmony with other colors in their neighborhood.   So that as the Scotch fir tree is combined or stationed, it forms a beautiful umbrage or a murky spot."

purpose of *variety ;* if they differ in two or three, they become *contrasts :* if in all, they are opposite, and seldom group well together. Those, on the contrary, which are of one character, and are distinguished only as the characteristic mark is strongly or faintly impressed upon them, form a beautiful mass, and unity is preserved without sameness."*

There is another circumstance connected with the color of trees, that will doubtless suggest itself to the improver of taste, the knowledge of which may sometimes be turned to valuable account. We mean the effects produced in the apparent coloring of a landscape by distance, which painters term *aërial perspective.* Standing at a certain position in a scene, the coloring is deep, rich, and full in the foreground, more tender and mellow in the middle-ground, and softening to a pale tint in the distance.

> " Where to the eye three well marked distances
> Spread their peculiar coloring, vivid green,
> Warm brown, and black opake the foreground bears
> Conspicuous: sober olive coldly marks
> The second distance; thence the third declines
> In softer blue, or lessening still, is lost
> In fainted purple. When thy taste is call'd
> To deck a scene where nature's self presents
> All these distinct gradations, then rejoice
> As does the Painter, and like him apply
> Thy colors ; plant thou on each separate part
> Its proper foliage."

Advantage may occasionally be taken of this peculiarity in the gradation of color, in Landscape Gardening, by the creation as it were, of an *artificial distance.* In grounds

---

* Observations on Modern Gardening.

and scenes of limited extent, the apparent size and breadth may be increased, by planting a majority of the trees in the foreground, of dark tints, and the boundary with foliage of a much lighter hue.

An acquaintance, individually, with the different species of trees of indigenous and foreign growth, which may be cultivated with success in this climate, is absolutely essential to the amateur or the professor of Landscape Gardening. The tardiness or rapidity of their growth, the periods at which their leaves and flowers expand, the soils they love best, and their various habits and characters, are all subjects of the highest interest to him. In short, as a love of the country almost commences with a knowledge of its peculiar characteristics, the pure air, the fresh enamelled turf, and the luxuriance and beauty of the whole landscape; so the taste for the embellishment of Rural Residences must grow out of an admiration for beautiful trees, and the delightful effects they are capable of producing in the hands of persons of taste and lovers of nature.

Admitting this, we think, in the comparatively meagre state of general information on this subject among us, we shall render an acceptable service to the novice, by giving a somewhat detailed description of the character and habits of most of the finest hardy forest and ornamental trees. Among those living in the country, there are many who care little for the beauties of Landscape Gardening, who are yet interested in those trees which are remarkable for the beauty of their forms, their foliage, their blossoms, or their useful purposes. This, we hope, will be a sufficient explanation for the apparently disproportionate number of pages which we shall devote to this part of our subject.

SECTION IV.

DECIDUOUS ORNAMENTAL TREES.

The History and Description of all the finest hardy Deciduous Trees. REMARKS ON THEIR EFFECTS IN LANDSCAPE GARDENING, INDIVIDUALLY AND IN COMPOSITION. Their Cultivation, etc. The Oak. The Elm. The Ash. The Linden. The Beech. The Poplar. The Horse-chestnut. The Birch. The Alder. The Maple. The Locust. The Three-thorned Acacia. The Judas-tree. The Chestnut. The Osage Orange. The Mulberry. The Paper Mulberry. The Sweet Gum. The Walnut. The Hickory. The Mountain Ash. The Ailantus. The Kentucky Coffee. The Willow. The Sassafras. The Catalpa. The Persimon. The Pepperidge. The Thorn. The Magnolia. The Tulip. The Dogwood. The Salisburia. The Paulonia. The Virgilia. The Cypress. The Larch, etc.

> O gloriosi spiriti de gli boschi,
> O Eco, o antri foschi, o chiare linfe,
> O faretrate ninfe, o agresti Pani,
> O Satiri e Silvani, o Fauni e Driadi,
> Naiadi ed Amadriadi, o Semidee
> Oreadi e Napee.—

SANNAZZARO.

> " O spirits of the woods,
> Echoes and solitudes and lakes of light;
> O quivered virgins bright, Pan's rustical
> Satyrs and sylvans all, dryads and ye
> That up the mountains be; and ye beneath
> In meadow or in flowery heath."

THE OAK. *Quercus.*

Nat. Ord. Corylaceæ.   *Lin. Syst.* Monœcia, Polyandria.

 H E Arcadians believed the oak to have been the first created of all trees; and when we consider its great and surpassing utility and beauty, we are fully disposed to concede it the first rank among the denizens of the

forest.   Springing up with a noble trunk, and stretching
out its broad limbs over the soil,

> " These monarchs of the wood,
> Dark, gnarled, centennial oaks,"

seem proudly to bid defiance to time ; and while generations
of man appear and disappear, they withstand the storms of
a thousand winters, and seem only to grow more venerable
and majestic.   They are mentioned in the oldest histories ;
we are told that Absalom was caught by his hair in " the
thick boughs of a great oak ;" and Herodotus informs us
that the first oracle was that of Dodona, set up in the
celebrated oak grove of that name.   There, at first, the
oracles were delivered by the priestesses, but, as was afterwards believed, by the inspired oaks themselves—

> " Which in Dodona did enshrine,
> So faith too fondly deemed, a voice divine."

Acorns, the fruit of the oak, appear to have been held in
considerable estimation as an article of food among the
ancients.   Not only were the swine fattened upon them, as
in our own forests, but they were ground into flour, with
which bread was made by the poorer classes.   Lucretius
mentions, that before grain was known they were the common food of man ; but we suppose the fruit of the chestnut
may also have been included under that term.

> " That oake whose acornes were our foode before
> The Cerese seede of mortal man was knowne."
>
> SPENSER.

The civic crown, given in the palmy days of Rome to
the most celebrated men, was also composed of oak leaves

It should not be forgotten that the oak was worshipped by the ancient Britons. Baal or Yiaoul (whence Yule) was the god of fire, whose symbol was an oak. Hence at his festival, which was at Christmas, the ceremony of kindling the Yule log was performed among the ancient Druids. This fire was kept perpetual throughout the year, and the hearths of all the people were annually lighted from these sacred fires every Christmas. We believe the curious custom is still extant in some remote parts of England, where the "Yule log" is ushered in with much glee and rejoicing once a year.

As an ornamental object we consider the oak the most varied in expression, the most beautiful, grand, majestic, and picturesque of all deciduous trees. The enormous size and extreme old age to which it attains in a favorable situation, the great space of ground that it covers with its branches, and the strength and hardihood of the tree, all contribute to stamp it with the character of dignity and grandeur beyond any other compeer of the forest. When young its fine foliage (singularly varied in many of our native species) and its thrifty form render it a beautiful tree. But it is not until the oak has attained considerable size that it displays its true character, and only when at an age that would terminate the existence of most other trees that it exhibits all its magnificence. Then its deeply furrowed trunk is covered with mosses ; its huge branches, each a tree, spreading out horizontally from the trunk with great boldness, its trunk of huge dimension, and its " high top, bald with dry antiquity ;" all these, its true characteristics, stamp the oak, as Virgil has expressed it in his Georgics—

> " Jove's own tree,
> That holds the woods in awful sovereignty
> For length of ages lasts his happy reign,
> And lives of mortal man contend in vain.
> Full in the midst of his own strength he stands,
> Stretching his brawny arms and leafy hands,
> His shade protects the plains, his head the hills commands."
>   DRYDEN'S TRANS.

"The oak," says Gilpin, "is confessedly the most picturesque tree in itself, and the most accommodating in composition. It refuses no subject either in natural or in
artificial landscape. It is suited to the grandest, and may
with propriety be introduced into the most pastoral. It
adds new dignity to the ruined tower and the Gothic arch;
and by stretching its wild, moss-grown branches athwart
their ivied walls, it gives them a kind of majesty coeval
with itself; at the same time its propriety is still preserved
if it throws its arms over the purling brook or the mantling
pool, where it beholds

> " Its reverend image in the expanse below."

Milton introduces it happily even in the lowest scene—

> " Hard by a cottage chimney smokes,
> From between two aged oaks."

The oak is not only one of the grandest and most picturesque objects as a single tree upon a lawn, but it is equally
unrivalled for groups and masses. There is a breadth about
the lights and shadows reflected and embosomed in its
foliage, a singular freedom and boldness in its outline, and
a pleasing richness and intricacy in its huge ramification
of branch and limb, that render it highly adapted to these
purposes. Some trees, as the willow or the spiry poplar

though pleasing singly, are monotonous to the last degree
when planted in quantities. Not so, however, with the
oak, as there is no tree, when forming a wood entirely by
itself, which affords so great a variety of form and disposition, light and shade, symmetry and irregularity, as this
king of the forests.

To arrive at its highest perfection, ample space on every
side must be allowed the oak. A free exposure to the sun
and air, and a deep mellow soil, are highly necessary to its
fullest amplitude. For this reason, the oaks of our forests,

[Fig. 30. The Charter Oak, Hartford.]

being thickly crowded, are seldom of extraordinary size;
and there are more truly majestic oaks in the parks of
England than are to be found in the whole cultivated portion of the United States. Here and there, however,
throughout our country may be seen a solitary oak of great

age and immense size, which attests the fitness of the soil
and climate, and displays the grandeur of our native species
The Wadsworth Oak near Geneseo, N. Y., of extraordinary
dimensions, the product of one of our most fertile valleys,
has attracted the admiration of hundreds of travellers on
the route to Niagara.   Its trunk measures thirty-six feet in
circumference.   The celebrated *Charter Oak* at Hartford,
which has figured so conspicuously in the history of New
England, is still existing in a green old age, one of the most
interesting monuments of the past to be found in the
country.

Near the village of Flushing, Long Island, on the farm
of Judge Lawrence, is growing one of the noblest oaks in
the country.   It is truly park-like in its dimensions, the
circumference of the trunk being nearly thirty feet, and its
majestic head of corresponding dignity.   In the deep
alluvial soil of the western valleys, the oak often assumes
a grand aspect, and bears witness to the wonderful fertility
of the soil in that region.

Different species of Oak.   This country is peculiarly
rich in various kinds of oak ; Michaux enumerating no less
than forty species indigenous to North America.   Of these
the most useful are the Live oak (*Quercus virens*), of such
inestimable value for ship-building ; the Spanish oak (*Q.
falcata*) ; the Red oak (*Q. rubra*), etc., the bark of which
is extensively used in tanning ; the Quercitron or Black
oak, which is highly valuable as affording a fine yellow or
brown dye for wool, silks, paper-hangings, etc. ; and the
White oak, which is chiefly used for timber.   We shall

here describe only a few of those which are most entitled
to the consideration of the planter, either for their valuable
properties or as ornamental trees, and calculated for planting in woods or single masses.

The White oak. (*Quercus alba.*) This is one of the most
common of the American oaks, being very generally distributed over the country, from Canada to the southern
states.   In good strong soils it forms a tree 70 or 80 feet
high, with wide extending branches; but its growth depends much upon this circumstance. It may readily be
known even in winter by its whitish bark, and by the dry
and withered leaves which often hang upon this species
through the whole of that season.   The leaves are about
four inches wide and six in length, divided uniformly into
rounded lobes without points; these lobes are deeper in
damp soils.   When the leaves first unfold in the spring
they are downy beneath, but when fully grown they are
quite smooth, and pale green on the upper surface and
whitish or glaucous below.   The acorn is oval and the cup
somewhat flattened at the base.   This is the most valuable
of all our native oaks, immense quantities of the timber
being used for various purposes in building ; and staves of
the white oak for barrels are in universal use throughout
the Union.   The great occasional size and fine form of this
tree, in some natural situations, prove how noble an object
it would become when allowed to expand in full vigor and
majesty in the open air and light of the park.   It more
nearly approaches the English oak in appearance than any
other American species.

Rock Chestnut oak. (*Q. Prinus Monticola.*) This is
one of the most ornamental of our oaks, and is found in
considerable abundance in the middle states.   It has the

peculiar advantage of growing well on the most barren and
rocky soils, and can therefore be advantageously employed
by the landscape gardener, when a steep, dry, rocky bank is
to be covered with trees. In deep, mellow soil, its growth
is wonderfully vigorous, and it rapidly attains a height of
50 or 60 feet, with a corresponding diameter. The head
is rather more symmetrical in form and outline than most
trees of this genus, and the stem, in free, open places, shoots
up into a lofty trunk. The leaves are five or six inches
long, three or four broad, oval and uniformly denticulated,
with the teeth more regular but less acute than the Chestnut white oak. When beginning to open in the spring
they are covered with a thick down; but when fully expanded they are perfectly smooth and of a delicate texture.
Michaux.

Chestnut White oak. (*Quercus Prinus palustris.*)
This species much resembles the last, but differs in
having longer leaves, which are obovate, and deeply
toothed. It is sparingly found in the northern states, and
attains its greatest altitude in the south, where it is often
seen 90 feet in height. Though generally found in the
neighborhood of swamps and low grounds, it grows with
wonderful rapidity in a good, moderately dry soil, and
from the beauty of its fine spreading head, and the
quickness of its growth, is highly deserving of introduction
into our plantations.

The Yellow oak. (*Q. Prinus acuminata.*) The
Yellow oak may be found scattered through our woods
over nearly the whole of the Union. Its leaves are
lanceolate, and regularly toothed, light green above, and
whitish beneath; the acorns small. It forms a stately
tree, 70 feet high; and the branches are more upright in

their growth, and more clustering, as it were, round the central trunk, than other species. The beauty of its long pointed leaves, and their peculiar mode of growth, recommend it to mingle with other trees, to which it will add variety.

The Pin oak. (*Q. palustris.*) The Pin oak forms a tree in moist situations, varying in height from 60 to 80 feet. The great number of small branches intermingled with the large ones, have given rise to the name of this variety. It is a hardy, free growing species, particularly upon moist soils. Loudon considers it, from its " far extending, drooping branches, and light and elegant foliage," among the most graceful of oaks. It is well adapted to small groups, and is one of the most thrifty growing and easily obtained of all our northern oaks.

The Willow oak. (*Q. Phellos.*) This remarkable species of oak may be recognised at once by its narrow, entire leaves, shaped almost like those of the willow, and about the same size, though thicker in texture. It is not found wild north of the barrens of New Jersey, where it grows plentifully, but thrives well in cultivation much further north. The stem of this tree is remarkably smooth in every stage of its growth. It is so different in appearance and character from the other species of this genus, that in plantations it would never be recognised by a person not conversant with oaks, as one of the family. It deserves to be introduced into landscapes for its singularity as an oak, and its lightness and elegance of foliage individually.

The Mossy-cup oak. (*Q. olivæformis*) This is so called because the scales of the cups terminate in a long, moss-like fringe, nearly covering the acorn. It is quite a

rare species, being only found on the upper banks of the
Hudson, and on the Genesee river.   The foliage is fine,
large, and deeply cut, and the lower branches of the tree
droop in a beautiful manner when it has attained some
considerable size.   *Quercus macrocarpa*, the Over-cup
White oak, is another beautiful kind found in the western
states, which a good deal resembles the Mossy-cup oak in
the acorn.   The foliage, however, is uncommonly fine,
being the largest in size of any American species; fifteen
inches long, and eight broad.   It is a noble tree, with fine
deep green foliage ; and the growth of a specimen planted
in our grounds has been remarkably vigorous.

Scarlet oak.   (*Quercus coccinea.*)   A native of the
middle states ; a noble tree, often eighty feet high.   The
leaves, borne on long petioles, are a bright lively green on
both surfaces, with four deep cuts on each side, widest at
the bottom.   The great and peculiar beauty of this tree,
we conceive to be its property of assuming a deep scarlet
tint in autumn.   At that period it may, at a great
distance, be distinguished from all other oaks, and indeed
from every other forest tree.   It is highly worthy of a
place in every plantation.

The Live oak.   (*Quercus virens.*)   This fine species
will not thrive north of Virginia.   Its imperishable timber
is the most valuable in our forests ; and, at the south, it is
a fine park tree, when cultivated, growing about 40 feet
nigh, with, however, a rather wide and low head.   The
thick oval leaves are evergreen, and it is much to be
regretted that this noble tree will not bear our northern
winters.

The English Royal oak.   (*Q. robur.*)   This is the great
representative of the family in Europe, and is one of the

most magnificent of the genus, growing often in the fine
old woods and parks of England, to eighty and one
hundred feet in height. The branches spread over a
great surface. " The leaves are petiolated, smooth, and
of a uniform color on both sides, enlarged towards the
summit, and very coarsely toothed." As a single tree for
park scenery, this equals any American species in *majesty*
of form, though it is deficient in individual beauty of
foliage to some of our oaks. It is to be found for sale in
our nurseries, and we hope will become well known
among us. The timber is closer grained and more
durable, though less elastic than the best American oak,
and Michaux, in his Sylva, recommends its introduction
into this country largely, on these accounts.

The Turkey oak. (*Q. Cerris.*) There are two
beautiful hybrid varieties of this species, which have
been raised in England by Messrs. Lucombe and Fulham,
which we hope will yet be found in our ornamental
plantations. They are partially evergreen in winter,
remarkably luxuriant in their growth, attaining a height
of seventy or eighty feet, and elegant in foliage and
outline. The Lucombe and Fulham oaks grow from one
to five feet in a season; the trees assume a beautiful
pyramidal shape, and as they retain their fine glossy
leaves till May, they would form a fine contrast to other
deciduous trees.

We might here enumerate a great number of other fine
foreign oaks; among which the most interesting are the
Holly or Holm oak (*Quercus Ilex*); and the Cork oak
(*Q. Suber*), of the south of France, which produces the
cork of commerce (both rather too tender for the north);
the Kermes oak (*Q. coccifera*), from which a scarlet dye

is obtained ; and the Italian Esculent oak (*Q. Esculus*), with sweet nutritious acorns. Those, however, who wish to investigate them, will pursue this subject further in European works; while that splendid treatise on our forest trees, the North American Sylva of Michaux, will be found to give full and accurate descriptions of all our numerous indigenous varieties, of which many are peculiar to the southern states.

The oak flourishes best on a strong loamy soil, rather moist than dry. Here at least the growth is most rapid. although, for timber, the wood is generally not so sound on a moist soil as a dry one, and the tree goes to decay more rapidly. Among the American kinds, however, some may be found adapted to every soil and situation, though those species which grow on upland soils, in stony, clayey, or loamy bottoms, attain the greatest size and longevity. When immense trees are desired, the oak should either be transplanted very young, or, which is preferable, raised from the acorn sown where it is finally to remain. This is necessary on account of the very large *tap roots* of this genus of trees, which are either entirely destroyed or greatly injured by removal. Transplanting this genus of trees should be performed either early in autumn, as soon as the leaves fall or become brown, or in spring before the abundant rains commence

----

THE ELM.   *Ulmus*

Nat. Ord. Ulmaceæ.   *Lin. Syst.* Pentandria, Digynia.

We have ascribed to the oak the character of pre-

eminent dignity and majesty among the trees of the forest.
Let us now claim for the elm the epithets graceful and
elegant. This tree is one of the noblest in the size of its
trunk, while the branches are comparatively tapering and
slender, forming themselves, in most of the species, into
long and graceful curves. The flowers are of a chocolate
or purple color, and appear in the month of April, before
the leaves. The latter are light and airy, of a pleasing
light green in the spring, growing darker, however, as the
season advances. The elm is one of the most common
trees in both continents, and has been well known for its
beauty and usefulness since a remote period. In the
south of Europe, particularly in Lombardy, elm trees are
planted in vineyards, and the vines are trained in festoons
from tree to tree in the most picturesque manner. Tasso
alludes to this in the following stanza:

> "Come olmo, a cui la pampinosa pianta
> Cupida s'avviticchi e si marite ;
> Se ferro il tronca, o fulmine lo schianta
> Trae seco a terra la compagna vite."
> *Gerusalemme Liberata*, 2. 326.

It is one of the most common trees for public walks
and avenues, along the highways in France and Germany,
growing with great rapidity, and soon forming a widely
extended shade. In Europe, the elm is much used for
keels in ship-building, and is remarkably durable in water ;
more extensive use is made of it there than of the
American kinds in this country, though the wood of the
Red American elm is more valuable than any other in
the United States for the blocks used in ship rigging.

For its graceful beauty the elm is entitled to high

regard. Standing alone as a single tree, or in a group
of at most three or four in number, it developes itself in
all its perfection. The White American elm we consider
the most beautiful of the family, and to this we more
particularly allude. In such situations as we have just
mentioned, this tree developes its fine ample form in the
most perfect manner. Its branches first spring up embracing the centre, then bend off in finely diverging lines,
until in old trees they often sweep the ground with their
loose pendent foliage. With all this lightness and peculiar
gracefulness of form, it is by no means a meagre looking
tree in the body of its foliage, as its thick tufted masses
of leaves reflect the sun and embosom the shadows as
finely as almost any other tree, the oak excepted. We
consider it peculiarly adapted for planting, in scenes
where the expression of elegant or classical beauty is
desired. In autumn the foliage assumes a lively yellow
tint, contrasting well with the richer and more glowing
colors of our native woods. Even in winter it is a
pleasing object, from the minute division of its spray and
the graceful droop of its branches. It is one of the most
generally esteemed of our native trees for ornamental
purposes, and is as great a favorite here as in Europe for
planting in public squares and along the highways.
Beautiful specimens may be seen in Cambridge, Mass.,
and very fine avenues of this tree are growing with great
luxuriance in and about New Haven.* The charming
villages of New England, among which Northampton
and Springfield are pre-eminent, borrow from the superb
and wonderfully luxuriant elms which decorate their fine

* The great elm of Boston Common is 22 feet in circumference

streets and avenues, the greater portion of their peculiar
loveliness. The elm should not be chosen where large
groups and masses are required, as the similarity of its
form in different individuals might then create a monotony; but as we have before observed, it is peculiarly
well calculated for small groups, or as a single object.
The roughness of the bark, contrasting with the lightness
of its foliage and the easy sweep of its branches, adds
much also to its effect as a whole.

We shall briefly describe the principal species of the
elm.

The American White elm.   (*Ulmus Americana.*)   This
is the best known and most generally distributed of our
native species, growing in greater or less profusion over
the whole of the country included between Lower Canada
and the Gulf of Mexico. It often reaches 80 feet in
height in fine soils, with a diameter of 4 or 5 feet. The
leaves are alternate, 3 or 4 inches long, unequal in size
at the base, borne on petioles half an inch to an inch in
length, oval, acuminate, and doubly denticulated. The
seeds are contained in a flat, oval, winged seed-vessel,
fringed with small hairs on the margin. The flowers,
of a dull purple color, are borne in small bunches on
short footstalks at the end of the branches, and appear
very early in the spring. This tree prefers a deep rich
soil, and grows with greater luxuriance if it be rather
moist, often reaching in such situations an altitude of
nearly 100 feet. It is found in the greatest perfection in
the alluvial soils of the fertile valleys of the Connecticut,
the Mississippi, and the Ohio rivers.

The Red or Slippery elm.   (*U. fulva.*)   A tree of

lower size than the White elm, attaining generally only
40 or 50 feet. According to Michaux, it may be
distinguished from the latter even in winter, by its buds,
which are larger and rounder, and which are covered a
fortnight before their development with a russet down
The leaves are larger, rougher, and thicker than those
of the White elm; the seed-vessels larger, destitute of
fringe; the stamens short, and of a pale rose color. This
tree bears a strong likeness to the Dutch elm, and the
bark abounds in mucilage, whence the name of Slippery
elm. The branches are less drooping than those of the
White elm.

The Wahoo elm (*U. alata*) is not found north of
Virginia. It may at once be known in every stage of
its growth by the fungous cork-like substance which
lines the branches on both sides. It is a very singular
and curious tree, of moderate stature, and grows rapidly
and well when cultivated in the northern states.

The common European elm. (*U. campestris.*) This
is the most commonly cultivated forest tree in Europe,
next to the oak. It is a more upright growing tree than
the White elm, though resembling it in the easy
disposition and delicacy of its branches. The flowers,
of a purple color, are produced in round bunches close
to the stem. The leaves are rough, doubly serrated,
and much more finely cut than those of our elms. It
is a fine tree, 60 or 70 feet high, growing with rapidity,
and is easily cultivated. The timber is more valuable
than the American sort, though the tree is inferior to
the White elm in beauty. There are some dozen or
more fine varieties of this species cultivated in the
English nurseries, among which the most remarkable are

the Twisted elm (*U. c. tortuosa*), the trunk of which is singularly marked with hollows and protuberances, and the grain of the wood curiously twisted together : the Kidbrook elm (*U. c. virens*), which is a sub-evergreen : the Gold and Silver striped elms, with variegated leaves, and the Narrow-leaved elm (*U. c. viminalis*), which resembles the birch : the Cork-barked elm (*U. c. suberosa*), the young branches of which are covered with cork, etc.

The latter is one of the hardiest and most vigorous of all ornamental trees in this climate. It thrives in almost every soil, and its rich, dark foliage, which hangs late in autumn, and its somewhat picturesque form, should recommend it to every planter.

The Scotch or Wych elm. (*U. montana.*) This is a tree of lower stature than the common European elm, its average height being about 40 feet. The leaves are broad, rough, pointed, and the branches extend more horizontally, drooping at the extremities. The bark on the branches is comparatively smooth. It is a grand tree, "the head is so finely massed and yet so well broken as to render it one of the noblest of park trees; and when it grows wild amid the rocky scenery of its native Scotland, there is no tree which assumes so great or so pleasing a variety of character."* In general appearance, the Scotch elm considerably resembles our White elm, and it is a very rapid grower. Its most ornamental varieties are the Spiry-topped elm (*U. m. fastigiata*), with singularly twisted leaves, and a very upright growth : the weeping Scotch elm (*U. m. pendula*), a very remarkable variety, the branches of which droop in a

---

* Sir Thos. Lauder, in Gilpin, 1. 91.

fan-like manner : and the Smooth-leaved Scotch elm (*U m. glabra*).

There is scarcely any soil to which some of the different elms are not adapted. The European species prefer a deep, dry soil; the Scotch or Wych elm will thrive well even in very rocky places; and the White elm grows readily in all soils, but most luxuriantly in moist places. All the species attain their maximum size when planted in a deep loam, rather moist than dry. They bear transplanting remarkably well, suffering but little even from the mistaken practice of those persons who reduce them in transplanting to the condition of bare poles, as they shoot out a new crop of branches, and soon become beautiful young trees in spite of the mal-treatment. As the elm scarcely produces a tap root, even large trees may be removed, when the operation is skilfully performed. In such cases, the recently-removed tree should be carefully and plentifully supplied with water until it is well established in its new situation. The elm is also easily propagated by seed, layers, or, in some species, by suckers from the root.

THE PLANE OR BUTTONWOOD TREE. *Platanus.*

Nat. Ord. Platanaceæ.   *Lin. Syst.* Monœcia, Polyandria.

The plane, *Platanus* derives its name from πλατυς, *broad*, on account of the broad, umbrageous nature of its branches. It is a well known tree of the very largest size, common to both hemispheres, and greatly prized for the fine shade afforded by its spreading head, in the warmer parts of Europe and Asia. No tree was in greater esteem with the ancients for this purpose; and we are told that the Academic groves, the neighborhood of the public schools, and all those favorite avenues where the Grecian philosophers were accustomed to resort, were planted with these trees; and beneath their shade Aristotle, Plato, and Socrates, delivered the choicest wisdom and eloquence of those classic days. The Eastern plane (*Platanus orientalis*) was first brought to the Roman provinces from Persia, and so highly was it esteemed that according to Pliny, the Morini paid a tribute to Rome for the privilege of enjoying its shade. To that author we are also indebted for the history of the great plane tree that grew in the province of Lycia, which was of so huge a size, that the governor of the province, Licinius Mutianus, together with eighteen of his retinue, feasted in the hollow of its trunk.

In the United States, the plane is not generally found growing in great quantities in any one place, but is more or less scattered over the whole country. In deep, moist, alluvial soils, it attains a size scarcely, if at all, inferior to that of the huge trees of the eastern continent; forming at least, in the body of its trunk, a larger circumference than any other of our native trees. The younger Michaux (*Sylva*, 1, 325) measured a tree near Marietta, Ohio, which at four feet from the ground was found to be forty-seven feet in circumference; and a specimen has lately been cut on the banks of the Genesee river, of such enormous size, that a section of the trunk was hollowed out and furnished as a small room, capable of containing fourteen persons.* On the margins of the great western rivers it sometimes rises up seventy feet, and then expands into a fine, lofty head, surpassing in grandeur all its neighbors of the forest. The large branches of the plane shoot out in a horizontal direction; the trunk generally ascending in a regular, stately, and uninterrupted manner The blossoms are small greenish balls appearing in spring, and the fertile ones grow to an inch in diameter, assuming a deep brownish color, and hang upon the tree during the whole winter. A striking and peculiar characteristic of the plane, is its property of throwing off or shedding continually the other coating of bark here and there in patches. Professor Lindley (*Introduction to the Natural System*, 2d ed. 187) says this is owing to its deficiency in the expansive power of the fibre common to the bark of other trees, or, in other words, to the rigidity of its tissue : being therefore incapable of stretching with the growth of the tree, it bursts open on different parts of the trunk, and is cast off. This gives the trunk quite a lively and picturesque look, extending more or less even to the extremity of the branches ; and makes this tree quite conspicuous in winter. Bryant, in his address to Green River, says :

> " Clear are the depths where its eddies play,
> And dimples deepen and whirl away,
> And the plane tree's *speckled arms* o'ershoot
> The swifter current that mines its root."

The great merit of the plane, or buttonwood, is its

* A buttonwood on the Montezuma estate, Jefferson, Cayuga Co., N. Y., is forty-seven and a half feet in circumference ; and the diameter of the hollow two feet from the ground, is fifteen feet. (*N. Y. Med. Repository, IV.* 427.)

extreme vigor and luxuriance of growth.   In a good soil it will readily reach a height of thirty-five or forty feet in ten years.   It is easily transplanted ; and in new residences, bare of trees, where an effect is desired speedily, we know of nothing better adapted quickly to produce abundance of foliage, shelter, and shade.   When the requisite foliage is obtained, and other trees of slower growth have reached a proper size, the former may be thinned out.   As the plane tree grows to the largest size, it is only proper for situations where there is considerable ground, and where it can without inconvenience to its fellows have ample room for its full development.   Then soaring up, and extending its wide-spread branches on every side, it is certainly a very majestic tree.   The color of the foliage is of a paler green than is usual in forest trees ; and although of large size, is easily wafted to and fro by the wind, thereby producing an agreeable diversity of light pleasing to the eye in summer.   In winter the branches are beautifully hung, even to their furthest ends, with the numerous round russet-balls, or seed-vessels, each suspended by a slender cord, and swinging about in the air. The outline of the head is pleasingly irregular, and its foliage against a sky outline is bold and picturesque.   It is not a tree to be planted in thick groves by itself, but to stand alone and detached, or in a group with two or three.   In avenues it is often happily employed, and produces a grand effect.   It also grows with great vigor in close cities, as some superb specimens in the square of the State-house, Pennsylvania Hospital, and other places in Philadelphia fully attest.

There is but a trifling difference in general effect between our plane or buttonwood and the Oriental plane. For the purposes of shade and shelter, the American is the finest, as its foliage is the longest and broadest. The Oriental plane (*Platanus orientalis*) has the leaves lobed like our native kind (*P. occidentalis*), but the segments are much more deeply cut; the footstalks of its leaves are green, while those of the American are of a reddish hue, and the fruit or ball is much smaller and rougher on the outer surface when fully grown. Both species are common in the nurseries, and are worthy the attention of the planter; the Oriental, as well for the interesting associations connected with it, being the favorite shade-tree of the east, etc., as for its intrinsic merits as a lofty and majestic tree.

Two of the varieties of P. occidentalis are sometimes cultivated, the chief of which is the Maple-leaved plane (*P. O. acerifolia*).

The Ash Tree. *Fraxinus.*

Nat. Ord. Oleaceæ.   *Lin. Syst.* Polygamia, Diœcia.

The name of the ash, one of the finest and most useful of forest trees, is probably derived from the Celtic *asc*, a pike—as its wood was formerly in common use for spears and other weapons. Homer informs us that Achilles was slain with an ashen spear. In modern times the wood is in universal use for the various implements of husbandry, for the different purposes of the wheelwright and carriage-maker, and in short for all purposes where great strength and elasticity are required; for in these qualities the ash is

second to no tree in the forest, the hickory alone excepted.
The ash is a large and lofty tree, growing, when surrounded
by other trees, sixty or seventy feet high, and three or more
in diameter. When exposed on all sides it forms a beautiful, round, compact head of loose, pinnated, light green
foliage, and is one of the most vigorous growers among the
hard-wooded trees. The American species of ash are
found in the greatest luxuriance and beauty on the banks
and margins of rivers where the soil is partially dry, yet
where the roots can easily penetrate down to the moisture.
The European ash is remarkable for its hardy nature, being
often found in great vigor on steep rocky hills, and amid
crevices where most other trees flourish badly. Southey
alludes to this in the following lines :—

> " Grey as the stone to which it clung, half root,
> Half trunk, the young ash rises from the rock."

As the ash grows strongly, and the roots, which extend
to a great distance, ramify near the surface, it exhausts the
soil underneath and around it to an astonishing degree.
For this reason the grass is generally seen in a very meagre
and starved condition in a lawn where the ash tree abounds.
Here and there a single tree of the ash will have an excellent effect, seen from the windows of the house ; but we
would chiefly employ it for the grand masses, and to intermingle with other large groups of trees in an extensive
plantation. When the ash is young it forms a well rounded
head ; but when older the lower branches bend towards
the ground, and then slightly turn up in a very graceful
manner. We take pleasure in quoting what that great
lover and accurate delineator of forest beauties, Mr. Gilpin,
says of the ash. " The ash generally carries its principal

stem higher than the oak, and rises in an easy flowing line.
But its chief beauty consists in the lightness of its whole
appearance.   Its branches at first keep close to the trunk
and form acute angles with it ; but as they begin to lengthen
they generally take an easy sweep, and the looseness of the
leaves corresponding with the lightness of the spray, the
whole forms an elegant depending foliage.   Nothing can
have a better effect than an old ash hanging from the corner
of a wood, and bringing off the heaviness of the other
foliage with its loose pendent branches."—(*Forest Scenery,
p.* 82.)

The highest and most characteristic beauty of the American White ash (and we consider it the finest of all the
species) is the coloring which its leaves put on in autumn.
Gilpin complains that the leaf of the European ash "decays
in a dark, muddy, unpleasing tint."   Not so the White ash.
In an American wood, such as often lines and overhangs
the banks of the Hudson, the Connecticut, and many of
our noble northern streams, the ash assumes peculiar beauty
in autumn, when it can often be distinguished from the
surrounding trees for four or five miles, by the peculiar and
beautiful deep brownish purple of its fine mass of foliage.
This color, though not lively, is so full and rich as to produce the most pleasing harmony with the bright yellows
and reds of the other deciduous trees, and the deep green
of the pines and cedars.

The ash, unlike the elm, starts into vegetation late in the
spring, which is an objection to planting it in the immediate
vicinity of the house.   In winter the long greyish white or
ash-colored branches are pleasing in tint, compared with
those of other deciduous trees.

The White ash. (*Fraxinus Americana.*) This species,
according to Michaux, is common to the colder parts of the
Union, and is most abundant north of the Hudson. It
owes its name to the light color of the bark, which on large
stocks is deeply furrowed, and divided into squares of one
to three inches in diameter. The trunk is perfectly straight,
and in close woods is often undivided to the height of more
than 40 feet. The leaves are composed of three or four
pairs of leaflets, terminated by an odd one; the whole
twelve or fourteen inches long. Early in spring they are
covered with a light down which disappears as summer
advances, when they become quite smooth, of a light green
color above and whitish beneath. The foliage, as well as
the timber of our White ash, is finer than that of the common European ash, and the tree is much prized in France
and Germany.

The Black ash (*F. sambucifolia*), sometimes called the
Water ash, requires a moist soil to thrive well, and is seen
n the greatest perfection on the borders of swamps. Its
buds are of a deep blue ; the young shoots of a bright green,
sprinkled with dots of the same color, which disappear as
the season advances. It may readily be distinguished from
the White ash by its bark, which is of a duller hue and less
deeply furrowed. The Black ash is altogether a tree of
less stature than the preceding.

The other native sorts are the Red ash (*F. tomentosa*),
with the bark of a deep brown tint, found in Pennsylvania :
the Green ash (*F. viridis*), which also grows in Pennsylvania, and is remarkable for the brilliant green of both sides
of the leaves : the Blue ash (*F. Quadrangulata*), a beautiful tree of Kentucky, 70 feet high, distinguished by the four
opposite membranes of a greenish color, found on the young

shoots : and the Carolina ash (*F. platycarpa*), a small tree,
the leaves of which are covered with a thick down in
spring.

The common European ash (*F. excelsior*) strongly resembles the White ash. It may, however, easily be known
by its very black buds, and longer, more serrated leaflets,
which are sessile, instead of being furnished with petioles
like the White ash. This fine tree, as well as the White
ash, grows to 80 or 90 feet in height, with a very handsome
head.

The Weeping ash, Fig. 31, is a very remarkable variety

[Fig. 31. The Weeping Ash.]

of the European ash, with pendulous or weeping branches;
and is worthy a place in every lawn for its curious ramification, as well as for its general beauty. It is generally
propagated by grafting on any common stock, as the White
ash, 7 or 8 feet high, when the branches immediately begin
to turn down in a very striking and peculiar manner. The
droop of the branches is hardly a graceful one, yet it is so

FIG. 32.—The EUROPEAN LINDEN, at Presqu-ile, the Residence of Mrs. Denning.
Age, 44 years.   Height, 57 feet.

unique, either when leafless, or in full foliage, that it has long been one of our greatest favorites.

The Flowering ash (*Fraxinus Ornus**) is a small tree of about 20 feet, growing plentifully in the south of Europe, and is also found sparingly in this country. Its chief beauty lies in the beautiful clusters of pale or greenish-white flowers, borne on the terminal branches in May and June. The foliage and general appearance of the tree are much like those of the common ash; but when in blossom it resembles a good deal the Carolina Fringe tree. In Italy a gummy substance called manna exudes from the bark, which is used in medicine.

THE LIME OR LINDEN TREE. *Tilia.*

Nat. Ord. Tilaceæ.   *Lin. Syst.* Polyandria, Monogynia.

This tree, or rather the American sort, is well known among us by the name of *basswood.* It is a rapidly growing, handsome, upright, and regularly shaped tree; and all the species are much esteemed, both in Europe and this country, for planting in avenues and straight lines, wherever the taste is in favor of geometric plantations. In Germany and Holland it is a great favorite for bordering their wide and handsome streets, and lining their long and straight canals. "In Berlin," Granville says in his travels, "there is a celebrated street called '*unter der Linden,*' (under the lime trees,) a gay and splendid avenue, planted with double

---

* *Ornus Europæus* of Persoon, and the European botanists. Beck remarks that the American kind is so little known, that it is difficult to determine whether it is a different species or only a mere variety of the European.

rows of this tree, which presented to my view a scene far more beautiful than I had hitherto witnessed in any town, either in France, Flanders, or Germany." In this country the European lime is also much planted in our cities; and some avenues of it may be seen in Philadelphia, particularly before the State-house in Chestnut-street. The basswood is a very abundant tree in some parts of the middle states, and is seen growing in great profusion, forming thick woods by itself in the interior of this state. With us the wood is considered too soft to be of much value, but in England it was formerly in high repute as an excellent material for the use of carvers. Some very beautiful specimens of old carving in lime wood may be seen in Windsor Castle and Trinity College.* The Russian bass mats, which find their way to every commercial country, are prepared from the inner bark of this tree. The sap affords a sugar like the maple, although in less quantities; and it is stated in the Encyclopædia of Plants (p. 467) " that the honey made from the flowers of the lime tree is reckoned the finest in the world. Near Knowno, in Lithuania, there are large forests chiefly of this tree, and probably a distinct variety. The honey produced in these forests sells at more than double the price of any other, and is used extensively in medicine and for liqueurs."

* The art of carving in wood, brought to such perfection by Gibbons, is now, we believe, much given up; therefore the lime has lost a most important branch of its usefulness. Perhaps the finest specimens of the works of Gibbons are to be seen at Chatsworth, the seat of the Duke of Devonshire, in Derbyshire. The execution of the flowers, fish, game, nets, etc., on the panelling of the walls is quite wonderful. It was of him that Walpole justly said, ' that he was the first artist who gave to wood the loose and airy lightness of flowers, and chained together the various productions of the elements, with a free disorder natural to each species.' The lime tree is still, however, used by the carver, and we hope that the art of wood carving may gradually be restored."—*Sir T. D. Lauder*

The leaves of the lime are large and handsome, heart-shaped in form, and pleasing in color.   The flowers, which open in June, hang in loose, pale yellow cymes or clusters, are quite ornamental and very fragrant.

> ——Sometimes
> A scent of violets and blossoming limes
> Loitered around us ; then of honey cells,
> Made delicate from all white flower bells.
>
> KEATS.

It was a favorite tree in the ancient style of gardening, as it bore the shears well, and was readily clipt into all manner of curious and fantastic shapes.   When planted singly on a lawn, and allowed to develope itself fully on every side, the linden is one of the most beautiful of trees. Its head then forms a fine pyramid of verdure, while its lower branches sweep the ground and curve upwards in the most pleasing form.   For this reason, though the linden is not a picturesque tree, it is very happily adapted for the graceful landscape, as its whole contour is full, flowing, and agreeable.   The pleasant odor of its flowers is an additional recommendation, as well as its free growth and handsome leaves.   Were it not that of late it is so liable to insects, we could hardly say too much in its praise as a fine ornament for streets and public parks.   There, its regular form corresponds well with the formality of the architecture ; its shade affords cool and pleasant walks, and the delightful odor of its blossoms is doubly grateful in the confined air of the city.   Our basswood has rather less of uniformity in its outline than the European lindens, but the general form is the same.

The American lime, or basswood (*Tilia Americana*), is the most robust tree of the genus, and produces much more vigorous shoots than the European species. It prefers a deep and fertile soil, where the trunk grows remarkably straight, and the branches form a handsome, well-rounded summit. The flowers are borne on long stalks, and are pendulous from the branches. The leaves are large, heart-shaped, finely cut on the margin, and terminated by a point at the extremity. The seeds, which ripen in autumn, are like small peas, round and greyish.

The white lime (*T. alba*) is rare in the eastern states, but common in Pennsylvania and the states south of it. It is not a tree of the largest size, but its flowers are the finest of our native sorts. The leaves are also very large, deep green on the upper surface, and white below; they are more obliquely heart-shaped than those of the common basswood. The young branches are covered with a smooth silvery bark. This species is very common on the Susquehannah river.

The Downy lime tree. (*T. pubescens.*) The under side of the leaves, and the fruits of this species, are, as its name denotes, covered with a short down. Its flowers are nearly white; the serratures of the leaves wider apart, and the base of the leaf obliquely truncated. It is a handsome large tree, a native of Florida, though hardy enough, as experience proves, to bear our northern winters.

The European lime (*T. Europœa*) is distinguished from the American sorts, by its smaller and more regularly cordate and rounded leaves. Unlike our native species, the flowers are not furnished with inner scale-like petals. The foliage is rather deeper in hue than the native sorts, and the branches of the head rather more regular in form and disposition. There are two pretty varieties of the English lime which are well known in this country, viz. the Red-barked, or corallina (*var. rubra*), with red branches ; and the Golden-barked (*var aurea*), with handsome yellow branches. These trees are peculiarly beautiful in winter, when a few of them mingled with other deciduous trees make a pleasing variety of coloring in the absence of foliage. The broad-leaved European lime is the finest for shade and ornament. The whitish foliage of *Tilia alba*, which probably is also a variety, has a beautiful appearance, somewhat like the Abele tree, in a gentle breeze.

These trees grow well on any good friable soil, and readily endure transplantation. They bear trimming remarkably well ; and when but little root is obtained the head may be shortened in proportion, and the tree will soon make vigorous shoots again. All the species are easily increased by layers.

The Beech Tree. *Fagus.*

Nat. Ord. Corylaceæ. *Lin. Syst.* Monœcia, Polyandria.

The Beech is a large, compact, and lofty tree, with a greyish bark and finely divided spray, and is a common inhabitant of the forest in all temperate climates. In the United States, this tree is generally found congregated in very great quantities, wherever the soil is most favorable ; hundreds of acres being sometimes covered with this single kind of timber. Such tracts are familiarly known as "beech woods." The leaves of the beech are remarkably thin in texture, glazed and shining on the upper surface, and so thickly set upon the numerous branches, that it forms the darkest and densest shade of any of our deciduous forest trees. It appears to have been highly valued by the ancients as a shade tree ; and Virgil says in its praise, in a well-known Eclogue :

> " Tityre, tu patulæ recubans sub tegmine *fagi*,
> Sylvestrem tenui musam meditaris avena."

It bears a small compressed nut or mast, oily and sweet, which once was much valued as an article of food. The most useful purpose to which we have heard of their being applied, is in the manufacture of an oil, scarcely inferior to olive oil. This is produced from the mast of the beech forests in the department of Oise, France, in immense quantities; more than a million of sacks of the nuts having been collected in that department in a single season. They are reduced, when perfectly ripe, to a fine paste, and the oil is extracted by gradual pressure. The product of oil, compared with the crushed nuts, is about sixteen per cent. (*Michaux, N. American Sylva.*)

In Europe, the wood of the beech is much used in the manufacture of various utensils ; but here, where our forests abound in woods vastly superior in strength, durability, and firmness, that of the beech is comparatively little esteemed.

The beech is quite handsome and graceful when young, and when large it forms one of the heaviest and grandest of *beautiful* park trees. From this massy quality, however, it is excellently adapted to mingle with other trees when a thick and impenetrable mass of foliage is desired ;

and, on account of its density, it is also well suited to shut out unsightly buildings, or other objects.

The leaves of many beech trees hang on the tree, in a dry and withered state, during the whole winter. This is chiefly the case with young trees; but we consider it as greatly diminishing its beauty at that season, as the tree is otherwise very pleasing to the eye, with its smooth, round, grey stem, and small twisted spray. A deciduous tree, we think, should as certainly drop its leaves at the approach of cold weather, as an evergreen should retain them; more especially if its leaves have a dead and withered appearance, as is the case with those of the beech in this climate.

The White beech (*Fagus Sylvatica*) is the common beech tree of the middle and western states. It is found in the greatest perfection in a cool situation and a moist soil. The bark is smooth and grey, even upon the oldest stocks. The leaves oval, smooth, and shining, coarsely cut on the edges, and margined with a soft down in the spring.

The Red beech (*F. ferruginea*), so called on account of the color of its wood, loves a still colder climate than the other, and is found in the greatest perfection in British America. The leaves are divided into coarser teeth on the margin than the foregoing species. The nuts are much smaller, and the whole tree forms a lower and more spreading head.

The European beech (*F. sylvatica*) is thought by many botanists to be the same species as our white beech, or at most only a variety. Its average height in Europe is about fifty feet; the buds are shorter, and the leaves not so coarsely toothed as our native sorts. The Purple beech is a very ornamental variety of the European beech, common in the gardens.   Both surfaces of the leaves, and even the young shoots, are deep purple ; and although the growth is slow, yet it is in every stage of its progress, and more par ticularly when it reaches a good size, one of the strangest anomalies among trees, in the hue of its foliage.   There is also a variety called the copper-colored beech, with paler purple leaves ;* and a more rare English variety (*F. s. pendula*), the Weeping beech, with graceful pendent branches

THE HORNBEAM (*Carpinus Americana*), and the IRON-WOOD (*Ostrya Virginica*), are both well known small trees, belonging to the same natural family as the beech.   They are of little value in ornamental plantations ; but from their thick foliage, they might perhaps be employed to advantage in making thick verdant screens for shelter or concealment.

THE POPLAR TREE. *Populus.*

Nat. Ord. Salicaceæ.   *Lin. Syst.* Diœcia, Octandria.

Arbor Populi, or the people's tree, was the name given in the ancient days of Rome to this tree, as being peculiarly appropriated to those public places most frequented by the people : some ingenious authors have still further justified the propriety of the name, by adding, that its trembling leaves are like the *populace*, always in motion.

The poplars are light-wooded, rapid-growing trees ; many

* The finest Copper Beech in America is growing in the grounds of Thomas Ash, Esq., Throgs Neck, Westchester Co., N. Y.   It is more than fifty feet high, with a broad and finely formed head.

of them of huge size, and all with pointed, heart-shaped leaves. The tassel-like catkins, or male blossoms, of a red or brownish hue, appear early in the spring. Some of the American kinds, as the Balsam and Balm of Gilead poplars, have their buds enveloped in a fragrant gum; others, as the Silver poplar, or Abele, are remarkable for the snowy whiteness of the under side of the foliage; and the Lom bardy poplar, which

> " Shoots up its spire, and shakes its leaves in the sun,"
>
> PROCTOR.

for its remarkably conical or spire-like manner of growth. The leaves of all the species, being suspended upon long and slender footstalks, are easily put in motion by the wind. This, however, is peculiarly the case with the aspen, the leaves of which may often be seen trembling in the slightest breeze, when the foliage of the surrounding trees is motion-less. There is a popular legend in Scotland respecting this tree, which runs thus :

> " Far off in the Highland wilds 'tis said
> (But truth now laughs at fancy's lore),
> That of this tree the cross was made,
> Which erst the Lord of Glory bore ;
> And of that deed its leaves confess,
> E'er since, a troubled consciousness."

In Landscape Gardening the poplar is not highly esteemed ; but it is a valuable tree when judiciously employed, and produces a given quantity of foliage and shade sooner perhaps than any other. Some of the American kinds are majestic and superb trees when old, particularly the Cotton-wood and Balsam poplars. One of the handsomest sorts is the Silver poplar. At some distance, the downy under surfaces of the leaves, turned up by the wind, give it very much the aspect of a tree covered with white blossoms. This effect is the more striking, when it is situated in front of a group or mass of the darker foliage of other trees. It is valuable for retaining its leaves in full beauty to the latest possible period in the autumn. Its growth is very rapid, forming a fine rounded head of thirty feet in height, in six or eight years.

The Lombardy poplar is a beautiful tree, and in certain situations produces a very elegant effect ; but it has been planted so indiscriminately, in some parts of this country, in close monotonous lines before the very doors of our houses, and in many places in straight rows along the high ways for miles together, to the neglect of our fine native trees, that it has been tiresome and disgusting. This tree may, however, be employed with singular advantage in giving life, spirit, and variety to a scene composed entirely of round-headed trees, as the oak, ash, etc.,—when a tall poplar, emerging here and there from the back or centre of the group, often imparts an air of elegance and animation to the whole. It may, also, from its marked and striking contrast to other trees, be employed to fix or direct the attention to some particular point in the landscape. When large poplars of this kind are growing near a house of but moderate dimensions, they have a very bad effect by com-pletely overpowering the building, without imparting any of that grandeur of character conferred by an old oak, or other spreading tree. It should be introduced but sparingly in landscape composition, as the moment it is made com-mon in any scene, it gives an air of sameness and formality, and all the spirited effect is lost which its sparing introduc-tion among other trees produces. The Lombardy poplar ıs so well adapted to confined situations, as its branches require less lateral room than those of almost any other large deciduous tree.

It is an objection to some of the poplars, that in any cultivated soil they produce an abundance of suckers For this reason they should be planted only in grass ground, or in situations where the soil will not be disturbed, or where the suckers will not be injurious. Indeed, we conceive them to be chiefly worthy of introduction in grounds of large extent, to give variety to plantations of other and more valuable trees. They grow well in almost every soil, moist or dry, and some species prefer quite wet and springy places.

The chief American poplars are the Tachamahaca or Balsam poplar (*Populus balsamifera*), chiefly found in Northern America; a large tree, 80 feet high, with fragrant gummy buds and lanceolate-oval leaves; the Balm of Gilead poplar (*P. candicans*), resembling the foregoing in its buds, but with very large, broad, heart-shaped foliage. From these a gum is sometimes collected, and used medicinally for the cure of scurvy. The American aspen (*P. tremuloides*), about 30 feet high, a common tree with very tremulous leaves and greenish bark; the large American aspen (*P. grandidentata*), 40 feet high, with large leaves bordered with coarse teeth or denticulations; the Cotton tree (*P. argentea*), 60 or 70 feet, with leaves downy in a young state; the American Black poplar of smaller size, having the young shoots covered with short hair; the Cottonwood (*P. Canadensis*), found chiefly in the western part of this state, a fine tree, with smooth, unequally-toothed, wide cordate leaves; and the Carolina poplar (*P. angulata*), an enormous tree of the swamps of the south and west, considerably resembling the Cotton tree, but without the resinous buds of that species.

Among the European kinds, the most ornamental, as we have already remarked, is the Silver aspen, White poplar, or Abele tree (*P. alba*), which grows to a great size on a deep loamy soil in a very short time. The leaves are divided into lobes, and toothed on the margin, smooth and very deep green above, and densely covered with a soft, close, white down beneath. There are some varieties of this species known abroad, with leaves more or less downy, etc. Sir J. E. Smith remarks in his English Flora, that the wood, though but little used, is much firmer than that of any other British poplar ; making as handsome floors as the best Norway fir, with the additional advantage that they will not readily take fire, like any resinous wood.

The English aspen (*P. tremula*) considerably resembles our native aspen ; but the buds are somewhat gummy. The Athenian poplar (*P. Græca*) is a tree about 40 feet high, with smaller, more rounded, and equally serrated foliage. The common Black European poplar (*P. nigra*) is also a large, rapidly growing tree, with pale-green leaves slightly notched : the buds expand later than most other poplars, and the young leaves are at first somewhat reddish in color. The Necklace-bearing poplar (*P. monilifera*), sc called from the circumstance of the catkins being arranged somewhat like beads in a necklace, is supposed to have been derived from Canada, but there are some doubts respecting its origin : in the south it is generally called the Virginia poplar.

The Lombardy poplar (*P. dilatata*), a native of the banks of the Po, where it is sometimes called the Cypress poplar from its resemblance to that tree, is too well known among us to need any description.   Only one sex, the female, has hitherto been introduced into this country ; and it has consequently produced no seeds here, but has been entirely propagated by suckers from the root.

The Horse-chestnut Tree. *Æsculus.*

Nat. Ord. Æsculaceæ.   *Lin. Syst.* Heptandria, Monogynia.

A large, showy, much admired, ornamental tree, bearing large leaves composed of seven leaflets, and, in the month of May, beautiful clusters of white flowers, delicately mottled with red and yellow.   It is a native of Middle Asia, but flourishes well in the temperate climates of both hemispheres.   It was introduced into England, probably from Turkey, about the year 1575 : in that country the nuts are often ground into a coarse flour, which is mixed with other food and given to horses that are broken-winded ; and from this use the English name of the tree was derived.

A starch has been extracted in considerable quantity from the nuts.   The wood is considered valueless in the United States.

The Horse-chestnut is by no means a picturesque tree, being too regularly rounded in its outlines, and too compact and close in its surface, to produce a spirited effect in light and shade.   But it is nevertheless one of the most *beautiful* exotic trees which will bear the open air in this climate.   The leaves, each made of clusters of six or seven leaflets, are of a fine dark-green color ; the whole head of foliage has much grandeur and richness in its depth of hue and massiness of outline ; and the regular, rounded, pyramidal shape, is something so different from that of most of our indigenous trees, as to strike the spectator with an air of novelty and distinctness. The great beauty of the Horse-chestnut is the splendor of its inflorescence, surpassing that of almost all our native forest trees : the huge clusters of gay blossoms, which every spring are distributed with such luxuriance and profusion over the surface of the foliage, and at the extremity of the branches, give the whole tree the aspect rather of some monstrous flowering shrub, than of an ordinary tree of the largest size.   At that season there can be no more beautiful object to stand singly upon the lawn, particularly if its branches are permitted to grow low down the trunk, and (as they naturally will as the tree advances) sweep the green sward with their drooping foliage. Like the lime tree, however, care must be taken, in the modern style, to introduce it rather sparingly in picturesque plantations, and then only as a single tree, or upon the margin of large groups, masses, or plantations ; but it may be more freely used in grounds in the graceful style, for which it is highly suitable.   When handsome avenues or straight lines are wanted, the Horse-chestnut is again admirably suited, from its symmetry and regularity.   It is, therefore, much and justly valued for these purposes in our towns and cities, where its deep shade and beauty of blossom are peculiarly desirable, the only objection to it being the early fall of its leaves.   The Horse-chestnut is very interesting in its mode of growth.   The large buds are thickly covered in winter with a resinous gum, to protect them from the cold and moisture ; in the spring these burst open, and the whole growth of the young shoots, leaves, flowers, and all, is completed in about three or four weeks When the leaves first unfold, they are clothed with a copious cotton-like down, which falls off when they have attained their full size and development.

The growth of the Horse-chestnut is slow for a soft-wooded tree, when the trees are young; after five or six years, however, it advances with more rapidity, and in twenty years forms a beautiful and massy tree. It prefers a strong, rich, loamy soil, and is easily raised from the large nuts, which are produced in great abundance.

There are several species of Horse-chestnut, but the common one (*Æsculus Hippocastanum*) is incomparably the finest. The American sorts are the following: (*Æsculus Ohioensis*,) or Ohio Buckeye, as it is called in the western states; a small sized tree, with palmated leaves consisting of *five* leaflets, and pretty, bright yellow flowers, with red stamens. The fruit is about half the size of the exotic species. The Red-flowered Horse-chestnut (*Æsculus rubicunda*) is a small tree with scarlet flowers; and the Smooth-leaved (*Æ. glabra*) has pale yellow flowers. All the foregoing have prickly fruit. Besides these are two small Horse-chestnuts with smooth fruit, which thence properly belong to the genus *Pavia*, viz. the Yellow-flowered Pavia (*P. lutea*) of Virginia and the southern states; and the Red-flowered (*P. rubra*), with pretty clusters of reddish flowers; both these have leaves resembling those of the Horse-chestnut, except in being divided into five leaflets, instead of seven. There are some other species, which are, however, rather shrubs than trees.

The Birch Tree. *Betula.*

Nat. Ord. Betulaceæ. *Lin. Syst.* Monœcia, Polyandria.

The Birch trees are common inhabitants of the forests of all cold and elevated countries. They are remarkable for their smooth, silvery-white, or reddish colored stems, delicate and pliant spray, and small, light foliage. There is no deciduous tree which will endure a more rigorous climate, or grow at a greater elevation above the level of the sea. It is found growing in Greenland and Kamschatka, as far north as the 58th and 60th degree of latitude, and on the Alps in Switzerland, according to that learned botanist, M. DeCandolle, at the elevation of 4,400 feet. It is undoubtedly the most useful tree of northern climates. Not only are cattle and sheep sometimes fed upon the leaves, but the Laplander constructs his hut of the branches; the Russian forms the bark into shoes, baskets, and cordage for harnessing his reindeer; and the inhabitants of Northern Siberia, in times of scarcity, grind it to mix with their oatmeal for food. In this country the birch is no less useful. The North American Indian, and all who are obliged to travel the wild, unfrequented portions of British America,—who have to pass over rapids, and make their way through the wilderness from river to river,—find the canoe made of the birch bark, the lightest, the most durable, and convenient vessel, for these purposes, in the world.*

* The following interesting description of their manufacture, we quote from Michaux. " The most important purpose to which the Canoe birch is applied and one in which its place is supplied by no other tree, is the construction of

The wood of our Black birch is by far the finest ; and, as it assumes a beautiful rosy color when polished, and is next in texture to the wild Cherry tree, it is considerably esteemed among cabinet-makers in the eastern states, for chairs, tables, and bedsteads.

In Europe, the sap of the birch is collected in the spring, in the same manner as that of the maple in this country, boiled with sugar and hops, and fermented with the aid of yeast. The product of the fermentation is called *birch wine*, and is described as being a remarkably pleasant and healthy beverage.

Though perhaps too common in some districts of our country to be properly regarded as an ornamental tree, yet in others where it is less so, the birch will doubtless be esteemed as it deserves. With us it is a great favorite ; and we regard it as a very elegant and graceful tree, not less on account of the silvery white bark of several species, than from the extreme delicacy of the spray, and the pleasing lightness and airiness of the foliage. In all the species, the branches have a tendency to form those graceful curves which contribute so much to the beauty

canoes. To procure proper pieces, the largest and smoothest trunks are selected ; in the spring, two circular incisions are made several feet apart, and two longitudinal ones, on opposite sides of the tree: after which, by introducing a wedge, the bark is easily detached. These plates are usually ten or twelve feet long, and two feet nine inches broad. To form canoes, they are stitched together with fibrous roots of the white spruce, about the size of a quill, which are deprived of the bark, split, and suppled in water. The seams are coated with resin of the Balm of Gilead. Great use is made of these canoes by the savages, and the French Canadians, in their long journeys through the interior of the country: they are light, and very easily transported on the shoulders from one lake to another, which is called the portage. A canoe calculated for four persons, with their baggage, weighs from forty to fifty pounds ; and some of them are made to carry fifteen passengers."

of trees; but the European weeping birch is peculiarly pleasing as it grows old, on that account. It is this variety which Coleridge pronounces,

> "————Most beautiful
> Of forest trees—the Lady of the woods."

And Bernard Barton, speaking of our native species, says,

> ————" See the beautiful Birch tree fling
> Its shade on the grass beneath—
> Its glossy leaf, and its silvery stem ;
> Dost thou not love to look on them ?"

The American sorts, and particularly the Black birch, start into leaf very early in the spring, and their tender green is agreeable to the eye at that season; while the swelling buds and young foliage in many kinds, give out a delicious, though faint perfume. Even the blossoms, which hang like little brown tassels from the drooping branches, are interesting to the lover of nature.

> " The fragrant birch above him hung
> Her tassels in the sky,
> And many a vernal blossom sprung,
> And nodded careless by."
>
> BRYANT.

Nothing can well be prettier, seen from the windows of the drawing-room, than a large group of trees, whose depth and distance is made up by the heavy and deep masses of the ash, oak, and maple ; and the portions nearest the eye or the lawn terminated by a few birches, with their sparkling white stems, and delicate, airy, drooping foliage. Our White birch, being a small tree, is very handsome in such situations, and offers the most pleasing variety to the eye, when

seen in connexion with other foliage. Several kinds, as
the Yellow and the Black birches, are really stately trees,
and form fine groups by themselves. Indeed, most beautiful and varied masses might be formed by collecting
together all the different kinds, with their characteristic
barks, branches, and foliage.

As an additional recommendation, many of these trees
grow on the thinnest and most indifferent soils, whether
moist or dry ; and in cold, bleak, and exposed situations,
as well as in warm and sheltered places.

We shall enumerate the different kinds as follows :—

The Canoe birch, *Boleau à Canot*, of the French Canadians (*B. papyracea*), sometimes also called the Paper birch,
is, according to Michaux, most common in the forests of the
eastern states, north of latitude **43°**, and in the Canadas
There it attains its largest size, sometimes seventy feet in
height, and three in diameter. Its branches are slender,
flexible, covered with a shining brown bark, dotted with
white ; and on trees of moderate size, the bark of the trunk
is of a brilliant white ; it is often used for roofing houses,
for the manufacture of baskets, boxes, etc., besides its most
important use for canoes, as already mentioned. The leaves,
borne on petioles four or five lines long, are of a middling
size, oval, unequally denticulated, smooth, and of a dark
green color.

The White birch (*B. populifolia*) is a tree of much
smaller size, generally from twenty to thirty-five feet in
height : it is found in New York and the other middle
states, as well as at the north. The trunk, like the foregoing, is covered with silvery bark : the branches are
slender, and generally drooping when the tree attains con
siderable size. The leaves are smooth on both surfaces

heart-shaped at the base, very acuminate, and doubly and irregularly toothed. The petioles are slightly twisted, and the leaves are almost as tremulous as those of the aspen It is a beautiful small tree for ornamental plantations.

The common Black or Sweet birch. (*B. lenta.*) This is the sort most generally known by the name of the birch, and is widely diffused over the middle and southern states. In color and appearance the bark much resembles that of the cherry tree; on old trees, at the close of winter, it is frequently detached in transverse portions, in the form of hard ligneous plates six or eight inches broad. The leaves, for a fortnight after their appearance, are covered with a thick silvery down, which disappears soon after. They are about two inches long, serrate, heart-shaped at the base, acuminate at the summit, and of a pleasing tint and fine texture. The wood is of excellent quality, and Michaux recommends its introduction largely into the forests of the north of Europe.

The Yellow birch (*B. lutea*) grows most plentifully in Nova Scotia, Maine, and New Brunswick, on cool, rich soils, where it is a tree of the largest size. It is remarkable for the color and arrangement of its outer bark, which is of a brilliant golden yellow, and is frequently seen divided into fine strips rolled backwards at the end, but attached in the middle. The leaves are about three and a half inches long, two and a half broad, ovate, acuminate, and bordered with sharp and irregular teeth. It is a beautiful tree, with a trunk of nearly uniform diameter, straight, and destitute of branches for thirty or forty feet.

The Red birch (*B. rubra*) belongs chiefly to the south, being scarcely ever seen north of Virginia. It prefers the moist soil of river banks, where it reaches a noble height

It takes its name from the cinnamon or reddish color of the outer bark on the young trees ; when old it becomes rough, furrowed, and greenish. The leaves are light green on the upper surface, whitish beneath, very pointed at the end, and terminated at the base in an acute angle. The twigs are long, flexible, and pendulous ; and the limbs of a brown color, spotted with white.

The European White birch. (*B. alba.*) This species, the common birch tree of Europe, is intermediate in appearance and qualities between our Canoe birch and White birch. The latter it resembles in its foliage, the former in its large size and the excellence of its wood. There is a distinct variety of this, to which we have alluded, called the Weeping birch (*Var. pendula*), which is very rapid in its growth, and highly graceful in its form. From the great beauty of our native species, this is perhaps the only European sort which it is very desirable to introduce into our collections

----

The Alder Tree. *Alnus.*

Nat. Ord. Betulaceæ.   *Lin. Syst.* Monœcia, Tetrandria.

The alder tree is a native of the whole of Europe, where it grows to the altitude of from thirty to sixty feet. Our common Black alder (*A. glauca*), and Hazel-leaved alder (*A. serrulata*), are low shrubs of little value or interest. This, however, is a neat tree, remarkable for its love of moist situations, and thriving best in places even too wet for the willows ; although it will also flourish on dry and elevated soils The leaves are roundish in form, wavy, and

serrated in their margins, and dark green in color. The
tree rapidly forms an agreeable pyramidal head of foliage.
when growing in damp situations. As it is a foreign tree
we shall quote from Gilpin its character in scenery. "The
alder," says he, "loves a low, moist soil, and frequents the
banks of rivers, and will flourish in the poorest forest
swamps where nothing else will grow. It is perhaps the
most picturesque of any of the aquatic tribe, except the
weeping willow. He who would see the alder in perfection
must follow the banks of the Mole in Surrey, through the
sweet vales of Dorking and Mickleham, into the groves of
Esher. The Mole, indeed, is far from being a beautiful
river; it is a silent and sluggish stream, but what beauty
it has it owes greatly to the alder, which everywhere fringes
its meadows, and in many places forms very pleasing scenes.
It is always associated in our minds with river scenery,
both of that tranquil description most frequently to be met
with in the vales of England, and with that wider and more
stirring cast which is to be found amidst the deep glens and
ravines of Scotland; and nowhere is this tree found in
greater perfection than on the wild banks of the river Find-
horn and its tributary streams, where scenery of the most
romantic description everywhere prevails."*

Although the beauty of the alder is of a secondary kind,
it is worth occasional introduction into landscapes where
there is much water to be planted round, or low running
streams to cover with foliage. In these damp places, like
the willow, it grows very well from truncheons or large
limbs, stuck in the ground, which take root and become
trees speedily. There are two principal varieties, the

* Lauder's Gilpin, i. p. 136.

common alder (*A. glutinosa*), and the cut-leaved alder (*A. glutinosa laciniata*). The latter is much the handsomer tree, and is also the rarest in our nurseries.

———

The Maple Tree. *Acer.*

Nat. Ord. Aceraceæ.   *Lin. Syst.* Polygamia, Monœcia.

The great esteem in which the maples are held in the middle states, as ornamental trees, although they are by no means uncommon in every piece of woods of any extent, is a high proof of their superior merits for such purposes. These consist in the rapidity of their growth, the beauty of their form, the fine verdure of their foliage, and in some sorts, the elegance of their blossoms. Among all the species, both native and foreign, we consider the Scarlet-flowering maple as decidedly the most ornamental species. In the spring this tree bursts out in gay tufts of red blossoms, which enliven both its own branches and the surrounding scene long before a leaf is seen on other deciduous trees, and when the only other appearances of vegetation are a few catkins of some willows or poplars swelling into bloom. At that season of the year the Scarlet maple is certainly the most beautiful tree of our forests. Besides this, it grows well either in the very moist soil of swamps, or the dry one of upland ridges, forms a fine clustering head of foliage, and produces an ample and delightful shade; while it is also as little infected by insects of any description as any other tree. The latter advantage, the Sugar maple and our other varieties equally possess. As a handsome spreading tree, perhaps the White maple deserves most praise, its outline and surface being, in many cases, quite picturesque. There is no quality, however, for which the American maples are entitled to higher consideration as desirable objects in scenery, than for the exquisite beauty which their foliage assumes in autumn, as it fades and gradually dies off. At the first approach of cold we can just perceive a bright yellow stealing over the leaves, then a deeper golden tint, then a few faint blushes, until at length the whole mass of foliage becomes one blaze of crimson or orange.

> " Tints that the maple woods disclose
> Like opening buds or fading rose,
> Or various as those hues that dye
> The clouds that deck a sunset sky."

The contrast of coloring exhibited on many of our fine river shores in a warm dry autumn, is perhaps superior to anything of the kind in the world : and the leading and most brilliant colors, viz. orange and scarlet, are produced by maples. Even in Europe, they are highly valued for this autumnal appearance, so different from that of most of the trees of the old world. Very beautiful effects can be produced by planting the Scarlet and Sugar maples in the near neighborhood of the ash, which, as we have already noticed, assumes a fine brownish purple ; of the sycamore, which is yellow, and some of the oaks, which remain green for a long time : if to these we add a few evergreens, as the White pine and hemlock, to produce depth, we shall have a kind of kaleidoscope ground, harmonious and beautiful as the rainbow.

When the maple is planted to grow singly on the lawn, or in small groups, it should never be trimmed up ten or twenty feet high, a very common practice in some places, as this destroys half its beauty ; but if it be suffered to branch out quite low down, it will form a very elegant head.   The maple is well suited to scenes expressive of graceful beauty, as they unite to a considerable variation of surface, a pleasing softness and roundness of outline. In bold or picturesque scenes, they can be employed to advantage by intermingling them with the more striking and majestic forms of the oak, etc., where variety and contrast is desired.   The European sycamore, which is also a maple, has a coarser foliage, and more of strength in its growth and appearance : it perhaps approaches nearer in general expression and effect to the plane tree, than to our native maples.

It is unnecessary for us to recommend this tree for avenues, or for bordering the streets of cities, as its general prevalence in such places sufficiently indicates its acknow-
.edged claims for beauty, shade, and shelter.   It bears pruning remarkably well, and is easily transplanted, even when of large size, from its native woods or swamps.   The finest trees, however, are produced from seed.

The Sugar maple (*Acer saccharinum*) is a very abundant tree in the northern states and the Canadas, where it sometimes forms immense forests.   The bark is white ; the leaves four or five inches broad, and five-lobed ; varying, however, in size according to the age of the tree.   The flowers are small, yellowish, and suspended by slender drooping peduncles.   The seed is contained in two capsules united at the base, and terminated in a membranous wing ; they are ripe in October.   From certain parts of the trunks of old Sugar maples, the fine wood called *bird's-eye maple*

is taken, which is so highly prized by the cabinet-makers
and the sap, which flows in abundance from holes bored in
the stem of the tree early in March, produces the well-
known *maple sugar.* This can be clarified, so as to equal
that of the cane in flavor and appearance; and it has been
demonstrated that the planting of maple orchards, for the
production of sugar, would be a profitable investment.*

The Scarlet-flowering maple (*A. rubrum*) is found
chiefly on the borders of rivers, or in swamps; the latter
place appears best suited to this tree, for it there often
attains a very large size: it is frequently called the Soft
maple or Swamp maple. The blossoms come out about
the middle of April while the branches are yet bare of
leaves, and their numerous little pendulous stamens appear
like small tufts of scarlet or purple threads. The leaves
somewhat resemble those of the Sugar maple, but are
rather smaller, and only three or four lobed, glaucous or
whitish underneath, and irregularly toothed on the margin.
This tree may easily be distinguished when young from the
former, by the bark of the trunk, which is grey, with large
whitish spots. Its trunk, in the choicest parts, furnishes the
beautiful wood known as the *curled maple.*

The White or Silver-leaved maple. (*A. eriocarpum.*)
This species somewhat resembles the Scarlet-flowering
maple. West of the Alleghany mountains it is seen in
perfection, and is well known as the White maple. Its
flowers are pale; the leaves are divided into four lobes,
and have a beautiful white under surface. Michaux,
speaking of this tree, says: "In no part of the United

---

* *A. nigrum* is a variety omitted by Mr. Downing, though quite well known
at the time he wrote. It differs from *A. saccharinum*, in having much larger
leaves, and the bark of a darker color; besides which, the sap is more abundant, and much sweeter, and is considered at the West much the finer tree of
the two.—H. W. S.

States is it more multiplied than in the western country, and nowhere is its vegetation more luxuriant than on the banks of the Ohio.   There, sometimes alone and sometimes mingled with the willow, which is found along these waters, it contributes singularly, by its magnificent foliage, to the embellishment of the scene.   The brilliant white of the leaves beneath, forms a striking contrast with the bright green above ; and the alternate reflection of the two surfaces in the water, heightening the beauty of this wonderful moving mirror, aids in forming an enchanting picture, which, during my long excursions in a canoe in these re- gions of solitude and silence, I contemplated with unwearied admiration."* There, on those fine, deep, alluvial soils, it often attains twelve or fifteen feet in circumference.

As an ornamental variety, the Silver-leaved maple is one of the most valuable.   It is exceedingly rapid in its growth, often making shoots six feet long in a season ; and the silvery hue of its foliage, when stirred by the wind, as well as its fine, half drooping habit, render it highly interesting to the planter.   Admirable specimens of this species may be seen in the wide streets of Burlington, N. J.

The Moose wood, or Striped maple (*A. striatum*), is a small tree with beautifully striped bark.   It is often seen on the mountains which border the Hudson, but abounds most profusely in the north of the continent.   *Acer nigrum* is the Black sugar tree of Genesee.   *A. Negundo*,† the Ash- leaved maple, has handsome pinnated foliage of a light green hue ; it forms a pleasing tree of medium size. These are our principal native species ‡

---

* N. A. Sylva, i. 214.   † *Negundo fraxinifolium.*

‡ Mr. Douglas has discovered a very superb maple (*A. macrophyllum*), on the Columbia river, with very large leaves, and fine fragrant yellow blossoms

Among the finest foreign sorts is the Norway maple (*A. platanoides*), with leaves intermediate in appearance between those of the plane tree and Sugar maple. The bark of the trunk is brown, and rougher in appearance than our maples, and the tree is more loose and spreading in its growth; it also grows more rapidly, and strongly resembles at a little distance, the button-wood in its young state. Another interesting species is the sycamore tree or Great maple (*A. pseudo-platanus*). The latter also considerably resembles the plane; but the leaves, like those of the common maple, are smoother. They are five-lobed, acute in the divisions, and are placed on much longer petioles than those of most of the species. The flowers, strung in clusters like those of the common currant, are greenish in color. It is much esteemed as a shade-tree in Scotland and some parts of the Continent, and grows with vigor, producing a large head, and widely spreading branches.

THE LOCUST TREE. *Robinia.*

Nat. Ord. Leguminosæ.   *Lin. Syst.* Diadelphia, Decandria.

This is a well-known American tree, found growing wild in all of the states west of the Delaware River. It is a tree of secondary size, attaining generally the height of forty or fifty feet. The leaves are pinnated, bluish-green in color, and are thinly scattered over the branches. The white blossoms appear in June, and are highly fragrant and beautiful; and from them the Paris perfumers distil an *extrait* which greatly resembles orange-flower water, and is used for the same purposes.

As an ornamental tree we do not esteem the locust highly. The objections to it are, 1st, its meagreness and lightness of foliage, producing but little shade ; secondly, the extreme brittleness of its branches, which are liable to be broken and disfigured by every gale of wind ; and lastly the abundance of suckers which it produces. Notwith. standing these defects, we would not entirely banish the locust from our pleasure-grounds ; for its light foliage of a fresh and pleasing green may often be used to advantage in producing a variety with other trees ; and its very fragrant blossoms are beautiful, when in the beginning of summer they hang in loose pendulous clusters from among its light foliage. These will always speak sufficiently in its favor to cause it to be planted more or less, where a variety of trees is desired. It should, however, be remembered that the foliage comes out at a late period in spring, and falls early in autumn, which we consider objections to any tree that is to be planted in the close vicinity of the mansion. It is valuable for its extremely rapid growth when young ; as during the first ten or fifteen years of its life it exceeds in thrifty shoots almost all other forest trees : but it is comparatively short-lived, and in twenty years' time many other trees would completely overtop and outstrip it. It is easily propagated by seed, which is by far the best mode of raising it, and it prefers a deep, rich, sandy loam.

The locust can be cultivated to advantage as a timber tree, only upon deep, mellow, and rather rich, *sandy* soils ; there, its growth is wonderfully vigorous, and an immense number may be grown upon a small area of ground.

There are but two distinct species of locust which attain

the size of trees in this country, viz. the Yellow locust
(*R. pseud-acacia*), so called from the color of its wood ; and
the Honey locust (*R. viscosa*), a smaller tree, with reddish
flowers, and branches covered with a viscid honey-like gum.
Some pretty varieties of the former have been originated
in gardens abroad, among which the Parasol locust (*Var.
umbraculifera*) is decidedly the most interesting. We
recollect some handsome specimens which were imported
by the late M. Parmentier, and grew in his garden at
Brooklyn, Long Island. They were remarkable for their
unique, rounded, umbrella-like heads, when grafted ten or
twelve feet high on the common locust.

There are two pretty distinct varieties of the common
Yellow locust, cultivated on the Hudson. That most frequently seen is the *White* variety, which forms a tall and
narrow head ; the other is the *Black* locust, with a broad
and more spreading head, and larger trunk ; the latter may
be seen in fine condition at Clermont. It is a much finer
ornamental tree, and appears less liable to the borer than
the White variety.

The Three-thorned Acacia Tree. *Gleditschia.*

Nat. Ord. Leguminosæ.   *Lin. Syst.* Polygamia, Diœcia.

This tree is often called the Three-thorned locust, from
some resemblance to the latter tree. Its delicate, doubly
pinnate leaves, however, are much more like those of the
Acacias, a family of plants not hardy enough to bear our
climate. It is a much finer tree in appearance than the
common locust, although the flowers are greenish, and
inconspicuous, instead of possessing the beauty and fra-

grance of the latter. There is, however, a peculiar elegance about its light green and beautiful foliage, which
wafts so gracefully in the summer breeze, and folds up on
the slightest shower, that it stands far above that tree in
our estimation, for the embellishment of scenery. The
branches spread out rather horizontally, in a fine, broad
and lofty head; there are none of the dead and unsightly
branches so common on the locust; and the light feathery
foliage, lit up in the sunshine, has an airy and transparent
look, rarely seen in so large a tree, which sometimes produces very happy effects in composition with other trees.
The bark is of a pleasing brown, smooth in surface the
branches are studded over with curious, long, triply-pointed
thorns, which also often jut out in clusters, in every direction from the trunk of the tree, to the length of four or five
inches, giving it a most singular and forbidding look. In
winter, these and the long seed-pods, five or six inches in
length, which hang upon the boughs at that season, give the
whole tree a very distinct character. These pods contain
a sweetish substance, somewhat resembling honey;
whence the tree has in some places obtained the name of
Honey locust, which properly belongs to *Robinia viscosa.*

Another recommendation of this tree, is the variety of
picturesque shapes which it assumes in growing up; sometimes forming a tall pyramidal head of 50 or 60 feet, sometimes a low horizontally branched tree, and at others it
expands into a wide irregular head, quite flattened at the
summit. It does not produce suckers like the locust, and
may therefore be introduced into any part of the grounds.
When but a limited extent is devoted to a lawn or garden,
this tree should be among the first to obtain a place; as
one or two Three-thorned Acacias, mingled with other

larger and heavier foliage, will at once produce a charming variety.

The Three-thorned Acacia has been strongly recom· mended for hedges. It is too liable to become thin at the bottom, to serve well for an outer inclosure, but if kept well trimmed, it forms a capital farm fence and protection against the larger animals, growing up in much less time than the hawthorn. Like the locust, it has the disadvantage of expanding its foliage late in the spring. In the strong rich soils which it prefers, it grows very vigorously, and is easily propagated from seeds.

The Three-thorned Acacia (*G. triacanthos*) is the principal species, and is indigenous to the states west of the Alleghanies. *G. monosperma* is another kind, which is scarcely distinguishable from the Three-thorned, except in having one-seeded pods. The seedlings raised from *G. triacanthos* are often entirely destitute of thorns.

There is a fine species called the Chinese (*G. horrida*), with larger and finer foliage, and immense triple thorns, which is interesting from its great singularity. A tree of this kind which we imported, has stood our coldest winters perfectly uninjured, and promises to be beautiful and very hardy. Some noble specimens of the common Three-thorned Acacia may be seen upon the lawn at Hyde Park, the fine seat of the late Dr. Hosack.

————

THE JUDAS TREE. *Cercis.*

Nat. Ord. Leguminosæ.   *Lin. Syst.* Decandria, Monogynia.

A handsome low tree, about 20 feet in height, which is

found scattered sparsely through warm sheltered valleys, along the Hudson and other rivers of the northern sections of the United States, but most abundantly on the Ohio. It is valuable as an ornamental tree, no less on account of its exceedingly neat foliage, which is exactly heart-shaped, or cordiform, and of a pleasing green tint, than for its pretty pink blossoms. These, which are pea-shaped, are produced in little clusters close to the branches, often in great profusion, early in the spring, before the leaves have expanded. From the appearance of the limbs at that period, it has in some places obtained the name of *Redbud*. It is then one of the most ornamental of trees, and, in company with the Dog-wood, serves greatly to enliven the scene, and herald the advent of the floral season. These blossoms, according to Loudon (*Encycl. of Plants*), having an agreeable poignancy, are frequently eaten in salads abroad, and pickled by the French families in Canada. The name of Judas tree appears to have been whimsically bestowed by Gerard, an old English gardener, who described it in 1596, and relates that "this is the tree whereon Judas did hange himselfe ; and not upon the elder tree, as it is said."

There are two species in common cultivation; the American (*C. Canadensis*) and the European (*C. Siliquastrum*). The latter much resembles our native tree. The flowers, however, are deeper in color; the leaves darker, and less pointed at the extremity. It also produces blossoms rather more profusely than the American tree. Both species are highly worthy of a place in the garden, or near the house, where their pleasing vernal influences may be observed.

THE CHESTNUT TREE. *Castanea.*

Nat. Ord. Corylaceæ.   *Lin. Syst.* Monœcia, Polyandria.

The chestnut, for its qualities in Landscape Gardening ranks with that king of the forest, the oak. Like that tree, it attains an enormous size, and its longevity in some cases is almost equally remarkable. Its fine massy foliage, and sweet nuts, have rendered it a favorite tree since a very remote period. Among the ancients, the latter were a common article of food.

> ———" Sunt nobis mitia poma,
> *Castaneæ* molles, et pressi copia lactis."
>
> VIRG. ECL. 1.

They appear to have been in general use, both in a raw and cooked state. In times of scarcity, they probably supplied in some measure the place of bread-stuffs, and were thence highly valued:

> " As for the thrice three angled beech nut shell,
> Or Chestnut's armed huske and hid kernell,
> No squire durst touch, the law would not afford,
> Kept for the court, and for the king's own board."
>
> *Bp. Hall, Sat. B. III.* 1.

Even to this day, in those parts of France and Italy nearest the great chestnut forests of the Appenines, these nuts form a large portion of the food which sustains the peasantry, where grain is but little cultivated, and potatoes almost unknown. There a sweet and highly nutritious flour is prepared from them, which makes a delicious bread. Large quantities of the fruit are therefore annually collected in those countries, and dried and stored

away for the winter's consumption. Old Evelyn **says,**
"the bread of the flour is exceedingly nutritive : it is a
robust food, and makes women well complexioned, as 1
have read in a good author.   They also make fritters of
chestnut flour, which they wet with rose-water, and
sprinkle with grated parmigans, and so fry them in fresh
butter for a delicate."   The fruit of the chestnut abounds
in saccharine matter ;   and we learn from a French
periodical, that experiments have been made, by which it
is ascertained that the kernel yields nearly sixteen pei
cent. of good sugar.

As a timber tree, this is greatly inferior to the oak, being
looser grained, and more liable to decay ; and the
American wood is more open to this objection than that
produced on the opposite side of the Atlantic.   It is,
however, in general use among us, for posts and rails in
fencing ; and when the former are charred, they are found
to be quite durable.

The finest natural situations for this tree appear to be
the mountainous slopes of mild climates, where it attains
the greatest possible perfection.   Michaux informs us, that
the most superb and lofty chestnuts in America are to be
found in such situations, in the forests of the Carolinas.
Abroad, every one will call to mind the far-famed chestnuts
of Mount Etna, of wonderful age and extraordinary size.
The great chestnut there, has excited the surprise of
numerous travellers ; at present, however, it appears to be
scarcely more than a mere shell, the wreck of former
greatness.   When visited by M. Houel (*Arboretum Brit.*),
it was in a state of decay, having lost the greater part of
its branches, and its trunk was quite hollow.   A house was
erected in the interior, and some country people resided in

it, with an oven, in which, according to the custom of the country, they dried chestnuts, filberts, and other fruits, which they wished to preserve for winter use; using as fuel, when they could find no other, pieces cut with a hatchet from the interior of the tree. In Brydone's time, in 1770, this tree measured two hundred and four feet in circumference. He says it had the appearance of five distinct trees ; but he was assured that the space was once filled with solid timber, and there was no bark on the inside. This circumstance of an old trunk, hollow in the interior, becoming separated so as to have the appearance of being the remains of several distinct trees, is frequently met with in the case of very old mulberry trees in Great Britain, and olive trees in Italy. Kircher, about a century before Brydone, affirms that an entire flock of sheep might be inclosed within the Etna chestnut, as in a fold.* (*Arboretum Brit. p.* 1988.)

* One of the most celebrated Chestnut trees on record, is that called the Tortworth Chestnut, in England. In 1772, Lord Ducie, the owner, had a portrait of it taken, which was accompanied by the following description: " The east view of the ancient Chestnut tree at Tortworth, in the county of Gloucester, which measures nineteen yards in circumference, and is mentioned by Sir Robert Aikins in his history of that county, as a famous tree in King John's reign : and by Mr. Evelyn in his Sylva, to have been so remarkable in the reign of King Stephen, 1135, as then to be called the great Chestnut of Tortworth ; from which it may reasonably be presumed to have been standing before the Conquest, 1066." This tree is still standing.

On the estate of Marshall S. Rice, Esq., at Newton Centre, is a venerable, though still vigorous and beautiful chestnut tree, the dimensions of which are believed to exceed any tree of the same species in New England. In proof of this, we are informed that a correspondence has recently been going on, through the medium of one of our agricultural papers, between the owner of the above tree, and several gentlemen in this and other States, none of whom have shown figures exceeding the following: size of the " Rice Tree"--circumference at base of trunk, 24 3-10 feet; height, 76 feet: spread of limbs, 93 feet. This tree is very prolific, and has never been known to fail of bearing a large crop of nuts. About five feet from the ground, the trunk divides into two well-formed shafts, which run up to the height of thirty feet, without a branch.— H. W. S.

In considering the chestnut as highly adapted to ornament the grounds of extensive country residences, much that we have already said of the oak will apply to this tree. When young, its smooth stem, clear and bright foliage, and lively aspect, when adorned with the numerous light greenish yellow blossoms, which project beyond the mass of leaves, render it a graceful and beautiful tree.

It has long been a favorite with the poets for its grateful shade; and as the roots run deep, the soil beneath it is sufficiently rich and sheltered to afford an asylum for the minutest beauties of the woods. Tennyson sweetly says :—

> " That slope beneath the chestnut tall
> Is wooed with choicest breaths of air,
> Methinks that I could tell you all
> The cowslips and the king cups there."

When old, its huge trunk, wide-spread branches, lofty head, and irregular outline, all contribute to render it a picturesque tree of the very first class. In that state, when standing alone, with free room to develope itself on every side, like the oak, it gives a character of dignity, majesty, and grandeur, to the scene, beyond the power of most trees to confer. It is well known that the favorite tree of Salvator Rosa, and one which was most frequently introduced with a singularly happy effect into his wild and picturesque compositions, was the chestnut; sometimes a massy and bold group of its verdure, but oftener an old and storm-rifted giant, half leafless, or a barren trunk coated with a rich verdure of mosses and lichens.

The chestnut in maturity, like the oak, has a great variety of outline ; and no trees are better fitted than these for the formation of grand groups, heavy masses, or wide outlines of foliage. A higher kind of beauty, with more dignity and variety, can be formed of these two genera of trees when disposed in grand masses, than with any other forest trees of temperate climates; perhaps we may say of any climate.

There is so little difference in the common Sweet chestnut (*Castanea vesca*) of both hemispheres, that they are generally considered the same species. Varieties have been produced in Europe, which far surpass our common chestnuts of the woods in size, though not in delicacy and richness of flavor. Those cultivated for the table in France, are known by the name of *marrons*. These improved sorts of the Spanish chestnut bear fruit nearly as large as that of the Horse-chestnut, inferior in sweetness, when raw, to our wild species, but delicious when roasted. The Spanish chestnut thrives well, and forms a large tree, south of the Highlands of the Hudson, but is rather tender north of this neighborhood. A tree in the grounds at Presque Isle, the seat of William Denning, Esq., Dutchess Co., is now 40 feet high. They may be procured from the nurseries, and we can hardly recommend to our planters more acceptable additions to our nut-bearing forest trees.

The Chinquapin, or Dwarf chestnut (*C. pumila*), is a curious low bush, from four to six feet high. The leaves are nearly the size of the ordinary chestnut, or rather smaller, and the fruit about two-thirds as large. It is indigenous to all the states south of Pennsylvania, and is often found in great abundance. It is a curious little tree, or more properly a shrub, and merits a place in the garden; or it may be advantageously planted for underwood in a group of large trees.

As the chestnut, like the oak, forms strong tap-roots, it is removed with some difficulty. The finest trees are produced from the nut, and their growth is much more rapid when young, than that of the transplanted tree. It prefers a deep sandy loam, rather moist than dry; and will not, like many forest trees, accommodate itself to wet and low situations.

The Osage Orange Tree. *Maclura.*

Nat. Ord. Urticaceæ.   *Lin. Syst.* Diœcia, Tetrandria.

This interesting tree is found growing wild on the Arkansas River, and other western tributaries of the Mississippi, south of St. Louis, where, according to Mr. Nuttall, it attains the height of 50 or 60 feet. The branches are rather light-colored, and armed with spines (produced at every joint) about an inch and a half long. The leaves are long, ovate, and acuminate, or pointed at the extremity; they are deep green, and more glossy and bright than those of the orange. The blossoms are greenish; and the fruit is about the shape and size of a large orange, but the surface much rougher than that fruit. In the south, we are told, it assumes a deep yellow color, and, at a short distance, strikingly resembles the common orange; the specimens of fruit which we have seen growing in Philadelphia, did not assume that fine color; but the appearance of the tree laden with it, is not unlike that of a large orange tree. It was first transplanted into our gardens from a village of the Osage tribe of Indians, whence the common name of Osage orange. The introduction of this tree was one of the favorable results of

Lewis and Clarke's Expedition. It was named by them in honor of the late Wm. Maclure, Esq., President of the American Academy of Natural Sciences.

The wood is fine grained, yellow in color, and takes a brilliant polish. It is also very strong and elastic, and on this account the Indians of the wide district to which this tree is indigenous, employ it extensively for bows, greatly preferring it to any other timber. Hence its common name among the white inhabitants is *Bodac*, a corruption of the term *bois d'arc* (*bow-wood*), of the French settlers. A fine yellow dye is extracted from the wood, similar to that of the Fustic.

As the Osage orange belongs to the monœcious class of plants, it does not perfect its fruit unless both the male and female trees are growing in the same neighborhood. Many have believed the fruit to be eatable, both from its fine appearance, and from its affinity with and resemblance to that of the bread-fruit; but all attempts to render it pleasant, either cooked or in a raw state, have hitherto failed : it is therefore probably inedible, though not injurious. Perhaps when fully ripened, some mode of preparing it by baking or otherwise, may render it palatable.

As an ornamental tree, the Osage orange is rather too loose in the disposition of its wide-spreading branches, to be called beautiful in its form. But the bright glossy hue of its foliage, and especially the unique appearance of a good sized tree when covered with the large, orange-like fruit, render it one of the most interesting of our native trees ; while it has the same charm of rarity as an exotic, since it was introduced from the far west, and is yet but little planted in the United States. On a small lawn, where but few trees are needed, and where it is desirable that the species employed should all be as distinct as possible, to give the whole as much variety as can be obtained in a limited space, such trees should be selected as will not only be ornamental, but combine some other charm, association, or interest. Among such trees, we would by all means give the Osage orange a foremost place. It has the additional recommendation of being a fine shade tree and of producing an excellent and durable wood.*

The stout growth and strong thorns of this tree have been thought indicative of its usefulness for the making of hedges : a method of fencing, which sooner or later must be adopted in many parts of this country and from the experiments which we have seen made with plants of the Osage orange, we think it likely to answer a very valuable purpose ; especially in the middle and southern states. The Messrs. Landreth of Philadelphia have lately offered many thousands of them to the public at a low rate, and we hope to see the matter fairly tested in various parts of the Union.

A rich deep loam is the soil best adapted to the growth of this tree ; and as it is rather tender when young (though quite hardy when it attains a considerable size) it should, as far as possible, be planted in a rather sheltered situation. A dry soil is preferable, if it must be placed in a cold

* A very superb effect may be produced with this tree, by cutting it severely back for several years, and compelling it, as the English call it, to stole, by sending out a dozen leading shoots, instead of one ; a plant treated in this way, becomes, after a few years, a gigantic bush, round-headed, and most luxuriant, and when covered with its golden fruit, peeping out from amidst its exquisitely green foliage, it is the most superb floral ornament to a lawn that can be conceived. We recollect a surprisingly fine specimen of an Osage Orange treated in this way, at the late Dr. Edmondston's, near Baltimore, where a plant about twenty-four years old measured in circumference, *one hundred and sixty-five feet!* the limbs lying about with a profusion of growth positively wonderful, and covered with fruit.—H. W. S.

aspect, as all plants not perfectly hardy are much injured by the late growth, caused by an excess of moisture and consequent upon an immature state of the wood, which is unable to resist the effects of a severe winter.

THE MULBERRY TREE. *Morus.*

Nat. Ord. Urticaceæ.   *Lin. Syst.* Monœcia, Tetrandria.

The three principal species of the Mulberry, are the common Red American, the European Black, and the White mulberries.   None of them are truly handsome in scenery; and the two latter are generally low spreading trees, valued entirely for the excellency of the fruit, or the suitableness of the foliage for feeding silkworms.   Our common mulberry, however, in free, open situations, forms a large, wide-spreading, horizontally branched, and not inelegant tree: the rough, heart-shaped leaves with which it is thickly clothed, afford a deep shade; and it groups well with the lime, the catalpa, and many other round-headed trees.   We consider it, therefore, duly entitled to a place in all extensive plantations; while the pleasant flavor of its slightly acid, dark red fruit, will recommend it to those who wish to add to the delicacies of the dessert.   The timber of our wild mulberry tree is of the very first quality , when fully seasoned, it takes a dull lemon-colored hue, and is scarcely less durable than the locust or Live oak.   Like those trees, it is much valued by ship-builders; and at Philadelphia and Baltimore it commands a high price, for the frame-work, knees, floor-timbers, and tree-nails of vessels.   The Red mulberry is much slower in its growth

than the locust; but so far as we are aware it is not liable
to the attacks of any insect destructive to its timber; and
it would probably be found profitable to cultivate it as a
timber tree. The locust, it will be remembered, grows
thriftily only on peculiar soils, loose, dry, and mellow; the
Red mulberry prefers deep, moist, and rich situations. No
extensive experiments, so far as we can learn, have been
made in its culture; but we would recommend it to the
particular attention of those who have facilities for planta
tions of this kind.

The Black mulberry of Europe (*Morus nigra*)*is a low,
slow-growing tree, with rough leaves, somewhat resembling
those of our Red mulberry, but more coarsely serrated, and
often found divided into four or five lobes; while the leaves,
which are not heart-shaped on our nat've species, are gene·
rally three-lobed. The European mulberry bears a fruit
four or five times as large as the American, full of rich,
sweet juice. It has long been a favorite in England, and
is one of the most healthy and delicious fruits of the season,
Glover says:

> ———" There the flushing peach,
> The apple, citron, almond, pear, and date,
> Pomegranates, *purple mulberry*, and fig,
> From interlacing branches mix their hues
> And scents, the passengers' delight."

LEONID. B. II.

We regret that so excellent a fruit should be so little
cultivated here. It succeeds extremely well in the middle

* Further experience has shown, that this tree is not to be depended upon,
at least as far north as the middle portion of the Hudson River. An admirable
substitute for the fruit, is Downing's Seedling Mulberry, raised some years ago
by Mr. Charles Downing, of Newburgh, and while being an excellent fruit,
has, we believe, the additional merit of being ever-bearing.—H. W. S.

states ; and as it ripens at the very period in midsummer when fruits are scarcest, there can be no more welcome addition to our pomonal treasures, than its deep purple and luscious berries. According to Loudon, it is a tree of great durability ; in proof of which he quotes a specimen at Sion House, 300 years old, which is supposed to have been planted in the 16th century by the botanist Turner.

The White mulberry (*M. alba*) is the species upon the leaves of which the silkworms are fed. The fruit is insipid and tasteless, and the tree is but little cultivated to embellish ornamental plantations, though one of the most useful in the world, when its importance in the production of silk is taken into account. There are a great number of varieties of this species to be found in the different nurseries and silk plantations ; among them the Chinese mulberry (*M. multicaulis*) grows rapidly, but scarcely forms more than a large shrub at the north ; and its very large, tender, and soft green foliage is interesting in a large collection. The fruit is, we believe, of no importance ; but it is the most valuable of all mulberries as food for the silkworm, while its growth is the most vigorous, and its leaves more easily gathered than those of any other tree of the genus.

The Paper Mulberry Tree.   *Broussonetia.*

Nat. Ord. Urticaceæ.   *Lin. Syst.* Diœcia, Tetrandria.

The Paper mulberry is an exotic tree of a low growth, rarely exceeding twenty-five or thirty feet, indigenous to Japan and the South Sea Islands, but very common in our gardens. It is remarkable for the great variety of forms exhibited in its foliage ; as upon young trees it is almost in possible to find two exactly alike, though the prevailing outlines are either heart-shaped, or more or less deeply cut or lobed.   These leaves are considered valueless for feeding the silkworm; but in the South Seas the bark is woven into dresses worn by the females; and in China and Japan extensive use is made of it in the manufacture of a paper of the softest and most beautiful texture.   This is fabricated from the inner bark of the young shoots, which is first boiled to a soft pulp, and then submitted to processes greatly similar to those performed in our paper-mills.   This tree blossoms in spring and ripens its fruit in the month of August.   The latter is dark scarlet, and quite singular and ornamental, though of no value.   The genus is diœcious; and the reason why so few fruit-bearing trees are seen in the United States, is because we generally cultivate only one of the sexes, the female.   M. Parmentier, however, who introduced the male plant from Europe, disseminated it in several parts of the country; and the beauty of the tree has thereby been augmented by the interest which it possesses when laden with its long, hairy berries.

The value of the Paper mulberry, in ornamental plantations, arises from its exotic look, as compared with other trees, from the singular diversity of its foliage, the beauty of its reddish berries, and from the rapidity of its growth. It is deficient in hardiness for a colder climate than that of New York; but further south it is considerably esteemed as a shade-tree for lining the side-walks in cities.   In winter its light fawn or ash-colored bark, mottled with patches of a darker grey, contrasts agreeably with other trees.   It has little picturesque beauty, and should never be planted in quantities, but only in scattered specimens, to give interest and variety to a walk in the lawn or shrubbery.

THE SWEET GUM TREE. *Liquidambar.*

Nat. Ord. Platanaceæ.   *Lin. Syst.* Monœcia, Polyandria.

According to Michaux,* the Sweet gum is one of our
most extensively diffused trees.   On the seashore it is seen
as far north as Portsmouth ; and it extends as far south as
the Gulf of Mexico and the Isthmus of Darien.   In many
of the southern states it is one of the commonest trees of the
forest; it is rarely seen, however, along the banks of the
Hudson (except in New Jersey), or other large streams of
New York.   It is not unlike the maple in general appearance, and its palmate, five-lobed leaves are in outline much
like the Sugar maple, though darker in color and firmer in
texture.   It may also be easily distinguished from that tree,
by the curious appearance of its secondary branches, which
have a peculiar roughness, owing to the bark attaching
itself in plates edgewise to the trunk, instead of laterally, as
in the usual manner.   The fruit is globular, somewhat
resembling that of the buttonwood, but much rougher, and
bristling with points.   The male and female catkins appear
on different branches of the same tree early in spring.

This tree grows in great perfection in the forests of New
Spain.   It was first described by a Spanish naturalist, Dr.
Hernandez, who observed that a fragrant and transparent
gum issued from its trunk in that country, to which, from
its appearance, he gave the name of liquid amber.   This is
now the common name of the tree in Europe ; and the gum
is at present an article of export from Mexico, being chiefly
valued in medicine as a styptic, and for its healing and
balsamic properties.   " This substance, which in the shops

* N. A. Sylva, i. 315.

is sometimes called the white balsam of Peru, or liquid storax, is, when it first issues from the tree, perfectly liquid and clear, white, with a slight tinge of yellow, quite balsamic ; and having a most agreeable fragrance, resembling that of ambergris or styrax. It is stimulant and aromatic, and has long been used in France as a perfume, especially for gloves."* In the middle states a fragrant substance sometimes exudes from the leaves, and, by incision, small quantities of the gum may be procured from the trunk ; but a warmer climate appears to be necessary to its production in considerable quantities.

We hardly know a more *beautiful* tree than the Liquid amber in every stage of its growth, and during every season of the year. Its outline is not picturesque or graceful, but simply beautiful, more approaching that of the maple than any other : it is, therefore, a highly pleasing, round-headed or tapering tree, which unites and harmonizes well with almost any others in composition ; but the chief beauty lies in the foliage. During the whole of the summer months it preserves, unsoiled, that dark glossy freshness which is so delightful to the eye ; while the singular, regularly palmate form of the leaves readily distinguishes it from the common trees of a plantation. But in autumn it assumes its gayest livery, and is decked in colors almost too bright and vivid for foliage ; forming one of the most brilliant objects in American scenery at that period of the year. The prevailing tint of the foliage is then a deep purplish red, unlike any symptom of decay, and quite as rich as is commonly seen in the darker blossoms of a Dutch parterre. This is sometimes varied by a shade deeper or lighter, and occasionally an orange tint is assumed. When planted in the

* Arboretum Brit. 2051.

neighborhood of our fine maples, ashes, and other trees remarkable for their autumnal coloring, the effect, in a warm, dry autumn, is almost magical. Whoever has travelled through what are called the pine barrens of New Jersey in such a season, must have been struck with the gay tints of the numberless forest trees, which line the roads through those sandy plains, and with the conspicuous beauty of the Sweet gum, or Liquidamber.

The bark of this tree when full grown, or nearly so, is exceedingly rough and furrowed, like that of the oak. The wood is fine-grained, and takes a good polish in cabinet work; though it is not so durable, nor so much esteemed for such purposes, as that of the Black walnut and some other native trees. The average height of full grown trees is about 35 or 40 feet.

Liquidambar styraciflua is the only North American species. It grows most rapidly in moist or even wet situations, though it will accommodate itself to a drier soil.

The Walnut Tree. *Juglans.*

Nat. Ord. Juglandaceæ.   *Lin. Syst.* Monœcia, Polyandria.

The three trees which properly come under this head and belong to the genus Juglans, are the Black walnut, the European walnut, and the Butternut.

The Black walnut is one of the largest trees of our native forests. In good soils it often attains a stature of 60 or 70 feet, and a diameter of three or four feet in the trunk, with a corresponding amplitude of branches. The leaves, about a foot or eighteen inches in length, are composed of six or eight pairs of opposite leaflets, terminated by an odd one They contain a very strong aromatic odor, which is emitted plentifully when they are bruised. The large nut, always borne on the extremity of the young shoots, is round, and covered with a thick husk ; which, instead of separating into pieces, and falling off like those of the hickory, rots away and decays gradually. The kernel of the Black walnut, too well known to need any description here, is highly esteemed, and is even considered by some persons to possess a finer flavor than any other walnut.

The timber of this tree is very valuable : when well seasoned it is as durable as the White oak, and is less liable to the attacks of sea-worms, etc., than almost any other ; it is, therefore, highly esteemed in naval architecture for certain purposes. But its great value is in cabinet work. Its color, when exposed to the air, is a fine, rich, dark brown, beautifully veined in certain parts ; and as it takes a brilliant polish, it is coming into general use in the United States for furniture, as well as for the interior finishing of houses.

The Black walnut has strong claims upon the Landscape Gardener, as it is one of the grandest and most massive trees which he can employ. When full grown it is scarcely inferior in the boldness of its ramification or the amplitude of its head to the oak or chestnut ; and what it lacks in spirited outline when compared with those trees, is fully compensated, in our estimation, by its superb and heavy masses of foliage, which catch and throw off the broad lights and shadows in the finest manner. When the Black walnut stands alone on a deep fertile soil it becomes a truly majestic tree ; and its lower branches often sweep the ground in a graceful curve, which gives additional beauty to its whole expression. It is admirably adapted to exten-

sive lawns, parks, or plantations, where there is no want
of room for the attainment of its full size and fair proportions.   Its rapid growth and umbrageous foliage also
recommend it for wide public streets and avenues.

The European walnut (*J. regia*)* or, as it is generally
termed here, the *Madeira nut*, is one of the most common
cultivated trees of Europe, where it was introduced originally from Persia.   It differs from our Black walnut (which,
however, it much resembles) in the smooth, grey bark of
the stem, the leaves composed of three or four pair of
leaflets, and in the very thin-shelled fruit, which, though
not exceeding the Black walnut in size, yet contains a
much larger kernel, which is generally considered more
delicate in flavor.   In the interior of France orchards of
the walnut are planted, and a considerable commerce is
carried on in its products, consisting chiefly of the fruit, of
which large quantities are consumed in all parts of Europe.
The wood is greatly used in the manufacture of gun-stocks,
and in cabinet-making (though it is much inferior to the
American walnut for this purpose) ; and the oil extracted
from the kernel is in high estimation for mixing with delicate colors used in painting and other purposes.

The European walnut is a noble tree in size, and thickly
clad in foliage.   It is much esteemed as a shade tree by the
Dutch ; and Evelyn, who is an enthusiastic admirer of its
beauties, mentions their fondness for this tree as in the highest degree praiseworthy.   " The *Bergstras* [*Bergstrasse*],
which extends from Heidelberg to Darmstadt, is all planted
with walnuts ; for as by an ancient law the Borderers were
obliged to nurse up and take care of them, and that chiefly
for their ornament and shade, so as a man may ride for

* (*Juglans laciniata*), Cutleaf Walnut, is a new and curious variety, with
large scalloped leaves.—H. W. S.

many miles about that country under a continual arbor or close walk,—the traveller both refreshed with the fruit and shade. How much such public plantations improve the glory and wealth of a nation! In several places betwixt Hanau and Frankfort in Germany, no young farmer is permitted to marry a wife till he bring proof that he hath planted, and is the father of a stated number of walnut trees."*

The nuts are imported into this country in great quantities; and as they are chiefly brought from Spain and the Madeiras, they are here almost entirely known by the name of the Madeira nut. The tree is but little cultivated among us, though highly deserving more extensive favor, both on account of its value and beauty. It grows well in the climate of the middle states, and bears freely; a specimen eighteen or twenty years old, in the garden of the author, has reached thirty-five feet in height, and bears two or three bushels of fine fruit annually; from which we have already propagated several hundred individuals. It is not perfectly hardy north of this.

As an ornamental tree, Gilpin remarks, that the warm russet hue of its young foliage makes a pleasing variety among the vivid green of other trees, about the end of May; and the same variety is maintained in summer, by the contrast of its yellowish hue, when mixed in any quantity with trees of a darker tint. It stands best alone, as the early loss of its foliage is then of less consequence, and its ramification is generally beautiful.

The Butternut (*J. cathartica*) belongs to this section, and is chiefly esteemed for its fruit, which abounds in oil, and is very rich and sweet. The foliage somewhat

* Hunter's Evelyn, p. 168.

resembles that of the Black walnut, though the leaflets are
smaller and narrower. The form of the nut, however, is
strikingly different, being oblong, oval, and narrowed to a
point at the extremity. Unlike the walnut, the husk is
covered with a sticky gum, and the surface of the nut is
much rougher than any other of the walnut genus. The
bark of the butternut is grey, and the tops of old trees
generally have a flattened appearance. It is frequently
an uncouth, ill-shapen, and ugly tree in form, though
occasionally, also, quite striking and picturesque. And it
is well worthy of a place for the excellence of its fruit.*

THE HICKORY TREE. *Carya.*

Nat. Ord. Juglandaceæ.   *Lin. Syst.* Monœcia, Polyandria.

The hickories are fine and lofty North American trees,
highly valuable for their wood, and the excellent fruit
borne by some of the species. The timber is extremely
elastic, and very heavy, possessing great strength and
tenacity. It is not much employed in architecture, as it is
peculiarly liable to the attacks of worms, and decays
quickly when exposed to moisture. But it is very extensively employed for all purposes requiring great elasticity
and strength ; as for axletrees, screws, the wooden rings
used upon the rigging of vessels, whip-handles, and axe-

* Loudon errs greatly in his Arboretum, in supposing the butternut to be
identical with the Black walnut : no trees in the whole American forest are
more easily distinguished at first sight. He also states the fruit to be rancid
and of little value ; but no American lad of a dozen years will accord with
him in this opin on.

handles ; and an immense quantity of the young poles are employed in the manufacture of hoops, for which they are admirably adapted.

For fuel, no American wood is equal to this in the brilliancy with which it burns, or in the duration or amount of heat given out by it : it therefore commands the highest price in market for that purpose.

The hickories are nearly allied to the walnuts; the chief botanical distinction consisting in the covering to the nut, or husk ; which in the hickories separates into four valves, or pieces, when ripe, instead of adhering in a homogeneous coat, as upon the Black walnut and butternut. In size and appearance, the hickories rank with the first class of forest trees ; most of them growing vigorously to the height of 60 or 80 feet, with fine straight trunks, well balanced and ample heads, and handsome, lively, pinnated foliage. When confined among other trees in the forest, they shoot up 50 or 60 feet without branches ; but when standing singly, they expand into a fine head near the ground and produce a noble, lofty pyramid of foliage, rather rounded at the top. They have all the qualities which are necessary to constitute fine, graceful park trees, and are justly entitled to a place in every considerable plantation.

The most ornamental species are the Shellbark hickory, the Pignut, and the Pecan-nut. The former and the latter produce delicious nuts, and are highly worthy of cultivation for their fruit alone ; while all of them assume very handsome shapes during every stage of their growth, and ultimately become noble trees. Varieties of the Shellbark hickory are sometimes seen producing nuts of twice or thrice the ordinary size ; and we have not the least doubt that the fruit might be so improved in size and delicacy of flavor by careful cultivation, as greatly to surpass the European walnut, for the table. This result will probably be attained by planting the nuts of the finest varieties found in our woods, in rich moist soil, kept in high cultivation; as all improved varieties of fruit have been produced in this way, and not, as many suppose, by cultivating the original species. These remarks also apply to the Pecan-nut; a western sort, which thrives well in the middle states, and which produces a nut more delicate in flavor than any other of this continent.

These trees form strong tap-roots, and are, therefore, somewhat difficult to transplant; but they are easily reared from the nut; and, for the reason stated above, this method should be adopted in preference to any other, except in particular cases.

The principal species of the hickory are the following:

The Shellbark hickory (*C. alba*), so called on account of the roughness of its bark, which is loosened from the trunk in long scales or pieces, bending outwards at the extremity, and remaining attached by the middle; this takes place, however, only on trees of some size. The leaves are composed of two pair of leaflets, with an odd or terminal one. The scales which cover the buds of the Shellbark in winter, adhere only to the lower half, while the upper half of the bud is left uncovered, by which this sort is readily distinguished from the other species. The hickory nuts of our markets are the product of this tree; they are much esteemed in every part of the Union, and are exported in considerable quantities to Europe. Among many of the descendants of the original Dutch settlers of

New York and New Jersey, the fruit is commonly known by the appellation of the *Kisky-tom nut.**

The Pecan-nut (*Pacainer* of the French), (*C. olivæformis*) is found only in the western states. It abounds on the Missouri, Arkansas, Wabash, and Illinois Rivers, and a portion of the Ohio: Michaux states that there is a swamp of 800 acres on the right bank of the Ohio, opposite the Cumberland river, entirely covered with it. It is a handsome, stately tree, about 60 or 70 feet in height, with leaves a foot or eighteen inches long, composed of six or seven pairs of leaflets much narrower than those of our hickories. The nuts are contained in a thin, somewhat four-sided husk; they are about an inch or an inch and a half long, smooth, cylindrical, and thin-shelled. The kernel is not, like most of the hickories, divided by partitions, and it has a very delicate and agreeable flavor. They form an object of petty commerce between Upper and Lower Louisiana. From New Orleans, they are exported to the West Indies, and to the ports of the United States.†

Besides these two most valuable species, our forests produce the Pignut hickory (*C. porcina*), a lofty tree with five to seven pairs of leaflets, so called from the comparative worthlessness of its fruit; which is very thick-shelled, and generally is left on the ground for the swine, squirrels, etc., to devour. It is easily distinguished in winter by the smaller size of its brown shoots, and its small oval buds. Its wood is considered the toughest and strongest of any of the trees of this section. The thick Shellbark hickory

---

* In some parts, pleasant social parties which meet at stated times during the winter season, are called Kisky-toms, from the regular appearance of these nuts among the refreshments of the evening.

† N. A. Sylva, i. 168.

(*C. laciniosa*) resembles much in size and appearance the common Shellbark; but the nuts are double the size, the shell much thicker and yellowish, while that of the latter is white. It is but little known except west of the Alleghanies. The Mockernut hickory (*C. tomentosa*) is so called from the deceptive appearance of the nuts, which are generally of large size, but contain only a very small kernel. The leaves are composed of but four pairs of sessile leaflets, with an odd one at the end. The trunk of the old trees is very rugged, and the wood is one of the best for fuel.

The Bitternut hickory (*C. amara*), sometimes called the White hickory, grows 60 feet high in New Jersey. The husk which covers the nut of this species, has four winged appendages on its upper half, and never hardens like the other sorts, but becomes soft and decays. The shell is thin, but the kernel is so bitter that even the squirrels refuse to eat it. The Water Bitternut (*C. aquatica*) is a very inferior sort, growing in the swamps and rice fields of the southern states. The leaflets are serrated, and resemble in shape the leaves of the peach tree. Both the fruit and timber are much inferior to those of all the other hickories.

The Mountain Ash Tree. *Pyrus.**

Nat. Ord. Rosaceæ.   *Lin. Syst.* Icosandria, Di-Pentagynia.

The European Mountain ash (*Pyrus aucuparia*) is an elegant tree of the medium size, with an erect stem,

* *Sorbus* of the old Botanists.

smooth bark, and round head. The leaves are pinnated, four or five inches in length, and slightly resemble those of the ash. The snow-white flowers are produced in large flat clusters, in the month of May, which are thickly scattered over the outer surface of the tree, and give it a lively appearance. These are succeeded by numerous bunches of berries, which in autumn turn to a brilliant scarlet, and are then highly ornamental. For the sake of these berries, this tree is a great favorite with birds ; and in Germany it is called the *Vogel Beerbaum*, i. e. bird's berry tree, and is much used by bird catchers to bait their springs with.

Twenty-five feet is about the average height of the Mountain ash in this country. Abroad it grows more vigorously ; and in Scotland, where it is best known by the name of the Roan or Rowan tree, it sometimes reaches the altitude of 35 or 40 feet. The lower classes throughout the whole of Britain, for a long time attributed to its branches the power of being a sovereign charm against witches ; and Sir Thomas Lauder informs us that this superstition is still in existence in many parts of the Highlands, as well as in Wales. It is probable that this tree was a great favorite with the Druids ; for it is often seen growing near their ancient mystical circles of stones. The dairymaid, in many parts of England, still preserves the old custom of driving her cows to pasture with a switch of the roan tree, which she believes has the power to shield them from all evil spells.* "Evelyn mentions that it is customary in Wales to plant this tree in churchyards ; and Miss Kent in her Sylvan Sketches, makes the following remarks :—' In former times this tree was supposed to be

* Lightfoot, Flora Scotica.

possessed of the property of driving away witches and evil spirits ; and this property is alluded to in one of the stanzas of a very ancient song, called the *Laidley Worm of Spindleton's Heughs.*

> ' Their spells were vain ; the boys return'd
> To the Queen in sorrowful mood,
> Crying that " witches have no power
> Where there is rowan-tree wood ?"

" The last line of this stanza leads to the true reading of a stanza in Shakspeare's tragedy of Macbeth. The sailor's wife, on the witch's requesting some chestnuts, hastily answers, ' A rown-tree, witch !'—but many of the editions have it, ' aroint thee, witch !' which is nonsense, and evidently a corruption."*

The European Mountain ash is quite a favorite with cultivators here, and deservedly so. Its foliage is extremely neat, its blossoms pretty, and its blazing red berries in autumn communicate a cheerfulness to the season, and harmonize happily with the gay tints of our native forest trees. It is remarkably well calculated for small plantations or collections, as it grows in almost any soil or situation, takes but little room, and is always interesting. " In the Scottish Highlands," says Gilpin, " on some rocky mountain covered with dark pines and waving birch, which cast a solemn gloom on the lake below, a few Mountain ashes joining in a clump and mixing with them, have a fine effect. In summer the light green tint of their foliage, and in autumn the glowing berries which hang clustering upon them, contrast beautifully with the deeper green of the pines : and if they are happily blended, and not in too large a proportion, they add some of the most picturesque furni-

* Arboretum et Fruticetum, p. 918.

ture with which the sides of those rugged mountains are invested." We have seen the Mountain ash, here, display-ing itself in great beauty, mingled with a group of hemlocks from among the deep green foliage of which, the coral berries of the former seemed to shoot out; their color heightened by the dark back ground of evergreen boughs.

The American Mountain ash (*Pyrus Americana*) is a native of the mountains along the banks of the Hudson, and other cold and elevated situations in the north of the United States: on the Catskill we have seen some handsome speci-mens near the Mountain House ; but generally it does not grow in so comely a shape, or form so handsome a tree as the foreign sort. In the general appearance of the leaves and blossoms, however, it so nearly resembles the European as to be thought merely a variety by some botanists. The chief difference between them appears to be in the color of the fruit, which on our native tree is copper colored or dull purplish red. It may probably assume a handsome shape when cultivated.

The Sorb or Service tree (*Pyrus Sorbus*) is an interest-ing species of Pyrus, a native of Europe, which is sometimes seen in our gardens, and deserves a place for its handsome foliage and its clusters of fruit ; which somewhat resemble those of the Mountain ash, and are often eaten when in a state of incipient decay. The leaves are coarser than those of the Mountain ash, and the tree is larger, often attaining the height of 50 or 60 feet in its native soil.

The White Beam (*Pyrus Aria*) is another foreign species, also bearing bunches of handsome scarlet berries, and clus-ters of white flowers. The leaves, however, are not pin-nated, but simply serrated on the margin. It grows 30 feet high, and as the foliage is dark green on the upper side, and downy white beneath, it presents an effect greatly resembling that of the Silver poplar in a slight breeze. Abroad, the timber is considered valuable; but here it is chiefly planted to produce a pleasing variety among other trees, by its peculiar foliage, and scarlet autumnal fruit.

All the foregoing trees grow naturally in the highest, most exposed, and often almost barren situations. When, however, a rapid growth is desired, they should be planted in a more moist and genial soil. They are easily propagated from the seed, and some of the sorts may be grafted on the pear or hawthorn. The seeds, in all cases, should be sown in autumn.

The Ailantus Tree. *Ailantus.*

Nat. Ord. Xanthoxylaceœ.   *Lin. Syst.* Polygamia, Monœcia.

Ailanto is the name of this tree in the Moluccas, and is said to signify Tree of Heaven; an appellation probably bestowed on account of the rapidity of its growth, and the great height which it reaches in the East Indies, its native country. When quite young it is not unlike a sumac in appearance; but the extreme rapidity of its growth and the great size of its pinnated leaves, four or five feet long, soon distinguish it from that shrub. During the first half dozen years it outstrips almost any other deciduous tree in vigor of growth, and we have measured leading stems which had grown twelve or fifteen feet in a single season. In four or five years, therefore, it forms quite a bulky head, but after that period it advances more slowly, and in 20 years would probably be overtopped by the poplar, the plane, or any other fast growing tree. There are, as yet, no specimens in this country more than 70 feet high; but the trunk shoots up in a fine column, and the head is massy and irregular in outline. In this country it is planted purely for ornament, but we learn that in Europe its wood has been applied to cabinet work; for which, from its close grain and bright satin-like lustre, it is well adapted.* The male and female flowers are borne on separate trees, and both sexes are now common, especially in New York. The male forms the finer ornamental tree, the female being rather low, and spreading in its head.

In New York and Philadelphia, the Ailantus is more generally known by the name of the *Celestial tree*, and is much planted in the streets and public squares. For such situations it is admirably adapted, as it will insinuate its strong roots into the most meagre and barren soil, where few other trees will grow, and soon produce an abundance of foliage and fine shade. It appears also to be perfectly free from insects; and the leaves, instead of dropping slowly, and for a long time, fall off almost immediately when frost commences.

The Ailantus is a picturesque tree, well adapted to produce a good effect on the lawn, either singly or grouped; as its fine long foliage catches the light well, and contrasts strikingly with that of the round-leaved trees. It has a troublesome habit of producing suckers, however, which must exclude it from every place but a heavy sward, where the surface of the ground is never stirred by cultivation.

The branches of this tree are entirely destitute of the small spray so common on most forest trees, and have a singularly naked look in winter, well calculated to fix the attention of the spectator at that dreary season.

* Annales de la Societé d'Horticulture.

The largest Ailantus trees in America are growing in Rhode Island, where it was introduced from China, under the name of the Tillou tree. It has since been rapidly propagated by suckers, and is now one of the commonest ornamental trees sold in the nurseries. The finest trees, however, are those raised from seed.*

THE KENTUCKY COFFEE TREE. *Gymnocladus.*

Nat. Ord. Leguminosæ.   *Lin. Syst.* Diœcia, Decandria.

This unique tree is found in the western part of the State of New York, and as far north as Montreal, in Canada. But it is seen in the greatest perfection, in the fertile bottoms of Kentucky and Tennessee. Sixty feet is the usual height of the Coffee tree in those soils; and judging from specimens growing under our inspection, it will scarcely fall short of that altitude, in well cultivated situations, anywhere in the middle states.

When in full foliage, this is a very beautiful tree. The whole leaf, doubly compound and composed of a great number of bluish-green leaflets, is generally three feet long, and of two-thirds that width on thrifty trees; and the whole foliage hangs in a well-rounded mass, that would look almost too heavy, were it not lightened in effect by

---

* We think public opinion has very much changed about this tree, since the early editions of this work. Being then but newly introduced, and having (to Americans) the very great merit of growing with remarkable rapidity, it was very much sought after, and is now, we think, as universally neglected. The exceedingly disagreeable odor of its flowers and young wood, and the troublesome habit of suckering, have quite thrown it into disfavor, especially since its place can be now supplied by a much more effective tree, from the same country (Japan): the *Paulownia*—growing with equal rapidity, and having an early Spring bloom, of great beauty and sweetness of perfume.—H. W. S.

the loose, tufted appearance of each individual leaf. The
flowers, which are white, are borne in loose spikes, in
the beginning of summer ; and are succeeded by ample
brown pods, flat and somewhat curved, which contain six
or seven large grey seeds, imbedded in a sweet pulpy
substance. As the genus is diœcious, it is necessary that
both sexes of this tree should be growing near each other,
in order to produce seed.

When Kentucky was first settled by the adventurous
pioneers from the Atlantic States, who commenced their
career in the primeval wilderness, almost without the
necessaries of life, except as produced by them from the
fertile soil, they fancied that they had discovered a
substitute for coffee in the seeds of this tree, and
accordingly the name of Coffee tree was bestowed upon
it : but when a communication was established with the
seaports, they gladly relinquished their Kentucky beverage
for the more grateful flavor of the Indian plant ; and no
use is at present made of it in that manner. It has,
however, a fine, compact wood, highly useful in building or
cabinet-work.

The Kentucky Coffee tree is well entitled to a place in
every collection. In summer, its charming foliage and
agreeable flowers render it a highly beautiful lawn tree ;
and in winter, it is certain y one of the most novel trees,
in appearance, in our whole native sylva. Like the
Ailantus, it is entirely destitute of small spray, but it also
adds to this the additional singularity of thick, blunt,
terminal branches, without any perceptible buds. Altogether it more resembles a dry, dead, and withered
combination of sticks, than a living and thrifty tree.
Although this would be highly monotonous and displeasing,
were it the common appearance of our deciduous trees

in winter ; yet, as it is not so, but a rare and very unique
exception to the usual beautiful diversity of spray and
ramification, it is highly interesting to place such a tree as
the present in the neighborhood of other full-sprayed
species, where the curiosity which it excites will add
greatly to its value as an interesting object at that period
of the year.*

[Fig. 83. The Kentucky Coffee Tree.]

The seeds vegetate freely, and the tree is usually
propagated in that manner. It prefers a rich, strong soil,
like most trees of the western states.

---

* There are some very fine specimens upon the lawn at Dr. Hosack's seat
Hyde Park, N. Y., which have fruited for a number of years. *See Fig.* 83.

The Willow Tree. *Salix.*

Nat. Ord. Salicaceæ. *Lin. Syst.* Diœcia, Diandria.

A very large genus, comprising plants of almost **every** stature, from minute shrubs of three or four inches in height, to lofty and wide-spreading trees of fifty or sixty feet.* They are generally remarkable for their narrow leaves, and slender, round, and flexible branches.

There are few of these willows which are adapted to add to the beauty of artificial scenery; but among them are three or four trees, which, from their peculiar character, deserve especial notice. These are the Weep-ing, or Babylonian willow (*Salix Babylonica*), the White, or Huntington willow (*S. alba*), the Golden willow (*S. vitellina*), the Russell willow (*S. Russelliana*), and the profuse Flowering willow (*S. caprea*).

The above are all foreign sorts, which, however (except the last), have long ago been introduced, and are now quite common in the United States. All of them except the first, have an upright or wavy, spreading growth, and form lofty trees, considerably valued abroad for their timber. The White willow and the Russell willow are very rapid in their growth, and have a pleasing light green foliage. The Golden willow is remarkable for its bright yellow bark, which renders it quite ornamental, even in winter. It is a middle sized tree, and is often seen growing along the road-sides in the eastern and middle states. *Salix caprea* is deserving a place in collections for the beauty of its abundant blossoms at an early and cheerless period in the spring.

* Dr. Barratt of Middletown, Conn., who has paid great attention to the willow, enumerates 100 species, as growing in North America, either indigenous or introduced.

The chief, and indeed almost the only value of these willows in Landscape Gardening, is to embellish low grounds, streams of water, or margins of lakes. When mingled with other trees, they often harmonize so badly from their extremely different habits, foliage, and color, that unless very sparingly introduced, they cannot fail to have a bad effect. On the banks of streams, however, they are extremely appropriate, hanging their slender branches over the liquid element, and drawing genial nourishment from the moistened soil.

> " Le saule incliné sur la rive penchante,
> Balançant mollement sa tête blanchissante."

In the middle distance of a scene, also, where a stream winds partially hidden, or which might otherwise wholly escape the eye, these trees, if planted along its course, connected as they are in our minds with watery soils, will not fail to direct the attention and convey forcibly the impression of a brook or river, winding its way beneath their shade.

In landscapes, the Weeping willow is peculiarly express-ive of grace and softness. Although a highly beautiful tree, great care must be used in its introduction, to preserve the harmony and propriety of the whole ; as nothing could be more strikingly inappropriate than to intermix it frequently with trees expressive of dignity or majesty, as the oak, etc.; where the violent contrast exhibited in the near proximity of the two opposite forms, could only produce discord. The favorite place, where it is most true to nature and itself, is near water, where

> ———— " it dips
> Its pendent boughs, stooping as if to drink."   COWPER.

There, when properly introduced, not in too great abun-dance, hanging over some rustic bridge, or cool jutting spring, and supported, and brought into harmony with surrounding vegetation by such other graceful and light-sprayed trees as the Birch and Weeping elm, its effect is often surpassingly beautiful and appropriate.   There it is one of the first in the vernal season to burst its buds, and mirror its soft green foliage in the flood beneath, and one of the last in autumn to yield its leafy vesture to the chilling frosts, or fitful gusts of approaching winter.

We consider the Weeping willow ill calculated for a place near a mansion which has any claims to size, mag-nificence, or architectural beauty; as it does not in any way contribute by its form or outline to add to or strengthen such characteristics in a building.   The only place where it can be happily situated in this way, is in the case of very humble or inconspicuous cottages, which we have seen much ornamented by being completely hidden, as it were, beneath the soft veil of its streaming foliage.

There is a very singular variety of the Weeping willow cultivated in our gardens, under the name of the Ringlet willow; which is so remarkable in the form of its foliage, and so different from all other trees, that it is well worth a place as a curiosity.   Each leaf is curled round like a ring or hoop, and the appearance of a branch in full foliage is not unlike a thinly curled ringlet; whence its common name.   It forms a neat, middle-sized tree, with drooping branches, though hardly so pendent as the Weeping willow.

The uses of the willow are extremely numerous.   Abroad it is extensively cultivated in coppices, for timber and fuel, for hoops, ties, etc. ; and we are informed, that in the north ern parts of Europe, and throughout the Russian Empire, the twigs are employed in manufacturing domestic uten· sils, harness, cables, and even for the houses of the pea· santry themselves. From the fibres of the bark, it is said that a durable cloth is woven by the Tartars ; and the bark is used for tanning in various parts of the eastern continent.

But by far the most extensive use to which this plant is applied, is in the manufacture of baskets. From the earliest periods it has been devoted to this purpose, and large plantations, or osier-fields, as they are called, are devoted to the culture of particular kinds for this purpose, both in Europe and America. The common Basket willow, an European species (*S. viminalis*), is the sort usually grown for this purpose, but several others are also employed. For the culture of the basket willows, a deep, moist, though not inundated soil is necessary ; such as is generally found on the margins of small streams, or low lands. " Ropes and baskets made from willow twigs, were probably among the very earliest manufactures, in countries where these trees abound. The Romans used the twigs for binding their vines, and tying their reeds in bundles, and made all sorts of baskets of them. A crop of willows was consi- dered so valuable in the time of Cato, that he ranks the Salictum, or willow field, next in value to the vineyard and the garden. (Art. *Salix. Arb. Brit.*)

Among us, the European Basket willow is extensively cultivated, and very large plantations are to be seen in the low grounds of New Jersey and Pennsylvania. The wood of some of the tree willows, and particularly that of the Yellow willow, and the Shining willow (*S. lucida*), is greatly used in making charcoal for the manufacture of gunpowder.

It is almost unnecessary to say that all the willows grow readily from slips or truncheons planted in the ground.   So tenacious of life are they, that examples are known where small trees have been taken up and completely inverted, by planting the branches and leaving the roots exposed, which have nevertheless thrown out new roots from the former tops, and the roots becoming branches, the tree grew again with its ordinary vigor.

The Sassafras Tree.   *Laurus.*

Nat. Ord.   Lauraceæ.   *Lin. Syst.*   Enneandria, Monogynia.

The Sassafras is a neat tree of the middle size, belonging to the same family as the European laurel or Sweet bay; it is found, more or less plentifully, through the whole territory of the United States.   In favorable soils, along the banks of the Hudson, it often grows to 40 or 50 feet in height; but in the woods it seldom reaches that altitude. The flowers are yellow, and appear in small clusters in May, and the fruit is a small, deep blue berry, seated on a red footstalk or cup.   The bark of the wood and roots has an agreeable smell and taste, and is a favorite ingredient, with the branches of the spruce, in the small beer made by the country people.   Medicinally, it is considered antiscorbutic and sudorific; and is thought efficacious in purifying the blood.   It was formerly in great repute with practitioners abroad, and large quantities of the bark of the roots were shipped to England; but the demand has of late greatly decreased.

The Sassafras is a very agreeable tree to the eye, decked as it is with its glossy, deep green, oval, or three-lobed leaves.   When fully grown, it is also quite picturesque for a tree of so moderate a size ; as its branches generally have an irregular, somewhat twisted look, and the head is partially flattened, and considerably varied in outline After ten years of age, this tree always looks older than it really is, from its rough, deeply cracked, grey bark, and rather crooked stem.   It often appears extremely well on the borders of a plantation, and mixes well with almost any of the heavier deciduous trees.   As it is by no means so common a tree as many of those already noticed, it is generally the more valued, and may frequently be seen growing along the edges of cultivated fields and pastures, appearing to thrive well in any good mellow soil.

<hr />

The Catalpa Tree. *Catalpa.*

Nat. Ord. Bignoniaceæ.   *Lin. Syst.* Diandria, Monogynia.

A native of nearly all the states south and west of Virginia, this tree has become naturalized also throughout the middle and eastern sections of the Union, where it is generally planted for ornament.

In Carolina it is called the Catawba tree, after the Catawba Indians, a tribe that formerly inhabited that country; and it is probable that the softer epithet now generally bestowed upon it in the north, is only a corruption of that original name.

The leaves of this tree are very large, often measuring six or seven inches broad; they are heart-shaped in form, smooth, and pale green on the upper side, slightly downy beneath. The blossoms are extremely beautiful, hanging, like those of the Horse-chestnut, in massy clusters beyond the outer surface of the foliage. The color is a pure and delicate white, and the inner part of the corolla is delicately sprinkled over with violet, or reddish and yellow spots; indeed, the individual beauty of the flowers is so great when viewed closely, that one almost regrets that they should be elevated on the branches of a large forest tree. When these fall, they are succeeded by bean-like capsules or seed-vessels, which grow ten or twelve inches long, become brown, and hang pendent upon the branches during the greater part of the winter.

The Catalpa never, or rarely, takes a symmetrical form when growing up; but generally forms a wide-spreading head, forty or fifty feet in diameter. Its large and abundant foliage affords a copious shade, and its growth is quite rapid, soon forming a large and bulky tree. In ornamental plantations it is much valued on account of its superb and showy flowers, and is therefore deserving a place in every lawn. It is generally seen to best advantage when standing alone, but it may also be mingled with other large round-leaved trees, as the basswood, etc., when it produces a very pleasing effect. The branches are rather brittle, like those of the locust, and are therefore somewhat liable to be broken by the wind. Accustomed to a warmer climate, the leaves expand late in the spring, and wither hastily when frost approaches; but the soft tint of their luxuriant vegetation is very grateful to the eye, and it appears to be uninjured by the hottest rays of summer. North of this place the Catalpa is rather too tender for exposed situations.

We have seen the Catalpa employed to great advantage in fixing and holding up the loose soil of river banks, where, if planted, it will soon insinuate its strong roots, and retain the soil firmly. In Ohio, experiments have been made with the timber for the posts used in fencing; and it is stated on good authority that it is but little inferior, when well seasoned, to that of the locust in durability.

Michaux mentions that he has been assured that the honey collected from the flowers is poisonous; but this we are inclined to doubt; or at least we have witnessed no ill effects from planting it in abundance in the middle States, in those neighborhoods where bees are kept in considerable numbers.

The Catalpa is very easily propagated from seeds sown in any light soil; and the growth of the young plants is extremely rapid. *C. syringafolia* is the only species.*

———

THE PERSIMON TREE. *Diospyros.*

Nat. Ord. Ebenaceæ.   *Lin. Syst.* Polygamia, Diœcia.

The Highlands of the Hudson, and about the same latitude on the Connecticut, may be considered the northern limits of this small tree. It generally forms a spreading loose head, of some twenty or thirty feet high, in good soils in the middle states; but we have seen a

* This was quite true when the above chapter was written. Since when, we have *C. bungei, C. kœmferi,* and *C. himmalayensis* — the first two being dwarfs.

specimen of nearly eighty feet, in the old Bartram Garden
at Philadelphia; and fifty feet is probably the average
growth on deep fertile lands in the southern states.

The Persimon bears a small, round, dull red fruit, about
an inch in diameter, containing six or seven stones; it is
insufferably austere and bitter, until the autumnal frosts have
mellowed it and lessened its harshness, when it becomes
quite palatable. Considerable quantities of the fruit are
annually brought into New York market and its vicinity,
from New Jersey, and sold: the produce is very abundant,
a single tree often yielding several bushels. A strong
brandy has been distilled from them; and in the south they
are said to enter into the composition of the country beer.
For the latter purpose they are pounded up with bran, dried,
and kept for use till wanted.

The foliage of the Persimon is handsome; the leaves
being four or five inches long, simple, oblong, dark green,
and glossy, like those of the orange. The blossoms are
green and inconspicuous.

The Persimon has no importance as a tree to recommend
it; but it may be admitted in all good collections for its
pleasing shining foliage, and the variety which its singular
fruit adds to the productions of a complete country residence. The common sort (*D. Virginiana*) grows readily
from the seed.

There is an European Species (*Dyosporus Lotus*), with
yellow fruit about the size of a cherry, rather less palatable
than our native kind. The specimens of this tree, which
we have imported, appear too tender to bear our winters
unprotected, so that it will probably not prove hardy in the
northern states.

THE PEPERIDGE TREE. *Nyssa.*

Nat. Ord. Santalaceæ.   *Lin. Syst.* Polygamia, Diœcia.

The Peperidge, Tupelo, or sour gum tree, as it is callea
:n various parts of the Union, grows to a moderate size,
and is generally found in moist situations, though we have
seen it in New York State, thriving very well in dry upland
soils. The diameter of the trunk is seldom more than
eighteen inches, and the general height is about forty or
fifty feet. The flowers are scarcely perceptible, but the
fruit borne in pairs, is about the size of a pea, deep blue,
and ripens in October.

The leaves are oval, smooth, and have a beautiful gloss
on their upper surface. The branches diverge from the
main trunk almost horizontally, and sometimes even bend
downwards like those of some of the Pine family, which
gives the tree a very marked and picturesque character.

The Peperidge when of moderate size is not difficult to
transplant, and we consider it a very fine tree, both on
account of its beautiful, dark green, and lustrous foliage in
summer, and the brilliant fiery color which it takes when
the frost touches it in autumn. In this respect it is fully
equal in point of beauty to that of the Liquidambar or Sweet
gum, and the maples which we have already described ;
and so fine a feature do we consider this autumnal beauty
of foliage that we would by all means advise the introduction of such trees as the Peperidge into the landscape for
that reason alone, were it not also valuable for its peculiar
form and polished leaves in summer.

Besides the Peperidge there are three other Nyssas,
natives of this continent, viz. the Black gum (*N. Sylvatica*),

a tree of greater dimensions, and larger, more elongated leaves, whose northern boundary is the neighborhood of Philadelphia; the Large Tupelo (*N. grandidentata*), a tree of the largest size, with large, coarsely toothed foliage, and a large blue fruit, three-fourths of an inch long, which is sometimes called the wild olive; and the sour Tupelo (*N. capitata*), with long, smooth, laurel-like leaves, and light red, oval fruit, called the Wild Lime, from its abounding in a strong acid, resembling that of the latter fruit. Both the latter trees are natives of the southern states, and are little known north of Philadelphia.

The wood of all the foregoing trees is remarkable for the peculiar arrangement of its fibres; which, instead of running directly through the stem in parallel lines, are curiously twisted and interwoven together. Owing to this circumstance it is extremely difficult to split, and is therefore often used in the manufacture of wooden bowls, trays, etc. That of the Peperidge is also preferred for the same reason, and for its toughness, by the wheel-wrights, in the construction of the naves of wheels, and for other similar purposes.

Michaux remarks that he is unable to give any reason why the names of Sour gum, Black gum, etc., have been bestowed upon these trees, as they spontaneously exude no sap or fluid which could give rise to such an appellation. We suspect that the term has arisen from a comparison of the autumnal tints of these trees belonging to the genus Nyssa, with those of the Sweet gum or Liquidambar, which, at a short distance, they so much resemble in the early autumn.

The Thorn Tree. *Crategus.*

Nat. Ord. Rosaceæ.　　*Lin. Syst.* Icosandria, Di-pentagynia.

A tree of the smallest size; but though many of the sorts attain only the stature of ordinary shrubs, yet some of our native species, as well as the English Hawthorn (*C. oxycantha*), when standing alone, will form neat, spreading-topped trees, of twenty or thirty feet in height. Although the thorn is not generally viewed among us as a plant at all conducive to the beauty of scenery, yet we are induced to mention it here, and to enforce its claims in that point of view, as they appear to us highly entitled to consideration. First, the foliage—deep green, shining, and often beautifully cut and diversified in form —is prettily tufted and arranged upon the branches; secondly, the snowy blossoms—often produced in such quantities as to completely whiten the whole head of the tree, and which in many sorts have a delightful perfume —present a charming appearance in the early part of the season; and thirdly, the ruddy crimson or purple haws or fruit, which give the whole plant a rich and glowing appearance in and among our fine forests, open glades, or wild thickets, in autumn.

The most ornamental and the strongest growing indigenous kinds are the Scarlet Thorn tree (*C. coccinea*), and its varieties, the Washington Thorn (*C. populifolia*), and the Cockspur Thorn (*C. crus-galli*); all of which, in good soil, will grow to the height of twenty or thirty feet, and can readily be transplanted from their native sites.

The English Hawthorn is not only a beautiful small tree, but it is connected in our minds with all the elegant, poetic, and legendary associations which belong to it in England ; for scarcely any tree is richer in such than this. With the floral games of *May*, this plant, from its blooming at that period, and being the favorite of the season, has become so identified, that the blossoms are known in many parts of Britain chiefly by that name. Among the ancient Greeks and Romans, they were dedicated to Flora, whose festival began on the first of that month ; and in the olden times of merry England, the May-pole, its top decked with the gayest garlands of these blossoms, was raised amid the shouts of the young and old assembled to celebrate this happy rustic festival. *Chaucer* alludes to the custom, and describes the hawthorn thus :

> Marke the faire blooming of the Hawthorne tree,
> Which finely cloathed in a robe of white,
> Fills full the wanton eye with May's delight.
>
> COURT OF LOVE.

And *Herrick* has left us the following lines to " Corrina *going a Maying :*"

> " Come, my Corrina, come ; and coming marke
> How eche field turns a street, eche street a park
> Made green, and trimmed with trees ; see how
> Devotion gives eche house a bough
> Or branch ; eche porch, eche doore ere this,
> An arke, a tabernacle is,
> Made up of Hawthorne, neatly interwove,
> As if here were those cooler shades of love."

The following lines descriptive of the English species, we extract from the " *Romance of Nature.*"

> " Come let us rest this hawthorn tree beneath,
> And breathe its luscious fragrance as it flies,

And watch the tiny petals as they fall,
Circling and winnowing down our sylvan hall."

The berries, or *haws,* as they are called, have a very rich
and coral-like look when the tree, standing alone, is completely covered with them in October. There are some
elegant varieties of this species, which highly deserve cultivation for the beauty of their flowers and foliage. Among
them we may particularly notice the Double White, with
beautiful blossoms like small white roses; the Pink and the
Scarlet flowering, both single and double, and the Variegated-leaved hawthorn, all elegant trees; as well as the
Weeping hawthorn, a rarer variety, with pendulous
branches.

The Hawthorn is most agreeable to the eye in composition when it forms the undergrowth or thicket, peeping
out in all its green freshness, gay blossoms, or bright fruit,
from beneath and between the groups and masses of trees;
where, mingled with the hazel, etc., it gives a pleasing
intricacy to the whole mass of foliage. But the different
species display themselves to most advantage, and grow
also to a finer size, when planted singly, or two or three
together, along the walks leading through the different parts
of the pleasure-ground or shrubbery.

The Magnolia Tree. *Magnolia.*

Nat. Ord. Magnoliaceæ.   *Lin. Syst.* Polyandria, Polygynia.

The North American trees composing the genus Magnolia
are certainly among the most splendid productions of the
forests in any temperate climate; and when we consider

the size and fragrance of their blossoms, or the beauty of their large and noble foliage, we may be allowed to doubt whether there is a more magnificent and showy genus of deciduous trees in the world. With the exception of a few shrubs or smaller trees, natives of China and the mountains of Central Asia, it belongs exclusively to this continent, as no individuals of this order are indigenous to Europe or Africa. The American species attracted the attention of the first botanists who came over to examine the riches of our native flora, and were transplanted to the gardens of England and France more than a hundred years ago, where they are still valued as the finest hardy trees of that hemisphere.

The Large Evergreen Magnolia (*M. grandiflora*), or Big Laurel, as it is sometimes called, is peculiarly indigenous to that portion of our country south of North Carolina, where its stately trunk, often seventy feet in height, and superb pyramid of deep green foliage, render it one of the loveliest and most majestic of trees. The leaves, which are evergreen, and somewhat resemble those of the laurel in form, are generally six or eight inches in length, thick in texture and brilliantly polished on the upper surface. The highly fragrant flowers are composed of about six petals, opening in a wide cup-like form, of the most snowy whiteness of color. Scattered among the rich foliage, their effect is exquisitely beautiful. The seeds are borne in an oval, cone-like carpel or seed-vessel, composed of a number of cells which split longitudinally, when the stony seed, covered with a bright red pulp, drops out. There are several varieties, which have been raised from the seed of this species abroad; the most beautiful is the Exmouth Magnolia, with fine foliage, rusty beneath; it produces its flowers much earlier and more abundantly than the original sort.

We regret that this tree is too tender to bear the open air north of Philadelphia, as it is one of the choicest evergreens. At the nurseries of the Messrs. Landreth, and at the Bartram Botanic Garden of Col. Carr, near that city, some good specimens of this Magnolia and its varieties are growing thriftily; but in the State of New York, and at the east, it can only be considered a green-house plant.

The Cucumber Magnolia (*C. acuminata*), (so called from the appearance of the young fruit, which is not unlike a green cucumber) takes the same place in the north, in point of majesty and elevation, that the Big Laurel occupies in the south. Its northern limit is Lake Erie; and it abounds along the whole range of the Alleghanies to the southward, in rich mountain acclivities, and moist sheltered valleys. There it often measures three or four feet in diameter, and eighty in height. The leaves, which are deciduous, like those of all the Magnolias except the *M. grandiflora*, are also about six inches long and four broad, acuminate at the point, of a bluish green on the upper surface. The flowers are six inches in diameter, of a pale yellow, much like those of the Tulip tree, and slightly fragrant. The fruit is about three inches long, and cylindrical in shape. Most of the inhabitants of the country bordering on the Alleghanies, says Michaux, gather these cones about midsummer, when they are half ripe, and steep them in whiskey; the liquor produced, they take as an antidote against the fevers prevalent in those districts.

The Umbrella Magnolia (*M. tripetala*), though found

sometimes in the northwest of New York, is rare there and abounds most in the south and west. It is a smaller tree than the preceding kinds, rarely growing more than thirty feet high. The leaves on the terminal shoots are disposed three or four in a tuft, which has given rise to the name of Umbrella tree. They are of fine size, eighteen inches or two feet long, and seven or eight broad, oval, pointed at both ends ; the flowers are also large, white, and numerous ; and the conical fruit-vessel containing the seeds, assumes a beautiful rose-color in autumn. From its fine tufted foliage, and rapid growth, this is one of the most desirable species for our pleasure-grounds.

The Large-leaved Magnolia (*M. macrophylla*) is the rarest of the genus in our forests, being only found as yet in North Carolina. The leaves grow to an enormous size when the tree is young, often measuring three feet long, and nine or ten inches broad. They are oblong, oval, and heart-shaped at the base. The flowers are also immense, opening of the size of a hat-crown, and diffusing a most agreeable odor. The tree attains only a secondary size, and is distinguished in winter by the whiteness of its bark, compared with the others. It is rather tender north of New York.

The Heart-leaved Magnolia (*M. cordata*) is a beautiful southern species, distinguished by its nearly round, heart-shaped foliage, and its yellow flowers about four inches in diameter. It blooms in the gardens very young, and very abundantly, often producing two crops in a season.

Magnolia auriculata grows about forty feet high, and is also found near the southern Alleghany range of mountains. The leaves are light green, eight or nine inches long, widest at the top, and narrower towards the base, where they are rounded into lobes. The flowers are not so fine as those of the preceding kinds, but still are handsome, pale greenish white, and about four inches in diameter.

Besides these, there is a smaller American Magnolia, which is the only sort that in the middle or eastern sections of the Union grows within 150 miles of the sea-shore. This is the Magnolia of the swamps of New Jersey and the South (*M. glauca*), of which so many fragrant and beautiful bouquets are gathered in the season of its inflorescence, brought to New York and Philadelphia, and exposed for sale in the markets. It is rather a large bush, than a tree; with shining, green, laurel-like leaves, four or five inches long, somewhat mealy or glaucous beneath. The blossoms, about three inches broad, are snowy white, and so fragrant that where they abound in the swamps, their perfume is often perceptible for the distance of a quarter of a mile.

The foreign sorts introduced into our gardens from China, are the Chinese purple (*M. purpurea*), which produces an abundance of large delicate purple blossoms early in the season ; the Yulan or Chinese White Magnolia (*M. conspicua*), a most abundant bloomer, bearing beautiful white, fragrant flowers in April, before the leaves appear ; and Soulange's Magnolia (*M. Soulangiana*), a hybrid between the two foregoing, with large flowers delicately tinted with white and purple. These succeed well in sheltered situations, in our pleasure-grounds, and add greatly to their beauty early in the season. Grafted on the cucumber tree, they form large and vigorous trees of great beauty.

The Magnolia, in order to thrive well, requires a deep

rich soil; which in nearly all cases, to secure their luxuriance, should be improved by adding thereto some leaf mould or decayed vegetable matter from the woods When transplanted from the nursery, they should be preferred of small or only moderate size, as their succulent roots are easily injured, and they recover slowly when large. Most of them may be propagated from seed ; but they flower sooner, grow more vigorously, and are much hardier when grafted upon young stocks of the Cucumber Magnolia. This we have found to be particularly the case with the Chinese species and varieties.

All these trees are such superbly beautiful objects upon a lawn in their rich summer garniture of luxuriant foliage, and large odoriferous flowers, that they need no further recommendation from us to insure their regard and admiration from all persons who have room for their culture. If possible, situations somewhat sheltered either by buildings or other trees, should be chosen for all the species, except the Cucumber Magnolia, which thrives well in almost any aspect not directly open to violent gales of wind.

THE WHITE-WOOD, OR TULIP TREE. *Liriodendron.*

Nat. Ord. Magnoliaceæ.   *Lin. Syst.* Polyandria, Polygynia.

The Tulip tree belongs to the same natural order as the Magnolias, and is not inferior to most of the latter in all that entitles them to rank among our very finest forest trees.

The taller Magnolias, as we have already remarked, do

not grow naturally within 100 or 150 miles of the sea-
coast; and the Tulip tree may be considered as in some
measure supplying their place in the middle Atlantic
states. West of the Connecticut river, and south of the
sources of the Hudson, this fine tree may be often seen
reaching in warm and deep alluvial soils 80 or 90 feet in
height. But in the western states, where indeed the
growth of forest trees is astonishingly vigorous, this tree
far exceeds that altitude. The elder Michaux mentions
several which he saw in Kentucky, that were fifteen and
sixteen feet in girth; and his son confirms the measurement of one, three miles and a half from Louisville, which,
at five feet from the ground, was found to be twenty-two
feet and six inches in circumference, with a corresponding
elevation of 130 feet.

The foliage is rich and glossy, and has a very peculiar
form; being cut off, as it were, at the extremity, and
slightly notched and divided into two-sided lobes. The
breadth of the leaves is six or eight inches. The flowers,
which are shaped like a large tulip, are composed of six
thick yellow petals, mottled on the inner surface with red
and green. They are borne singly on the terminal shoots,
have a pleasant, slight perfume, and are very showy.
The seed-vessel, which ripens in October, is formed of a
number of scales surrounding the central axis in the form
of a cone. It is remarkable that young trees under 30 or
35 feet high, seldom or never perfect their seeds.

Whoever has once seen the Tulip tree in a situation
where the soil was favorable to its free growth, can
never forget it. With a clean trunk, straight as a
column, for 40 or 50 feet, surmounted by a fine, ample
summit of rich green foliage, it is, in our estimation,

decidedly the most *stately* tree in North America. When standing alone, and encouraged in its lateral growth, it will indeed often produce a lower head, but its tendency is to rise, and it only exhibits itself in all its stateliness and majesty when, supported on such a noble columnar trunk, it towers far above the heads of its neighbors of the park or forest. Even when at its loftiest elevation, its large specious blossoms, which, from their form, one of our poets has likened to the chalice ;

> ———Through the verdant maze
> The Tulip tree
> Its golden chalice oft triumphantly displays.
>
> PICKERING.

jut out from amid the tufted canopy in the month of June, and glow in richness and beauty. While the tree is less than a foot in diameter, the stem is extremely smooth, and it has almost always a refined and finished appearance. For the lawn or park, we conceive the Tulip tree eminently adapted : its tall upright stem, and handsome summit, contrasting nobly with the spreading forms of most deciduous trees. It should generally stand alone, or near the border of a mass of trees, where it may fully display itself to the eye, and exhibit all its charms from the root to the very summit; for no tree of the same grandeur and magnitude is so truly beautiful and graceful in every portion of its trunk and branches. Where there is a taste for avenues, the Tulip tree ought by all means to be employed, as it makes a most magnificent overarching canopy of verdure, supported on trunks almost architectural in their symmetry. The leaves also, from their bitterness, are but little liable to the attacks of any insect.

This tree was introduced into England about 1668 ; and
is now to be found in almost every gentleman's park on the
Continent of Europe, so highly is it esteemed as an
ornamental tree of the first class. We hope that the fine
native specimens yet standing, here and there, in farm lands
along our river banks, may be sacredly preserved from
the barbarous infliction of the axe, which formerly
despoiled without mercy so many of the majestic denizens
of our native forests.

In the western states, where this tree abounds, it is much
used in building and carpentry. The timber is light and
yellow, and the tree is commonly called the Yellow Poplar
in those districts, from some fancied resemblance in the
wood, though it is much heavier and more durable than
that of the poplar.

When exposed to the weather, the wood is liable to
warp, but as it is fine grained, light, and easily worked, it is
extensively employed for the panels of coaches, doors,
cabinet-work, and wainscots. The Indians who once
inhabited these regions, hollowed out the trunks, and made
their canoes of them. There are two sorts of timber
known ; viz. the Yellow and the White Poplar, or Tulip
tree. These, however, it is well known are the same
species (*L. tulipifera*) ; but the variation is brought about
by the soil, which if dry, gravelly, and elevated, produces
the white, and if rich, deep, and rather moist, the yellow
timber.

It is rather difficult to transplant the Tulip tree when it
has attained much size, unless the roots have undergone
preparation, as will hereafter be mentioned ; but it is easily
propagated from seed, or obtained from the nurseries, and
the growth is then strong and rapid.

THE DOGWOOD TREE. *Cornus.*

Nat. Ord. Cornaceæ.   *Lin. Syst.* Tetrandria, Monogynia.

There are a number of small shrubs that belong to this genus, but the common Dogwood (*Cornus florida*) is the only species which has any claims to rank as a tree. In the middle states, where it abounds, as well as in most other parts of the Union, the maximum height is thirty-five feet, while its ordinary elevation is about twenty feet.

The Dogwood is quite a picturesque small tree, and owes its interest chiefly to the beauty of its numerous blossoms and fruit. The leaves are oval, about three inches long, dark green above, and paler below. In the beginning of May, while the foliage is beginning to expand rapidly, and before the tree is in full leaf, the flowers unfold, and present a beautiful spectacle, often covering the whole tree with their snowy garniture. The principal beauty of these consists in the involucrum or calyx, which, instead of being green, as is commonly the case, in the Dogwood takes a white or pale blue tint. The true flowers may be seen collected in little clusters, and are, individually, quite small, though surrounded by the involucrum, which produces all the effect of a fine white blossom.

In the early part of the season, the Dogwood is one of the gayest ornaments of our native woods. It is seen at that time to great advantage in sailing up the Hudson river. There, in the abrupt Highlands, which rise boldly many hundred feet above the level of the river, patches of the Dogwood in full bloom gleam forth in snowy whiteness from among the tender green of the surrounding young foliage, and the gloomier shades of the dark evergreens, which clothe with a rich verdure the rocks and precipices that overhang the moving flood below.

The berries which succeed these blossoms become quite' red and brilliant in autumn ; and, as they are plentifully borne in little clusters, they make quite a display. When the sharp frosts have lessened their bitterness, they are the food of the robin, which, at that late season, eats them greedily.

The foliage in autumn is also highly beautiful, and must be considered as contributing to the charms of this tree. The color it assumes is a deep lake-red ; and it is at that season as easily known at a distance by its fine coloring, as the Maple, the Liquidambar, and the Nyssa, of which we have already spoken. Taking into consideration all these ornamental qualities, and also the fact that it is every day becoming scarcer in our native wilds, we think the Dogwood tree should fairly come under the protection of the picturesque planter, and well deserves a place in the pleasure-ground and shrubbery.

The wood is close-grained, hard, and heavy, and takes a good polish.   It is too small to enter into general use, but is often employed for the lesser utensils of the farm.   The bark has been very successfully employed by physicians in Philadelphia, and elsewhere, and is found to possess nearly the same properties as the Peruvian bark.   Bigelow states in his American Botany, that its use in fevers has been known and practised in many sections of the Union by the country people, for more than fifty years.

Besides this native species there is an European dogwood (*Cornus mascula*), commonly called the Cornelian cherry, which is now planted in many of our gardens, and grows to the height of twenty or thirty feet.   The small

yellow flowers come out close to the branches in March or
April, and the whole tree is quite handsome in autumn,
from the size and color of its fine oval scarlet berries.
These are as large as a small cherry, transparent, and hang
for a long time upon the tree.   The leaves are much like
those of the common Dogwood.   Although the blossoms
are produced when the plant is quite a bush, yet it must
attain some age before the fruit sets.   Altogether, the
Cornelian cherry is one of the most desirable of small
trees.*

THE SALISBURIA, OR GINKO TREE.

Nat. Ord. Taxaceæ.   *Lin. Syst.* Monœcia, Polyandria.

This fine exotic tree, which appears to be perfectly hardy
in this climate, is one of the most singular in its foliage that
has ever come under our observation.   The leaves are
wedge-shaped, or somewhat triangular, attached to the
petioles at one of the angles, and pale yellowish green in
color ; the ribs or veins, instead of diverging from the
central mid-rib of the leaf, as is commonly the case in
dicotyledonous plants, are all parallel ; in short, they almost
exactly resemble (except in being three or four times as
large) those of the beautiful Maiden hair fern (*Adiantum*)
common in our woods : being thickened at the edges and
notched on the margin in a similar manner.   The male
flowers are yellow, sessile catkins ; the female is seated in a
curious kind of cup, formed by the enlargement of the summit of the peduncle.   The fruit is a drupe, about an inch
in length, containing a nut, which, according to Dr. Abel,
is almost always to be seen for sale in the markets of China

* (*Cornus variegata*), the Variegated Dogwood, with leaves curiously blotched
with white, and (*C. sanguinea*), with its young shoots of a bright scarlet—very
showy in Winter, are both very desirable varieties.—H. W. S.

and Japan, the native country of this tree. They are eaten after having been roasted or boiled, and are considered excellent.

The Salisburia was introduced into this country by that zealous amateur of horticulture and botany, the late Mr. Hamilton, of Woodlands, near Philadelphia, who brought it from England in 1784, where it had been received from Japan about thirty years previous. There are several of these now growing at Woodlands ; and the largest measures sixty feet in height, and three feet four inches in circumference. The next largest specimen which we have seen is now standing on the north side of that fine public square, the Boston Common. It originally grew in the grounds of Gardiner Green, Esq., of Boston ; but though of fine size, it was, about three years since, carefully removed to its present site, which proves its capability for bearing transplanting. Its measurement is forty feet in elevation, and three in circumference. There is also a very handsome tree in the grounds of Messrs. Landreth, Philadelphia, about thirty-five feet high and very thrifty.

We have not learned that any of these trees have yet borne their blossoms ; at any rate none but male blossoms have yet been produced. Abroad, the Salisburia has fruited in the South of France, and young trees have been reared from the nuts.

The bark is somewhat soft and leathery, and on the trunk and branches assumes a singular tawny yellow or greyish color. The tree grows pretty rapidly, and forms an exceedingly neat, loose, conical, or tapering head. The timber is very solid and heavy ; and the tree is said to grow to enormous size in its native country. Bunge, who accompanied the mission from Russia to Pekin, states that he saw near a Pagoda, an immense Ginko tree, with a trunk nearly forty feet in circumference, and still in full vigor of vegetation.*

Although nearly related to the Pine tribe, and forming, apparently, the connecting link between the *coniferæ* and exogenous trees, yet, unlike the former tribe, the wood of the tree is perfectly free from resin.

The Ginko tree is so great a botanical curiosity, and is so singularly beautiful when clad with its fern-like foliage, that it is strikingly adapted to add ornament and interest to the pleasure ground. As the foliage is of that kind which must be viewed near by to understand its peculiarity, and as the form and outline of the tree are pleasing, and harmonize well with buildings, we would recommend that it be planted near the house, where its unique character can be readily seen and appreciated.

Salisburia adiantifolia is the only species. In the United States it appears to flourish best in a rich fertile soil, rather dry than otherwise. South of Albany it is perfectly hardy, and may therefore be considered a most valuable acquisition to our catalogue of trees of the first class. It has hitherto been propagated chiefly from layers; but cuttings of the preceding year's growth, planted early in the spring, in a fine sandy loam, and kept shaded and watered, will also root without much difficulty. When the old trees already mentioned (which have doubtless been raised from seed) begin to blossom, plants reared from them by cuttings or grafts, will, of course, produce blossoms and fruit much more speedily than when reared from the nut.

* Bull. de la Soc. d'Agr. du départ de l'Herault.   Arb. Brit.

The American Cypress Tree. *Taxodium.*

Nat. Ord. Coniferæ.   *Lin. Syst.* Monœcia, Monadelphia.

The Southern or Deciduous cypress (*Taxodium disti-chum*)* is one of the most majestic, useful, and beautiful trees of the southern part of North America. Naturally, it is not found growing north of Maryland, or the south part of Delaware, but below that boundary it becomes extremely multiplied. The low grounds and alluvial soils subject to inundations, are constantly covered with this tree ; and on the banks of the Mississippi and other great western rivers, for more than 600 miles from its mouth, those vast marshes, caused by the periodical bursting and overflowing of their banks, are filled with huge and almost endless growths of this tree, called Cypress swamps. Beyond the boundaries of the United States its geographical range extends to Mexico; and Michaux estimates that it is found more or less abundantly, over a range of country more than 3000 miles in extent.

" In the swamps of the southern states and the Floridas, on whose deep, miry soil a new layer of vegetable mould is deposited every year by the floods, the Cypress attains its utmost development. The largest stocks are 120 feet in height, and from 25 to 40 feet in circumference above the conical base, which at the surface of the earth is always three or four times as large as the continued diameter of the trunk ; in felling them, the negroes are obliged to raise themselves upon scaffolds five or six feet from the ground The roots of the largest stocks, particularly of such as are

* Cupressus disticha.

most exposed to inundation, are charged with conical protuberances, commonly from eighteen to twenty-four inches,
and sometimes four or five feet in thickness; these are
always hollow, smooth on the surface, and covered with a
reddish bark, like the roots, which they resemble also in the
softness of their wood; they exhibit no sign of vegetation,
and I have never succeeded in obtaining shoots by wound-
ing their surface and covering them with the earth. No
cause can be assigned for their existence : they are peculiar
to the Cypress, and begin to appear when it is twenty or
twenty-five feet in height; they are not made use of except
by the negroes for bee-hives."

"The foliage is open, light, and of a fresh, agreeable
tint; each leaf is four or five inches long, and consists of
two parallel rows of leaflets, upon a common stem. The
leaflets are small, fine, and somewhat arching, with the
convex side outwards. In the autumn, they change from
a light green to a dull red, and are shed soon after."

"The Cypress blooms in Carolina about the first of
February. The male and female flowers arc borne
separately, by the same tree ; the first in flexible pendulous
aments, and the second in bunches, scarcely apparent.
The cones are about as large as the thumb, hard, round,
of an uneven surface, and stored with small, irregular,
ligneous seeds, containing a cylindrical kernel ; they are
ripe in October, and retain their productive virtue for two
years."*

Such is the account given of the Cypress in its native
soils. In the middle states it is planted only as an ornamental tree ; and while, in the South, its great abundance

* N. A. Sylva. ii. **332.**

causes it to be neglected or disregarded as such, its rarity here allows us fully to appreciate its beauty. North of the 43° of latitude it will not probably stand the winter without protection; but south of that, it will attain a good size. The finest planted specimen which we have seen, and one which is probably equal in grandeur to almost any in their native swamps, is growing in the Bartram Botanic Garden, near Philadelphia. That garden was founded by the father of American botanists, John Bartram, who explored the southern and western territories, then vast wilds, at the peril of his life, to furnish the *savans* and gardens of Europe, with the productions of the new world, and who commenced the living collection, now unequalled, of American trees, in his own garden. In the lower part of it stands the *great Cypress*, a tree of noble dimensions, measuring at this time 130 feet in height and 25 in circumference. The tree was held by Bartram's son, William, while his father assisted in planting it, *ninety-nine* years ago. The elder Bartram at the time expressed to his son, the hope that the latter might live to see it a large tree. Long before he died (not many years since), it had become the prodigy of the garden, and great numbers from the neighboring city annually visit it, to admire its vast size, and recline beneath its ample shade.

The foliage of the Cypress is peculiar; for while it has a resemblance to the Hemlock, Yew, and other evergreen trees, its cheerful, bright green tint, and loose airy tufts of foliage, give it a character of great lightness and elegance. In young trees, the form of the head is pyramidal or pointed; but when they become old, Michaux remarks, the head becomes widely spread, and even depressed, thus assuming a remarkably picturesque aspect. This is also heightened by the deep furrows or channels in the trunk, and the singular excrescences or knobs already described, which, jutting above the surface of the ground, give a strange ruggedness to the surface beneath the shadow of its branches. A single Cypress standing alone, like that in the Bartram Garden, is a grand object, uniting with the expression of great elegance and lightness in its foliage, that of magnificence, when we perceive its extraordinary height, and huge stem and branches.

In composition, the Cypress produces the happiest effect, when it is planted with the hemlock and firs, with which it harmonizes well in the form of its foliage, while its soft light green hue is beautifully opposed to the richer and darker tints of those thickly-clad evergreens. Wherever there is a moist and rather rich soil, the Cypress may be advantageously planted : for although we have seen it thrive well on a fertile dry loam, yet to attain all its lofty proportions, it requires a soil where its thirsty roots can drink in a sufficient supply of moisture. There its growth is quite rapid ; and although it may, at first, suffer a little from the cold at the north, in severe winters, yet it continues its progress, and ultimately becomes a stately tree.

In many parts of the southern states, the timber of this tree, which is of excellent quality, is extensively used in the construction of the framework and outer covering of houses. It is also esteemed for shingles ; and a large trade has long been carried on from the south in Cypress shingles. Posts made of this tree are found to be very lasting ; and it is also employed for water-pipes, masts of vessels, etc. In the north, its place is supplied by the Pine

timber, but in many southern cities, particularly New
Orleans, it will be found to enter into the composition of
almost every building.

In the nurseries, the Cypress is usually propagated from
the seed; and as it sends down strong roots, it should be
transplanted where it is finally to grow before it attains too
great a development.

The European Cypress (*Cupressus sempervirens*), a
beautiful evergreen tree, shaped like a small Lombardy
poplar, which is the principal ornament of the churchyards
and cemeteries abroad, is unfortunately too tender to
endure the winter in any of the states north of Virginia.
South of that state, it may probably become naturalized,
and serve to add to the catalogue of beautiful indigenous
evergreen trees.

From its dark and sombre tint, and perpetual verdure, it
is peculiarly the emblem of grief:

> " Binde you my brows with *mourning* Cyparesse,
>   And palish twigs of deadlier poplar tree,
>   Or if some sadder shades ye can devise,
>   Those sadder shades vaile my light-loathing eyes."
>
> BP. HALL.

THE LARCH TREE. *Larix.*

Nat. Ord. Coniferæ.   *Lin. Syst.* Monœcia, Monadelphia.

The Larch is a resinous, cone-bearing tree, belonging
to the Pine family, but differing from that genus in the
annual shedding of its leaves like other deciduous trees.
In Europe it is a native of the coldest parts of the Alps
and Appenines; and in America, is indigenous to the most

northern parts of the Union, and the Canadas.   The leaves
are collected in little bunches, and the branches shoot out
from the main stem in a horizontal, or, more generally
in a declining position.

[Fig. 34. The European Larch.]

For picturesque beauty, the Larch is almost unrivalled.
Unlike most other trees which must grow old, uncouth, and
misshapen before they can attain that expression, this is
singularly so, as soon almost as it begins to assume the
stature of a tree.   It can never be called a beautiful tree,
so far as beauty consists in smooth outlines, a finely rounded
head, or gracefully drooping branches.   But it has what is
perhaps more valuable, as being more rare,—the expression
of boldness and picturesqueness peculiar to itself, and

which it seems to have caught from the wild and rugged chasms, rocks, and precipices of its native mountains. There its irregular and spiry top and branches, harmonize admirably with the abrupt variation of the surrounding hills, and suit well with the gloomy grandeur of those frowning heights.

Like all highly expressive and characteristic trees, much more care is necessary in introducing the Larch into artificial scenery judiciously, than round-headed trees. If planted in abundance, it becomes monotonous, from the similitude of its form in different specimens; it should therefore be introduced sparingly, and always for some special purpose. This purpose may be either to give spirit to a group of other trees, to strengthen the already picturesque character of a scene, or to give life and variety to one naturally tame and uninteresting. All these objects can be fully effected by the Larch; and although it is by far the most suited to harmonize with and strengthen the expression of scenery naturally grand, or picturesque, with which it most readily enters into combination; yet, in the hands of taste, there can be no reason why so marked a tree should not be employed in giving additional expression to scenery of a tamer character.

The extremely rapid growth of this tree when planted upon thin, barren, and dry soils, is another great merit which it possesses as an ornamental tree; and it is also a necessary one to enable it to thrive well on those very rocky and barren soils, where it is most in character with the surrounding objects. It is highly valuable to produce effect or shelter suddenly, on portions of an estate, too thin or meagre in their soil to afford the sustenance necessary to the growth of many other deciduous trees.

The Larch is the great timber tree of Europe. Its wood is remarkably heavy, strong, and durable, exceeding in all those qualities the best English oak. To these, it is said to add the peculiarity of being almost uninflammable, and resisting the influence of heat for a long time. Vitruvius relates that when Cæsar attacked the castle of Larignum, near the Alps, whose gate was commanded by a tower built of this wood, from the top of which the besieged annoyed him with their stones and darts, he commanded his army to surround it with fagots, and set fire to the whole. When, however, all the former were consumed, he was astonished to find the Larch tower uninjured.*

The Larch is unquestionably the most enduring timber that we have. It is remarkable, that whilst the red wood or heart wood is not formed at all in the other resinous trees, till they have lived for a good many years, the Larch, on the contrary, begins to make it soon after it is planted; and while you may fell a Scotch fir of thirty years old, and find no red wood in it, you can hardly cut down a young Larch large enough to be a walking stick, without finding just such a proportion of red wood compared to its diameter as a 'ree, as you will find in the largest Larch tree in the forest, compared to its diameter. To prove the value of the Larch as a timber tree, several experiments were made in the river Thames. Posts of equal thickness and strength, some of Larch and others of oak, were driven down facing the river wall, where they were alternately covered with water by the effect of the tide, and then left dry by its fall. This species of alternation is the most trying of all circumstances for the endurance of timber; and accordingly the oaken posts decayed, and were twice renewed in the course of a very few years,

* Newton's Vitruvius, p. 40.

while those that were made of the Larch remained altogether unchanged.

Besides the foregoing species (*Larix Europea*)*we have two native sorts much resembling it; which are chiefly found in the states of Maine, Vermont, and New Hampshire. These are known by the names of the Red Larch (*L. Microcarpa*) and the Black Larch (*L. pendula*), which latter is often called *Hackmatack*. In the coldest parts of the Union, these often grow to 80 and 100 feet high; but in the middle states they are only seen in the swamps, and appear not to thrive so well except in such situations. For this reason the European Larch is of course greatly preferable when plantations are to be made, either for profit or ornament. The latter is generally increased from seed in the nurseries.

The American Larches are well worthy a place where sufficient moisture can be commanded, as their peculiar forms are striking, though not so finely picturesque as that of the European species.

* A very curious and remarkable addition to the varieties of this genus is (*Larix pendula*) the Weeping Larch, differing from our (*Pendula Americana*) American Weeping Larch, and much more extraordinary. When worked ten or fifteen feet high, the inclination of the branches and spray is immediately downward, and when gently swayed by the wind, it is excessively graceful and pretty. We do not know a more distinctive and striking tree, or one more rare. It seems difficult to transplant—at least this is our experience—and it can only be increased by grafting by approach. Nurserymen are apt to work it too low: it should never be grafted at a less distance than ten to twelve feet --and for some years, it should be supported by a stout stake, as the tree is apt to be top-heavy. This curious variety was found accidentally, if we remember right, some ten to fifteen years since, in a nursery near Hereford, England, by a Mr. Godsall, and is known in English nurseries as *Larix communis pendula Godsalii*. *Larix Griffithii*, the Sikkin Larch, and *Abies kœmferi* (though at present classed as an *Abies*, we believe may prove to be Larch), are two very new varieties, too expensive at present to be generally introduced. A *Kœmferi*, known also as the Golden Pine of China, is very highly extolled for its beautiful green in Summer, and golden color in Autumn or Winter.—H. W. S.

FIG. 35.—WEEPING LARCH, at Wodenethe. Age, 8 yrs. Height, 12 ft. Clr. 35 ft.

FIG. 36.—LARGE-LEAVED MAGNOLIA, at Laurel Hill Cemetery. Age, 10 yrs. Ht. 39 ft.

In the upper part of Massachusetts, we have observed them in their native soils growing 70 or 80 feet high, and assuming a highly pleasing appearance. Their foliage is bluish-green, and more delicate; yet altogether the American Larch appears to be more stiff and formal (except far north) than the foreign tree.

THE VIRGILIA TREE. *Virgilia.**

Nat. Ord. Leguminaceæ.   *Lin. Syst.* Decandria, Monogynia.

This fine American tree, still very rare in our ornamental plantations, is a native of West Tennessee, and the banks of the Kentucky river, and in its wild localities seems confined to rather narrow limits. It was named, when first discovered, after the poet Virgil, whose agreeable *Georgics* have endeared him to all lovers of nature and a country life.

The Virgilia is certainly one of the most beautiful of all that class of trees bearing papilionaceous, or pea-shaped flowers, and pinnate leaves, of which the common locust may serve as a familiar example. It grows to a fine, rather broad head, about 30 or 40 feet high, with dense and luxuriant foliage—much more massy and finely tufted than that of most other pinnated-leaved trees. Each leaf is composed of seven or eight leaflets, three or four inches long, and half that breadth, the whole leaf being more than a foot in length. These expand rather late in the spring, and are, about the middle of May, followed by numerous terminal racemes, or clusters, of the most delicate and charming pea-shaped blossoms, of a pure white. These

* Cladeastris tinctoria. *Torrey and Gray.*

clusters are six or eight inches in length, and quite broad, the flowers daintily formed, and arranged in a much more graceful, loose, and easy manner, than those of the locust. They have a very agreeable, slight perfume, especially in the evening, and the whole effect of the tree, when standing singly on a lawn and filled with blossoms, is highly elegant.

When the blossoms disappear, they are followed by the pods, about the fourth of an inch wide, and three or four inches long, containing a few seeds. These ripen in July or August.

This tree is frequently called the *Yellow-wood* in its native haunts—its heart wood abounding in a fine yellow coloring matter, which, however, is said to be rather difficult to fix, or render permanent. The bark is beautifully smooth, and of a greenish grey color. In autumn, the leaves, when they die off, take a lively yellow tint.

This tree grows pretty rapidly, and is very agreeable in its form and foliage, even while young. It commences flowering when about ten or fifteen feet high, and we can recommend it with confidence to the amateur of choice trees as worthy of a conspicuous place in the smallest collection.

The only species known is *Virgilia lutea.* It was first described by Michaux, and was sent to England about the year 1812. Quite the finest planted specimens within our knowledge are growing in some of the old seats in the northern suburbs of Philadelphia, where there are several thirty or forty feet in height, and exceedingly beautiful, both in their form and blossoms. A small specimen on our lawn, eighteen feet high, blossoms now very pro-fusely.

The Paulownia Tree. *Paulownia.*

Nat. Ord. Scrophulariaceæ.   *Lin. Syst.* ——— ———

The Paulownia is an entirely new ornamental tree, very lately introduced into our gardens and pleasure-grounds from Japan, and is likely to prove hardy here, wherever the Ailantus stands the winter, being naturally from the same soil and climate as that tree. It is remarkable for the large size of its foliage, and the great rapidity of its growth. The largest leaves are more than two feet in diameter, slightly rough or hairy, and serrated on the edges. They are heart-shaped, and have been likened to those of the Catalpa, but they perhaps more nearly resemble those of the common Sun-flower.

In its growth, this tree, while young, equals or exceeds the *Ailantus.* In rich soils, near Paris, it has produced shoots, in a single season, 12 or 14 feet in length. After being two or three years planted, it commences yielding its blossoms in panicled clusters. These are bluish lilac, of an open mouthed, tubular form, are very abundantly distributed, and, together with the large foliage, and the robust habit of growth, give this tree a gay and striking appearance. Its flower buds open during the last of April, or early in May, and have a slight, syringa-like perfume.

Should the Paulownia prove as hardy as (from our fine dry summers for ripening its wood) we confidently anticipate * it will be worthy of a prominent place in every arrangement of choice ornamental trees.

* We doubt if this tree proves quite as hardy as Mr. Downing believed. Our own trees, some of the oldest in the country, have missed their bloom for three years—though previously, they had blossomed regularly and well. It is not impossible that, as the tree gets older, and its growth less rampant, it may ripen off its wood better, and thus be in a better condition to resist Spring frosts.—H. W. S.

SECTION V.

EVERGREEN ORNAMENTAL TREES.

The History and Description of all the finest Hardy Evergreen Trees. REMARKS on THEIR EFFECTS in LANDSCAPE GARDENING, INDIVIDUALLY AND IN COMPOSITION. Their Cultivation, etc. The Pines. The Firs. The Cedar of Lebanon, and the Deodar Cedar. The Red Cedar. The Arbor Vitæ. The Holly. The Yew, etc.

> Beneath the forest's skirt I rest,
> ·Whose branching Pines rise dark and high,
> And hear the breezes of the West
> Among the threaded foliage sigh.
>
> BRYANT.

THE PINE TREE. *Pinus.*

Nat. Ord. Coniferæ.   *Lin. Syst.* Monœcia, Monodelphia.

H E Pines compose by far the most important genus of evergreen trees. In either continent they form the densest and most extensive forests known, and their wood in civil and naval architecture, and for various other purposes, is more generally used than any other. In the United States and the Canadas, there are ten species; in the territory west of the Mississippi, to the Pacific, including Mexico, there are fourteen; in Europe fourteen; in Asia, eight, and in Africa, two species. All the colder parts of the old world

—the mountains of Switzerland and the Alps, the shores of the Baltic, vast tracts in Norway, Sweden, Germany, Poland, and Russia, as well as millions of acres in our own country, abound with immense and interminable forests of Pine. Capable of enduring extreme cold, growing on thin soils, and flourishing in an atmosphere, the mean temperature of which is not greater than 37° or 38° *Fahrenheit,* they are found as far north as latitude 68° in Lapland; while on mountains they grow at a greater elevation than any other arborescent plant. On Mount Blanc, the Pines grow within 2,800 feet of the line of perpetual snow.* In Mexico, also, Humboldt found them higher than any other tree; and Lieut. Glennie describes them as growing in thick forests on the mountain of Popocatapetl, as high as 12, 693 feet, beyond which altitude vegetation ceases entirely.†

The Pines are, most of them, trees of considerable magnitude and lofty growth, varying from 40 to 150 or even 200 feet in height in favorable situations, rising with a perpendicular trunk, which is rarely divided into branches bearing much proportionate size to the main stem, as in most deciduous trees. The branches are much more horizontal than those of the latter class (excepting the Larch). The leaves are linear or needle-shaped, and are always found arranged in little parcels of from two to six, the number varying in the different species. The blossoms are produced in spring, and the seeds, borne in cones, are not ripened, in many sorts, until the following autumn. Every part of the stem abounds in a resinous juice, which is extracted, and forms in the

* Edinburgh Phil. Journ.
† Proc. Geological Soc Lond.   Arb. Brit.

various shapes of tar, pitch, rosin, turpentine, balsam, **etc.** a considerable article of trade and export.

As ornamental trees, the Pines are peculiarly valuable for the deep verdure of their foliage, which, unchanged by the severity of the seasons, is beautiful at all periods, and especially so in winter ; for the picturesque forms which many of them assume when fully grown ; and for the effectual shelter and protection which they afford in cold, bleak, and exposed situations. We shall here particularize those species, natives of either hemisphere, that are most valuable to the planter, and are also capable of enduring the open air of the middle states.

The White Pine (*P. strobus*), called also Sapling Pine and Apple Pine, in various parts of this country, and Weymouth Pine abroad, is undoubtedly the most beautiful North American tree of the genus. The foliage is much lighter in color, more delicate in texture, and the whole tufting of the leaves more airy and pleasing than that of the other species. It is also beautiful in every stage of its growth, from a plant to a stately tree of 150 feet. When it grows in strong soil, it becomes thick and compact in its head ; but its most beautiful form is displayed when it stands in a dry and gravelly site ; there it shoots up with a majestic and stately shaft, studded every six or eight feet with horizontal tiers of branches and foliage. The hue of the leaves is much paler and less sombre than that of the other native sorts ; and being less stiffly set upon the branches, is more easily put in motion by the wind ; the murmuring of the wind among the Pine tops is, poetically thought to give out rather a melancholy sound —

" The pines of Mœnalus were heard to mourn,
And sounds of woe along the grove were borne,"

says Virgil, speaking of the European Pine. But the murmur of the slight breeze among the foliage of the White Pine gives out a remarkably soothing and agreeable sound, which agrees better with the description of Leigh Hunt:

> " And then there fled by me a rush of air
> That stirr'd up all the other foliage there,
> Filling the solitude with panting tongues,
> At which the Pines woke up into their songs,
> Shaking their *choral locks.*"

Pickering, one of our own poets, thus characterizes the melody:

> " The overshadowing pines alone, through which I roam,
> Their verdure keep, although it darker looks ;
> And hark ! as it comes sighing through the grove,
> The exhausted gale, a spirit there awakens,
> That wild and melancholy music makes."

This species—the White Pine—seldom becomes flattened or rounded on the summit in old age, like many other sorts, but preserves its graceful and tapering form entire. From its pleasing growth and color, we consider it by far the most desirable kind for planting in the proximity of buildings, and its growth for an evergreen is also quite rapid.

The leaves of the White Pine are thickly disposed on the branches, in little bundles or parcels of five. The cones are about five inches long: they hang, when nearly ripe, in a pendulous manner from the branches, and open, to shed their seeds, about the first of October. The bark on trees less than twenty years old is remarkably smooth, but becomes cracked and rough, like that of the other

Pines, when they grow old, although it never splits and separates itself from the trunk in scales, as in other species. The great forests of White Pine lie in the northern parts of the Union ; and the geographical range of this tree is comprised chiefly between New York and the 47th degree of north latitude, it being neither capable of resisting the fierce heat of the south, nor the intense cold of the extreme northern regions. In Maine, New Hampshire, and Vermont, the White Pine abounds in various situations, adapting itself to every variety of soil, from dry, gravelly upland, to swamps constantly wet. Michaux measured two trunks near the river Kennebec, one of which was 154 feet long, and 54 inches in diameter ; the other 144 feet long, and 44 inches in diameter, at three feet from the ground. Dr. Dwight also mentions a specimen on the Kattskill 249 feet long, and several on the Unadilla 200 feet long, and three in diameter.* These, though they are remarkable specimens, show the stately altitude which this fine species sometimes attains, equalling in majesty the grandest specimens of the old world :

> ———The rougher rinded Pine,
> The great Argoan ship's brave ornament,
> Which, coveting with his high top's extent
> To make the mountains touch the stars divine,
> Decks all the forest with embellishment.
>
> SPENSER.

The Yellow Pine (*P. mitis*) is a fine evergreen, usually reaching a stature of 50 or 60 feet, with a nearly uniform diameter of about 18 inches for two-thirds of its length. The branches generally take a handsome conical shape, and the whole head considerably resembles that of the spruce.

* Dwight's Travels, Vol. iv. p. 21—26.

whence it is sometimes called the *Spruce Pine.* The term Yellow Pine arises from the color of the wood as contrasted with that of the foregoing sort, which is white. The leaves of this species are long and flexible, arranged in pairs upon the branches, and have a fine dark green color. The cones are very small, scarcely measuring an inch and a half in length, and are clothed on the exterior with short spines. The growth is quite slow.

The Yellow Pine is rarely found above Albany to the northward, but it extends as far south as the Floridas. It grows in the greatest abundance in New Jersey, Maryland, and Virginia, and sometimes measures five or six feet in circumference. In plantations, it has the valuable property to recommend it, of growing on the very poorest lands.

The Pitch Pine (*P. rigida*) is a very distinct sort, common in the whole of the United States east of the Alleghanies. It is very stiff and formal in its growth when young, but as it approaches maturity, it becomes one of the most picturesque trees of the genus. The branches, which shoot out horizontally, bend downwards at the extremities, and the top of the tree, when old, takes a flattened shape. The whole air and expression of the tree is wild and romantic, and is harmonious with portions of scenery where these characters predominate. The leaves are collected in threes, and the color of the foliage is a dark green. The cones are pyramidal, from one to three inches long, and armed with short spines.

The bark of this kind of Pine is remarkably rough, black, and furrowed, even upon young trees; and the wood is filled with resinous sap, from which pitch and tar are copiously supplied. The trees grow in various parts of the country, both on the most meagre soils and in moist swamps, with almost equal facility. In the latter situations they are, however, comparatively destitute of resin, but the stems often rise to 80 feet in elevation.

The foregoing are the finest and most important species of the north. The Red Pine (*Pinus rubra*) and the Grey Pine are species of small or secondary size, chiefly indigenous to British America. The Jersey Pine (*P. inops*) is a dwarfish species, often called the Scrub Pine, which seldom grows more than 25 feet high.

There are some splendid species that are confined to the southern states, where they grow in great luxuriance. Among the most interesting of these is the Long-leaved Pine (*P. Australis*), a tree of 70 feet elevation, with superb wandlike foliage, borne in threes, often nearly a foot in length. The cones are also seven or eight inches long, containing a kernel or seed of agreeable flavor. As this tree grows as far north as Norfolk in Virginia, we are strongly inclined to believe that it might be naturalized in the climate of the middle states, and think it would become one of the most valuable additions to our catalogue of evergreen trees. The Loblolly Pine (*P. Tæda*) of Virginia has also fine foliage, six inches or more in length, and grows to 80 feet in height. Besides these already named, the southern states produce the Pond Pine (*P. Serotina*), which resembles considerably the Pitch Pine, with, however, longer leaves, and the Table Mountain Pine (*P. Pungens*), which grows 40 or 50 feet high, and is found exclusively upon that part of the Alleghany range.

We must not forget in this enumeration of the Pines of North America, the magnificent species of California and the North-West coast. The most splendid of these was discovered in Northern California, and named the *Pinus*

Lambertiana, in honor of that distinguished botanist, A. B. Lambert, Esq., of London, the author of a superb work on this genus of trees. It is undoubtedly one of the finest evergreens in the world, averaging from 100 to 200 feet in height. Its discoverer, Mr. Douglass, the indefatigable collector of the Horticultural Society of London, measured one of these trees that had blown down, which was two hundred and fifteen feet in length, and fifty-seven feet nine inches in circumference, at three feet from the root; while at one hundred and thirty-four feet from the root, it was seventeen feet five inches in girth. This, it is stated, is by no means the maximum height of the species. The cones of the Lambert Pine measure sixteen inches in length; and the seeds are eaten by the natives of those regions, either roasted or made into cakes, after being pounded. The other species found by Mr. Douglass grow naturally in the mountain valleys of the western coast, and several of them, as the *Pinus grandis* and *nobilis,* are almost as lofty as the foregoing sort; while *Pinus monticola* and *P. Sabiniana* are highly beautiful in their forms and elegant in foliage. The seeds of nearly all these sorts were first sent to the garden of the London Horticultural Society, where many of the young trees are now growing; and we hope that they will soon be introduced into our plantations, which they are so admirably calculated, by their elegant foliage and stupendous magnitude, to adorn.

The European Pines next deserve our attention. The most common species in the north of Europe is the Scotch Pine (*P. sylvestris*), a dark, tall, evergreen tree, with bluish foliage, of 80 feet in height, which furnishes most of the deal timber of Europe. It is one of the most rapid of all the Pines in its growth, even on poor soils, and is therefore

valuable in new places. The Stone Pine (*P. pinea*) is a
native of the South of Europe, where it is decidedly the
most picturesque evergreen tree of that continent. It
belongs peculiarly to Italy, and its "vast canopy, supported
on a naked column of great height, forms one of the chief
and peculiar beauties in Italian scenery, and in the living
landscapes of Claude." We regret that it is too tender to
bear our winters, but its place may in a great measure be
supplied by the Pinaster or Cluster Pine (*P. pinaster*),
which is quite hardy, and succeeds well in the United
States. This has much of the same picturesque expression,
depressed or rounded head, and tall columnar stem, which
mark the Stone Pine; while its thickly massed foliage,
clustering cones, and rough bark, render it distinct and
strikingly interesting.

The Corsican Pine (*P. laricio*) is a handsome, regular
shaped, pyramidal tree, with the branches disposed in tiers
like those of the White Pine. It grows to a large size, and
is valued for its extremely dark green foliage, thickly spread
upon the branches. It is also one of the most rapid growers
among the foreign sorts, and has been found to grow
remarkably well upon the barren chalk downs of England.
Pinus cembra is a very slow growing, though valuable
kind, indigenous to Switzerland, and hardy here.

These are the principal European species that deserve
notice here for their ornamental qualities. Some splendid
additions have been made to this genus, by the discovery
of new species on the Himalaya mountains of Asia; and
from the great elevation at which they are found growing
wild, we have reason to hope that they will become naturalized in our climate.

We must not leave this extensive family of trees without

adverting to their numerous and important uses. In the United States, full four-fifths of all the houses built are constructed of the White and Yellow Pine, chiefly of the former. Soft, easily worked, light and fine in texture, it is almost universally employed in carpentry, and for all the purposes of civil architecture; while the tall stately trunks furnish masts and spars, not only for our own vessels, but many of those of England. A great commerce is therefore carried on in the timber of this tree, and vast quantities of the boards, etc., are annually exported to Europe. The Yellow and Pitch Pine furnish much of the enormous supplies of fuel consumed by the great number of steamboats employed in navigating our numerous inland rivers. The Long-leaved Pine is the great timber tree of the southern states; and when we take into account all its various products, we must admit it to be the most valuable tree of the whole family. The consumption of the wood of this tree in building, in the southern states, is immense; and its sap furnishes nearly all the turpentine, tar, pitch, and rosin, used in this country, or exported to Europe. The *turpentine* flows from large incisions made in the trunk (into boxes fastened to the side of the trees for that purpose) during the whole of the spring and summer. *Spirit of turpentine* is obtained from this by distillation. *Tar* is procured by burning the dead wood in kilns, when it flows out in a current from a conduit made in the bottom. *Pitch* is prepared by boiling tar until it is about one half diminished in bulk; and *rosin* is the residuum of the distillation when spirit of turpentine is made. The Carolinas produce all these in the greatest abundance, and so long ago as 1807, the exportation of them to England alone amounted to nearly $800,000 in that single year.

THE FIR TREES. *Abies.*

Nat Ord. Coniferæ.   *Lin. Syst.* Monœcia, Monadelphia.

The Fir trees differ from the Pines, to which they are nearly related, in having much shorter leaves, which are placed *singly* upon the branches, instead of being collected in little bundles or parcels of two, three, or five, as is the case in all Pines. They generally grow in a more conical manner than the latter, and in ornamental plantations owe their beauty in most cases more to their symmetrical regularity of growth than to picturesque expression.

The Balsam, or Balm of Gilead Fir (*A. balsamea*), sometimes also called the American Silver Fir, is one of the most ornamental of our native evergreens. It is found most abundantly in Maine and Nova Scotia, but is scattered more or less on the mountain tops, and in cold swamps, through various other parts of the Union. At Pine Orchard, near the Catskill Mountain-house, it flourishes well, though never seen below the elevation of 1,800 feet. When standing singly, it forms a perfect pyramid of fine dark green foliage, 30 or 40 feet high, regularly clothed from the bottom to the top. The leaves about half or three-fourths of an inch long, are silvery white on the under surface, though dark green above ; and are inserted both on the sides and tops of the branches. It is one of the most beautiful evergreens for planting in grounds near the house, and is perhaps more cultivated for that purpose than any other in the Union. The cones, which are four or five inches long, like those of the European Silver Fir point upwards. However small the plants of this Fir may be, they are still interesting, as they

FIG 87.—The SILVER FIR, at the Residence of Dr. Johnson, Germantown, Pa.
Age, 57 years. Height, ‵00 feet.

display the same symmetry as full grown trees. The deep green color of the verdure of the Balm of Gilead Fir is retained unchanged in all its beauty through the severest winters, which causes it to contrast agreeably with the paler tints of the Spruces. On the trunks of trees of this species are found small vesicles or blisters, filled with a liquid resin, which is extracted and sold under the name of Balm of Gilead,* for its medicinal virtues.

The European Silver Fir (*A. picea*) strongly resembles, when young, the Balsam Fir. But its leaves are longer and coarser, and the cones are much larger, while it also attains twice or three times the size of the latter. In the forests of Germany it sometimes rises over 100 feet ; and it always becomes a large tree in a favorable soil. It grows slowly during the first twenty years, but afterwards advances with much more rapidity. It thrives well, and is quite hardy in this country.

The Norway Spruce Fir (*A. communis*†) is by far the handsomest of that division of the Firs called the Spruces. It generally rises with a perfectly straight trunk to the height of from 80 to 150 feet. It is a native, as its name denotes, of the colder parts of Europe, and consequently grows well in the northern states. The branches hang down with a fine graceful curve or sweep ; and although the leaves are much paler than those of the foregoing kinds, yet the thick fringe-like tufts of foliage which clothe the branches, give the whole tree a rich, dark appearance. The large cones, too, always nearly six inches long, are

---

* The true Balm of Gilead is an Asiatic herb, *Amyris gileadensis.*

† *Abies excelsa.*

beautifully pendent, and greatly increase the beauty of an old tree of this kind.

The Norway Spruce is the great tree of the Alps; and as a park tree, to stand alone, we scarcely know a more beautiful one. It then generally branches not quite down to the ground; and its fine, sweeping, feathery branches hang down in the most graceful and pleasing manner. There are some superb specimens of this species in various gardens of the middle states, 80 or 100 feet high.

The Black, or Double Spruce (*A. nigra*), sometimes also called the Red Spruce, is very common in the north; and, according to Michaux, forms a third part of the forests of Vermont, Maine, New Hampshire, as well as New Brunswick and Lower Canada. The leaves are quite short and stiff, and clothe the young branches around the whole surface; and the whole tree, where it much abounds, has rather a gloomy aspect. In the favorable humid black soils of those countries, the Black Spruce grows 70 feet high, forming a fine tall pyramid of verdure. But it is rarely found in abundance further south, except in swamps, where its growth is much less strong and vigorous. Mingled with other evergreens, it adds to the variety, and the peculiar coloring of its foliage gives value to the livelier tints of other species of Pine and Fir.

The White or Single Spruce (*A. alba*) is a smaller and less common tree than the foregoing, though it is often found in the same situations. The leaves are more thinly arranged on the young shoots, and they are longer and project more from the branches. The color, however, is a distinguishing characteristic between the two sorts; for while in the Black Spruce it is very dark, in this species it is of a light bluish green tint. The cones are also much larger on the White Spruce tree.

The Hemlock Spruce, or, as it is more commonly called, the *Hemlock* (*A. canadensis*), is one of the finest and most distinct of this tribe of trees. It is most abundantly multiplied in the extreme northern portions of the Union; and abounds more or less, in scattered groups and thickets, throughout all the middle states, while at the south it is confined chiefly to the mountains.

It prefers a soil, which, though slightly moist, is less humid than that where the Black Spruce succeeds best; and it thrives well in the deep cool shades of mountain valleys. In the Highlands of the Hudson it grows in great luxuriance; and in one locality, the sides of a valley near Crow's nest, the surface is covered with the most superb growths of this tree, reaching up from the water's edge to the very summit of the hill, 1,400 feet high, like a rich and shadowy mantle, sprinkled here and there only with the lighter and more delicate foliage of deciduous trees.

The average height of the Hemlock in good soils is about 70 or 80 feet; and when standing alone, or in very small groups, it is one of the most beautiful coniferous trees. The leaves are disposed in two rows on each side of the branches, and considerably resemble those of the Yew, though looser in texture, and livelier in color. The foliage, when the tree has grown to some height, hangs from the branches in loose pendulous tufts, which give it a peculiarly graceful appearance. When young, the form of the head is regularly pyramidal; but when the tree attains more age, it often assumes very irregular and picturesque forms.

Sometimes it grows up in a thick, dense, dark mass of foliage, only varied by the pendulous branches, which project beyond the grand mass of the tree ; at others it forms a loose, airy, and graceful top, permeable to the slightest breeze, and waving its loose tufts of leaves to every passing breath of air. In almost all cases, it is extremely ornamental, and we regret that it is not more generally employed in decorating the grounds of our residences. It should be transplanted (like all of this class of trees) quite early in the spring, the roots being preserved as nearly entire as possible, and not suffered to become the least dried, before they are replaced in the soil.

The uses of the Fir tree are important. The Norway Spruce Fir furnishes the white deal timber so extensively employed in Europe for all the various purposes of building; and its tall, tapering stems afford fine masts for vessels. The Black Spruce timber is also highly valuable, and is thought by many persons to surpass in excellence that of the Norway Spruce. The young shoots also enter into the composition of the celebrated *Spruce beer* of this country, a delightful and very healthful beverage. And the Hemlock not only furnishes a vast quantity of the joists used in building frame-houses, but supplies the tanners with an abundance of bark, which, when mixed with that of the oak, is highly esteemed in the preparation of leather.

We regret that the fine evergreen trees both of this country and Europe, which compose the Pine and Fir tribes, have not hitherto received more of the attention of planters. It is inexpressible how much they add to the beauty of a country residence in winter. At that season, when, during three or four months the landscape is bleak and covered with snow, these noble trees, properly intermingled with the groups in view from the window, or those surrounding the house, give an appearance of verdure and life to the scene which cheats winter of half its dreariness. In exposed quarters, also, and in all windy and bleak situations, groups of evergreens form the most effectual shelter at all seasons of the year, while many of them have the great additional recommendation of growing upon the most meagre soils.

In fine country residences abroad, it is becoming customary to select some extensive and suitable locality, where all the species of Pines and Firs are collected together, and allowed to develope themselves in their full beauty of proportion. Such a spot is called a *Pinetum ;* and the effect of all the different species growing in the same assemblage, and contrasting their various forms, heights, and peculiarities, cannot but be strikingly elegant. One of the largest and oldest collections of this kind is the Pinetum of Lord Grenville, at Dropmore, near Windsor, England. This contains nearly 100 kinds, comprising all the sorts known to English botanists, that will endure the open air of their mild climate. The great advantage of these Pinetums is, that many of the more delicate species, which if exposed singly would perish, thrive well, and become quite naturalized under the shelter of the more hardy and vigorous sorts.

THE CEDAR OF LEBANON TREE. *Cedrus*

Nat. Ord. Coniferæ.   *Lin. Syst.* Monœcia, Monadelphia.

The Cedar of Lebanon is universally admitted by European authors to be the noblest evergreen tree of the old world. Its native sites are the elevated valleys and ridges of Mount Lebanon and the neighboring heights of the lofty groups of Asia Minor. There it once covered immense forests, but it is supposed these have never recovered from the inroads made upon them by the forty score thousand hewers employed by Solomon to procure the timber for the erection of the Temple. Modern travellers speak of them as greatly diminished in number, though there are still specimens measuring thirty-six feet in circumference. Mount Lebanon is inhabited by numerous Maronite Christians, who hold annually a celebration of the Transfiguration under the shade of the existing trees, which they call the " *Feast of Cedars.*"

The Cedar of Lebanon is nearly related to the Larch, having its leaves collected in parcels like that tree, but differs widely in the circumstance of its foliage being *evergreen*. It is remarkable for the wide extension of its branches, and the immense surface covered by its overshadowing canopy of foliage. In the sacred writings it is often alluded to as an emblem of great strength, beauty, and duration. "Behold the Assyrian was a Cedar in Lebanon, with fair branches, and with a shadowing shroud, and of an high stature ; and his top was among the thick boughs. His boughs were multiplied, and his branches became long. The fir trees were not like his boughs, nor

FIG. 38.—CEDAR OF LEBANON, at Woodlawn, near Princeton, N. J. Height, 36 ft.

the chestnut trees like his branches, nor any tree in the garden of God like unto him in beauty."*

In England the Cedar of Lebanon appears to have become quite naturalized. There it is considered by far the most ornamental of all the Pine tribe,—possessing, when full grown, an air of dignity and grandeur beyond any other tree. To attain the fullest beauty of development, it should always stand alone, so that its far-spreading horizontal branches can have full room to stretch out and expand themselves on every side. Loudon, in his Arboretum, gives a representation of a superb specimen now growing at Sion House, the seat of the Duke of Northumberland, which is 72 feet high, 24 in circumference, and covers an area, with its huge depending branches, of 117 feet. There are many other Cedars in England almost equal to this in grandeur. Sir T. D. Lauder gives an account of one at Whitton, which blew down in 1779: it then measured 70 feet in height, 16 feet in circumference, and covered an area of 100 feet in diameter. To show the rapidity of the growth of this tree, he quotes three Cedars of Lebanon, which were planted at Hopetoun House, Scotland, in the year 1748. The measurement is the circumference of the trunks, and shows the rapid increase *after* they have attained a large size.

	1801.		1820.		1825.		1833.		Increase in 32 years.	
	ft.	in.	ft.	in.	ft.	in.	ft.	in.	ft.	in.
First Cedar,	10	0	13	1½	14	0	15	1	5	1
Second do.	8	6	10	9½	11	4	12	3	3	9
Third do.	7	10	9	9½	10	8	11	6	3	8

A Chestnut measured at the same periods, only increased 2 7

* Ezekiel xxxi.

From the above table, it will be seen how congenial even the cold climate of Scotland is to the growth of this tree. Indeed in its native soils, the tops of the surrounding hills are almost perpetually covered with snow, and it is, therefore, one of the very hardiest of the evergreens of the old world. There is no reason why it should not succeed admirably in many parts of the United States ; and when we consider its great size, fine dark green foliage, and wide spreading limbs which

> " ———Overarching, frame
> Most solemn domes within,"
>
> SHELLEY.

as well as the many interesting associations connected with it, we cannot but think it better worth our early attention, and extensive introduction, than almost any other foreign tree. Evergreens are comparatively difficult to import, and as we have made the experiment of importing Cedars of Lebanon from the English nurseries with but indifferent success, we would advise that persons attempting its cultivation should procure the cones containing the seeds from England, when they may be reared directly in our own soil, which will of course be an additional advantage to the future growth of the tree.*

The situations found to be most favorable to this Cedar, in the parks and gardens of Europe, are sandy or gravelly soils, either with a moist subsoil underneath, or in the neighborhood of springs, or bodies of water. In such places it is found to advance with a rapidity equal to the Larch,

---

* The finest Cedar of Lebanon in the Union, is growing in the grounds of T. Ash, Esq., of Westchester Co., N. Y., being 50 feet high and of corresponding breadth. It stands near a Purple-leaved Beech, equally large and beautiful.

one of the fastest growing timber trees, as we have already noticed.

The Deodara, or Indian Cedar (*Cedrus Deodara*), is a magnificent species of this tree, recently introduced from the high mountains of Nepal and Indo-Tartary. It stands the climate of Scotland, and appears likely to succeed here wherever the Cedar of Lebanon will flourish. In its native country it is described as being a lofty and majestic tree, frequently attaining the height of 150 feet, with a trunk 30 feet in circumference. The leaves are larger than those of the Cedar of Lebanon, of a deeper bluish green, covered with a silvery bloom; the cones, borne in pairs, are of a reddish brown color, and are both longer and broader than those of the latter species. In some parts of Upper India it is considered a sacred tree (*Deodara*—tree of God), and is only used to burn as incense in days of high ceremony; but in others it is held in the highest esteem as a timber tree, having all the good qualities of the Cedar of Lebanon —its great durability being attested by its sound state in the roofs of temples of that country, which cannot have been built less than 200 years.

We have but just introduced the Deodara into the United States, and can therefore say little of its growth or beauty here, though we have little doubt that it will prove one of the noblest evergreen trees for our pleasure grounds. Loudon says, "the specimens in England are yet small; but the feathery lightness of its spreading branches, and the beautiful glaucous hue of its leaves, render it, even when young, one of the most ornamental of the coniferous trees; and all the travellers who have seen it full grown, agree that it unites an extraordinary degree of majesty and grandeur with its beauty. The tree thrives in every part of

Great Britain where it has been tried, even as far north as Aberdeen, where, as in many other places, it is found hardier than the Cedar of Lebanon.   It is readily propa-gated by seeds, which preserve their vitality when imported in the cones.   It also grows freely by cuttings, which appear to make as handsome free-growing plants as those raised from seed." The soil and culture for this tree are pre-cisely those for the Cedar of Lebanon.

The Red Cedar Tree. *Juniperus.*

Nat. Ord. Coniferæ.   *Lin. Syst.* Diœcia, Monadelphia.

The Red Cedar is a very common tree, indigenous to this country, and growing in considerable abundance from Maine to Florida; but thriving with the greatest luxuriance in the sea-board states.   When fully grown, the Red Cedar is about 40 feet in height, and little more than a foot in diameter.   The leaves are very small, composed of minute scales, and lie pretty close to the branches.   Small blue berries, borne thickly upon the branches of the female trees in autumn and winter, contain the seeds.   These are covered with a whitish exudation, and are sometimes used, like those of the foreign juniper, in the manufacture of gin.

The Red Cedar has less to recommend it to the eye than most of the evergreens which we have already described. The color of the foliage is dull and dingy at many seasons, and the form of the young tree is too compactly conical to please generally.   When old, however, we have seen it throw off this formality, and become an interesting, and indeed a picturesque tree.   Then its branches shooting out in a horizontal direction, clad with looser and more pendent foliage, give the whole tree quite another character. The twisted stems, too, when they become aged, have a singular, dried-looking, whitish bark, which is quite unique and peculiar. There is a very fine natural avenue of Red Cedars near Fishkill landing, in Duchess Co., composed of two rows of noble trees 35 or 40 feet high, which is a very agreeable walk in winter and early spring. This has given the name of *Cedar Grove* to the country seat in question, where the Red Cedar grows spontaneously upon a slate subsoil with great luxuriance. There the trees are disseminated widely by the birds, which feed with avidity upon the berries.

The Red Cedar is well known to every person as one of our very best timber trees. It takes its name from the reddish hue of the perfect wood. This has a fragrant odor, and is not only light, fine-grained, and close in texture, but extremely durable. It is therefore much employed (though of late it is becoming scarcer) in conjunction with Live oak, which is too heavy alone, in ship-building. It is also valued for its great durability as posts for fencing; and is exported to Europe, to be used in the manufacture of pencils, and other useful purposes.

———

THE ARBOR VITÆ TREE. *Thuja.*

Nat. Ord. Coniferæ.   *Lin. Syst.* Monœcia, Monadelphia.

The Arbor Vitæ (*Thuja occidentalis*), sometimes also called Flat Cedar, or White Cedar, is distinguished from most evergreens by its flat foliage, composed of a great number of scales closely imbricated, or overlaying each other, which give the whole a compressed appearance. The seeds are borne in a small cone, usually not more than half an inch in length.

This tree is extremely formal and regular in outline in almost every stage of growth ; generally assuming the shape of an exact cone or pyramid of close foliage, of considerable extent at the base, close to the ground, and narrowing upwards to a sharp point. So regular is their outline in many cases, when they are growing upon favorable soils, that at a short distance they look as if they had been subjected to the clipping-shears. The sameness of its form precludes the employment of this evergreen in so extensive a manner as most others ; that is, in intermingling it promiscuously with other trees of less artificial forms. But the Arbor Vitæ, from this very regularity, is well suited to support and accompany scenery when objects of an avowedly artificial character predominate, as buildings, etc., where it may be used with a very happy effect. There is also no evergreen tree indigenous or introduced, which will make a more effectual, close, and impervious screen than this : and as it thrives well in almost every soil, moist, dry, rich, or poor, we strongly recommend it whenever such thickets are desirable. We have ourselves tried the experiment with a hedge of it about 200 feet long, which was transplanted about five or six feet high from the native *habitats* of the young trees, and which fully answers our expectations respecting it, forming a perfectly thick screen, and an excellent shelter on the north of a range of buildings at all seasons of the year, growing perfectly thick without trimming, from the very ground upwards.

The only fault of this tree as an evergreen, is the comparatively dingy green hue of its foliage in winter But to compensate for this, it is remarkably fresh looking in its spring, summer, and autumn tints, comparing well at those seasons even with the bright verdure of deciduous trees.

The Arbor Vitæ is very abundant in New Brunswick, Vermont, and Maine. In New York, the shores of the Hudson, at Hampton landing, 70 miles above the city of New York, are lined on both sides with beautiful specimens of this tree, many of them being perfect cones in outline; and it is here much more symmetrical and perfect in its growth than we have seen it. Forty feet is about the maximum altitude of the Arbor Vitæ, and the stem rarely measures more than ten or twelve inches in diameter.

The wood is very light, soft, and fine-grained, but is reputed to be equally durable with the Red Cedar. It is consequently employed for various purposes in building and fencing, where, in the northern districts, it grows in sufficient abundance, and of suitable size.

The Chinese Arbor Vitæ (*T. orientalis*) is a tree of much smaller and more feeble growth. It cannot, therefore, as an ornamental tree, be put in competition with our native species. Bnt it is a beautiful evergreen for the garden and shrubbery, where it finds a more suitable and sheltered site, being rather tender north of New York.

The White Cedar (*Thuja spheroida**), which belongs to the same genus as the Arbor Vitæ, is a much loftier

* *Cupressus thuyoides* of the old botanists.

tree, often growing 80 feet high. It can hardly be
considered a tree capable of being introduced into
cultivated situations, as it is found only in thick swamps
and wet grounds. The foliage considerably resembles
that of the common Arbor Vitæ, though rather narrower
and more delicate in texture. The cones are small and
rugged, and change from green to a blue or brown tint in
autumn. In the south it is often called the Juniper.

The White Cedar furnishes excellent shingles, much
more durable than those made of either Pine or Cypress ;
in Philadelphia the wood is much esteemed and greatly
used in cooperage. "Charcoal," according to Michaux,
"highly esteemed in the manufacture of gunpowder, is
made of young stocks, about an inch and a half in
diameter, deprived of their bark ; and the seasoned wood
affords beautiful lamp-black, lighter and more intensely
colored than that obtained from the Pine."

The American Holly Tree. *Ilex.*

Nat. Ord. Aquifoliaceæ.   *Lin. Syst.* Diœcia, Tetrandria.

The European Holly is certainly one of the *evergreen
glories* of the English gardens. There its deep green,
glossy foliage, and bright coral berries, which hang on for
a long time, are seen enlivening the pleasure-grounds and
shrubberies throughout the whole of that leafless and
inactive period in vegetation—winter. It is also, in our
mother tongue, inseparably connected with the delightful
associations of merry Christmas gambols and feastings,
when both the churches and the dwelling-houses are

decorated with its boughs. We have much to regret, therefore, in the severity of our winters, which will not permit the European Holly to flourish in the middle or eastern states, as a hardy tree. South of Philadelphia, it may become acclimated; but it appears to suffer greatly further north.

A beautiful succedaneum, however, may, we believe, be found in the American Holly (*Ilex opaca*), which indeed very closely resembles the foreign species in almost every particular. The leaves are waved or irregular in surface and outline, though not so much so as those of the latter, and their color is a much lighter shade of green. Like those of the foreign plant, they are armed on the edges with thorny prickles, and the surface is brilliant and polished. The American Holly is seen in the greatest perfection on the eastern shore of Maryland and Virginia, and the lower part of New Jersey. There it thrives best upon loose, dry, and gravelly soils. Michaux says it is also common through all the extreme southern states, and in West Tennessee, in which latter places it abounds on the margins of shady swamps, where the soil is cool and fertile. In such spots it often reaches forty feet in height, and twelve or fifteen inches in diameter.

Although the growth of the Holly is slow, yet it is *always* beautiful; and we regret that the American sort, which may be easily brought into cultivation, is so very rarely seen in our gardens or grounds. The seeds are easily procured, and if scalded and sowed in autumn, immediately after being gathered, they vegetate freely. For hedges the Holly is altogether unrivalled; and it was also one of the favorite plants for *verdant sculpture*, in the ancient style of gardening. Evelyn, in the edition of his

Sylva, published in London in 1664, thus bursts out in eloquent praise of it: "Above all natural greens which enrich our home-born store, there is none certainly to be compared to the Holly ; insomuch that I have often wondered at our curiosity after foreign plants and expen sive difficulties, to the neglect of the culture of this vulgar but incomparable tree,—whether we will propagate it for use and defence, or for sight and ornament. Is there under heaven a more glorious and refreshing object of the kind, than an impregnable hedge of one hundred and sixty-five feet in length, seven high, and five in diameter, which I can show in my poor gardens, at any time of the year, glittering with its armed and varnished leaves ? The taller standards at orderly distances blushing with their natural coral. It mocks the rudest assaults of the weather, beasts, or hedge-breaker :—

'Et illum nemo impune lacessit.' "

THE YEW TREE. *Taxus.*

Nat. Ord. Taxaceæ.   *Lin. Syst.* Monœcia, Monadelphia.

The European Yew is a slow-growing, evergreen tree, which often, when full grown, measures forty feet in height, and a third more in the diameter of its branches. The foliage is flat, linear, and is placed in two rows, like that of the Hemlock tree, though much darker in color. The flowers are brown or greenish, and inconspicuous, but they are succeeded by beautiful scarlet berries, about half or three-fourths of an inch in diameter, which are open at the end, where a small nut or seed is deposited. These berries have an exquisitely delicate, waxen appearance, and contribute highly to the beauty of the tree.

The growth of this tree, even in its native soil, is by no means rapid. In twenty years, says Loudon, it will attain the height of fifteen or eighteen feet, and it will continue growing for one hundred years; after which it becomes comparatively stationary, but will live many centuries.

When young, the Yew is rather compact and bushy in its form; but as it grows old, the foliage spreads out in fine horizontal masses, the outline of the tree is irregularly varied, and the whole ultimately becomes highly venerable and picturesque. When standing alone, it generally shoots out into branches at some three or four feet above the surface of the ground, and is ramified into a great number of close branches.

[Fig. 39. The English Yew.]

In England, it has been customary, since the earliest settlement of that island by the Britons, to plant the Yew in churchyards; and it is therefore as decidedly conse- crated to this purpose there, as the Cypress is in the south of Europe. For the decoration of places of burial it is well adapted, from the deep and perpetual verdure of its foliage, which, conjointly with its great longevity, may be considered as emblematical of immortality. The Yew, like the Holly, makes an excellent evergreen hedge—close, dark green, and beautiful when clad in the rich scarlet berries. We desire, however, rather to see this tree naturalized in our gardens and lawns as an evergreen tree of the first class, than in any other form. Judging from specimens which we have growing in our own grounds, we should consider it quite hardy anywhere south of the 41° of latitude. And although it is somewhat slow in its growth, yet, like many other evergreens, it is as beautiful when a small bush or a thrifty young tree, as it is venerable and picturesque when ages or even centuries have witnessed its never failing verdure. It appears to grow most vigorously and thrive best on a rich and heavy soil, and in situations rather shaded than exposed to a burning sun.

There are several beautiful varieties of the Yew (*Taxus baccata*) cultivated in the nurseries; the Irish Yew (*T. b. fastigiata*), remarkable for its dark green foliage, and very handsome, upright growth, and the Yellow berried Yew (*T. b. fructo-flava*), are the most ornamental.

The North American Yew (*T. canadensis*) is a low trailing shrub, scarcely rising above the height of four or six feet, though the branches extend to a considerable distance. In foliage, berries, etc., it so strongly resembles the European plant, that many botanists consider it only a dwarf variety. The leaves are nevertheless shorter and narrower, and the male flowers always solitary It is found in shady, rocky places, in the Highlands, and various other localities from Canada to Virginia

SECTION VI.

VINES AND CLIMBING PLANTS.

Value of this kind of Vegetation. Fine natural effects. The European Ivy. Th? Virginia Creeper. The Wild Grape Vine. The Bittersweet. The Trumpet Creeper. The Pipe Vine, and the Clematis. The Wistarias. The Honeysuckles and Woodbines. The Jasmine and the Periploca. Remarks on the proper mode of introducing vines. Beautiful effects of climbing plants in connexion with buildings.

> Quite over-canopied with lush woodbine,
> With sweet musk roses, and with eglantine.
>
> SHAKSPEARE.

 I N E S and climbing plants are objects full of interest for the Landscape Gardener, for they seem endowed with the characteristics of the graceful, the beautiful, and the picturesque, in their luxuriant and ever-varying forms. When judiciously introduced, therefore, nothing can so easily give a spirited or graceful air to a fine or even an ordinary scene, as the various plants which compose this group of the vegetable kingdom. We refer particularly now to those which have woody and perennial stems, as all annual or herbaceous stemmed plants are too short-lived to afford any lasting or permanent addition to the beauty of the lawn or pleasure-ground.

Climbing plants may be classed among the *adventitious beauties of trees.* Who has not often witnessed with delight in our native forests, the striking beauty of a noble tree, the old trunk and fantastic branches of which were enwreathed with the luxuriant and pliant shoots and rich foliage of some beautiful vine, clothing even its decayed limbs with verdure, and hanging down in gay festoons or loose negligent masses, waving to and fro in the air. The European Ivy (*Hedera Helix*) is certainly one of the finest, if not the very finest climbing plant (or more properly, creeping vine, for by means of its little fibres or rootlets on the stems, it will attach itself to trees, walks, or any other substance), with which we are acquainted. It possesses not only very fine dark green palmated foliage in great abundance, but the foliage has that agreeable property of being evergreen,—which, while it enhances its value tenfold, is at the same time so rare among vines. The yellow flowers of the Ivy are great favorites with bees, from their honied sweetness ; they open in autumn, and the berries ripen in the spring. When planted at the root of a tree, it will often, if the head is not too thickly clad with branches, ascend to the very topmost limbs ; and its dark green foliage, wreathing itself about the old and furrowed trunk, and hanging in careless drapery from the lower branches, adds greatly to the elegance of even the most admirable tree. Spenser describes the appearance of the Ivy growing to the tops of the trees,

> " Emongst the rest, the clamb'ring Ivie grew,
> Knitting his wanton arms with grasping hold,
> Lest that the poplar happely should renew
> Her brother's strokes, whose boughs she doth enfold
> With her lythe twigs, till they the top survew,
> And paint with pallid green her buds of gold."

The fine contrasts between the dark coloring of the leaves of the Ivy, and the vernal and autumnal tints of the foliage of deciduous trees, are also highly pleasing. Indeed this fine climbing plant may be turned to advantage in another way ; in reclothing dead trees with verdure Sir T. D. Lauder says, that "trees often die from causes which we cannot divine, and there is no one who is master of extensive woods, who does not meet with many such instances of unexpected and unaccountable mortality. Of such dead individuals we have often availed ourselves, and by planting Ivy at their roots, we have converted them into more beautiful objects than they were when arrayed in their own natural foliage."

The Ivy is not only ornamental upon trees, but it is also remarkably well adapted to ornament cottages, and even large mansions, when allowed to grow upon the walls, to which it will attach itself so firmly by the little rootlets sent out from the branches, that it is almost impossible to tear it off. On wooden buildings, it may perhaps be injurious, by causing them to decay; but on stone buildings, it fastens itself firmly, and holds both stone and mortar together like a coat of cement. The thick garniture of foliage with which it covers the surface, excludes stormy weather, and has, therefore, a tendency to preserve the walls, rather than accelerate their decay. This vine is the inseparable accompaniment of the old

The Ivy is not a native of America; nor is it by any means a very common plant in our gardens, though we know of no apology for the apparent neglect of so beautiful a climber. It is hardy south of the latitude of 42°, and we have seen it thriving in great luxuriance as far north as Hyde Park, on the Hudson, eighty miles above New York. One of the most beautiful growths of this plant, which has

ever met our eyes, is that upon the old mansion in the
Botanic Garden at Philadelphia, built by the elder Bartram.
That picturesque and quaint stone building is beautifully
overrun by the most superb mantle of Ivy, that no one who
has once seen can fail to remember with admiration. The
dark grey of the stone-work is finely opposed by the rich
verdure of the plant, which falls away in openings here and
there, around the windows, and elsewhere. It never thrives
well if suffered to ramble along the ground, but needs the
support of a tree, a frame, or a wall, to which it attaches
itself firmly, and grows with vigorous shoots. Bare walls
or fences may thus be clothed with verdure and beauty
equal to the living hedge, in a very short period of time, by
planting young Ivy roots at the base.

The most desirable varieties of the common Ivy are : the
Irish Ivy, with much larger foliage than the common sort,
and more rapid in its growth ; the Silver-striped and the
Gold-striped leaved Ivy, both of which, though less vigorous,
are much admired for the singular color of their leaves.
The common English Ivy is more hardy than the others
in our climate.

Although, as we have said, the Ivy is not a native of this
country, yet we have an indigenous vine, which, at least
in summer, is not inferior to it. We refer to the Virginia
Creeper (*Ampelopsis hederacea*), which is often called the
American Ivy. The leaves are as large as the hand,
deeply divided into five lobes, and the blossoms are succeeded by handsome, dark blue berries. The Virginia
Creeper is a most luxuriant grower, and we have seen it
climbing to the extremities of trees 70 or 80 feet in height.
Like the Ivy it attaches itself to whatever it can lay hold
of, by the little rootlets which spring out of the branches ;

and its foliage, when it clothes thickly a high wall, or folds itself in clustering wreaths around the trunk and branches of an open tree, is extremely handsome and showy. Although the leaves are not evergreen, like those of the Ivy, yet in autumn they far surpass those of that plant in the rich and gorgeous coloring which they then assume. Numberless trees may be seen in the country by the roadside, and in the woods, thus decked in autumn in the borrowed glories of the Virginia Creeper; but we particularly remember two as being remarkably striking objects; one, a wide-spread elm—the trunk and graceful diverging branches completely clad in scarlet by this beautiful vine, with which its own leaves harmonized well in their fine deep yellow dress; the other, a tall and dense Cedar, through whose dark green boughs gleamed the rich coloring of the Virginia Creeper, like a half-concealed, though glowing fire.

In the American forests nothing adds more to the beauty of an occasional tree, than the tall canopy of verdure with which it is often crowned by the wild Grape vine. There its tall stems wind themselves about until they reach the very summit of the tree, where they cluster it over, and bask their broad bright green foliage in the sunbeams. As if not content with this, they often completely overhang the head of the tree, falling like ample drapery around on every side, until they sweep the ground. We have seen very beautiful effects produced in this way by the grape in its wild state, and it may easily be imitated. The delicious fragrance of these wild grape vines when in blossom, is unsurpassed in delicacy; and we can compare it to nothing but the delightful perfume which exhales from a huge bed of Mignonette in full bloom. The Bittersweet (*Celastrus scandens*) is another well known climber, which ornaments our wild trees. Its foliage is very bright and shining, and the orange-colored seed-vessels which burst open, and display the crimson seeds in winter, are quite ornamental. It winds itself very closely around the stem, however, and we have known it to strangle or compress the bodies of young trees so tightly as to put an end to their growth.

The Trumpet Creeper (*Bignonia radicans*) is a very picturesque climbing plant. The stem is quite woody, and often attains considerable size ; the branches, like those of the Ivy and Virginia Creeper, fasten themselves by the roots thrown out. The leaves are pinnated, and the flowers, which are borne in terminal clusters on the ends of the young shoots about midsummer, are exceedingly showy. They are tubes five or six inches long, shaped like a trumpet, opening at the extremity, of a fine scarlet color on the outside, and orange within. The Trumpet Creeper is a native of Virginia, Carolina, and the states further south, where it climbs up the loftiest trees. It is a great favorite in the northern states as a climbing plant, and very beautiful effects are sometimes produced by planting it at the foot of a tall-stemmed tree, which it will completely surround with a pillar of verdure, and render very ornamental by its little shoots, studded with noble blossoms.

One of the most singular and picturesque climbing shrubs or plants which we cultivate, is the Pipe-vine, or Birthwort (*Aristolochia sipho*). It is a native of the Alleghany mountains, and is one of the tallest of twining plants, growing on the trees there to the height of 90 or 100 feet, though in gardens it is often kept down to a frame of four or five feet high. The leaves are of a noble size, being eight or nine inches broad, and heart-shaped in outline. The flowers, about an inch or a little more in length, are very singular. They are dark yellow, spotted with brown, in shape like a bent siphon-like tube, which opens at the extrem·ty, the whole flower resembling, as close as possible, a very small *Dutchman's pipe*, whence the vine is frequently so called by the country people. It flowers in the beginning of summer, and the foliage, during the whole growing season, has a very rich and luxuriant appearance. *Aristolochia tomentosa* is a smaller species, with leaves and flowers of less size, the former downy or hairy on the under surface.

The various kinds of Clematis, though generally kept within the precincts of the garden, are capable of adding to the interest of the pleasure ground, when they are planted so as to support themselves on the branches of trees. The common White Clematis or Virgin's Bower (*C. virginica*) is one of the strongest growing kinds, often embellishing with its pale white blossoms, the whole interior and even the very tops of our forest trees in the middle states. After these have fallen, they are succeeded by large tufts of brown, hairy-like plumes, appendages to the clusters of seeds, which give the whole a very unique and interesting look. The Wild *Atragene*, with large purple flowers, which blossom early, has much the same habit as the Clematis, to which, indeed, it is nearly related. Among the finest foreign species of this genus are, the Single and Double-flowered purple Clematis (*C. viticella* and its varieties), which, though slender in their stems, run to considerable height, are very pretty, and blossom profusely. The sweet scented and the Japan Clematis (*C flammula* and *C. florida*), the former very fragrant, and the latter beautiful, are perhaps too tender, except for the garden, where they are highly prized.

The Glycine or Wistaria (*Wistaria pubescens*) is a very beautiful climbing plant, and adds much to the gracefulness of trees, when trained so as to hang from their lower branches. The leaves are pinnate, and the light purple flowers, which bloom in loose clusters like those of the Locust, are universally admired. The Chinese Wistaria (*W. sinensis*) is a very elegant species of this plant, which appears to be quite hardy here ; and when loaded with its numerous large clusters of pendent blossoms, is highly ornamental. It grows rapidly, and, with but little care, will mount to a great height. These vines with pinnated foliage, would be remarkably appropriate when climbing up, and hanging from the branches of such light airy trees as the Three-thorned Acacia, the Locust, etc.

We must not forget to enumerate here the charming family of the Honeysuckles ; some of them are natives of the old world, some of our own continent ; and all of them are common in our gardens, where they are universally prized for their beauty and fragrance. In their native localities they grow upon trees, and trail along the rocks. The species which ascends to the greatest height, is the common European Woodbine,* which twines around the stems, and hangs from the ends of the longest branches of trees :

> " As Woodbine weds the plant within her reach,
> Rough Elm, or smooth-grained Ash, or glossy Beech,
> In spiral rings ascends the trunk, and lays
> Her golden tassels on the leafy sprays."
>   COWPER.

---

* *Woodbind* is the original name, derived from the habit of the plant of winding itself around trees, and binding the branches together.

The Woodbine (*Lonicera periclymenum*) has separate, opposite leaves, and buff-colored or paler yellow and red blossoms. There is a variety, the common monthly Woodbine, which produces its flowers all summer, and is much the most valuable plant. Another (*L. p. belgicum*), the Dutch Honeysuckle, blossoms quite early in spring; and a third (*L. p. quercifolium*) has leaves shaped like those of the oak tree.

The finest of our native sorts are the Red and Yellow trumpet Honeysuckle (*L. sempervirens* and *L. flava*), which have the terminal leaves on each branch joined together at the base, or perfoliate, making a single leaf. They blossom in the greatest profusion during the whole summer and autumn, and their rich blossom tubes, sprinkled in numerous clusters over the exterior of the foliage, as well as an abundance of scarlet berries in autumn, entitle them to high regard. There is also a very strong and vigorous species, called the Orange pubescent Honeysuckle (*L. pubescens*), with large, hairy, ciliate leaves, and fine large tawny or orange-colored flowers. It is a very luxuriant plant in its habit, and a very distinct species to the eye. All these native sorts have but very slight fragrance.

The Chinese twining Honeysuckle (*L. flexuosa*) is certainly one of the finest of the genus. In the form of the leaf it much resembles the common Woodbine ; but the foliage is much darker colored, and is also sub-ever-green, hanging on half the winter, and in sheltered spots, even till spring. It blossoms when the plant is old, several times during the summer, bearing an abundance of beautiful flowers, open at the mouth, red outside, and striped with red, white, or yellow within. It grows remarkably fast, climbing to the very summ t of trees in a short time ; and the flowers, which first appear in June, are deliciously fragrant. In all its varieties the Honey-suckle is a charming plant, either to adorn the porch of the cottage, the latticed bower of the garden—to both of which spots they are especially dedicated—or to climb the stem of the old forest tree, where—

> " With clasping tendrils it invests the branch,
> Else unadorn'd, with many agay festoon,
> And fragrant chaplet ; recompensing well
> The strength it borrows with the grace it lends."

There it diffuses through the air a delicious breath, that renders a walk beneath the shade of the tall trees doubly delightful, while its flowers give a gaiety and brightness to the park, which forest trees, producing usually but inconspicuous blossoms, could not alone impart.

Some of the climbing Roses are very lovely objects in the pleasure-grounds. Many of them, at the north, as the Multifloras, Noisettes, etc., require some covering in the winter, and are therefore better fitted for the garden. At the south, where they are quite hardy, they are, however, most luxuriant and splendid objects. But there are two classes of Roses that are perfectly hardy climbers, and may therefore be employed with great advantage by the Landscape Gardener—the Michigan and the Boursalt trees. The single Michigan is a most compact and vigorous grower, and often, in its wild haunts in the west, clambers over the tops of tall forest trees, and decks them with its abundant clusters of pale purple flowers. There are now in our gardens several beautiful double varieties of this, and among them, one, called *Beauty of the Prairies*, is

most admired for its large rich buds and blossoms of a deep
rose color.

The Boursalt roses are remarkable for their profusion of
flowers, and for their shining, reddish stems, with few
thorns. The common Purple or Crimson Boursalt is quite
a wonder of beauty in the latter part of May, when trained
on the wall of a cottage, being then literally covered with
blossoms ; and it is so hardy that scarcely a branch is ever
injured by the cold of winter. The Blush and the Elegans
are still richer and finer varieties of this class of roses, all
of which are well worthy of attention.

We have to regret that the inclemency of our winters
will not permit us to cultivate the White European
Jasmine (*Jasminum officinale*) out of the garden, as even
there it requires a slight protection in winter. Below the
latitude of Philadelphia, however, it will probably succeed
well. In the southern states they have a most lovely plant,
the Carolina Jasmine (*Gelseminum*), which hangs its
beautiful yellow flowers on the very tree tops, and the
woods there in spring are redolent with their perfume.

The connoisseur in vines will not forget the curious
Periploca, which grows very rapidly to the height of 40
or 50 feet, and bears numerous branches of very curious
brown or purple flowers in summer; or the Double-
blossoming Brambles, both pink and white, which often
make shoots of 20 or 30 feet long in a season, and bear
pretty clusters of double flowers in June. All these fine
climbers, and several others to be found in the catalogues,
may, in the hands of a person of taste, be made to
contribute in a wonderful degree to the variety, elegance,
and beauty of a country residence ; and to neglect to
introduce them would be to refuse the aid of some of the

most beautiful accessories that are capable of being combined with trees, as well as with buildings, gardens, and fences.

The reader must not imagine, from the remarks which we have here made on the beauty and charms of climbing plants, that we would desire to see every tree in an extensive park wreathed about, and overhung with fantastic vines and creepers. Such is by no means our intention. We should consider such a proceeding something in the worst possible taste. There are some trees whose rugged and ungraceful forms would refuse all such accompaniment ; and others from whose dignity and majesty it would be improper to detract even by adding the gracefulness of the loveliest vine.

Although we are not now writing of buildings, it is not inappropriate here to remark how much may be done in the country, and indeed even in town, by using vines and creepers to decorate buildings. The cottage in this country too rarely conveys the idea of comfort and happiness which we wish to attach to such a habitation, and chiefly because so often it stands bleak, solitary, and exposed to every ray of our summer sun, with a scanty robe of foliage to shelter it. How different such edifices, however humble. become when the porch is overhung with climbing plants.

Almost every man feels prouder of his home when it is a pleasant spot for the eye to rest upon, than when it is situated in a desert, or overgrown with weeds. Besides this, tasteful embellishment has a tendency to refine the feelings of every member of the family ; and every leisure hour spent in rendering more lovely and agreeable even the humblest cottage, is infinitely better employed than in lounging about in idle and useless dissipation.

SECTION VII.

TREATMENT OF GROUND.—FORMATION OF WALKS.

Nature of operations on Ground.   Treatment of flowing and irregular surfaces to heighten their expression; flats, or level surfaces.   Rocks, as materials in Landscape. Laying out Roads and Walks: Directions for the Approach: Rules by Repton.   The Drive, and minor walks.   The introduction of fences and verdant hedges

———" Strength may wield the ponderous spade,
May turn the clod and wheel the compost home;
But elegance, chief grace the garden shows,
And most attractive, is the fair result
Of thought, the creature of a polished mind."

COWPER.

R O U N D is undoubtedly the most un-wieldy and ponderous material that comes under the care of the Landscape Gardener. It is not only difficult to remove, the operations of the leveller rarely extending below two or three feet of the surface; but the effect produced by a given quantity of labor expended upon it, is generally much less than when the same has been bestowed in the formation of plantations, or the erection of buildings. The achievements of art upon ground appear so trifling, too, when we behold the apparent facility with which nature has arranged it in such a variety of forms, that the former sink into insignificance when compared with the latter.

For these reasons, the operations to be performed

upon ground in this country, will generally be limited
to the neighborhood of the house, or the scenery directly
under the eye. Here, by judicious levelling and smooth-
ing in some cases, or by raising gentle eminences with
interposing hollows in others, much may be done at a
moderate expense, to improve the beauty of the surrounding landscape.

Roads and walks are so directly connected with operations on the surface of the ground, and with the disposition
of plantations, which we have already made familiar to the
reader, that we shall introduce in this place a few remarks
relative to their direction and formation.

The *Approach* is by far the most important of these
routes. It is the private road, leading from the public
highway, directly to the house itself. It should therefore
bear a proportionate breadth and size, and exhibit marks
of good keeping, in accordance with the dignity of the
mansion.

In the ancient style of gardening, the Approach was so
formed as to enter directly in front of the house, affording
a full view of that portion of the edifice, and no other. A
line drawn as directly as possible, and evenly bordered on
each side with a tall avenue of trees, was the whole
expenditure of art necessary in its formation. It is true,
the simplicity of design was often more than counter-
balanced by the difficulty of levelling, grading, and altering
the surface, necessary to please the geometric eye ; but the
rules were as plain and unchangeable, as the lines were
parallel and undeviating.

In the present more advanced state of Landscape
Gardening, the formation of the Approach has become
equally a matter of artistical skill with other details of the
art. The house is generally so approached, that the eye
shall first meet it in an angular direction, displaying not

only the beauty of the architectural *façade* but also one of the *end* elevations, thus giving a more complete idea of the size, character, or elegance of the building : and instead of leading in a direct line from the gate to the house, it curves in easy lines through certain portions of the park or lawn, until it reaches that object.

If the point where the Approach is to start from the highway be not already determined past alteration, it should be so chosen as to afford a sufficient drive through the grounds before arriving at the house, to give the stranger some idea of the extent of the whole property : to allow an agreeable *diversity* of surface over which to lead it : and lastly in such a manner as not to interfere with the convenience of ready access to and from the mansion.

This point being decided, and the other being the mansion and adjacent buildings, it remains to lay out the road in such gradual curves as will appear easy and graceful, without verging into rapid turns or formal stiffness.   Since the modern style has become partially known and adopted here, some persons appear to have supposed that nature "has a horror of straight lines," and consequently, believing that they could not possibly err, they immediately ran into the other extreme, filling their grounds with zig-zag and regularly serpentine roads, still more horrible : which can only be compared to the contortions of a wounded snake dragging its way slowly over the earth.

There are two guiding principles which have been laid down for the formation of Approach roads.   The first, that the curves should never be so great, or lead over surfaces so unequal, as to make it disagreeable to drive upon them ; and the second, that the road should *never curve without some reason,* either real or apparent.

The most natural method of forming a winding Approach
where the ground is gently undulating, is to follow, in some
degree, the depressions of surface, and to curve round the
eminences. This is an excellent method, so long as it does
not lead us in too circuitous a direction, nor, as we before
hinted, make the road itself too uneven. When either of
these happens, the easy, gradual flow of the curve in the
proper direction, must be maintained by levelling or
grading, to produce the proper surface.

Nothing can be more unmeaning than to see an Approach, or any description of road, winding hither and
thither, through an extensive level lawn, towards the
house, without the least apparent reason for the curves.
Happily, we are not, therefore, obliged to return to the
straight line; but gradual curves may always be so arranged as to appear necessarily to wind round the *groups of
trees*, which otherwise would stand in the way. Wherever
a bend in the road is intended, a cluster or group of
greater or less size and breadth, proportionate to the
curve, should be placed in the projection formed. These
trees, as soon as they attain some size, if they are properly
arranged, we may suppose to have originally stood there,
and the road naturally to have curved, to avoid destroying
them.

This arrangement of trees bordering an extended
Approach road, in connexion with the various other
groups, masses, and single trees, in the adjacent lawn, will
in most cases have the effect of concealing the house from
the spectator approaching it, except, perhaps, from one or
two points. It has, therefore, been considered a matter
worthy of consideration, at what point or points the *first*

view of the house shall be obtained. If seen at too great a distance, as in the case of a large estate, it may appear more diminutive and of less magnitude than it should ; or, if first viewed at some other position, it may strike the eye of a stranger, at that point, unfavorably. The best, and indeed the only way to decide the matter, is to go over the whole ground covered by the Approach route carefully, and select a spot or spots sufficiently near to give the most favorable and striking view of the house itself. This, if openings are to be made, can only be done in winter ; but when the ground is to be newly planted, it may be prosecuted at any season.

The late Mr. Repton, who was one of the most celebrated English practical landscape gardeners, has laid down in one of his works, the following rules on the subject, which we quote, not as applying in all cases, but to show what are generally thought the principal requisites of this road in the modern style.

First. It ought to be a road to the house, and to that principally.

Secondly. If it be not naturally the nearest road possible, it ought artificially to be made to appear so.

Thirdly. The artificial obstacles which make this road the nearest, ought to appear natural.

Fourthly. Where an approach quits the high road, it ought not to break from it at right angles, or in such a manner as to rob the entrance of importance, but rather at some bend of the public road, from which a lodge or gate may be more conspicuous ; and where the high road may appear to branch from the approach, rather than the approach from the high road.

Fifthly. After the approach enters the park, it should avoid skirting along its boundary, which betrays the want of extent or unity of property.

Sixthly. The house, unless very large and magnificent, should not be seen at so great a distance as to make it appear much less than it really is.

Seventhly. The first view of the house should be from the most pleasing point of sight.

Eighthly. As soon as the house is visible from the approach, there should be no temptation to quit it (which will ever be the case if the road be at all circuitous), unless sufficient obstacles, such as water or inaccessible ground, appear to justify its course.*

Although there are many situations where these rules must be greatly modified in practice, yet the improver will do well to bear them in mind, as it is infinitely more easy to make occasional deviations from general rules, than to carry out a tasteful improvement without any guiding principles.

There are many fine country residences on the banks of the Hudson, Connecticut, and other rivers, where the proprietors are often much perplexed and puzzled by the *situation* of their houses; the building presenting really *two fronts*, while they appear to desire only one. Such is the case when the estate is situated between the public road on one side, and the river on the other; and we have often seen the Approach artificially tortured into a long circuitous route, in order finally to arrive at what the proprietor considers the true front, viz. the side nearest the river. When a building is so situated, much the most

---

* Repton's Inquiry into the Changes of Taste in Landscape Gardening, p. 109.

elegant effect is produced by having two fronts : one, the *entrance front*, with the porch or portico nearest the road, and the other, the *river front*, facing the water. The beauty of the whole is often surprisingly enhanced by this arrangement, for the visitor, after passing by the Approach through a considerable portion of the grounds, with perhaps but slight and partial glimpses of the river, is most agreeably surprised on entering the house, and looking from the drawing-room windows of the other front, to behold another beautiful scene totally different from the last, enriched and ennobled by the wide-spread sheet of water before him. Much of the effect produced by this agreeable surprise from the interior, it will readily be seen, would be lost, if the stranger had already driven round and alighted on the river front.

The *Drive* is a variety of road rarely seen among us, yet which may be made a very agreeable feature in some of our country residences, at a small expense. It is intended for exercise more secluded than that upon the public road, and to show the interesting portions of the place from the carriage, or on horseback. Of course it can only be formed upon places of considerable extent ; but it enhances the enjoyment of such places very highly, in the estimation of those who are fond of equestrian exercises. It generally commences where the approach terminates, viz. near the house : and from thence, proceeds in the same easy curvilinear manner through various parts of the grounds, farm or estate. Sometimes it sweeps through the pleasure grounds, and returns along the very beach of the river, beneath the fine overhanging foliage of its projecting bank ; sometimes it proceeds towards some favorite point of view, or interesting spot on the landscape ; or at others it

leaves the lawn and traverses the farm, giving the proprietor an opportunity to examine his crops, or exhibit
his agricultural resources to his friends.

Walks are laid out for purposes similar to Drives, but
are much more common, and may be introduced into every
scene, however limited. They are intended solely for
promenades, or exercise on foot, and should therefore be
dry and firm, if possible, at all seasons when it is desirable
to use them. Some may be open to the south, sheltered
with evergreens, and made dry and hard for a warm promenade in winter; others formed of closely mown turf,
and thickly shaded by a leafy canopy of verdure, for a cool
retreat in the midst of summer. Others again may lead to
some sequestered spot, and terminate in a secluded rustic
seat, or conduct to some shaded dell or rugged eminence,
where an extensive prospect can be enjoyed. Indeed, the
genius of the place must suggest the direction, length, and
number of the walks to be laid out, as no fixed rules can be
imposed in a subject so everchanging and different. It
should, however, never be forgotten, that the walk ought
always to correspond to the scene it traverses, being rough
where the latter is wild and picturesque, sometimes scarcely
differing from a common footpath, and more polished as
the surrounding objects show evidences of culture and high
keeping. In *direction*, like the approach, it should take
easy flowing curves, though it may often turn more
abruptly at the interposition of an obstacle. The chief
beauty of curved and bending lines in walks, lies in the
new scenes which by means of them are opened to the
eye. In the straight walk of half a mile the whole is seen
at a glance, and there is too often but little to excite the
spectator to pursue the search; but in the modern style, at

every few rods, a new turn in the walk opens a new prospect to the beholder, and "leads the eye," as Hogarth graphically expressed it, "a kind of wanton chase," continually affording new refreshment and variety.

Fences are often among the most unsightly and offensive objects in our country seats. Some persons appear to have a passion for subdividing their grounds into a great number of fields; a process which is scarcely ever advisable even in common farms, but for which there can be no apology in elegant residences. The close proximity of fences to the house gives the whole place a confined and mean character. "The mind," says Repton, "feels a certain disgust under a sense of confinement in any situation, however beautiful." A wide-spread lawn, on the contrary, where no boundaries are conspicuous, conveys an impression of ample extent and space for enjoyment. It is frequently the case that, on that side of the house nearest the outbuildings, fences are, for convenience, brought in its close neighborhood, and here they are easily concealed by plantations ; but on the other sides, open and unobstructed views should be preserved, by removing all barriers not absolutely necessary.

Nothing is more common, in the places of cockneys who become inhabitants of the country, than a display immediately around the dwelling of a spruce paling of carpentry, neatly made, and painted white or green ; an abomination among the fresh fields, of which no person of taste could be guilty. To fence off a small plot around a fine house, in the midst of a lawn of fifty acres, is a perversity which we could never reconcile, with even the lowest perception of beauty. An old stone wall covered with creepers and climbing plants, may become a picturesque barrier a thousand times superior to such a fence. But there is never one instance in a thousand where any barrier is necessary. Where it is desirable to separate the house from the level grass of the lawn, let it be done by an architectural terrace of stone, or a raised platform of gravel supported by turf, which will confer importance and dignity upon the building, instead of giving it a petty and trifling expression.

Verdant hedges are elegant substitutes for stone or wooden fences, and we are surprised that their use has not been hitherto more general. We have ourselves been making experiments for the last ten years with various hedge-plants, and have succeeded in obtaining some hedges which are now highly admired. Five or six years will, in this climate, under proper care, be sufficient to produce hedges of great beauty, capable of withstanding the attacks of every kind of cattle ; barriers, too, which will outlast many generations. The common *Arbor Vitæ* (or flat Cedar), which grows in great abundance in many districts, forms one of the most superb hedges, without the least care in trimming; the foliage growing thickly down to the very ground, and being evergreen, the hedge remains clothed the whole year. Our common Thorns, and in particular those known in the nurseries as the Newcastle and Washington thorns, form hedges of great strength and beauty. They are indeed much better adapted to this climate than the English Hawthorn, which often suffers from the unclouded radiance of our midsummer sun. In autumn, too, it loses its foliage much sooner than our native sorts, some of which assume a brilliant scarlet when the foliage is fading in autumn. In New England, the Buckthorn is preferred from its rapid and luxuriant growth ;* and in the middle states, the Maclura, or Osage Orange, is becoming a favorite for its glossy and polished foliage. The Privet, or Prim, is a rapid growing shrub, well fitted for interior divisions. Picturesque hedges are easily formed by intermingling a variety of flowering shrubs, sweet briers, etc., and allowing the whole to grow together in rich masses. For this purpose the Michigan rose is admirably adapted at the north, and the Cherokee rose at the south. In all cases where hedges are employed in the natural style of landscape (and not in close connexion with highly artificial objects, buildings, etc.), a more agreeable effect will be produced by allowing the hedge to grow somewhat irregular in form, or varying it by planting near it other small trees and shrubs to break the outline, than by clipping it in even and formal lines. Hedges may be obtained in a single season, by planting long shoots of the osier willow, or any other tree which throws out roots easily from cuttings.

A simple and pleasing barrier, in good keeping with cottage residences, may be formed of *rustic work*, as it is termed. For this purpose, stout rods of any of our native forest trees are chosen (Cedar being preferable) with the bark on, six to ten feet in length ; these are sharpened and driven into the ground in the form of a lattice, or wrought into any figures of trellis that the fancy may suggest. When covered with luxuriant vines and climbing plants, such a barrier is often admirable for its richness and variety.

* The Buckthorn is perhaps the best plant where a thick screen is very speedily desired. It is not liable to the attack of insects ; grows very thickly at the bottom, at once ; and will make an efficient screen sooner than almost any other plant.

The sunken fence, fosse, or *ha-ha*, is an English in
vention, used in separating that portion of the lawn neai
the house, from the part grazed by deer or cattle, and is
only a ditch sufficiently wide and deep to render communication difficult on opposite sides. When the ground
slopes from the house, such a sunk fence is invisible to a
person near the latter, and answers the purpose of a
barrier without being in the least obtrusive.

In a succeeding section we shall refer to terraces with
their parapets, which are by far the most elegant barriers
for a highly decorated flower garden, or for the purpose of
maintaining a proper connexion between the house and the
grounds, a subject which is scarcely at all attended to, or
its importance even recognised as yet among us.

SECTION VIII.

TREATMENT OF WATER.

Beautiful effects of this element in nature. In what cases it is desirable to attempt the formation of artificial pieces of water. Regular forms unpleasing. Directions for the formation of ponds or lakes in the irregular manner. Study of natural lakes. Islands Planting the margin. Treatment of natural brooks and rivulets. Cascades and water-falls. Legitimate sphere of the art in this department.

——The dale
With woods o'erhung, and shagg'd with mossy rocks,
Whence on each hand the gushing waters play,
And down the rough cascade white-dashing fall,
Or gleam in lengthened vista through the trees.

THOMSON.

 H E delightful and captivating effects of water in landscapes of every description, are universally known and admitted. The boundless sea, the broad full river, the dashing noisy brook, and the limpid meandering rivulet, are all possessed of their peculiar charms ; and when combined with scenes otherwise finely disposed and well wooded, they add a hundred fold to their beauty. The soft and trembling shadows of the surrounding trees and hills, as they fall upon a placid sheet of water—the brilliant light which the crystal surface reflects in pure sunshine, mirroring, too, at times in its resplendent bosom, all the cerulean depth and snowy whiteness of the overhanging sky, give it an almost

magical effect in a beautiful landscape. The murmur of
the babbling brook, that

"In linked sweetness long drawn out,"

falls upon the ear in some quiet secluded spot, is inexpressibly soothing and delightful to the mind ; and the
deeper sound of the cascade that rushes, with an almost
musical dash, over its bed of moss-covered rock, is one of
the most fascinating of the many elements of enjoyment
in a fine country seat. The simplest or the most monotonous view may be enlivened by the presence of water in
any considerable quantity ; and the most picturesque and
striking landscape will, by its addition, receive a new
charm, inexpressibly enhancing all its former interest.
In short, as no place can be considered perfectly complete
without either a water view or water upon its own
grounds, wherever it does not so exist and can be *easily*
formed by artificial means, no man will neglect to take
advantage of so fine a source of embellishment as is this
element in some of its varied forms.

"——— Fleuves, ruisseaux, beaux lacs, claires fontaines,
Venez, portez partout la vie et la fraîcheur ?
Ah ! qui peut remplacer votre aspect enchanteur ?
De près il nous amuse, et de loin nous invite :
C'est le premier qu'on cherche, et le dernier qu'on quitte.
Vous fécondez les champs ; vous répétez les cieux ;
Vous enchantez l'oreille, et vous charmez les yeux."

In this country, where the progress of gardening and
improvements of this nature, is rather shown in a simple
and moderate embellishment of a large number of villas
and country seats, than by a lavish and profuse expenditure on a few entailed places, as in the residences of the
English nobility, the formation of large pieces of water

at great cost and extreme labor, would be considered both absurd and uncalled for. Indeed, when nature has so abundantly spread before us such an endless variety of superb lakes, rivers, and streams of every size and description, the efforts of man to rival her great works by *mere imitation*, would, in most cases, only become ludicrous by contrast.

When, however, a number of perpetual springs cluster together, or a rill, rivulet, or brook, runs through an estate in such a manner as *easily* to be improved or developed into an elegant expanse of water in any part of the grounds, we should not hesitate to take advantage of so fortunate a circumstance. Besides the additional beauty conferred upon the whole place by such an improvement, the proprietor may also derive an inducement from its utility : for the possession of a small lake, well stocked with carp, trout, pickerel, or any other of the excellent pond fish, which thrive and propagate extremely well in clear fresh water, is a real advantage which no one will undervalue.

There is no department of Landscape Gardening which appears to have been less understood in this country than the management of water. Although there have not been many attempts made in this way, yet the occasional efforts that have been put forth in various parts of the country, in the shape of square, circular, and oblong pools of water, indicate a state of knowledge extremely meagre, in·the art of Landscape Gardening. The highest scale to which these pieces of water rise in our estimation is that of respectable horse-ponds ; beautiful objects they certainly are not. They are generally round or square, with perfectly smooth, flat banks on every side, and resemble a huge basin set down in the middle of a green lawn.

Lakes or ponds are the most beautiful forms in which water can be displayed in the grounds of a country residence.* They invariably produce their most pleasing effects when they are below the level of the house ; as, if above, they are lost to the view, and if placed on a level with the eye, they are seen to much less advantage. We conceive that they should never be introduced where they do not naturally exist, except with the concurrence of the following circumstances. First, a sufficient quantity of running water to maintain *at all times* an overflow, for nothing can be more unpleasant than a stagnant pool, as nothing is more delightful than pure, clear, limpid water ; and secondly, some natural formation of ground, in which the proposed water can be expanded, that will not only make it appear natural, but diminish, a hundred fold, the expense of formation.

The finest and most appropriate place to form a lake, is in the bottom of a small valley, rather broad in proportion to its length. The soil there will probably be found rather clayey and retentive of moisture ; and the rill or brook, if not already running through it, could doubtless be easily diverted thither. There, by damming up the lower part of the valley with a head of greater or less height, the water may be thrown back so as to form the whole body of the lake.

The first subject which will demand the attention, after the spot has been selected for the lake or pond, and the

---

* Owing to the immense scale upon which nature displays this fine element in North America, every sheet of water of moderate or small size is almost universally called a *pond*. And many a beautiful, limpid, natural expanse, which in England would be thought a charming lake, is here simply a pond. The term may be equally correct, but it is by no means as elegant.

height of the head and consequent depth of water determined upon, is the proposed *form* or *outline* of the whole
And, as we have already rejected all regular and geometric
forms, in scenes where either natural or picturesque beauty
is supposed to predominate, we must turn our attention to
examples for imitation in another direction.

If, then, the improver will recur to the most beautiful
small *natural* lake within his reach, he will have a subject
to study and an example to copy well worthy of imitation.
If he examine minutely and carefully such a body of water,
with all its accompaniments, he will find that it is not only
delightfully wooded and overshadowed by a variety of
vegetation of all heights, from the low sedge that grows
on its margin, to the tall tree that bends its branches over
its limpid wave ; but he will also perceive a striking peculiarity in its *irregular outline*. This, he will observe, is
neither round, square, oblong, nor any modification of these
regular figures, but full of bays and projections, sinuosities,
and recesses of various forms and sizes, sometimes bold,
and reaching a considerable way out into the body of the
lake, at others, smaller and more varied in shape and connexion. In the heights of the banks, too, he will probably
observe considerable variety. At some places, the shore
will steal gently and gradually away from the level of the
water, while at others it will rise suddenly and abruptly, in
banks more or less steep, irregular, and rugged. Rocks and
stones covered with mosses, will here and there jut out
from the banks, or lie along the margin of the water, and
the whole scene will be full of interest from the variety
intricacy, and beauty of the various parts. If he will
accurately note in his mind all these varied forms—their
separate outlines, the way in which they blend into one

another, and connect themselves together, and the effect which, surrounding the water, they produce as a whole, he will have some tolerably correct ideas of the way in which an artificial lake ought to be formed.

Let him go still further now, in imagination, and suppose the banks of this natural lake, without being otherwise altered, entirely denuded of grass, shrubs, trees, and verdure of every description, remaining characterized only by their original form and outline ; this will give him a more complete view of the method in which his labors must commence ; for uncouth and apparently mis-shapen as those banks are and must be, when raw and unclothed, to exhibit all their variety and play of light and shadow when verdant and complete, so also must the original form of the banks and margin of the piece of artificial water, in order finally to assume the beautiful or picturesque, be made to assume outlines equally rough and harsh in their raw and incomplete state.

It occasionally happens, though rarely, that around the hollow or valley where it is proposed to form the piece of water, the ground rises in such irregular form, and is so undulating, receding, and projecting in various parts, that when the water is dammed up by the head below, the natural outline formed by the banks already existing, is sufficiently varied to produce a pleasing effect without much further preparatory labor.   This, when it occurs, is exceedingly fortunate ; but the examples are so unfrequent, that we must here make our suggestions upon a different supposition.

When, therefore, it is found that the form of the intended lake would not be such as is desirable, it must be made so by digging.   In order to do this with any exactness the improver should take his stand at that part of the ground where the dam or head is to be formed, and raising his levelling instrument to the exact height to which the intended lake will rise, sweep round with his eye upon the surrounding sides of the valley, and indicate by placing marks there, the precise line to which the water will reach. This can easily be done throughout the whole circumference by a few changes of position.

When the outline is ascertained in this way, and marked out, the improver can, with the occasional aid of the leveller, easily determine where and how he can make alterations and improvements. He will then excavate along the new margin, until he makes the water line (as shown by the instrument) penetrate to all the various bays, inlets, and curves of the proposed lake. In making these irregular variations, sometimes bold and striking, at others fainter and less perceptible, he can be guided, as we have already suggested, by no fixed rules, but such as he may deduce from the operations of nature on the same materials, or by imbuing his mind with the beauty of forms in graceful and refined art. In highly polished scenery, elegant curves and graceful sweeps should enter into the composition of the outline ; but in wilder or more picturesque situations, more irregular and abrupt variations will be found most suitable and appropriate.

The intended water outline once fully traced and under-stood, the workmen can now proceed to form the banks. All this time the improver will keep in mind the supposed appearance of the bank of a natural lake stripped of its vegetation, etc., which will greatly assist him in his progress. In some places the banks will rise but little from the water at others one or two feet, and at others perhaps three, four,

or six times as much. This they will do, not in the same
manner in all portions of the outline, sloping away with a
like gradual rise on both sides, for this would inevitably
prcduce tameness and monotony, but in an irregular and
varied manner; sometimes falling back gradually, sometimes starting up perpendicularly, and again overhanging
the bed of the lake itself.

All this can be easily effected while the excavations of
those portions of the bed which require deepening are
going on. And the better portions of the soil obtained
from the latter, will serve to raise the banks when they are
too low.

It is of but little consequence how roughly and
irregularly the projections, elevations, etc., of the banks
and outlines are at first made, so that some general form
and connexion is preserved. The danger lies on the other
side, viz. in producing a whole too tame and insipid ; for
we have found by experience, how difficult it is to make
the best workmen understand how to operate in any othei
way than in regular curves and straight lines. Besides,
newly moved earth, by settling and the influence of rains,
etc., tends, for some time, towards greater evenness and
equality of surface.

In arranging these outlines and banks, we should study
the effect at the points from which they will generally be
viewed. Some pieces of water in valleys, are looked
down upon from other and higher parts of the demesne ;
others (and this is most generally the case) are only seen
from the adjoining walk, at some point or points where the
latter approaches the lake. They are most generally seen

from one, and seldom from more than two sides. When a lake is viewed from above, its contour should be studied as a whole; but when it is only seen from one or more sides or points, the beauty of the *coup d'œil* from those positions can often be greatly increased by some trifling alterations in arrangement. A piece of water which is long and comparatively narrow, appears extremely different in opposite points of view; if seen lengthwise from either extremity, its apparent breadth and extent is much increased ; while, if the spectator be placed on one side and look across, it will seem narrow and insignificant. Now, although the form of an artificial lake of moderate size should never be much less in breadth than in length, yet the contrary is sometimes unavoidably the case ; and being so, we should by all means avail ourselves of those well known laws in perspective, which will place them in the best possible position, relative to the spectator.

If the improver desire to render his banks still more picturesque, resembling the choicest *morçeaux* of natural banks, he should go a step further in arranging his materials before he introduces the water, or clothes the margin with vegetation. In analysing the finest poitions of natural banks, it will be observed that their peculiar characteristics often depend on other objects besides the mere ground of the surrounding banks, and the trees and verdure with which they are clothed. These are, rocks of various size, forms, and colors, often projecting out of or holding up the bank in various places ; stones sometimes imbedded in the soil, sometimes lying loosely along the shore ; and lastly, old stumps of trees with gnarled roots, whose decaying hues are often extremely mellow and agreeable to the eye. All these have much to do with the expression of a truly picturesque bank, and cannot be excluded or taken away from it without detracting largely from its character. There is no reason, therefore, in an imitation of nature, why we should not make use of all her materials to produce a similar effect; and although in the raw and rude state of the banks at first, they may have a singular and rather *outré* aspect, stuck round and decorated here and there with large rocks, smaller stones, and old stumps of trees; yet it must be remembered that this is only the chaotic state, from which the new creation is to emerge more perfectly formed and completed; and also that the appearance of these rocks and stumps, when covered with mosses, and partially overgrown with a profusion of luxuriant vegetation and climbing plants, will be as beautifully picturesque after a little time has elapsed, as it is now uncouth and uninviting.

Islands generally contribute greatly to the beauty of a piece of water. They serve, still further, to increase the variety of outline, and to break up the wide expanse of liquid into secondary portions, without injuring the effect of the whole. The striking contrast, too, between their verdure, the color of their margins, composed of variously tinted soils and stones, and the still, smooth water around them,—softened and blended as this contrast is, by their shadows reflected back from the limpid element, gives additional richness to the picture.

The distribution of islands in a lake or pond requires some judgment. They will always appear most natural when sufficiently near the shore, on either side, to maintain in appearance some connexion with it. Although islands do sometimes occur near the middle of natural lakes, yet the effect is by no means good, as it not only breaks and distracts the effects of the whole expanse by dividing it into two distinct parts, but it always indicates a shallowness or want of depth where the water should be deepest.

There are two situations where it is universally admitted that islands may be happily introduced. These are, at the inlet and the exit of the body of water. In many cases where the stream which supplies the lake is not remarkable for size, and will add nothing to the appearance of the whole view from the usual points of sight, it may be concealed by an island or small group of islands, placed at some little distance in front of it. The head or dam of a lake, too, is often necessarily so formal and abrupt, that it is difficult to make it appear natural and in good keeping with the rest of the margin. The introduction of an island or two, placed near the main shore, on either side, and projecting as far as possible before the dam, will greatly diminish this disagreeable formality, particularly if well clothed with a rich tuft of shrubs and overhanging bushes.

Except in these two instances, islands should be generally placed *opposite the salient points* of the banks, or near those places where small breaks or promontories run out into the water. In such situations, they will increase the irregularity of the outline, and lend it additional spirit and animation. Should they, on the other hand, be seated in or near the marginal curve and indentations, they will only serve to clog up these recesses; and while their own figures are lost in these little bays where they are hidden, by lessening the already existing irregularities, they will render the whole outline tame and spiritless.

On one or two of these small islands, little rustic habitations, if it coincide with the taste of the proprietor, may be made for different aquatic birds or waterfowl, which will much enliven the scene by their fine plumage. Among these the *swan* is pre-eminent, for its beauty and gracefulness. Abroad, they are the almost constant accompaniments of water in the ground of country residences ; and it cannot be denied that, floating about in the limpid wave, with their snow-white plumage and superbly curved necks, they are extremely elegant objects.

After having arranged the banks, reared up the islands, and completely formed the bed of the proposed lake, the improver will next proceed, at the proper period, to finish his labors by clothing the newly formed ground, in various parts, with vegetation. This may be done immediately, if it be desirable ; or if the season be not favorable, it may be deferred until the banks, and all the newly formed earth, have had time to settle and assume their final forms, after the dam has been closed, and the whole basin filled to its intended height.

Planting the margins of pieces of water, if they should be of much extent, must evidently proceed upon the same leading principle that we have already laid down for ornamental plantations in other situations. That is, there must be trees of different heights and sizes, and underwood and shrubs of lower growth, disposed sometimes singly, at others in masses, groups, and thickets : in all of which forms, *connexion* must be preserved, and the whole must be made to blend well together, while the different sizes and contours will prevent any sameness and confusion. On the retreating dry banks, the taller and more sturdy deciduous and evergreen trees, as the oak, ash, etc., may be planted, and nearer by, the different willows, the elm, the alder, and other trees that love a moister situation, will thrive well. It is indispensably necessary, in order to

produce breadth of effect and strong rich contrasts, that
underwood should be employed to clothe many parts of the
banks. Without it, the stems of trees will appear loose
and straggling, and the screen will be so imperfect as to
allow a free passage for the vision in every direction. For
this purpose, we have in all our woods, swamps, and along
our brooks, an abundance of hazels, hawthorns, alders,
spice woods, winter berries, azaleas, spireas, and a hundred
other fine low shrubs, growing wild, which are by nature
extremely well fitted for such sites, and will produce
immediate effect on being transplanted. These may be
intermingled, here and there, with the swamp button-bush
(*Cephalanthus*), which bears handsome white globular heads
of blossoms, and the swamp magnolia, which is highly
beautiful and fragrant. On cool north banks, among
shelves of proper soil upheld by projecting ledges of rock,
our native Kalmias and Rhododendrons, the common and
mountain laurels, may be made to flourish. The Virginia
Creeper, and other beautiful wild vines, may be planted at
the roots of some of the trees to clamber up their stems,
and the wild Clematis so placed that its luxuriant festoons
shall hang gracefully from the projecting boughs of some of
the overarching trees. Along the lower banks and closer
margins, the growth of smaller plants will be encouraged,
and various kinds of wild ferns may be so planted as
partially to conceal, overrun, and hide the rocks and
stumps of trees, while trailing plants, as the periwinkle and
moneywort (*Lysamachia nummularia*), will still further
increase the intricacy and richness of such portions. In
this way, the borders of the lake will resemble the finest
portions of the banks of picturesque and beautiful natural
dells and pieces of water, and the effect of the whole when

time has given it the benefit of its softening touches, if it
has been thus properly executed, will not be much inferior
to those matchless bits of fine landscape. A more striking
and artistical effect will be produced by substituting for
native trees and shrubs, common on the banks of streams
and lakes in the country, only rare *foreign* shrubs, vines,
and aquatic plants of hardy growth, suitable for such
situations. While these are arranged in the same manner
as the former, from their comparative novelty, especially
in such sites, they will at once convey the idea of refined
and elegant art.

If any person will take the trouble to compare a piece of
water so formed, when complete, with the square or circular
sheets or ponds now in vogue among us, he must indeed be
little gifted with an appreciation of the beautiful, if he do
not at once perceive the surpassing merit of the natural
style. In the old method, the banks, level, or rising on all
sides, without any or but few surrounding trees, carefully
gravelled along the edge of the water, or what is still worse,
walled up, slope away in a tame, dull, uninteresting grass
field. In the natural method, the outline is varied, sometimes receding from the eye, at others stealing out, and
inviting the gaze—the banks here slope off gently with a
gravelly beach, and there rise abruptly in different heights,
abounding with hollows, projections, and eminences, showing various colored rocks and soils, intermingled with a
luxuriant vegetation of all sizes and forms, corresponding to
the different situations. Instead of allowing the sun to
pour down in one blaze of light, without any objects to
soften it with their shade, the thick overhanging groups and
masses of trees cast, here and there, deep cool shadows.
Stealing through the leaves and branches, the sun-beams

quiver and play upon the surface of the flood, and are reflected back in dancing light, while their full glow upon the broader and more open portions of the lake is relieved, and brought into harmony by the cooler and softer tints mirrored in the water from the surrounding hues and tints of banks, rocks, and vegetation.

Natural brooks and rivulets may often be improved greatly by a few trifling alterations and additions, when they chance to come within the bounds of a country residence. Occasionally, they may be diverted from their original beds when they run through distant and unfrequented parts of the demesne, and brought through nearer portions of the pleasure grounds or lawn. This, however, can only be done with propriety when there is a natural indication in the grounds through which it is proposed to divert it—as a succession of hollows, etc., to form the future channel. Sometimes, a brisk little brook can be divided into smaller ones for some distance, again uniting at a point below, creating additional diversity by its varying form.*

Brooks, rivulets, and even rills may frequently be greatly improved by altering the form of their beds in various places. Often by merely removing a few trifling obstructions, loose stones, branches, etc., or hollowing away the

---

* The Abbe Délille has given us a fine image of a brook thus divided, in the following lines:—

> " Plus loin, il se sépare en deux ruisseaux agiles,
> Qui, se suivant l'un l'autre avec rapidité,
> Disputent de vitesse et de limpidité ;
> Puis, rejoignant tous deux le lit qui les rassemble,
> Murmurent enchantés de voyager ensemble.
> Ainsi, toujours errant de détour en détour,
> Muet, bruyant, paisible, inquiet tour à tour,
> Sous mille aspects divers son cours se renouvelle."

adjoining bank for a short distance, fine little expanses or
pools of still water may be formed, which are happily contrasted with the more rugged course of the rest of the
stream. Such improvements of these minor water courses
are much preferable to widening them into flat, insipid,
tame canals or rivers, which, though they present greater
surface to the eye, are a thousand times inferior in the
impetuosity of motion, and musical, "babbling sound," so
delightful in rapid brooks and rivulets.*

Cascades and water-falls are the most charming features
of natural brooks and rivulets. Whatever may be their
size they are always greatly admired, and in no way is the
peculiar stillness of the air, peculiar to the country, more
pleasingly broken, than by the melody of falling water.
Even the gurgling and mellow sound of a small rill, leaping
over a few fantastic stones, has a kind of lulling fascination
for the ear, and when this sound can be brought so near as
to be distinctly heard at the residence itself, it is peculiarly
delightful.† Now any one who examines a small cascade
at all attentively, in a natural brook, will see that it is often
formed in the simplest manner by the interposition of a few
large projecting stones, which partially dam up the current
and prevent the ready flow of the water. Such little cascades are easily imitated, by following exactly the same

* The most successful improvement of a natural brook that we have ever
witnessed, has been effected in the grounds of Henry Sheldon, Esq., of Tarrytown, N. Y. The great variety and beauty displayed in about a fourth of a
mile of the course of this stream, its pretty cascades, rustic bridges, rockwork,
etc., reflect the highest credit on the taste of that gentleman.

† The fine stream which forms the south boundary of Blithewood, on the
Hudson, the seat of R. Donaldson, Esq., affords two of the finest natural cata-
racts that we have seen in the grounds of any private residence. Fig. 41 is a
view of the larger cascade which falls about 60 feet over a bold, rocky bed.

course, and damming up the little brook artificially ; studiously avoiding, however, any formal and artificial disposition of the stones or rocks employed.

Larger water-falls and cascades cannot usually be made without some regular head or breastwork, to oppose more firmly the force of the current. Such heads may be formed of stout plank and well prepared clay ;* or, which is greatly preferable, of good masonry laid in water cement. After a head is thus formed it must be concealed entirely from the eye by covering it both upon the top and sides with natural rocks and stones of various sizes, so ingeniously disposed, as to appear fully to account for, or be the cause of the water-fall.

The axe of the original backwoodsman appears to have left such a mania for *clearing* behind it, even in those portions of the Atlantic states where such labor should be for ever silenced, that some of our finest places in the country will be found much desecrated and mutilated by its careless and unpardonable use ; and not only are fine plantations often destroyed, but the banks of some of our finest streams and prettiest rivulets partially laid bare by the aid of this instrument, guided by some tasteless hand. Wherever fine brooks or water courses are thus mutilated, one of the most necessary and obvious improvements is to reclothe them with plantations of trees and underwood. In planting their banks anew, much beauty and variety can often be produced by employing different growths, and arranging them as we have directed for the margins

---

* It is found that strong loam or any tenacious earth well prepared by *puddling* or beating in water is equally impervious to water as clay ; and may therefore be used for lining the sides or dams of bodies of made water when such materials are required.

of lakes and ponds. In some places where easy, beautiful slopes and undulations of ground border the streams, gravel, soft turf, and a few simple groups of trees, will be the most natural accompaniments ; in others where the borders of the stream are broken into rougher, more rocky, and precipitous ridges, all the rich wildness and intricacy of low shrubs, ferns, creeping and climbing plants, may be brought in to advantage. Where the extent to be thus improved is considerable, the trouble may be lessened by planting the larger growth, and sowing the seeds of the smaller plants mingled together. Prepare the materials, and time and nature, with but little occasional assistance, will mature, and soften, and blend together the whole, in their own matchless and inimitable manner.

From all that we have suggested in these limited remarks, it will be seen that we would only attempt in our operations with water, the graceful or picturesque imitations of natural lakes or ponds, and brooks, rivulets, and streams. Such are the only forms in which this unrivalled element can be displayed so as to harmonize agreeably with natural and picturesque scenery. In the latter, there can be no apology made for the introduction of straight canals, round or oblong pieces of water, and all the regular forms of the geometric mode ; because they would evidently be in violent opposition to the whole character and expression of natural landscape. In architectural, or flower gardens (on which we shall hereafter have occasion to offer some remarks), where a different and highly artificial arrangement prevails, all these regular forms, with various jets, fountains, etc., may be employed with good taste, and wil' combine well with the other accessories of such

places. But in the grounds of a residence in the modern
style, *nature*, if possible, still more purified, as in the great
chefs-d'œuvre of art, by an ideal standard, should be the
great aim of the Landscape Gardener. And with water
especially, only beautiful when allowed to take its own
flowing forms and graceful motions, more than with any
other of our materials, all appearance of constraint and
formality should be avoided. If art be at all manifest, it
should discover itself only, as in the admirably painted
landscape, in the reproduction of nature in her choicest
developments. Indeed, many of the most celebrated
authors who have treated of this subject, appear to agree
that the productions of the artist in this branch are most
perfect as they approach most nearly to fac-similes of
nature herself: and though art should have formed the
whole, its employment must be nowhere discovered by the
spectator ; or as *Tasso* has more elegantly expressed the
idea :

" L'ARTE CHE TUTTO FA, NULLA SI SCOPRE."

SECTION IX.

LANDSCAPE OR RURAL ARCHITECTURE.

Difference between a city and a country house. The characteristic features of a country house. Examination of the leading principles in Rural Architecture. The different styles. The Grecian style, its merits and defects, and its associations. The Roman and Italian styles. The Pointed or Gothic style. The Tudor Mansion. The English Cottage, or Rural Gothic style. These styles considered in relation to situation or scenery. Individual tastes. Entrance Lodges.

> " A house amid the quiet country's shades,
>   With length'ning vistas, ever sunny glades ;
>   Beauty and fragrance clustering o'er the wall,
>   A porch inviting, and an ample hall."

 R C H I T E C T U R E, either practically considered or viewed as an art of taste, is a subject so important and comprehensive in itself, that volumes would be requisite to do it justice. Buildings of every description, from the humble cottage to the lofty temple, are objects of such constant recurrence in every habitable part of the globe, and are so strikingly indicative of the intelligence. character, and taste of the inhabitants, that they possess in themselves a great and peculiar interest for the mind. To have a "local habitation,"—a permanent dwelling, that we can give the impress of our own mind, and identify with our own existence,—appears to be the ardent wish, sooner or later felt, of every man : excepting

only those wandering sons of Ishmael, who pitch their tents with the same indifference, and as little desire to remain fixed, in the flowery plains of Persia, as in the sandy deserts of Zahara or Arabia.

In a city or town, or in its immediate vicinity, where space is limited, where buildings stand crowded together, and depend for their attractions entirely upon the style and manner of their construction, mere architectural effect, after convenience and fitness are consulted, is of course the only point to be kept in view. There, the façade, which meets the eye of the spectator from the public street, is enriched and made attractive by the display of architectural style and decoration, commensurate to the magnitude or importance of the edifice ; and the whole, so far as the effect of the building is concerned, comes directly within the province of the architect alone.

With respect to this class of dwellings we have little complaint to make, for many of our town residences are highly elegant and beautiful. But how shall we designate that singular perversity of taste, or rather that total want of it, which prompts the man, who, under the name of a villa residence, piles up in the free open country, amid the green fields, and beside the wanton gracefulness of luxuriant nature, a stiff modern " three story brick," which, like a well bred cockney with a true horror of the country, doggedly seems to refuse to enter into harmonious combination with any other object in the scene, but only serves to call up the exclamation,

Avaunt, stiff pile ! why didst thou stray
From blocks congenial in Broadway !

Yet almost daily we see built up in the country huge

combinations of boards and shingles, without the least
attempt at adaptation to situation ; and square masses
of brick start up here and there, in the verdant slopes
of our village suburbs, appearing as if they had been
transplanted, by some unlucky incantation, from the close-
packed neighborhood of city residence, and left accidentally in the country, or, as Sir Walter Scott has remarked, "had strayed out to the country for an airing."

What then are the proper characteristics of a rural
residence ? The answer to this, in a few words, is, such
a dwelling, as from its various accommodations, not only
gives ample space for all the comforts and conveniences
of a country life, but by its varied and picturesque form
and outline, its porches, verandas, etc., also appears to
have some reasonable connexion, or be in perfect keeping,
with surrounding nature. *Architectural beauty* must be
considered conjointly with the *beauty of the landscape* or
situation. Buildings of almost every description, and
particularly those for the habitation of man, will be
considered by the mind of taste, not only as architectural
objects of greater or less merit, but as component parts
of the general scene ; united with the surrounding lawn,
embosomed in tufts of trees and shrubs, if properly
designed and constructed, they will even serve to impress
a character upon the surrounding landscape. Their effect
will frequently be good or bad, not merely as they are
excellent or indifferent examples of a certain style of
building, but as they are happily or unhappily combined
with the adjacent scenery. The intelligent observer will
readily appreciate the truth of this, and acknowledge the
value, as well as necessity, of something besides architectural knowledge. And he will perceive how much

more likely to be successful are the efforts of him, who, in composing and constructing a rural residence, calls in tc the aid of architecture, the genius of the landscape ;— whose mind is imbued with a taste for beautiful scenery, and who so elegantly and ingeniously engrafts art upon nature, as to heighten her beauties ; while by the harmonious union he throws a borrowed charm around his own creation.

The English, above all other people, are celebrated for their skill in what we consider *rural adaptation*. Their residences seem to be a part of the scenes where they are situated ; for their exquisite taste and nice perception of the beauties of Landscape Gardening and rural scenery, lead them to erect those picturesque edifices, which, by their varied outlines, seem in exquisite keeping with nature ; while by the numberless climbing plants, shrubs, and fine ornamental trees with which they surround them, they form beautiful pictures of rural beauty. Even the various offices connected with the dwelling, partially concealed by groups of foliage, and contributing to the expression of domestic comfort, while they extend out, and give importance to the main edifice, also serve to connect it, in a less abrupt manner, with the grounds.

The leading principles which should be our guide in Landscape or Rural Architecture, have been condensed by an able writer in the following heads. "1st, As a useful art, in FITNESS FOR THE END IN VIEW : 2d, as an art of design in EXPRESSION OF PURPOSE : 3d, as an art of taste, in EXPRESSION OF SOME PARTICULAR ARCHITEC- TURAL STYLE."

The most enduring and permanent source of satisfaction in houses is, undoubtedly, utility. In a country residence,

therefore, of whatever character, the comfort and con
venience of the various members of the family being the
first and most important consideration, the quality of
fitness is universally appreciated and placed in the first
rank. In many of those articles of furniture or apparel
which luxury or fashion has brought into use, fitness or
convenience often gives way to beauty of form or texture :
but in a habitation intended to shelter us from the heat
and cold, as well as to give us an opportunity to dispense
the elegant hospitalities of refined life—the neglect of the
various indispensable conveniences and comforts which
an advanced state of civilization requires, would be but
poorly compensated for by a fanciful exterior or a highly
ornate style of building. Further than this, *fitness* will
extend to the choice of situation ; selecting a sheltered
site, neither too high, as upon the exposed summit of bleak
hills, nor too low, as in the lowest bottoms of damp
valleys ; but preferring those middle grounds which, while
they afford a free circulation of air, and a fine prospect,
are not detrimental to the health or enjoyment of the
occupants. A proper exposure is another subject, worthy
of the attention of either the architect or proprietor, as
there are stormy and pleasant aspects or exposures in all
climates.

However much the principle of *fitness* may be appreciated and acted upon in the United States, we have
certainly great need of apology for the flagrant and almost
constant violation of the second principle, viz. *the expression of purpose.* By the expression of purpose in
buildings, is meant that architectural character, or
ensemble, which distinctly points out the particular use or
destination for which the edifice is intended. In a

dwelling-house, the expression of purpose is conveyed by the chimney-tops, the porch or veranda, and those various appendages indicative of domestic enjoyment, which are needless, and therefore misplaced, in a public building. In a church, the spire or the dome, when present, at once stamps the building with the expression of purpose ; and the few openings and plain exterior, with the absence of chimneys, are the suitable and easily recognised characteristics of the barn. Were any one to commit so violent an outrage upon the principle of the expression of purpose as to surmount his barns with the tall church spire, our feelings would at once cry out against the want of propriety. Yet how often do we meet in the northern states, with stables built after the models of Greek temples, and barns with elegant Venetian shutters—to say nothing of mansions with none but concealed chimney-tops, and without porches or append-ages of any kind, to give the least hint to the mind of the doubting spectator, whether the edifice is a chapel, a bank, a hospital, or the private dwelling of a man of wealth and opulence!

" The expression of the purpose for which every building is erected," says the writer before quoted, " is the first and most essential beauty, and should be obvious from its architecture, although independent of any particular style ; in the same manner as the reasons for things are altogether independent of the language in which they are conveyed. As in literary composition, no beauty of language can ever compensate for poverty of sense, so in architectural composition, no beauty of style can ever compensate for want of expression of purpose."

Applying this excellent principle to our own country

houses and their offices or out-buildings, we think every reasonable person will, at the first glance, see how lamentably deficient are many of the productions of our architects and builders, in one of the leading principles of the art. The most common form for an American country villa is the pseudo-Greek Temple ; that is, a rectangular oblong building, with the chimney-tops concealed, if possible, and instead of a pretty and comfortable porch, veranda, or piazza, four, six, or eight lofty wooden columns are seen supporting a portico, so high as neither to afford an agreeable promenade, nor a sufficient shelter from the sun and rain.

There are two features, which it is now generally admitted contribute strongly to the expression of purpose in a dwelling-house, and especially in a country residence. These are the chimney-tops and the entrance porch. Chimney-tops, with us, are generally square masses of brick, rising above the roof, and presenting certainly no very elegant appearance, which may perhaps serve as the apology of those who studiously conceal them. But in a climate where fires are requisite during a large portion of the year, chimney-tops are expressive of a certain comfort resulting from the use of them, which characterizes a building intended for a dwelling in that climate. Chimney-tops being never, or rarely, placed on those buildings intended for the inferior animals, are also undoubtedly strongly indicative of human habitations. Instead, therefore, of hiding or concealing them, they should be in all dwellings not only boldly avowed, but rendered ornamental; for whatever is a characteristic and necessary feature, should undoubtedly, if possible, be rendered elegant, or at least prevented from being ugly.

Much of the picturesque effect of the ola English and Italian houses, undoubtedly arises from the handsome and curious stacks of chimneys which spring out of their roofs. These, while they break and diversify the sky outline of the building, enrich and give variety to its most bare and unornamented part. Examples are not wanting, in all the different styles of architecture, of handsome and character istic chimneys, which may be adopted in any of our dwellings of a similar style. The Gothic, or old English chimney, with octagonal or cylindrical flues or shafts united in clusters, is made in a great variety of forms, either of bricks or artificial stone. The former materials, moulded in the required shape, are highly taxed in England, while they may be very cheaply made here.

A *Porch* strengthens or conveys expression of purpose, because, instead of leaving the entrance door bare, as in manufactories and buildings of an inferior description, it serves both as a note of preparation, and an effectual shelter and protection to the entrance. Besides this, it gives a dignity and importance to that entrance, pointing it out to the stranger as the place of approach. A fine country house, without a porch or covered shelter to the doorway of some description, is therefore as incomplete, to the correct eye, as a well printed book without a title page, leaving the stranger to plunge at once *in medias res*, without the friendly preparation of a single word of intro-duction. Porches are susceptible of every variety of form and decoration, from the embattled and buttressed portal of the Gothic castle, to the latticed arbor porch of the cottage, around which the festoons of luxuriant climbing plants cluster, giving an effect not less beautiful than the richly carved capitals of the classic portico.

In this country no architectural feature is more plainly expressive of purpose in our dwelling-houses than the *veranda*, or piazza. The unclouded splendor and fierce heat of our summer sun, render this very general appendage a source of real comfort and enjoyment ; and the long veranda round many of our country residences stands instead of the paved terraces of the English mansions as the place for promenade ; while during the warmer portions of the season, half of the days or evenings are there passed in the enjoyment of the cool breezes, secure under low roofs supported by the open colonnade, from the solar rays, or the dews of night. The obvious utility of the veranda in this climate (especially in the middle and southern states) will, therefore, excuse its adoption into any style of architecture that may be selected for our domestic uses, although abroad, buildings in the style in question, as the Gothic, for example, are not usually accompanied by such an appendage. An artist of the least taste or invention will easily compose an addition of this kind, that will be in good keeping with the rest of the edifice.

These various features, or parts of the building, with many others which convey *expression of purpose* in domestic architecture, because they recall to the mind the different uses to which they are applied, and the several enjoyments connected with them, also contribute greatly to the interest of the building itself, and heighten its good effect as part of a harmonious whole, in the landscape. The various projections and irregularities, caused by verandas, porticos, etc., serve to connect the otherwise square masses of building, by gradual transition with the ground about it.

The reader, who thus recognizes features as expressive

of purpose in a dwelling intended for the habitation of man, we think, can be at no great loss to understand what would be characteristic in out-buildings or offices, farm-houses, lodges, stables, and the like, which are necessary structures on a villa or mansion residence of much size or importance. A proper regard to the expression of use or purpose, without interfering with the beauty of style, will confer at all times another, viz. the beauty of truth, without which no building can be completely satisfactory ; as deceptions of this kind (buildings appearing to be what they are not) always go far towards destroying in the mind those pleasurable emotions felt on viewing any correct work of art, however simple in character or design.

We have now to consider rural architecture under the guidance of the third leading principle, as *an art of taste*. The expression of architectural *style* in buildings is undoubtedly a matter of the first importance, and proper care being taken not to violate fitness and expression of purpose, it may be considered as appealing most powerfully, at once, to the mind of almost every person. Indeed, with many, it is the only species of beauty which they perceive in buildings, and to it both convenience and the expression of purpose are often ignorantly sacrificed.

A marked style of architecture appears to us to have claims for our admiration or preference for rural residences, for several reasons. As it is intrinsically beautiful in itself ; as it interests us by means of the associations connected with it ; as it is fitted to the wants and comforts of country life ; and as it is adapted to, or harmonizes with, the locality or scenery where it is located.

The harmonious union of buildings and scenery, is a point of taste that appears to be but little understood in

any country ; and mainly, we believe, because the architect
and the landscape painter are seldom combined in the same
person, or are seldom consulted together. It is for this
reason that we so rarely see a country residence, or cottage
and its grounds, making such a composition as a landscape
painter would choose for his pencil. But it does not seem
difficult, with a slight recurrence to the leading principle
of unity of expression, to suggest a mode of immediately
deciding which style of building is best adapted to harmonize with a certain kind of scenery.

The reader is, we trust, already familiar with our
division of landscapes into two natural classes,—the
Beautiful and the Picturesque,—and the two accordant
systems of improvement in Landscape Gardening which
we have based upon these distinct characters. Now, in
order to render our buildings perfectly harmonious, we
conceive it only to be necessary to arrange (as we may
very properly do) all the styles of domestic architecture in
corresponding divisions.

Some ingenious writer has already developed this idea,
and, following a hint taken from the two leading schools
of literature and art, has divided all architecture into the
Classical and the *Romantic* schools of design. The
Classical comprises the Grecian style, and all its near and
direct offspring, as the Roman and Italian modes ; the
Romantic school, the Gothic style, with its numberless
variations of Tudor, Elizabethan, Flemish, and old English
modes.

It is easy to see, at a glance, how well these divisions
correspond with our Beautiful and Picturesque phases of
Landscape Gardening, so that indeed we might call the
Grecian or Classical style, Beautiful, and the Gothic or

Romantic style, the Picturesque schools in architecture. In classical buildings, as in beautiful landscape, we are led to admire simplicity of forms and outlines, purity of effect, and grace of composition. In the Romantic or Picturesque buildings, we are struck by the irregularity of forms and outlines, variety of effect, and boldness of composition. What, therefore, can be more evident in seeking to produce unity of effect than the propriety of selecting some variations of the classical style for Beautiful landscape, and some species of romantic irregular building for Picturesque landscape?

In a practical point of view, all buildings which have considerable simplicity of outline, a certain complete and graceful style of ornament, and a polished and refined kind of finish, may be considered as likely to harmonize best with all landscape where the expression is that of simple or graceful beauty—where the lawn or surface is level or gently undulating, the trees rich and full in foliage and form, and the general character of the scenery peaceful and beautiful. Such are the Grecian, Roman, Tuscan, and the chaster Italian styles.

On the other hand, buildings of more irregular outline, in which appear bolder or ruder ornaments, and a certain free and more rustic air in finishing, are those which should be selected to accompany scenery of a wilder or more picturesque character, abounding in striking variations of surface, wood, and water. And these are the Castellated, the Tudor, and the old English in all its forms.

There is still an intermediate kind of architecture, originally a variation of the classical style, but which, in becoming adapted to different and more picturesque situations, has lost much of its graceful character, and has become quite picturesque in its outlines and effects. Of this kind are the *Swiss* and the *bracketed* cottage, and the different highly irregular forms of the *Italian villa.* The more simple and regular variations of these modes of building, may be introduced with good effect in any plain country ; while the more irregular and artistical forms have the happiest effect only in more highly varied and suitable localities.

The *Egyptian*, one of the oldest architectural styles, characterized by its heavy colossal forms, and almost sublime expression, is supposed to have had its origin in caverns hewn in the rocks. The *Chinese* style, easily known by its waving lines, probably had its type in the eastern tent. The Saracenic, or Moorish style, rich in fanciful decoration, is striking and picturesque in its details, and is worthy of the attention of the wealthy amateur.

Neither of these styles, however, is, or can well be, thoroughly adapted to our domestic purposes, as they are wanting in fitness, and have comparatively few charms of association for residents of this country.

The only styles at present in common use for domestic architecture, throughout the enlightened portions of Europe and America, are the Grecian and Gothic styles, or some modifications of these two distinct kinds of building. These modifications, which of themselves are now considered styles by most authors, are, the *Roman* and *modern Italian* styles, which have grown out of Greek architecture ; the *Castellated,* the *Tudor,* the *Elizabethan,* and the *rurai Gothic* or old English cottage styles, all of which are variations of Gothic architecture.

Grecian or classic architecture was exhibited in its purity in those splendid temples of the golden days of

Athens, which still remain in a sufficient degree of preservation to bear ample testimony to the high state of architectural art among the Greeks. Each of the five orders was so nicely determined by their profound knowledge of the harmony of forms, and admirably executed, that all modern attempts at improving them have entirely failed, for they are, individually, complete models.

As it is admitted, then, that Grecian architecture is intrinsically beautiful in itself, and highly interesting in point of associations, it may be asked, what are the objections, if any, to its common introduction into domestic Rural Architecture?

We have already avowed that we consider fitness and expression of purpose two leading principles of the first importance in Rural Architecture, and Grecian architecture in its pure form—viz., the *temple*—when applied to the purposes of domestic life, makes a sad blow at both these established rules. The comforts of a country residence are so various, that verandahs, porches, wings of different sizes, and many other little accommodations expressive of purpose, become necessary, and, therefore, when **properly arranged**, add to the beauty of Rural Architecture. But the admirer of the true Greek models is obliged to forego the majority of these; and to come within the prescribed form of the rectangular parallelogram, his apartments must be of a given size and a limited number, while many things, both exterior and interior, which convenience might otherwise prompt, have to bow to the despotic sway of the pure Greek model. In a dwelling of moderate dimensions how great a sacrifice of room is made to enable the architect to display the *portico* alone!

[Fig. 40. Roman Residence.]

It has been well observed by modern critics, that there is no reason to believe the temple form was ever, even by the Greeks, used for private dwellings, which easily accounts for our comparative failure in constructing well arranged, small residences in this style.

The Romans, either unable to compose in the simple elegance and beauty of the Grecian style, or feeling its want of adaptation to the multifarious usages of a more

[Fig. 41. View at Presque Isle, the residence of Wm. Denning, Esq., Dutchess Co., N. Y.]

luxurious state of society, created for themselves what is generally considered a less beautiful and perfect, yet which is certainly a more rich, varied, and, if we may use the

term, *accommodating* style.   The *Roman style* is distinguished from its prototype by the introduction of arched
openings over the doors and windows, story piled over
story,—often with columns of different orders—instead of
the simple unbroken line of the Greek edifices. In
decoration, the buildings in this style vary from plain,
unornamented exteriors, to the most highly decorated
façades ; and instead of being confined to the few fixed
principles of the Greek, the greatest latitude is often
observed in the proportions, forms, and decorations of
buildings in the Roman style.   These very circumstances,
while they rendered the style less perfect as a fine art, or
for public edifices, gave it a pliability or facility of
adaptation, which fits it more completely for domestic
purposes.   For this reason, a great portion of the finest
specimens of the modern domestic architecture of the
other continent is to be found in the Roman style.*

The *Italian style* is, we think, decidedly the most
beautiful mode for domestic purposes, that has been the
direct offspring of Grecian art.   It is a style which has
evidently grown up under the eyes of the painters of more
modern Italy, as it is admirably adapted to harmonize with
general nature, and produce a pleasing and picturesque
effect in fine landscapes.   Retaining more or less of the
columns, arches, and other details of the Roman style, it
has intrinsically a bold irregularity, and strong contrast of
light and shadow, which give it a peculiarly striking and
painter-like effect.

* Perhaps the finest façade of a private residence, in America, is that of the
"Patroon's house," near Albany, the ancient seat of the Van Rensselaer
family, lately remodelled and improved by that skilful architect, Mr. Upjohn,
of New York.

"The villa architecture of modern Italy," says Mr. Lamb, an able architect,* "is characterized, when on a moderate scale, by scattered irregular masses, great contrasts of light and shade, broken and plain surfaces, and great variety of outline against the sky. The blank wall on which the eye sometimes reposes ; the towering campanile, boldly contrasted with the horizontal line of roof only broken by a few straggling chimney-tops : the row of equal sized, closely placed windows, contrasting with the plain space and single window of the projecting balcony ; the prominent portico, the continued arcade, the terraces, and the variously formed and disposed out-buildings, all combine to form that picturesque whole, which distinguishes the modern Italian villa from every other."†

A building in the Italian style may readily be known at first sight, by the peculiar appearance of its roofs. These are always projecting at the eaves, and deeply furrowed or

[Fig 42. A Villa in the Italian style.]

ridged, being formed abroad of semi-cylindrical tiles, which give a distinct and highly marked expression to this

* Loudon's Ency. of Arch. p. 951.
† In this country, owing to the greater number of fires, the effect would be improved by an additional number of chimney-tops.

portion of the building.* So many appliances of comfort
and enjoyment suited to a warm climate appear, too, in
the villas of this style, that it has a peculiarly elegant and
refined appearance. Among these are *arcades*, with the
Roman arched openings, forming sheltered promenades ;
and beautiful *balconies* projecting from single windows, or
sometimes from connected rows of windows, which are
charming places for a *coup d'œil*, or to enjoy the cool
breeze—as they admit, to shelter one from the sun, of a
fanciful awning shade, which may be raised or lowered at
pleasure. The windows themselves are bold, and well
marked in outline, being either round-arched at the tops,
or finished with a heavy architrave.

[Fig. 43. Residence of Gov. Morehead, North Carolina.]

All these balconies, arcades, etc., are sources of real
pleasure in the hotter portions of our year, which are quite
equal in elevation of temperature to summers of the south
of Europe ; while by increased thickness of walls and

* In some situations in this country, where it might be difficult to procure
tiles made in this form, their effect may be very accurately imitated by deeply
ridged zinc or tin coverings. The bold projection of the eaves, in the Italian
style, offers great protection to a house against storms and dampness.

closeness of window fixtures, the houses may also be made of the most comfortable description in winter.

The Italian chimney-tops, unlike the Grecian, are always openly shown and rendered ornamental; and as we have already mentioned, the irregularity in the masses of the edifice and shape of the roof, renders the sky outline of a building in this style, extremely picturesque. A villa, however small, in the Italian style, may have an elegant and expressive character, without interfering with convenient internal arrangements, while at the same time this style has the very great merit of allowing additions to be made in almost any direction, without

injuring the effect of the original structure; indeed such is the variety of sizes and forms which the different parts of an Italian villa may take, in perfect accordance with architec-

[Fig. 44.   The New Haven Suburban Villa.*]

tural propriety, that the original edifice frequently gains in beauty by additions of this description.   Those who are aware how many houses are every year erected in the United States by persons of moderate fortune, who would gladly make additions at some subsequent period, could this be done without injuring the effect or beauty of the main building, will, we think, acknowledge how much,

* New Haven abounds with tasteful residences. "Hillhouse Avenue," in particular, is remarkable for a neat display of Tuscan or Italian Suburban Villas. Moderate in dimension and economical in construction, these exceedingly neat edifices may be considered as models for this kind of dwelling. *Fig.* 44, without being a precise copy of any one of these buildings, may be taken as a pretty accurate representation of their general appearance.

even were it in this single point alone, the Italian style is superior to the Grecian for rural residences.

Pleasing associations are connected with Roman and Italian architecture, especially to those who have studied their effect in all the richness and beauty with which they are invested in the countries where they originated ; and they may be regarded with a degree of classic interest by every cultivated mind. The modern Italian style recalls images of that land of painters and of the fine arts, where the imagination, the fancy, and taste, still revel in a world of beauty and grace. The great number of elegant forms which have grown out of this long cultivated feeling for the beautiful in the fine arts,—in the shape of fine vases, statues, and other ornaments, which harmonize with, and are so well adapted to enrich, this style of architecture,— combine to render it in the fine terraced gardens of Florence and other parts of Italy, one of the richest and most attractive styles in existence. Indeed we can hardly imagine a mode of building, which in the hands of a man of wealth and taste, may, in this country, be made productive of more beauty, convenience, and luxury, than the modern Italian style ; so well suited to both our hot summers and cold winters, and which is so easily susceptible of enrichment and decoration, while it is at the same time so well adapted to the material in the most common use at present in most parts of the country,—wood. Vases, and other beautiful architectural ornaments, may now be procured in our cities, or imported direct from the Mediterranean, finely cut in Maltese stone, at very moderate prices, and which serve to decorate both the grounds and buildings in a handsome manner.

From the Italian style it is an easy transition to the Swiss mode, a bold and spirited one, highly picturesque and interesting in certain situations. To build an exact copy of a Swiss cottage in a smooth cultivated country, would, both as regards association and intrinsic want of fitness, be the height of folly. But in a wild and mountainons region, such as the borders of certain deep valleys and rocky glens in the Hudson Highlands, or rich bits of the Alleghanies, positions may be found where the Swiss cottage (Fig. 45), with its low and broad roof, shedding off the heavy snows, its ornamented exterior gallery, its strong and deep brackets, and its rough and rustic exterior, would be in the highest degree appropriate.

[Fig. 45. The Swiss Cottage.]

A modification, partaking somewhat of the Italian and Swiss features, is what we have described more fully in our "Cottage Residences" as the Bracketed mode. It possesses

a good deal of character, is capable of considerable picturesque effect, is very easily and cheaply constructed of
wood or stone, and is perhaps more entirely adapted to our

[Fig. 46. The Bracketed Mode.]

hot summers and cold winters than any other equally
simple mode of building. We hope to see this Bracketed
style becoming every day more common in the United
States, and especially in our farm and country houses,
when wood is the material employed in their construction.

Gothic, or more properly, *pointed architecture*, which
sprang up with the Christian religion, reached a point of
great perfection about the thirteenth century ; a period
when the most magnificent churches and cathedrals of
England and Germany were erected.   These wonderful
structures, reared by an almost magical skill and contrivance, with their richly groined roofs of stone supported in
mid-air ; their beautiful and elaborate tracery and carving
of plants, flowers, and animate objects ; their large windows

through which streamed a rich glow of rainbow light ; their
various buttresses and pinnacles, all contributing to
strengthen, and at the same time give additional beauty to
the exterior; their clustered columns, airy-like, yet firm ;
and, surmounting the whole, the tall spire, piled up to an
almost fearful height towards the heavens, are lasting
monuments of the genius, scientific skill, and mechanical
ingenuity of the artists of those times. That person, who,
from ignorance or prejudice, fully supposes there is no
architecture but that of the Greeks, would do well to study
one of these unrivalled specimens of human skill. In so
doing, unless he closes his eyes against the evidences of his
senses, he cannot but admit that there is far more genius,
and more mathematical skill, evinced in one of these
cathedrals, than would have been requisite in the construction of the most celebrated of the Greek temples. Though
they may not exhibit that simplicity and harmony of proportion which Grecian buildings display, they abound in
much higher proofs of genius, as is abundantly evinced in
the conception and execution of Cathedrals so abounding
in unrivalled sublimity, variety, and beauty.

Gothic architecture, in its purity, was characterized
mainly by the *pointed arch.* This novel feature in architecture, which, probably, in the hands of artists of great
mathematical skill, was suggested by the inefficiency of the
Roman arch first used, has given rise to all the superior
boldness and picturesqueness of this style compared with
the Grecian; for while the Greek artist was obliged to
cover his narrow openings with architraves, or solid blocks
of stone, resting on columns at short intervals, and filling
up the open space, the Gothic artist, by a single span of
his pointed arch, resting on distant pillars, kept the whole

area beneath free and unencumbered.   Applied, too, tc
openings for the admission of light, which were deemed
of comparatively little or no importance by the Greeks, the
arch was of immense value, making it possible to pierce
the solid wall with large and lofty apertures, that diffused
a magical brilliancy of light in the otherwise dim and
shadowy interior.

We have here adverted to the Gothic cathedral (as we
did to the Greek temple) as exhibiting the peculiar style in
question in its greatest purity.   For domestic purposes,
both, for the same reasons, are equally unfitted ; as they
were never so intended to be used by their original invent-
ors, and being entirely wanting in fitness for the purposes
of habitation in domestic life ; the Greek temple, as we
have already shown, from its massive porticoes and the
simple rectangular form of its interior ; and the Gothic
cathedral, from its high-pointed windows, and immense
vaulted apartments.   It would scarcely, however, be more
absurd to build a miniature cathedral, for a dwelling in the
Gothic style, than to make an exact copy of the Temple of
Minerva 30 by 50 feet in size, for a country residence, as
we often witness in this country.

The *Gothic Style*, as applied to Domestic Architecture,
has been varied and adapted in a great diversity of ways,
to the wants of society in different periods, from the 12th
century to the present time.   The baronial castle of feudal
days, perched upon its solitary, almost inaccessible height,
and built strongly for defence ; the Collegiate or monastic
abbey of the monks, suited to the rich fertile plains which
these jolly ascetics so well knew how to select ; the Tudor
or Elizabethan mansion, of the English gentleman, surrounded by its beautiful park, filled with old ancestral trees ;

and the pretty, rural, gabled cottage, of more humble pretensions; are all varieties of this multiform style, easily adapting itself to the comforts and conveniences of private life.

Contrasted with Classic Architecture and its varieties, in which horizontal lines are most prevalent, all the different Gothic modes or styles exhibit a preponderance of vertical or perpendicular lines. In the purer Gothic Architecture, the style is often determined by the form of the arch predominant in the window and door openings, which in all edifices (except Norman buildings) were lancet-shaped, or high pointed, in the 13th century ; four centred or low arched, in the times of Henry VII. and VIII. ; and finally square-headed, as in most domestic buildings of later date.

Castellated Gothic is easily known, at first sight, by the line of battlements cut out of the solid parapet wall, which surmounts the outline of the building in every part. These generally conceal the roof, which is low, and were originally intended as a shelter to those engaged in defending the

[Fig. 47. The Castellated Mode.]

building against assaults Modern buildings in the castellated style, without sacrificing almost everything to strength, as was once necessary, preserve the general character of the ancient castle, while they combine with it almost every modern luxury. In their exteriors, we perceive strong and massive octagonal or circular towers, rising boldly, with corbelled or projecting cornices, above the ordinary level of the building. The

windows are either pointed or square-headed, or perhaps a
mixture of both.   The porch rises into a turreted and
embattled gateway, and all the offices and out-buildings
connected with the main edifice, are constructed in a style
corresponding to that exhibited in the main body of the
building. The whole is placed on a distinct and firm
terrace of stone, and the expression of the edifice is that
of strength and security.

This mode of building is evidently of too ambitious and
expensive a kind for a republic, where landed estates are
not secured by entail, but divided, according to the dictates
of nature, among the different members of a family.   It is,
perhaps, also rather wanting in appropriateness, castles
never having been used for defence in this country.
Notwithstanding these objections, there is no very weighty
reason why a wealthy proprietor should not erect his
mansion in the castellated style, if that style be in unison
with his scenery and locality.   Few instances, however,
of sufficient wealth and taste to produce edifices of this
kind, are to be met with among us ; and the castellated
style is therefore one which we cannot fully recommend
for adoption here.   Paltry imitations of it, in materials less
durable than brick or stone, would be discreditable to any
person having the least pretension to correct taste.

The Castellated style never appears completely at home
except in wild and romantic scenery, or in situations where
the neighboring mountains, or wild passes, are sufficiently
near to give that character to the landscape.   In such
localities the Gothic castle affects us agreeably, because we
know that baronial castles were generally built in similar
spots, and because the battlements, towers, and other bold
features, combine well with the rugged and spirited

character of the surrounding objects. To place such a building in this country on a smooth surface in the midst of fertile plains, would immediately be felt to be bad taste by every one, as from the style not having been before our eyes from childhood, as it is in Europe, we immediately refer to its original purposes,—those of security and defence.

A mansion in the *Tudor Style* affords the best example of the excellence of Gothic architecture for domestic purposes. The roof often rises boldly here, instead of being concealed by the parapet wall, and the gables are either plain or ornamented with crockets. The windows are divided by mullions, and are generally enriched with tracery in a style less florid than that employed in churches, but still sufficiently elegant to give an appearance of decoration to these parts of the building. Sometimes the low, or Tudor arch, is displayed in the window-heads, but most commonly the square-headed window with the Gothic label is employed. Great latitude is allowed in this particular, as well as in the size of the window, provided the general details of style are attended to. Indeed, in the domestic architecture of this era, the windows and doors are often sources of great architectural beauty, instead of being left mere bare openings filled with glass, as in the Classic styles. Not only is each individual window divided by mullions into compartments whose tops are encircled by tracery ; but in particular apartments, as the dining-hall, library, etc., these are filled with richly stained glass, which gives a mellow, pleasing light to the apartment. Added to this, the windows, in the best Tudor mansions, affect a great variety of forms and sizes. Among these stand conspicuous the *bay* and *oriel* windows. The bay-

FIG. 48.—Mr. Paulding's Residence, Tarrytown, N. Y.

FIG. 49.—Residence of the Author, near Newburgh, N. Y.

window, which is introduced on the first or principal floor, in most apartments of much size or importance, is a window of treble or quadruple the common size, projecting from the main body of the room in a semi-octagonal or hexagonal form, thereby affording more space in the apartment, from the floor to the ceiling, as well as giving an abundance of light, and a fine prospect in any favorite direction. This, while it has a grander effect than several windows of moderate size, gives a variety of form and outline to the different apartments, that can never be so well attained when the windows are mere openings cut in the solid walls. The oriel-window is very similar to the bay-window, but projecting in a similar manner from the upper story, supported on corbelled mouldings. These windows are not only elegant in the interior, but by standing out from the face of the walls, they prevent any-thing like too great a formality externally, and bestow a pleasing variety on the different fronts of the building.

The sky outline of a villa in the Tudor Gothic style, is highly picturesque. It is made up of many fine features. The pointed gables, with their finials, are among the most striking, and the neat parapet wall, either covered with a moulded coping, or, perhaps, diversified with battlements; the latter not so massive as in the castellated style, but evidently intended for ornament only. The roof line is often varied by the ornamented gablet of a dormer window, rising here and there, and adding to the quaintness of the whole. We must not forget, above all, the highly enriched chimney shaft, which, in the English examples, is made of fancifully moulded bricks, and is carried up in clusters some distance above the roof. How much more pleasing for a dwelling must be the outline of such a building, than that of a simple square roof whose summit is one unbroken straight line !*

The inclosed entrance porch, approached by three or four stone steps, with a seat or two for servants waiting, is a distinctive mark of all the old English houses. This projects, in most cases, from the main body of the edifice, and opens directly into the *hall*. The latter apartment is not merely (as in most of our modern houses) an entry, narrow and long, running directly through the house, but has a peculiar character of its own, being rather spacious, the roof or ceiling ribbed or groined, and the floor often inlaid with marble tiles. A corresponding and suitable style of finish, with Gothic details, runs through all the different apartments, each of which, instead of being finished and furnished with the formal sameness here so prevalent, displays, according to its peculiar purposes— as the dining-room, drawing-room, library, etc.—a marked and characteristic air.

We have thus particularized the Tudor mansion, because we believe that for a cold country like England or the United States, it has strong claims upon the attention of large landed proprietors, or those who wish to realize in a country residence the greatest amount of comfort and enjoyment. With the addition, here, of a veranda, which the cool summers of England render needless, we believe the Tudor Gothic to be the most convenient and comfortable, and decidedly the most picturesque and striking

---

* Two miles south of Albany, on a densely wooded hill, is the villa of Joel Rathbone, Esq., Fig. 50, one of the most complete specimens of the Tudor style in the United States. It was built from the designs of Davis, and is to the amateur, a very instructive example of this mode of domestic architecture.

FIG. 50.—Residence of Joel Rathbone, Esq., near Albany, N. Y.

FIG. 51.—Cottage of S E. Lyon, Esq., White Plains, N. Y.

Fig. 52.—Cottage Residence of Thomas W. Ludlow, near Yonkers, N Y.

Fig. 53.—Sunnyside, Residence of Washington Irving, Esq , near Tarrytown, N Y.

style, for country residences of a superior class.* The materials generally employed in their construction in England, are stone aud brick; and of late years, brick and stucco has come into very general use.

The *Elizabethan Style*, that mode of building so common in England in the 17th century,—a mixture of Gothic and Grecian in its details—is usually considered as a barbarous kind of architecture, wanting in purity of taste. Be this as it may, it cannot be denied that in the finer specimens of this style, there is a surprising degree of richness and picturesqueness for which we may look in vain elsewhere. In short it seems, in the best examples, admirably fitted for a *bowery*, thickly foliaged country, like England, and for the great variety of domestic enjoyments of its inhabitants. In the most florid examples of this style, of which many specimens yet remain, we often meet with every kind of architectural feature and ornament, oddly, and often grotesquely combined—pointed gables, dormer-windows, steep and low roofs, twisted columns, pierced parapets, and broad windows with small lights. Sometimes the effect of this fantastic combination is excellent, but often bad. The florid Elizabethan style is, therefore, a very dangerous one in the hands of any one but an architect of profound taste; but we think in some of its simpler forms (Fig. 52), it may be adopted for country residences here in picturesque situations with a quaint and happy effect.†

* The residence of Samuel E. Lyon, Esq., at White Plains, N. Y., Fig. 51, is a very pleasing example of the *Tudor Cottage*.

The seat of Robert Gilmor, Esq., near Baltimore, in the Tudor style, is a very extensive pile of building.

† A highly unique residence in the old English syle, is Pelham Priory, the seat of the Rev. Robert Bolton, near New Rochelle, N. Y., Fig. 53. The

The English cottage style, or what we have denominated
Rural Gothic, contains within itself all the most striking
and peculiar elements of the beautiful and picturesque in
its exterior, while it admits of the greatest possible variety
of accommodation and convenience in internal arrangement. In its general composition, Rural Gothic really differs
from the Tudor style more in that general *simplicity*
which serves to distinguish a cottage or villa of moderate
size from a mansion, than in any marked character of its
own. The square-headed windows preserve the same
form, and display the Gothic label and mullions, though
the more expensive finish of decorative tracery is frequently omitted. Diagonal or latticed lights are also more
commonly seen in the cottage style than in the mansion.
The general form and arrangement of the building, though
of course much reduced, is not unlike that of the latter
edifice. The entrance porch is always preserved, and the
bay-window jutting out from the best apartment, gives
variety, and an agreeable expression of use and enjoyment,
to almost every specimen of the old English cottage.

Perhaps the most striking feature of this charming style
as we see it in the best old English cottages, is the pointed
gable. This feature, which grows out of the high roofs

exterior is massive and picturesque, in the simplest taste of the Elizabethan
age, and being built amidst a fine oak wood, of the dark rough stone of the
neighborhood, it has at once the appearance of considerable antiquity. The
interior is constructed and fitted up throughout in the same feeling,—with
harmonious wainscoting, quaint carving, massive chimney pieces, and old
furniture and armor. Indeed, we doubt if there is, at the present moment
any recent private residence, even in England, where the spirit of the antique
is more entirely carried out, and where one may more easily fancy himself in
one of those " mansions builded curiously " of our ancestors in the time of
" good Queen Bess "

adopted, not only appears in the two ends of the main building, but terminates every wing or projection of almost any size that joins to the principal body of the house. The gables are either of stone or brick, with a handsome moulded coping, or they are finished with the widely projecting roof of wood, and *verge boards*, carved in a fanciful and highly decorative shape. In either case, the point or apex is crowned by a finial, or ornamental octagonal shaft, rendering the gable one of the greatest sources of interest in these dwellings. The projecting roof renders the walls always dry.

The porch, the labelled windows, the chimney shafts, and the ornamented gables, being the essential features in the composition of the English cottage style, it is evident that this mode of building is highly expressive of purpose, for country residences of almost every description and size, from the humblest peasant's cottage, to the beautiful and picturesque villa of the retired gentleman of fortune. In the simple form of the cottage, the whole may be constructed of wood very cheaply, and in the more elaborate villa residence, stone, or brick and cement, may be preferred, as being more permanent. No style so readily admits of enrichment as that of the old English cottage when on a considerable scale ; and by the addition of pointed verandas, bay windows, and dormer-windows, by the introduction of mullions and tracery in the window openings, and indeed, by a multitude of interior and exterior enrichments generally applied to the Tudor mansions, a villa in the rural Gothic style may be made a perfect gem of a country residence. Of all the styles hitherto enumerated, we consider this one of the most suitable for this country, as, while it comes within the reach of all persons of moderate

means, it unites, as we before stated, so much of convenience and rural beauty.*

To the man of taste, there is no style which presents
greater attractions, being at once rich in picturesque
beauty, and harmonious in connexion with the surrounding
forms of vegetation. The Grecian villa, with its simple
forms and horizontal lines, seems to us only in good keeping
when it is in a smooth, highly cultivated, peaceful scene.
But the Rural Gothic, the lines of which point upwards, in
the pyramidal gables, tall clusters of chimneys, finials, and
the several other portions of its varied outline, harmonizes
easily with the tall trees, the tapering masses of foliage, or
the surrounding hills; and while it is seldom or never
misplaced in spirited rural scenery, it gives character and
picturesque expression to many landscapes entirely devoid
of that quality.

What we have already said in speaking of the Italian
style, respecting the facility with which additions may be
made to irregular houses, applies with equal, or even
greater force, to the varieties of the Gothic style, just
described. From the very fact that the highest beauty of
these modes of building arises from their irregularity
(opposed to Grecian architecture, which, in its chaste
simplicity, should be regular), it is evident that additions

---

* The only objection that can be urged against this mode of building, is that
which applies to all cottages with a low second story, viz. want of coolness in
the sleeping chambers during mid-summer. An evil which may be remedied
by constructing a false inner-roof—leaving a vacuity between the two roofs of
six or eight inches, which being occupied with air and ventilated at the top, will
almost entirely obviate the objection.

In our *Cottage Residences*, Design II., we have shown how the comfort of
a full second story, suitable for this climate, may be combined with the expres
sion of the English cottage style.

judiciously made will tend to increase this beauty, or afford more facility for its display ; while it is equally evident that in the interior arrangement, including apartments of every description, superior opportunities are afforded for attaining internal comfort and convenience, as well as external effect.

The ideas connected in our minds with Gothic architecture are of a highly *romantic* and *poetical* nature contrasted with the classical associations which the Greek and Roman styles suggest. Although our own country is nearly destitute of ruins and ancient time-worn edifices, yet the literature of Europe, and particularly of what we term the mother country, is so much our own, that we form a kind of delightful ideal acquaintance with the venerable castles, abbeys, and strongholds of the middle ages. Romantic as is the real history of those times and places, to our minds their charm is greatly enhanced by distance, by the poetry of legendary superstition, and the fascination of fictitious narrative. A castellated residence, therefore, in a wild and pictur-esque situation, may be interesting, not only from its being perfectly in keeping with surrounding nature, but from the delightful manner in which it awakens associations fraught with the most enticing history of the past.

The older domestic architecture of the English may be viewed in another pleasing light. Their buildings and residences have not only the recommendation of beauty and complete adaptation, but the additional charm of having been the homes of our ancestors, and the dwellings of that bright galaxy of English genius and worth, which illuminates equally the intellectual firmament of both hemispheres. He who has extended his researches, *can*

amore, into the history of the domestic life and habits of
those illustrious minds, will not, we are sure, forget that
lowly cottage by the side of the Avon, where the great
English bard was wont to dwell; the tasteful residence
of Pope at Twickenham; or the turrets and battlements
of the more picturesque Abbotsford; and numberless other
examples of the rural buildings of England, once the
abodes of renowned genius. In truth, the cottage and
villa architecture of the English has grown out of the
feelings and habits of a refined and cultivated people,
whose devotion to country life, and fondness for all its
pleasures, are so finely displayed in the beauty of their
dwellings, and the exquisite keeping of their buildings and
grounds.

It is this love of rural life, and this nice feeling of
the harmonious union of nature and art, that reflects
so much credit upon the English as a people, and which,
sooner or later, we hope to see completely naturalized in
this country. Our rural residences, evincing that love of
the beautiful and the picturesque, which, combined with
solid comfort, is so attractive to the eye of every beholder,
will not only become sources of the purest enjoyment to
the refined minds of the possessors, but will exert an
influence for the improvement in taste of every class in
our community. The ambition to build "shingle palaces"
in starved and meagre grounds, we are glad to see giving
way to that more refined feeling which prefers a neat villa
or cottage, tastily constructed, and surrounded by its proper
accessories, of greater or less extent, of verdant trees and
beautiful shrubbery.

It is gratifying to see the progressive improvement in
Rural Architecture, which within a few years past has
evinced itself in various parts of the country, and par-

Fig. 54.—A Mansion in the Elizabethan Style.

Fig. 55.—The Residence of the Rev. Robert Bolton, near New Rochelle, N. Y.

ticularly on the banks of the Hudson and Connecticut Rivers, as well as in the suburbs of our largest cities. Here and there, beautiful villas and cottages in the Italian or old English styles, are being erected by proprietors who feel the pre-eminent beauty of these modes for domestic architecture. And from the rapidity with which improve ments having just claims for public favor advance in our community, we have every reason to hope that our Rural Architecture will soon exhibit itself in a more attractive and agreeable form than it has hitherto generally assumed. We take pleasure in referring to a few of these buildings more in detail.

The cottage of Thomas W. Ludlow, Esq., near Yonkers, on the Hudson (Fig. 54), is one of the most complete examples on this river. The interior is very carefully and harmoniously finished, the apartments are agreeably arranged, and the general effect of the exterior is varied and pleasing.

There is scarcely a building or place more replete with interest in America, than the cottage of Washington Irving, near Tarrytown (Fig. 55). The "Legend of Sleepy Hollow," so delightfully told in the Sketch-Book, has made every one acquainted with this neighborhood, and especially with the site of the present building, there celebrated as the "Van Tassel House," one of the most secluded and delightful nooks on the banks of the Hudson. With characteristic taste, Mr. Irving has chosen this spot, the haunt of his early days, since rendered classic ground by his elegant pen, and made it his permanent residence. The house of "Baltus Van Tassel" has been altered and rebuilt in a quaint style, partaking somewhat of the English cottage mode, but retaining strongly marked symptoms of its Dutch origin   The quaint old weather-

cocks and finials, the crow-stepped gables, and the hall
paved with Dutch tiles, are among the ancient and
venerable ornaments of the houses of the original
settlers of Manhattan, now almost extinct among us.
There is also a quiet keeping in the cottage and the
grounds around it, that assists in making up the charm
of the whole ; the gently swelling slope reaching down
to the water's edge, bordered by prettily wooded ravines
through which a brook meanders pleasantly ; and threaded by foot-paths ingeniously contrived, so as sometimes
to afford secluded walks, and at others to allow fine
vistas of the broad expanse of river scenery.   The
cottage itself is now charmingly covered with ivy and
climbing roses, and embosomed in thickets of shrubbery.

Mr. Sheldon's residence, in the same neighborhood,
furnishes us with another example of the Rural Gothic
mode, worth the study of the amateur.   Captain Perry's
spirited cottage, near Sing Sing, partakes of the same features ; and we might add numerous other cottages now
building, or in contemplation, which show how fast the
feeling for something more expressive and picturesque
is making progress among us.

Mr. Warren's residence, at Troy, N. Y., is a very
pretty example of the English cottage, elegantly finished internally, as well as externally.   A situation in
a valley, embosomed with luxuriant trees, would have
given this building a more appropriate and charming
air than its present one, which, however, affords a
magnificent prospect of the surrounding country.

It is the common practice here to place a portion of
what are called the *domestic offices,* as the kitchen
pantries, etc., in the basement story of the house

directly beneath the living rooms. This has partly arisen from the circumstance of the comparative economy of this method of constructing them under the same roof; and partly from the difficulty of adding wings to the main building for those purposes, which will not mar the simplicity and elegance of a Grecian villa. In the better class of houses in England, the domestic offices, which include the kitchen and its appurtenances, and also the stable, coach-house, harness-room, etc., are in the majority of cases attached to the main body of the building on one side. The great advantage of having all these conveniences on the same floor with the principal rooms, and communicating in such a way as to be easily accessible at all times without going into the open air, is undeniable. It must also be admitted that these domestic offices, extending out from the main building, partly visible and partly concealed by trees and foliage, add much to the extent and importance of a villa or mansion in the country. In the old English style these appendages are made to unite happily with the building, which is in itself irregular. Picturesque effect is certainly increased by thus extending the pile and increasing the variety of its outline.

A blind partiality for any one style in building is detrimental to the progress of improvement, both in taste and comfort. The variety of means, habits, and local feelings, will naturally cause many widely different tastes to arise among us ; and it is only by the means of a number of distinct styles, that this diversity of tastes can be accommodated. There will always be a large class of individuals in every country who prefer a plain square house because it is more economical, and because they have little feeling for architectural, or, indeed, any other species of beauty. But besides such, there will always be found some men of finer natures, who have a sympatnetic appreciation of the beautiful in nature and art. Among these, the classical scholar and gentleman may, from association and the love of antiquity, prefer a villa in the Grecian or Roman style. He who has a passionate love of pictures and especially fine landscapes, will perhaps, very naturally, prefer the modern Italian style for a country residence. The wealthy proprietor, either from the romantic and chivalrous associations connected with the baronial castle, or from desire to display his own resources, may indulge his fancy in erecting a castellated dwelling. The gentleman who wishes to realize the *beau ideal* of a genuine old English country residence, with its various internal comforts, and its spirited exterior, may establish himself in a Tudor villa or mansion; and the lover of nature and rural life, who, with more limited means, takes equal interest in the beauty of his grounds or garden (however small) and his house—who is both an admirer of that kind of beauty called the picturesque, and has a lively perception of the effect of a happy adaptation of buildings to the landscape,—such a person will very naturally make choice of the rural cottage style.

Entrance Lodges are not only handsome architectural objects in the scenery of country residences of large size, but are in many cases exceedingly convenient, both to the family and the guests or visitors having frequent ingress and egress. The entrance lodge may further be considered a matter strictly useful, in serving as the dwelling of the

gardener or farmer and his family. In this point of view,
arrangements for the comfort and convenience of the
inmates should be regarded as more important than the
fanciful decoration of the exterior—as no exterior, however
charming, can, to a reflective and well regulated mind,
apologize for contracted apartments, and imperfect light
and ventilation, in human habitations.

Among the numerous entrance lodges which we remember
to have seen in the United States, we scarcely recall a single
example where the means, or rather the facility, of opening
and shutting the gate itself, has been sufficiently considered.
Most generally the lodge is at too great a distance from the
gate, consuming too much time in attendance, and exposing
the persons attending, generally women or children, to the
inclemencies of the weather.   Besides this, service of this
kind is less cheerfully performed in this country than in
Europe, from the very simple reason of the greater equality
of conditions here, and therefore everything which tends
to lessen labor, is worthy of being taken into account.

For these reasons we would place the gate very near the
lodge ; it would be preferable if it were part of the same
architectural composition : and if possible adopt the contrivance now in use at some places abroad, by which the
gate, being hung nearest the building, may be opened by
the occupant without the latter being seen, or being
scarcely obliged to leave his or her employment.*   This

* In *Fig.* 56, is shown the section of a gate arranged upon this plan. At
the bottom of the hanging post of the gate, is a bevelled iron pinion, that works
into another pinion, *b*, at the end of the horizontal shaft, *a*, which shaft is fixed
in a square box or tunnel under the road.   The part to the right of the partition
line, *f*, is the *interior* of the gate-keeper's house ; and by turning the winch, *e*,
the upright shaft, *c*, is put in motion, which moves by means of the bevelled
pinions, *g*, *d*, the shaft *a*, and therefore, through *d*, the back post of the gate,

is certainly the ultimatum of improvements in gate lodges ;
and where it cannot be attained, something may still be
done towards amelioration, by placing the gate within a
convenient distance, instead of half a dozen rods apart
from the lodge, as is frequently done.

That the entrance lodge should correspond in style with
the mansion, is a maxim insisted upon by all writers on
Rural Architecture.   Where the latter is built in a mixed
style, there is more latitude allowed in the choice of forms
for the lodge, which may be considered more as a thing by
itself.   But where the dwelling is a strictly architectural
composition, the lodge should correspond in style, and bear
evidence of emanating from the same mind.   A variation
of the same style may be adopted with pleasing effect, as a

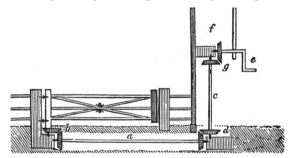

[Fig. 56.   Plan for opening the gate from the interior of the Lodge.]

lodge in the form of the old English cottage for a castellated

which is opened and shut by the motion of the winch, without obliging the
nmates to leave the house.

A very convenient way we have found of opening a gate from a lodge, when
at right angles to each other, is by passing a light chain from the latch of the gate
through the walls of the house into the usual sitting-room—here to turn on a
crank, or simply pulled hand over hand, as the sailors term it.   The gate
being hung a little out of plumb, is held open from the house, by the chain,
until a carriage passes, and falls back again, from its own inclination, against a
jog, or projection in the gate-pier to receive it.—H. W. S.

mansion, or a Doric lodge for a Corinthian villa ; but never
two distinct styles on the same place (a Gothic gate-house
and a Grecian residence) without producing in minds
imbued with correct principles a feeling of incongruity.
A certain correspondence in size is also agreeable ; where
the dwelling of the proprietor is simply an ornamental
cottage, the lodge, if introduced, should be more simple and
unostentatious ; and even where the house is magnificent,
the lodge should rather be below the general air of the
residence than above it, that the stranger who enters at a
showy and striking lodge may not be disappointed in the
want of correspondence between it and the remaining
portions of the demesne.

[Fig. 57. The New Gate Lodge at Blithewood.]

The gate-lodge at Blithewood, on the Hudson, the seat
of R. Donaldson, Esq., is a simple and effective cottage in
the bracketed style—octagonal in its form, and very compactly arranged internally.

Nearly all the fine seats on the North river have entrance

lodges—often simple and but little ornamented, or only

pleasingly embowered in foliage ; but, occasionally, highly picturesque and striking in appearance.

A view of the pretty gate lodge at Nether-wood, Duchess County N. Y., the seat of Gardi-

[Fig. 58. The Gate Lodge at Netherwood.]

ner Howland, Esq., is shown in Fig. 58. Half a mile north of this seat is an interesting lodge in the Swiss style, at the entrance to the residence of Mrs. Sheafe.

In Fig. 59, is shown an elevation of a lodge in the Italian style, with projecting eaves supported by cantilevers or brackets, round-headed windows with balconies, character-istic porch, and other leading features of this style.

[Fig. 59.　Gate Lodge in the Italian style.]

Mr. Repton has stated it as a principle in the composition of residences, that neither the house should be visible from the entrance nor the entrance from the house, if there be sufficient distance between them to make the approach through varied grounds, or a park, and not immediately into a court-yard.

Entrance lodges, and indeed all small ornamental buildings, should be supported, and partially concealed, by trees
and foliage ; naked walls, in the country, hardly admitting
of an apology in any case, but especially when the building
is ornamental, and should be considered part of a whole,
grouping with other objects in rural landscape.

NOTE.—To readers who desire to cultivate a taste for rural architecture, we
take pleasure in recommending the following productions of the English press.
Loudon's *Encyclopædia of Cottage, Farm, and Villa Architecture*, a volume
replete with information on every branch of the subject ; Robinson's *Rural
Architecture and Designs for Ornamental Villas ;* Lugar's *Villa Architecture ;* Goodwin's *Rural Architecture ;* Hunt's *Picturesque Domestic
Architecture, and Examples of Tudor Architecture ;* Pugin's *Examples of
Gothic Architecture,* etc. The most successful American architects in this
branch of the art, with whom we are acquainted, are Alexander J. Davis, Esq.,
of New York, and John Notman, Esq., of Philadelphia.

[Fig. 60. The Gardener's House, Blithewood.]

SECTION X.

EMBELLISHMENTS ; ARCHITECTURAL, RUSTIC, AND FLORAL.

Value of a proper connexion between the house and grounds. Beauty of the architectural terrace, and its application to villas and cottages. Use of vases of different descriptions Sun-dials. Architectural flower-garden. Irregular flower-garden. French flower-garden. English flower-garden. General remarks on this subject. Selection of showy plants, flowering in succession. Arrangement of the shrubbery, and selection of choice shrubs. The conservatory or green-house. Open and covered seats. Pavilions. Rustic seats. Prospect tower. Bridges. Rockwork. Fountains of various descriptions. Judicious introduction of decorations.

> Nature, assuming a more lovely face,
> Borrowing a beauty from the works of grace.
>
> COWPER.

> —— Each odorous bushy shrub
> Fenced up the verdant wall ; each beauteous flower ;
> Iris all hues, Roses and Jessamine
> Rear'd high their flourished heads between,
> And wrought Mosaic.
>
> MILTON.

N our finest places, or those country seats where much of the polish of pleasure ground or park scenery is kept up, one of the most striking defects is the want of *" union between the house and the grounds."*

We are well aware that from the comparative rarity of anything like a highly kept place in this country, the want of
this, which is indeed like the last finish to the residence, is
scarcely felt at all. But this only proves the infant state
of Landscape Gardening here, and the little attention that
has been paid to the highest details of the art.

If our readers will imagine, with us, a pretty villa, con-
veniently arranged and well constructed, in short, complete
in itself as regards its architecture, and at the same time,
properly placed in a smooth well kept lawn, studded with
groups and masses of fine trees, they will have an example
often to be met with, of a place, in the graceful school of
design, about which, however, there is felt to be a certain
incongruity between the house, a highly artificial object,
and the surrounding grounds, where the prevailing expression in the latter is that of beautiful nature.

Let us suppose, for further illustration, the same house
and grounds with a few additions. The house now rising
directly out of the green turf which encompasses it, we
will surround by a raised platform or terrace, wide enough
for a dry, firm walk, at all seasons; on the top of the wall
or border of this terrace, we will form a handsome *parapet*,
or balustrade, some two or three feet high, the details of
which shall be in good keeping with the house, whether
Grecian or Gothic. On the coping of this parapet, if the
house is in the classical style, we will find suitable places,
at proper intervals, for some handsome urns, vases, etc.
On the drawing-room side of the house, that is, the side
towards which the best room or rooms look, we will place
the flower-garden, into which we descend from the terrace
by a few steps. This flower-garden may be simply what
its name denotes, a place exclusively devoted to the culti-

vation of flowers, or (if the house is not in a very plain
style, admitting of little enrichment) it may be an architectural flower-garden.   In the latter case, intermingled
with the flowers, are to be seen vases, fountains, and sometimes even statues; the effect of the fine colors and deep
foliage of the former, heightened by contrast with the
sculptured forms of the latter.

If our readers will now step back a few rods with us and
take a second view of our villa residence, with its
supposed harmonizing accessories, we think they can hardly
fail to be impressed at once with the great improvement
of the whole.   The eye now, instead of witnessing the
sudden termination of the architecture at the base of the
house, where the lawn commences as suddenly, will be at
once struck with the increased variety and richness
imparted to the whole scene, by the addition of the architectural and garden decorations.   The mind is led
gradually down from the house, with its projecting porch
or piazzas, to the surrounding terrace crowned with its
beautiful vases, and from thence to the architectural
flower-garden, interspersed with similar ornaments.   The
various play of light afforded by these sculptured forms on
the terrace ; the projections and recesses of the parapet,
with here and there some climbing plants luxuriantly
enwreathing it, throwing out the mural objects in stronger
relief, and connecting them pleasantly with the verdure of
the turf beneath ; the still further rambling off of vases,
etc., into the brilliant flower-garden, which, through these
ornaments, maintains an avowed connexion with the
architecture of the house; all this, we think it cannot be
denied, forms a rich setting to the architecture, and unites

agreeably the forms of surrounding nature with the more regular and uniform outlines of the building.

The effect will not be less pleasing if viewed from another point of view, viz. the terrace, or from the apartments of the house itself. From either of these points, the various objects enumerated, will form a rich *foreground* to the pleasure-grounds or park—a matter which painters well know how to estimate, as a landscape is incomplete and unsatisfactory to them, however beautiful the middle or distant points, unless there are some strongly marked objects in the foreground. In fine, the intervention of these elegant accompaniments to our houses prevents us, as Mr. Hope has observed, " from launching at once from the threshold of the symmetric mansion, in the most abrupt manner, into a scene wholly composed of the most unsymmetric and desultory forms of mere nature, which are totally out of character with the mansion, whatever may be its style of architecture and furnishing."*

The highly decorated terrace, as we have here supposed it, would, it is evident, be in unison with villas of a somewhat superior style ; or, in other words, the amount of enrichment bestowed upon exterior decoration near the house, should correspond to the style of art evinced in the exterior of the mansion itself. An humble cottage with sculptured vases on its terrace and parapet, would be in bad taste ; but any Grecian, Roman, or Italian villa, where a moderate degree of exterior ornament is visible, or a Gothic villa of the better class, will allow the additional enrichment of the architectural terrace and its ornaments. Indeed the terrace itself, in so far as it denotes a raised dry

* *Essay on Ornamental Gardening,* by Thomas Hope.

platform around the house, is a suitable and appropriate appendage to every dwelling, of whatever class.

The width of a terrace around a house may vary from five to twenty feet, or more, in proportion as the building is of greater or less importance. The surrounding wall, which supports its level, may also vary from one to eight feet. The terrace, in the better class of English residences, is paved with smooth flag stones, or in place of this, a surface of firm well-rolled gravel is substituted. In residences where a parapet or balustrade would be thought too expensive, a square stone or plinth is placed at the angles or four corners of the terrace, which serves as the pedestal for a vase or urn. When a more elegant and finished appearance is desirable, the parapet formed of open work of stone, or wood painted in imitation of stone, rises above the level of the terrace two or three feet with a suitably bold coping. On this vases may be placed, not only at the corners, but at regular intervals of ten, twenty, or more feet. We have alluded to the good effect of climbers, here and there planted, and suffered to intermingle their rich foliage with the open work of the parapet and its crowning ornaments. In the climate of Philadelphia, the Giant Ivy, with its thick sculpturesque looking masses of foliage, would be admirably suited to this purpose. Or the Virginia Creeper (the Ivy of America) may take its place in any other portion of the Union. To these we may add, the Chinese twining Honeysuckle (Lonicera flexuosa) and the Sweet-scented Clematis, both deliciously fragrant in their blossoms, with many other fine climbers which will readily recur to the amateur.

There can be no reason why the smallest cottage, if its occupant be a person of taste should not have a terrace

decorated in a suitable manner. This is easily and cheaply
effected by placing neat flower-pots on the parapet, or
border and angles of the terrace, with suitable plants growing in them. For this purpose, the American or Century
Aloe, a formal architectural-looking plant, is exceedingly

well adapted, as it always preserves nearly the
same appearance. Or in place of this, the
Yuccas, or "*Adam's needle* and *thread*,"
which have something of the same character,
while they also produce beautiful heads of

[Fig. 61.] flowers, may be chosen. *Yucca flaccida* is a
fine hardy species, which would look well
in such a situation. An aloe in a common
flower pot is shown in Fig. 61; and a
Yucca in an ornamental flower-pot in
Fig. 62.

[Fig. 62.]

Where there is a terrace ornamented with urns or vases,
and the proprietor wishes to give a corresponding air of
elegance to his grounds, vases, sundials, etc., may be placed
in various appropriate situations, not only in the architec
tural flower-garden, but on the lawn, and through the
pleasure-grounds in various different points *near the house*
We say near the house, because we think so highly artificial and architectural an object as a sculptured vase, is
never correctly introduced unless it appear in some way
connected with buildings, or objects of a like architectural
character. To place a beautiful vase in a distant part of
the grounds, where there is no direct allusion to art, and
where it is accompanied only by natural objects, as the
overhanging trees and the sloping turf, is in a measure
doing violence to our reason or taste, by bringing two
objects so strongly contrasted, in direct union. But when

we see a statue or a vase placed in any part of the grounds where a near view is obtained of the house (and its accompanying statues or vases), the whole is accounted for, and we feel the distant vase to be only a part of, or rather a repetition of the same idea,—in other words, that it forms part of a whole, harmonious and consistent.

Vases of real stone, as marble or granite, are decorations of too costly a kind ever to come into general use among us. Vases, however, of equally beautiful forms, are manufactured of artificial stone, of fine pottery, or of cast iron, which have the same effect, and are of nearly equal durability, as garden decorations.

A vase should never, in the open air, be set down upon the ground or grass, without being placed upon a firm base of some description, either a *plinth* or a *pedestal*. Without a base of this kind it has a temporary look, as if it had been left there by mere accident, and without any intention of permanence. Placing it upon a pedestal, or square plinth (block of stone), gives it a character of art, at once more dignified and expressive of stability. Besides this, the pedestal in reality serves to preserve the vase in a perpendicular position, as well as to expose it fairly to the eye, which could not be the case were it put down, without any preparation, on the bare turf or gravel.

Figure 63 is a Gothic, and Figures 64, 65, are Grecian vases, commonly manufactured in plaster in our cities, but which are also made of Roman cement. They are here shown upon suitable pedestals—*a* being the vase, and *b* the pedestal. These with many other elegant vases and urns are manufactured in an artificial stone, as durable as

[Fig. 63.]

marble, by *Austin* of London, and together with a great

variety of other beautiful sculpturesque decorations, may
be imported at very reasonable prices.

Figures 64, 65, are beautiful vases of pottery ware
manufactured by Peake, of Staffordshire—and which may
be imported cheaply, or will be made to order at the Sala-
mander works, in New York.   These vases, when colored

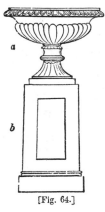

to imitate marble or other stone, are extremely durable and very ornamental.
As yet, we are unable to refer our readers
to any manufactory here, where these
articles are made in a manner fully equal
to the English ; but we are satisfied, it is
only necessary that the taste for such
articles should increase, and the consequent demand, to induce our artisans to
produce them of equal beauty and of

[Fig. 64.]

greater cheapness.

At Blithewood, the seat of R. Donaldson, Esq., on the
Hudson, a number of exquisite vases may
be seen in the pleasure-grounds, which are
cut in Maltese stone. These were imported
by the proprietor, direct from Malta, at very
moderate rates, and are not only ornamental, but very durable. Their color is a
warm shade of grey which harmonizes
agreeably with the surrounding vegetation.

[Fig. 65.]

Large vases are sometimes
filled with earth and planted with choice flowering plants, and the effect of the blossoms and
green leaves growing out of these handsome
[Fig. 66.] receptacles, is at least unique and striking

Loudon objects to it in the case of an elegant sculptured vase, "because it is reducing a work of art to the
level of a mere garden flower-pot, and dividing the
attention between the beauty of the form of the vase
and of its sculptured ornaments, and that of the plant
which it contains." This criticism is a just one in its
general application, especially when vases
are considered as architectural decorations.
Occasional deviations, however, may be permitted, for the sake of producing variety,
especially in the case of vases used as decorations in the flower-garden.

A very pretty and fanciful substitute for
the sculptured vase, and which may take its
place in the picturesque landscape, may be
found in vases or baskets of *rustic work*, con-   [Fig. 67.]
structed of the branches and sections of trees with the

bark attached. Figure 68 is a representation of a pleasing rustic vase
which we have constructed without
difficulty. A tripod of branches of trees
forms the pedestal. An octagonal box
serves as the body or frame of the vase;
on this, pieces of birch and hazel (small
split limbs covered with the bark) are

[Fig. 68.]

nailed closely, so as to form a sort of mosaic covering to the
whole exterior. Ornaments of this kind, which may be
made by the amateur with the assistance of a common
carpenter, are very suitable for the decoration of the
grounds and flower-gardens of cottages or picturesque
villas. An endless variety of forms will occur to an

ingenious artist in rustic work, which he may call in to the embellishment of rural scenes, without taxing his purse heavily.

Sundials (Fig. 69) are among the oldest decorations for the garden and grounds, and there are scarcely any which we think more suitable. They are not merely decorative, but have also an useful character, and may therefore be occasionally placed in distant parts of the grounds, should a favorite walk terminate there. When we meet daily in our walks for a number of years, with one of these silent monitors of the flight of time, we become in a degree attached to it, and really look upon it as gifted with a species of intelligence, beaming out when the sunbeams smile upon its dial-plate.

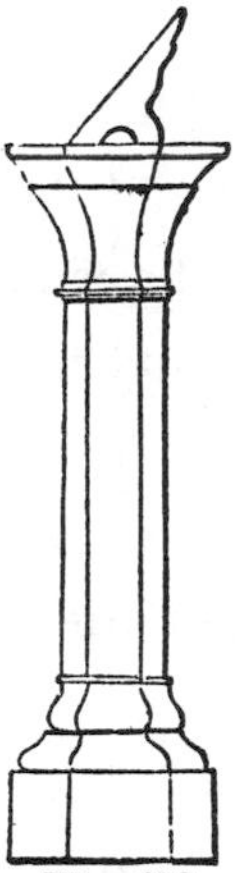

[Fig. 69.]

The *Architectural Flower-garden*, as we have just remarked, has generally a direct connexion with the house, at least on one side by the terrace. It may be of greater or less size, from twenty feet square to half an acre in extent. The leading characteristics of this species of flower-garden, are the regular lines and forms employed in its beds and walks. The flowers are generally planted in beds in the form of circles, octagons, squares, etc., the centre of the garden being occupied by an elegant vase, a sundial, or that still finer ornament, a fountain, or *jet d'eau*. In various parts of the garden, along the principal walks, or in the centre of parterres, pedestals supporting vases, urns, or handsome flower-pots with plants, are placed. When a highly marked character of art is intended, a balustrade or parapet, resembling that of the terrace to which it is connected, is continued round the whole of

this garden. Or in other cases the garden is surrounded
by a thicket of shrubs and low trees, partly concealing it
from the eye on all sides but one.

It is evident that the architectural flower-garden is
superior to the general flower-garden, *as an appendage
to the house*, on two accounts. First, because, as we
have already shown, it serves an admirable purpose
n effecting a harmonious union between the house and the
grounds. And secondly, because we have both the rich
verdure and gay blossoms of the flowering plants, and the
more permanent beauty of sculptured forms; the latter
heightening the effect of the former by contrast, as well as
by the relief they afford the eye in masses of light, amid
surrounding verdure.

There are several varieties of general flower-gardens,
which may be formed near the house. Among these we
will only notice the *irregular* flower-garden, the *old French*
flower-garden, and the *modern* or *English* flower-garden.

In almost all the different kinds of flower-gardens, two
methods of forming the beds are observed. One is, to cut
the beds out of the green turf, which is ever afterwards

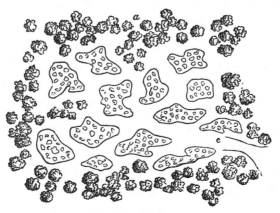

[Fig. 70. The Irregular Flower-garden.]

kept well-mown or cut for the walks, and the edges pared ; the other, to surround the beds with edgings of verdure, as box, etc., or some more durable material, as tiles, or cut stone, the walks between being covered with gravel. The turf is certainly the most agreeable for walking upon in the heat of summer, and the dry part of the day ; while the gravelled flower-garden affords a dry footing at nearly all hours and seasons.

The *irregular* flower-garden is surrounded by an irregular belt of trees and ornamental shrubs of the choicest species, and the beds are varied in outline, as well as irregularly disposed, sometimes grouping together, sometimes standing singly, but exhibiting no uniformity of arrangement. An idea of its general appearance may be gathered from the accompanying sketch (Fig. 70), which may be varied at pleasure. In it the irregular boundary of shrubs is shown at *a*, the flower-beds *b*, and the walks *e*.

This kind of flower-garden would be a suitable accompaniment to the house and grounds of an enthusiastic lover of the picturesque, whose residence is in the Rural Gothic style, and whose grounds are also eminently varied and picturesque. Or it might form a pretty termination to a distant walk in the pleasure-grounds, where it would be more necessary that the flower-garden should be in keeping with the surrounding plantations and scenery than with the house.

Where the flower-garden is a spot set apart, of any regular outline, not of large size, and especially where it is attached directly to the house, we think the effect is most satisfactory when the beds or walks are laid out in symmetrical forms. Our reasons for this are these : the flower-garden, unlike distant portions of the pleasure-ground scenery, is an appendage to the house, seen in the same view or moment with it, and therefore should exhibit something of the regularity which characterizes, in a greater or less degree, all architectural compositions; and when a given scene is so small as to be embraced in a single glance of the eye, regular forms are found to be more satisfactory than irregular ones, which, on so small a scale, are apt to appear unmeaning.

The *French* flower-garden is the most fanciful of the regular modes of laying out the area devoted to this purpose. The patterns or figures employed are often highly intricate, and require considerable skill in their formation. The walks are either of gravel or smoothly shaven turf, and the beds are filled with choice flowering plants. It is evident that much of the beauty of this kind of flower-garden, or indeed any other where the figures are regular and intricate, must depend on the outlines of the beds, or *parterres of embroidery*, as they are called, being kept distinct and clear. To do this effectually, low growing herbaceous plants or border flowers, perennials and annuals, should be chosen, such as will not exceed on an average, one or two feet in height.

In the English flower-garden, the beds are either in symmetrical forms and figures, or they are characterized by irregular *curved* outlines. The peculiarity of these gardens, at present so fashionable in England, is, that each separate bed is planted with a single variety, or at most two varieties of flowers. Only the most striking and showy varieties are generally chosen, and the effect, when the selection is judicious, is highly brilliant. Each bed, in its season, presents a mass of blossoms, and the contrast of rich colors is much more striking than in any other

arrangement. No plants are admitted that are shy bloom-
ers, or which have ugly habits of growth, meagre or starved
foliage ; the aim being brilliant effect, rather than the
display of a great variety of curious or rare plants. To
bring this about more perfectly, and to have an elegant
show during the whole season of growth, hyacinths and
other fine bulbous roots occupy a certain portion of the
beds, the intervals being filled with handsome herbaceous
plants, permanently planted, or with flowering annuals and
green-house plants renewed every season.

To illustrate the mode of arranging the beds and disposing
the plants in an English garden, we copy the plan and
description of the elegant flower-garden, on the lawn at
Dropmore, the beds being cut out of the smooth turf.

" As a general principle for regulating the plants in this
figure, the winter and spring flowers ought, as much as
possible, to be of sorts which admit of being in the ground
all the year : and the summer crop should be planted at
intervals between the winter plants. Or the summer crop,
having been brought forward in pots under glass, or by
nightly protection, may be planted out about the middle of
June, after the winter plants in pots are removed. A
number of hardy bulbs ought to be potted and plunged in
the beds in the months of October and November ; and
when out of bloom, in May or June, removed to the reserve

garden and plunged there, in order to perfect their foliage and mature their bulbs for the succeeding season."*

There cannot be a question that this method of planting the flower-garden in groups and masses, is productive of by far the most splendid effect. In England, where flower-gardens are carried to their greatest perfection, the preference in planting is given to exotics which blossom constantly throughout the season, and which are kept in the green-house during winter, and turned out in the beds in the early part of the season, where they flower in the greatest profusion until frost; as Fuchsias, Salvias,

[Fig. 72. English Flower-Garden.]

* Ency. of Gardening, 1000.

Lobelias, Scarlet Geraniums, etc., etc.* This mode can be adopted here where a small green-house or frame is kept. In the absence of these, nearly the same effect may be produced by choosing the most showy herbaceous plants, perennial and biennial, alternating them with hardy bulbs, and the finer species of annuals.

In Fig. 72, we give an example of a small cottage or villa residence of one or two acres, where the flower-beds are disposed around the lawn in the English style : their forms irregular, with curved outlines, affording a great degree of variety in the appearance as viewed from different points on the lawn itself. In this, the central portion is occupied by the lawn ; c, d, are the flower-beds, planted with showy border-flowers, in separate masses ; b, the conservatory. Surrounding the whole is a collection of choice shrubs and trees, the lowest near the walk, and those behind increasing in altitude as they approach the boundary wall or fence. In this plan, as there is supposed to be no exterior view worth preserving, the amphitheatre of shrubs and trees completely shuts out all objects but the lawn and its decorations, which are rendered as elegant as possible.

Where the proprietor of a country residence, or the ladies of a family, have a particular taste, it may be indulged at pleasure in other and different varieties of the flower-garden. With some families there is a taste for botany,

* In many English residences, the flower-garden is maintained in never-fading brilliancy by almost daily supplies from what is termed the *reserve garden.* This is a small garden out of sight, in which a great number of duplicates of the species in the flower-garden are grown in pots plunged in beds. As soon as a vacuum is made in the flower-garden by the fading of any flowers, the same are immediately removed and their places supplied by fresh plants just ready to bloom, from the pots in the reserve garden. This, which is the *ultimatum* of refinement in flower-gardening, has never, to our knowledge, been attempted in this country.

when a small botanic flower-garden may be preferred—the
herbaceous and other plants being grouped or massed 'n
beds after the *Linnæan*, or the *natural* method.   Some
persons have an enthusiastic fondness for florist flowers, as
Pansies, Carnations, Dahlias, Roses, etc.; others for buibous
roots, all of which may very properly lead to particular
modes of laying out flower-gardens.

The desideratum, however, with most persons is, to have
a continued display of blossoms in the flower-garden from
the opening of the crocus and snowdrop in the spring,
until the autumnal frosts cut off the last pale asters, or
blacken the stems of the luxuriant dahlias in November.
This may be done with a very small catalogue of plants if
they are properly selected : such as flower at different
seasons, continue long time in bloom, and present fine
masses of flowers.   On the other hand, a very large number of species may be assembled together ; and owing to
their being merely botanical rarities, and not bearing fine
flowers, or to their blossoming chiefly in a certain portion
of the season, or continuing but a short period in bloom,
the flower-garden will often have but an insignificant
appearance.   With a group of Pansies and spring bulbs, a
bed of ever-blooming China Roses, including the *Isle de
Bourbon* varieties, some few Eschscholtzias, the showy
Petunias, Gilias, and other annuals, and a dozen choice
double Dahlias, and some trailing Verbenas, a limited spot,
of a few yards in diameter, may be made productive of
more enjoyment, so far as regards a continued display of
flowers, than ten times that space, planted, as we often see
flower-gardens here, with a heterogeneous mixture of
everything the possesor can lay his hands on, or crowd
within the inclosure.

The *mingled* flower-garden, as it is termed, is by far the most common mode of arrangement in this country, though it is seldom well effected. The cbject in this is to dispose the plants in the beds in such a manner, that while there is no predominance of bloom in any one portion of the beds there shall be a general admixture of colors and blossoms throughout the entire garden during the whole season of growth.

To promote this, the more showy plants should be often repeated in different parts of the garden, or even the same parterre when large, the less beautiful sorts being suffered to occupy but moderate space. The smallest plants should be nearest the walk, those a little taller behind them, and the largest should be furthest from the eye, at the back of the border, when the latter is seen from one side only, or in the centre, if the bed be viewed from both sides. A neglect of this simple rule will not only give the beds, when the plants are full grown, a confused look, but the beauty of the humbler and more delicate plants will be lost amid the tall thick branches of sturdier plants, or removed so far from the spectator in the walks, as to be overlooked.

Considerable experience is necessary to arrange even a moderate number of plants in accordance with these rules. To perform it successfully, some knowledge of the habits of the plants is an important requisite ; their height, time of flowering, and the colors of their blossoms. When a gardener, or an amateur, is perfectly informed on these points, he can take a given number of plants of different species, make a plan of the bed or all the beds of a flower-garden upon paper, and designate the particular situation of each species.

The *shrubbery* is so generally situated in the neighborhood of the flower-garden and the house, that we shall
here offer a few remarks on its arrangement and distribution.

A collection of flowering shrubs is so ornamental, that
to a greater or less extent it is to be found in almost every
residence of the most moderate size : the manner in which
the shrubs are disposed, must necessarily depend in a great
degree upon the size of the grounds, the use or enjoyment
to be derived from them, and the prevailing character of
the scenery.

It is evident, on a moment's reflection, that shrubs being
intrinsically more ornamental than trees, on account of the
beauty and abundance of their flowers, they will generally
be placed near and about the house, in order that their gay
blossoms and fine fragrance may be more constantly
enjoyed, than if they were scattered indiscriminately over
the grounds.

Where a place is limited in size, and the whole lawn and
plantations partake of the *pleasure-ground* character,
shrubs of all descriptions may be grouped with good effect,
in the same manner as trees, throughout the grounds ; the
finer and rarer species being disposed about the dwelling,
and the more hardy and common sorts along the walks,
and in groups, in different situations near the eye.

When, however, the residence is of larger size, and the
grounds have a park-like extent and character, the introduction of shrubs might interfere with the noble and
dignified expression of lofty full grown trees, except
perhaps they were planted here and there, among large

groups, as *underwood;* or if cattle or sheep were allowed
to graze in the park, it would of course be impossible to
preserve plantations of shrubs there. When this is the
case, however, a portion near the house is divided from the
park (by a wire fence or some inconspicuous barrier) for
the pleasure-ground, where the shrubs are disposed in belts,
groups, etc., as in the first case alluded to.

There are two methods of grouping shrubs upon lawns
which may separately be considered, in combination with
beautiful and with *picturesque* scenery.

In the first case, where the character of the scene, of
the plantations of trees, etc., is that of polished beauty, the
belts of shrubs may be arranged similar to herbaceous
flowering plants, in arabesque beds, along the walks, as in
Fig. 70, page 372. In this case, the shrubs alone, arranged
with relation to their height, may occupy the beds; or if
preferred, shrubs and flowers may be intermingled. Those
who have seen the shrubbery at *Hyde Park*, the residence
of the late Dr. Hosack, which borders the walk leading
from the mansion to the hot-houses, will be able to recall
a fine example of this mode of mingling woody and
herbaceous plants. The belts or borders occupied by the
shrubbery and flower-garden there, are perhaps from 25 to
35 feet in width, completely filled with a collection of
shrubs and herbaceous plants; the smallest of the latter
being quite near the walk; these succeeded by taller species
receding from the front of the border, then follow shrubs
of moderate size, advancing in height until the background of the whole is a rich mass of tall shrubs and trees
of moderate size. The effect of this belt on so large a
scale, in high keeping, is remarkably striking and elegant.

Where *picturesque effect* is the object aimed at in the

pleasure-grounds, it may be attained in another way; that is, by planting irregular groups of the most vigorous and thrifty growing shrubs in lawn, without placing them in regular dug beds or belts; but instead of this, keeping the grass from growing and the soil somewhat loose, for a few inches round their stems (which will not be apparent at a short distance). In the case of many of the hardier shrubs, after they become well established, even this care will not be requisite, and the grass only will require to be kept short by clipping it when the lawn is mown.

As in picturesque scenes everything depends upon *grouping well*, it will be found that shrubs may be employed with excellent effect in connecting single trees, or finishing a group composed of large trees, or giving fulness to groups of tall trees newly planted on a lawn, or effecting a union between buildings and ground. It is true that it requires something of an artist's feeling and perception of the picturesque to do these successfully, but the result is so much the more pleasing and satisfactory when it is well executed.

When walks are continued from the house through distant parts of the pleasure-grounds, groups of shrubs may be planted along their margins, here and there, with excellent effect. They do not shut out or obstruct the view like large trees, while they impart an interest to an otherwise tame and spiritless walk. Placed in the projecting bay, round which the walk curves so as to appear to be a reason for its taking that direction, they conceal also the portion of the walk in advance, and thus enhance the interest doubly. The neighborhood of rustic seats, or resting points, are also fit places for the assemblage of a group or groups of shrubs.

For the use of those who require some guide in the

selection of species, we subjoin the accompanying list of hardy and showy shrubs, which are at the same time easily procured in the United States. A great number of additional species and varieties, and many more rare, might be enumerated, but such will be sufficiently familiar to the connoisseur already ; and what we have said respecting botanical rarities in flowering plants may be applied with equal force to shrubs, viz. that in order to produce a brilliant effect, a few well chosen species, often repeated, are more effective than a great and ill-assorted *mélange.*

In the following list, the shrubs are divided into two classes—No. 1 designating those of medium size, or low *growth,* and No. 2, those which are of the largest size.

FLOWERING IN APRIL.

1. *Daphne mezereum,* the Pink Mezereum, *D. M. album,* the white Mezereum.
2. *Shepherdia argentea,* the Buffalo berry ; yellow.
1. *Xanthorhiza apiifolia,* the parsley-leaved Yellow-root ; brown.
1. *Cydonia japonica,* the Japan Quince ; scarlet.
1. *Cydonia japonica alba,* the Japan Quince ; white.
2. *Amelanchier Botryapium,* the snowy Medlar.
1. *Ribes aureum,* the Missouri Currant ; yellow.
1. *Coronilla Emerus,* the Scorpion Senna ; yellow.
2. *Magnolia conspicua,* the Chinese chandelier Magnolia ; white.

MAY.

2. *Crategus oxycantha,* the scarlet Hawthorn.
2. *Crategus oxycantha, fl. pleno,* the double white Hawthorn.
2. *Chionanthus virginica,* the white Fringe tree.
1. *Chionanthus latifolius,* the broad-leaved Fringe tree ; white.
1. *Azalea,* many fine varieties ; red, white, and yellow.
1. *Calycanthus florida,* the Sweet-scented-shrub ; brown.
1. *Magnolia purpurea,* the Chinese purple Magnolia.
2. *Halesia tetraptera,* the silver Bell tree ; white.
2. *Syringa vulgaris,* the common white and red Lilacs.
1. *Syringa persica,* the Persian Lilac : white and purple.

1. *Syringa persica laciniata*, the Persian cut-leaved Lilac ; purple.
1. *Kerria* or *Corchorus japonica*, the Japan Globe flower ; yellow.
1. *Lonicera tartarica*, the Tartarian upright Honeysuckles ; red and white.
1. *Philadelphus coronarius*, the common Syringo, and the double Syringo ; white.
1. *Spiræa hypericifolia*, the St. Stephen's wreath ; white.
1. *Spiræa corymbosa*, the cluster flowering Spirea ; white.
1. *Ribes sanguineum*, the scarlet flowering Currant.
1. *Amygdalus pumila, pl.*, the double dwarf Almond ; pink.
1. *Caragana Chamlagu*, the Siberian Pea tree ; yellow.
2. *Magnolia soulangeana*, the Soulange Magnolia ; purple.
1. *Pæonia Moutan banksia*, and *rosea*, the Chinese tree Pæonia ; purple.
1. *Benthamia frugifera*, the red berried Benthamia ; yellow.

JUNE.

1. *Amorpha fruticosa*, the Indigo Shrub ; purple.
2. *Colutea arborescens*, the yellow Bladder-senna.
1. *Colutea cruenta*, the red Bladder-senna.
1. *Cytisus capitatus*, the cluster-flowered Cytisus ; yellow.
1. *Stuartia virginica*, the white Stuartia.
1. *Cornus sanguinea*, the bloody twig Dogwood ; white.
1. *Hydrangea quercifolia*, the oak-leaved Hydrangea ; white.
2. *Philadelphus grandiflorus*, the large flowering Syringo ; white.
2. *Viburnum Opulus*, the Snow-ball ; white.
2. *Magnolia glauca*, the swamp Magnolia ; white.
1. *Robinia hispida*, the Rose-acacia

JULY.

1. *Spiræa bella*, the beautiful Spirea ; red.
2. *Sophora japonica*, the Japan Sophora ; white.
2. *Sophora japonica pendula*, the weeping Sophora ; white.
2. *Rhus Cotinus*, the Venetian Fringe tree ; yellow. (Brown tufts.)
1. *Ligustrum vulgare*, the common Privet ; white.
2. *Cytisus Laburnum*, the Laburnum ; yellow.
2. *Cytisus l. quercifolia*, the oaked-leaved Laburnum ; white.
1. *Cytisus purpureus*, the purple Laburnum.
1. *Cytisus argenteus*, the silvery Cytisus ; yellow.
1. *Cytisus nigricans*, the black rooted Cytisus ; yellow.
2. *Kolreutria paniculata*, the Japan Kolreuteria ; yellow.

AUGUST AND SEPTEMBER.

1. *Clethra alnifolia,* the alder-leaved Clethra ; white.
1. *Symphoria racemosa,* the Snowberry ; (in fruit) white.
2. *Hibiscus syriacus,* the double purple, double white, double striped double blue, and variegated leaved Altheas.
1. *Spiræa tomentosa,* the tomentose Spirea ; red.
2. *Magnolia glauba thompsoniana,* the late flowering Magnolia white.
1. *Baccharis halimifolia,* the Groundsel tree ; white tufts.
2. *Euonymus europæus,* the European Strawberry tree (in fruit), red.
2. *Euonymus europæus alba,* the European Strawberry tree ; the fruit white.
2. *Euonymus latifolius,* the broad-leaved Strawberry tree ; red.
1. *Daphne mezereum autumnalis,* the autumnal Mezereum.

Besides the above, there are a great number of charming varieties of hardy roses, some of which may be grown in the common way on their own roots, and others grafted on stocks, two, three, or four feet high, as standards or tree-roses. The effect of the latter, if such varieties as *George the Fourth, La Cerisette, Pallagi,* or any of the new hybrid roses are grown as standards, is wonderfully brilliant when they are in full bloom. Perhaps the situation where they are displayed to the greatest advantage is, in the centre of small round, oval, or square beds in the flower-garden where the remainder of the plants composing the bed are of dwarfish growth, so as not to hide the stem and head of the tree-roses.

There are, unfortunately, but few evergreen shrubs that will endure the protracted cold of the winters of the northern states. The fine Hollies, Portugal Laurels, Laurustinuses, etc., which are the glory of English gardens in autumn and winter, are not hardy enough to endure the depressed temperature of ten degrees below zero. South of Philadelphia, these beautiful exotic evergreens may be acclimated with good success, and will add greatly to the interest of the shrubbery and grounds in winter.

Besides the Balsam firs and the Spruce firs, the Arbor Vitæ, and other evergreen trees which we have described in the previous pages of this volume, the following hardy species of evergreen shrubs may be introduced with advantage in the pleasure-ground groups, viz:—

Rhododendron maximum, the American rose bay or big Laurel ; white and pink, several varieties (in shaded places).

Kalmia latifolia, the common Laurel ; several colors.

Juniperus succia, the Swedish Juniper.

Juniperus communis, the Irish Juniper.

Buxus arborescens, the common Tree-box, the Gold striped Tree-box, and the Silver striped Tree-box.

Ilex opaca, the American Holly.

Crategus pyracantha, the Evergreen Thorn.

Mahonia aquifolium, the Holly leaved Berberry.

The *Conservatory* or the *Green-House* is an elegant and delightful appendage to the villa or mansion, when there is a taste for plants among the different members of a family. Those who have not enjoyed it, can hardly imagine the pleasure afforded by a well-chosen collection of exotic plants, which, amid the genial warmth of an artificial climate, continue to put forth their lovely blossoms, and exhale their delicious perfumes, when all out-of-door nature is chill and desolate. The many hours of pleasant and healthy exercise and recreation afforded to the ladies of a family, where they take an interest themselves in the growth and vigor of the plants, are certainly no trifling considerations where the country residence is the place of habitation throughout the whole year. Often during the inclemency of our winter and spring months, there are days when either the excessive cold, or the disagreeable state of the weather, prevents in a great measure many persons, and especially females, from taking exercise in the open air. To such, the conservatory would be an almost endless source of enjoyment and amusement; and if they are true amateurs, of active exertion also. The constant changes which daily growth and development bring about in vegetable forms, the interest we feel in the opening of a favorite cluster of buds, or the progress of the thrifty and luxuriant shoots of a rare plant, are such as serve most effectually to prevent an occupation of this nature from ever becoming monotonous or *ennuyant*.

The difference between the *green-house* and conserva tory is, that in the former, the plants are all kept in *pots* and arranged on stages, both to meet the eye agreeably, and for more convenient growth ; while in the *conservatory*, the plants are grown in a *bed* or border of soil precisely as in the open air.

When either of these plant habitations is to be attached to the house, the preference is greatly in favor of the conservatory. The plants being allowed more room, have richer and more luxuriant foliage, and grow and flower in a manner altogether superior to those in pots. The allusion to nature is also more complete in the case of plants growing in the ground ; and from the objects all being on the same level, and easily accessible, they are with more facility kept in that perfect nicety and order which an elegant plant-house should always exhibit.

On the other hand, the green-house will contain by far the largest number of plants, and the same may be more easily changed or renewed at any time ; so that for a particular taste, as that of a botanical amateur, who wishes to grow a great number of species in a small space, the green-house will be found preferable. Whenever either the conservatory or green-house is of moderate size, and intended solely for private recreation, we would in every case, when such a thing is not impossible, have it attached to the house; communicating by a glass door with the drawing-room, or one of the living rooms. Nothing can be more gratifying than a vista in winter through a glass door down the walk of a conservatory, bordered and overhung with the fine forms of tropical vegetation, golden oranges glowing through the dark green foliage, and gay corollas lighting up the branches of Camellias, and other floral favorites. Let us add the exulting song of a few Canaries, and the enchantment is complete. How much more refined and elevated is the taste which prefers such accessories to a dwelling, rather than costly furniture, or an extravagant display of plate!

The best and most economical form for a conservatory is a parallelogram—the deviation from a square being greater or less according to circumstances. When it is joined to the dwelling by one of its *sides* (in the case of the parallelogram form), the roof need only slope in one way, that is from the house. When one of the *ends* of the conservatory joins the dwelling, the roof should slope both ways from the centre. The advantage of the junction in the former case, is, that less outer surface of the conservatory being exposed to the cold, viz. only a side and two ends, less fuel will be required; the advantage in the latter case is, that the main walk leading down the conservatory will be exactly in the line of the vista from the drawing-room of the dwelling.

It is, we hope, almost unnecessary to state, that the roof of a conservatory, or indeed any other house where plants are to be well-grown, *must* be glazed. Opake roofs prevent the admission of perpendicular light, without which the stems of vegetation are drawn up weak and feeble, and are attracted in an unsightly manner towards the glass in front. When the conservatory joins the house by one of its ends, and extends out from the building to a considerable length, the effect will be much more elegant; and the plants will thrive more perfectly, when it is glazed on all of the three sides, so as to admit light in every direction.

The best aspect for a conservatory is directly south; southeast and southwest are scarcely inferior. Even east and west exposures will do very well, where there is plenty of glass to admit light; for though our winters are cold, yet there is a great abundance of sun, and bright clear atmosphere, both far more beneficial to plants than the moist, foggy vapor of an English winter, which, though mild, is comparatively sunless. When the conservatory adjoins and looks into the flower-garden, the effect will be appropriate and pleasing.

Some few hints respecting the construction of a con servatory may not be unacceptable to some of our readers In the first place, the roof should have a sufficient slope to carry off the rain rapidly, to prevent leakage; from 40 to 45 degrees is found to be the best inclination in our climate. The *roof* should by no means be glazed with large panes, because small ones have much greater strength, which is requisite to withstand the heavy weight of snow that often falls during winter, as well as to resist breakage by hail storms in summer. Four or eight inches by six, is the best size for roof-glass, and with this size the lap of the panes need not be greater than one-eighth of an inch, while it would require to be one-fourth of an inch, were the panes of the usual size. On the front and sides, the sashes may be handsome, and filled in with the best glass; even plate glass has been used in many cases to our knowledge here.

In the second place, some thorough provision must be made for warming the conservatory; and it is by far the best mode to have the apparatus for this purpose entirely independent of the dwelling house; that is (though the furnace may be in the basement), the flues and fire should be intended to heat the conservatory alone; for although a conservatory may, if small, be heated by the same fire which heats the kitchen or one of the living rooms, it is a much less efficient mode of attaining this object, and renders the conservatory more or less liable at all times to be too hot or too cold.

The common square flue, the sides built of bricks, and the top and bottom of tiles manufactured for that purpose, is one of the oldest, most simple, and least expensive methods of heating in use. Latterly, its place has been supplied by hot water circulated in large tubes of three or four inches in diameter from an open boiler, and by Perkins's mode as it is called, which employs small pipes of an inch in diameter, hermetically sealed. Economy of fuel and in the time requisite in attendance, are the chief merits of the hot water systems, which, however, have the great additional advantage of affording a more moist and genial temperature.

In a green-house, the flues, or hot water pipes, may be concealed under the stage. In conservatories they should by all means be placed out of sight also. To effect this, they are generally conducted into a narrow, hollow

Fig. 78.—The Conservatory and Flower Garden at Montgomery Place.

chamber, under the walk, which has perforated sides or a grated top, to permit the escape of heated air.*

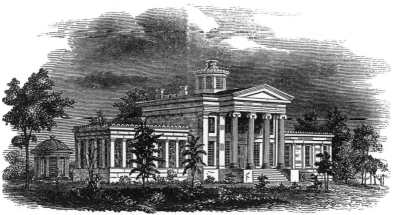

[Fig. 74. Villa at Brooklyn, N. Y., with the Conservatory attached.]

One of the most beautiful conservatories attached to the dwelling, to which we can refer our readers, for an example, is one built by J. W. Perry, Esq., Brooklyn, near New York (Fig. 74), forming the left wing of this elegant villa. Among the most magnificent detached conservatories are those of J. P. Cushing, Esq., at his elegant seat, *Belmont Place,* Watertown, near Boston; and that at Montgomery Place, the seat of Mrs. Edward Livingston, on the Hudson, Fig. 73.

A conservatory is frequently made an addition to a rectangular Grecian villa, as one of its wings—the other being a living or bed-room. The more varied and irregular outline of Gothic buildings enables them to receive an appendage of this nature with more facility in almost any direction, where the aspect is suitable.

* The circulation of warm air is greatly accelerated when an opening through the outer air is permitted to enter the hot air passage, thus becoming heated and passing into the conservatory.

Whatever be the style of the architecture of the house, that of the conservatory should in every case conform to it, and evince a degree of enrichment according with that of the main building.

Though a conservatory is often made an expensive luxury, attached only to tne better class of residences, there is no reason why cottages of more humble character should not have the same source of enjoyment on a more moderate scale. A small green-house, or *plant cabinet*, as it is sometimes called, eight or ten feet square, communicating with the parlor, and constructed in a simple style, may be erected and kept up in such a manner, as to be a source of much pleasure, for a comparatively trifling sum ; and we hope soon to see in this country, where the comforts of life are more equally distributed than in any other, the taste for enjoyments of this kind extending itself with the means for realizing them, into every portion of the northern and middle States.

Open and covered seats, of various descriptions, are among the most convenient and useful decorations for the pleasure-grounds of a country residence. Situated in portions of the lawn or park, somewhat distant from the house, they offer an agreeable place for rest or repose. If there are certain points from which are obtained agreeable prospects or extensive views of the surrounding country, a seat, by designating those points, and by affording us a convenient mode of enjoying them, has a double recommendation to our minds.

Open and covered seats are of two distinct kinds ; one *architectural*, or formed after artist-like designs, of stone or wood, in Grecian, Gothic, or other forms ; which may, if they are intended to produce an elegant effect, have

vases on pedestals as accompaniments ; the other, *rustic,*
as they are called, which are formed out of trunks and
branches of trees, roots, etc., in their natural forms.
There are particular sites where each of these kinds of
seats, or structures, is, in good taste, alone admissible. In
the proximity of elegant and decorated buildings where all
around has a polished air, it would evidently be doing
violence to our feelings and sense of propriety to admit
many rustic seats and structures of any kind ; but architectural decorations and architectural seats are there
correctly introduced. For the same reason, also, as we
have already suggested, that the sculptured forms of vases,
etc., would be out of keeping in scenes where nature is
predominant (as the distant wooded parts or walks of a
residence), architectural, or, in other words, highly artificial seats, would not be in character : but rustic seats
and structures, which, from the nature of the materials
employed and the simple manner of their construction,
appear but one remove from natural forms, are felt at once
to be in unison with the surrounding objects. Again, the
mural and highly artistical vase and statue, most properly
accompany the beautiful landscape garden ; while rustic
baskets, or vases, are the most fitting decorations of the
Picturesque Landscape Garden.

The simplest variety of covered architectural seat is the
latticed arbor for vines of various descriptions, with the
seat underneath the canopy of foliage ; this may with
more propriety be introduced in various parts of the
grounds than any other of its class, as the luxuriance and
natural gracefulness of the foliage which covers the arbor,
in a great measure destroys or overpowers the expression
of its original form. Lattice arbors, however, neatly

formed of rough poles and posts, are much more picturesque and suitable for wilder portions of the scenery.

The temple and the pavilion are highly
finished forms of covered seats, which are
occasionally introduced in splendid places,
[Fig. 75.] where classic architecture prevails. There is
a circular pavilion of this kind at the termination of one
of the walks at Mr. Langdon's residence, Hyde Park.
Fig. 75.

We consider rustic seats and structures as likely to be
much preferred in the villa and cottage residences of the
country. They have the merit of being tasteful and picturesque in their appearance, and are easily constructed
by the amateur, at comparatively little or no expense.

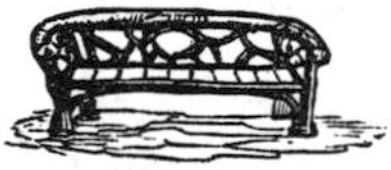

There is scarcely a prettier or more
pleasant object for the termination of a
[Fig. 76.] long walk in the pleasure-grounds or park,
than a neatly thatched structure of rustic work, with its
seat for repose, and a view of the landscape beyond. On
finding such an object, we are never tempted to think that
there has been a lavish expenditure to serve a trifling
purpose, but are gratified to see the exercise of taste and
ingenuity, which completely answers the end in view.

Figure 76 is an example of a simple rustic
seat formed of the crooked and curved branches
of the oak, elm, or any other of our forest trees
[Fig. 77.] Fig. 77 is a seat of the same character, made
at the foot of a tree, whose overhanging branches afford a
fine shade.

Figure 78 is a covered seat or rustic arbor, with a
thatched roof of straw. Twelve posts are set securely in
tne ground, which make the frame of this structure, the

[Fig. 78.]

openings between being filled in with branches (about
three inches in diameter) of different trees—the more
irregular the better, so that the perpendicular surface of
the exterior and interior is kept nearly equal.   In lieu of
thatch, the roof may be first tightly boarded, and then a
covering of bark or the slabs of trees with the bark on,
overlaid and nailed on.   The figure represents the structure as formed round a tree.   For the sake of variety this
might be omitted, the roof formed of an open lattice work
of branches like the sides, and the whole covered by a
grape, bignonia, or some other vine or creeper of luxuriant
growth.   The seats are in the interior.

Figure 79 represents a covered seat of another kind.

The central structure, which is circular, is
intended for a collection of minerals, shells,
or any other curious objects for which an
amateur might have a *penchant*.   Geological or mineralogical specimens of the
adjacent neighborhood, would be very proper for such a
cabinet.   The seat surrounds it on the outside, over which
is a thatched roof or veranda, supported on rustic pillars
formed of the trunks of saplings, with the bark attached.

[Fig. 79.]

Many of the English country places abound with admirable specimens of rustic work in their parks and pleasure-grounds. White Knight's, in particular, a residence of the Duke of Marlborough, has a number of beautiful structures of this kind. Figure 80 is a view of a

[Fig. 80. Rustic Covered Seat.]

round seat with thatched roof, in that demesne. Three or four rustic pillars support the architrave, and the whole of the exterior and interior (being first formed of frame-work) is covered with straight branches of the maple and larch. The seat on the interior looks upon a fine prospect; and the seat on the back of the exterior fronts the park.

There is no limit to the variety of forms and patterns in which these rustic seats, arbors, summer-houses, etc., can be constructed by an artist of some fancy and ingenuity. After the frame-work of the structure is formed of posts and rough boards, if small straight rods about an inch in diameter, of hazel, white birch, maple, etc., are selected in sufficient quantity, they may be nailed on in squares, diamonds, medallions, or other patterns, and have the effect of a *mosaic* of wood.

Among the curious results of this fancy for rustic work, we may mention the *moss-house*—erected in several places abroad. The skeleton or frame-work of the arbor or house is formed as we have just stated; over this small rods half an inch in diameter are nailed, about an inch from centre to centre; after the whole surface is covered with this sort of rustic lathing, a quantity of the softer wood-moss of different colors is collected; and taking small parcels in the hand at a time, the tops being evenly arranged, the bottoms or roots are crowded closely between the rods with a small wooden wedge. When this is done with some little skill, the tufted ends spread out and cover the rods entirely, showing a smooth surface of mosses of different colors, which has an effect not unlike that of a thick Brussels carpet.

The mosses retain their color for a great length of time, and when properly rammed in with the wedge, they cannot be pulled out again without breaking their tops. The prettiest example which we have seen of a handsome moss-house in this country, is at the residence of Wm. H. Aspinwall, Esq., on Staten Island.

A *prospect tower* is a most desirable and pleasant structure in certain residences. Where the view is comparatively limited from the grounds, on account of their surface being level, or nearly so, it often happens that the spectator, by being raised some twenty-five or thirty feet above the surface, finds himself in a totally different position, whence a charming *coup d'œil* or bird's-eye view of the surrounding country is obtained.

Those of our readers who may have visited the delightful garden and grounds of M. Parmentier, near Brooklyn, some half a dozen years since, during the lifetime of that amiable and zealous amateur of horticulture, will readily remember the rustic prospect-arbor, or tower

[Fig. 81.]

Fig. 81, which was situated at the extremity of his place. It was one of the first pieces of rustic work of any size, and displaying any ingenuity, that we remember to have seen here; and from its summit, though the garden walks afforded no prospect a beautiful reach of the neighborhood for many miles was enjoyed.

Figure 82 is a design for a rustic prospect tower of three

[Fig. 82.]

stories in height, with a double thatched roof. It is formed of rustic pillars or columns, which are well fixed in the ground, and which are filled in with a fanciful lattice of rustic branches. A spiral staircase winds round the interior of the platform of the second and upper stories, where there are seats under the open thatched roof.

On a *ferme ornée*, where the proprietor desires to give a picturesque appearance to the different appendages of the place, rustic work offers an easy and convenient method of attaining this end. The *dairy* is sometimes made a detached building, and in this country it may be built of logs in a tasteful manner with a thatched roof; the interior being studded, lathed, and plastered in the usual way. Or the ice-house, which generally shows but a rough gable and ridge roof rising out of the ground, might be covered with a neat structure in rustic work, overgrown with vines, which would give it a pleasing or picturesque air, instead of leaving it, as at present, an unsightly object which we are anxious to conceal.

A species of useful decoration, which is perhaps more naturally suggested than any other, is the *bridge*. Where a constant stream, of greater or less size, runs through the grounds, and divides the banks on opposite sides, a bridge of some description, if it is only a narrow plank over a rivulet, is highly necessary. In pieces of artificial water that are irregular in outline, a narrow strait is often purposely made, with the view of introducing a bridge for effect.

When the stream is large and bold, a handsome architectural bridge of stone or timber is by far the most suitable ; especially if the stream is near the house, or if it is crossed on the Approach road to the mansion ; because a character of permanence and solidity is requisite in such cases. But when it is only a winding rivulet or crystal brook, which meanders along beneath the shadow of tufts of clustering foliage of the pleasure-ground or park, a rustic bridge may

[Fig. 83.]

be brought in with the happiest effect. Fig. 83 is a rustic bridge erected under our direction. The foundation is made by laying down a few large square stones beneath the surface on both sides of the stream to be spanned ; upon these are stretched two round posts or sleepers with the bark on, about eight or ten inches in diameter. The rustic hand-rail is framed into these two sleepers. The floor of the bridge is made by laying down small posts of equal size, about four or six inches in diameter, crosswise upon the sleepers, and nailing them down securely. The bark is allowed to remain on in every piece of wood employed in the construction of this little bridge ; and when the wood is cut at the proper season (durable kinds being chosen), such a bridge, well made will remain in excellent order for many years.

Rockwork is another kind of decoration sometimes introduced in particular portions of the scenery of a residence Fig. 84. When well executed, that is, so as to have a natural and harmonious expression, the effect is highly pleasing. We have seen, however, in places where a high

[Fig. 84. Rockwork.]

keeping and good taste otherwise prevailed, such a barbarous *mélange*, or confused pile of stones mingled with soil, and planted over with dwarfish plants dignified with the name of rockwork, that we have been led to believe that it is much better to attempt nothing of the kind, unless there is a suitable place for its display, and at the same time, the person attempting it is sufficiently an artist, imbued with the spirit of nature in her various compositions and combinations, to be able to produce something higher than a caricature of her works.

The object of *rockwork* is to produce in scenery or portions of a scene, naturally in a great measure destitute of groups of rocks and their accompanying drapery of plants and foliage, something of the picturesque effect which such natural assemblages confer. To succeed in this, it is evident that we must not heap up little hillocks of mould and smooth stones, in the midst of an open lawn, or the centre of a flower-garden. But if we can make choice of a situation where a rocky bank or knoll already partially exists, or would be in keeping with the form of the ground and the character of the scene, then we may introduce such accompaniments with the best possible hope of success.

It often happens in a place of considerable extent, that somewhere in conducting the walks through the grounds, we meet with a ridge with a small rocky face, or perhaps with a large rugged single rock, or a bank where rocky summits just protrude themselves through the surface. The common feeling against such uncouth objects, would direct them to be cleared away at once out of sight. But let us take the case of the large rugged rock, and commence our picturesque operations upon it. We will begin by collecting from some rocky hill or valley in the neighborhood of the estate, a sufficient quantity of rugged rocks, in size from a few pounds to half a ton or more, if necessary, preferring always such as are already coated with mosses and lichens. These we will assemble around the base of a large rock, in an irregular somewhat pyramidal group, bedding them sometimes partially, sometimes almost entirely in soil heaped in irregular piles around the rock. The rocks must be arranged in a natural manner, avoiding all regularity and appearance of formal art, but placing them sometimes in groups of half a dozen together, overhanging each other, and sometimes half bedded in the soil, and a little distance apart. There are no *rules* to be given for such operations, but the study of natural groups, of a character similar to that which we wish to produce, will afford sufficient hints if the artist is

"Prodigue de génie,"

and has a perception of the natural beauty which he
desires to imitate.

The rockwork once formed, choice trailing, creeping, and
alpine plants, such as delight naturally in similar situations,
may be planted in the soil which fills the interstices between
the rocks: when these grow to fill their proper places,
partly concealing and adorning the rocks with their neat
green foliage and pretty blossoms, the effect of the whole,
if properly done, will be like some exquisite portion of a
rocky bank in wild scenery, and will be found to give an
air at once striking and picturesque to the little scene
where it is situated.

In small places where the grounds are extremely limited,
and the owner wishes to form a rockwork for the growth
of alpine and other similar plants, if there are no natural
indications of a rocky surface, a rockwork may sometimes
be introduced without violating good taste by *preparing
natural indications* artificially, if we may use such a term.
If a few of the rocks to be employed in the rockwork are
sunk half or three-fourths their depth in the soil near the
site of the proposed rockwork, so as to have the appearance of a rocky ridge just *cropping out,* as the
geologists say, then the rockwork will, to the eye of a
spectator, seem to be connected with, and growing out of
this rocky spur or ridge below: or, in other words, there
will be an obvious reason for its being situated there,
instead of its presenting a wholly artificial appearance.

In a previous page, when treating of the banks of pieces
of water formed by art, we endeavored to show how the
natural appearance of such banks would be improved by
the judicious introduction of rocks partially imbedded into

and holding them up. Such situations, in the case of a small lake or pond, or a brook, are admirable sites for rock-work. Where the materials of a suitable kind are abundant, and tasteful ingenuity is not wanting, surprising effects may be produced in a small space. Caves and grottoes, where ferns and mosses would thrive admirably with the gentle drip from the roof, might be made of the overarching rocks arranged so as to appear like small natural caverns. Let the exterior be partially planted with low shrubs and climbing plants, as the wild Clematis, and the effect of such bits of landscape could not but be agreeable in secluded portions of the grounds.

In many parts of the country, the secondary blue limestone abounds, which, in the small masses found loose in the woods, covered with mosses and ferns, affords the very finest material for artificial rockwork.*

After all, much the safest way is never to introduce rockwork of any description, unless we feel certain that it will have a good effect. When a place is naturally picturesque, and abounds here and there with rocky banks, etc., little should be done but to heighten and aid the expressions of these, if they are wanting in spirit, by adding something more ; or softening and giving elegance to the expression, if too wild, by planting the same with

* Our readers may see an engraving and description of a superb *extravaganza* in rockwork in a late number of Loudon's Gardener's Magazine. Lady Broughton, of Hoole House, Chester, England, has succeeded in forming, round a natural valley, an imitation of the hills, glaciers, and scenery of a *passage* in Switzerland. The whole is done in rockwork, the snow-covered summits being represented in white spar. The appropriate plants, trees, and shrubs on a small scale, are introduced, and the illusion, to a spectator standing in the valley surrounded by these glaciers, is said to be wonderfully striking and complete.

beautiful shrubs and climbers. On a tame sandy level,
where rocks of any kind are unknown, their introduction
in rockworks, nine times in ten, is more likely to give rise
to emotions of the ridiculous, than those of the sublime or
picturesque.

Fountains are highly elegant garden decorations, rarely
seen in this country ; which is owing, not so much, we
apprehend, to any great cost incurred in putting them up,
or any want of appreciation of their sparkling and
enlivening effect in garden scenery, as to the fact that there
are few artisans here, as abroad, whose business it is to
construct and fit up architectural, and other *jets d'eau.*

The first requisite, where a fountain is a desideratum, is
a constant supply of water, either from a natural source
or an artificial reservoir, some distance higher than the
level of the surface whence the jet or fountain is to rise.

[Fig. 85. Design for a Fountain.]

Where there is a pond, or other body of water, on a higher
level than the proposed fountain, it is only necessary to lay
pipes under the surface to conduct the supply of water to

the required spot; but where there is no such head of water, the latter must be provided from a reservoir artificially prepared, and kept constantly full.

There are two very simple and cheap modes of effecting this, which we shall lay before our readers, and one or the other of which may be adopted in almost every locality. The first is to provide a large flat cistern of sufficient size, which is to be placed under the roof in the upper story of one of the outbuildings, the carriage-house for example, and receive its supplies from the water collected on the roof of the building; the amount of water collected in this way from a roof of moderate size being much more than is generally supposed. The second is to sink a well of capacious size (where such is not already at command) in some part of the grounds where it will not be conspicuous, and over it to erect a small tower, the top of which shall contain a cistern and a small horizontal windmill; which being kept in motion by the wind more or less almost every day in summer, will raise a sufficient quantity of water to keep the reservoir supplied from the well below. In either of these cases, it is only necessary to carry leaden pipes from the cistern (under the surface, below the reach of frost) to the place where the jet is to issue; the supply in both these cases will, if properly arranged, be more than enough for the consumption of the fountain during the hours when it will be necessary for it to play, viz. from sunrise to evening.

The steam-engine is often employed to force up water for the supply of fountains in many of the large public and royal gardens; but there are few cases in this country where private expenditures of this kind would be justifiable.

But where a small stream, or even the overflow of a

perpetual spring, can be commanded, the *Hydraulic Ram* is the most perfect as well as the simplest and cheapest of all modes of raising water. A supply pipe of an inch in diameter is in many cases sufficient to work the Ram and force water to a great distance; and where sufficien to fill a "driving pipe" of two inches diameter can be commanded, a large reservoir may be kept constantly filled. As the Hydraulic Ram is now for sale in all our cities we need not explain its action.

"In conducting the water from the cistern or reservoir to the jet or fountain, the following particulars require to be attended to : In the first place, all the pipes must be laid sufficiently deep in the earth, or otherwise placed and protected so as to prevent the possibility of their being reached by frost; next, as a general rule, the diameter of the orifice from which the jet of water proceeds, technically called the bore of the quill, ought to be four times less than the bore of the conduit pipe; that is, the quill and the pipe ought to be in a quadruple proportion to each other. There are several sorts of quills or spouts, which throw the water up or down, into a variety of forms : such as fans, parasols, sheaves, showers, mushrooms, inverted bells, etc. The larger the conduit pipes are, the more freely will the jets display their different forms; and the fewer the holes in the quill or jet (for sometimes this is pierced like the rose of a watering pot) the greater certainty there will be of the form continuing the same; because the risk of any of the holes choking up will be less. The diameter of a conduit pipe ought in no case to be less than one inch; but for jets of very large size, the diameter ought to be two inches. Where the conduit pipes are of great length, say upwards of 1000 feet, it is found advantageous to begin, at the reservoir or cistern with pipes of a diameter somewhat greater than those which deliver the water to the quills, because the water, in a pipe of uniform diameter of so great a length, is found to lose much of its strength, and become what is tech nically called sleepy: while the different sizes quicken it, and redouble its force. For example, in a conduit pipe of 1800 feet in length, the first six hundred feet may be laid with pipes of eight inches in diameter, the next 600 feet with pipes of six inches in diameter, and the last 600 feet with pipes of four inches in diameter. In conduits not exceeding 900 feet, the same diameter may be continued throughout. When several jets are to play in several fountains, or in the same, it is not necessary to lay a fresh pipe from each jet to the reservoir ; a main of sufficient size, with branch pipes to each jet, being all that is required. Where the conduit pipe enters the reservoir or cistern, it ought to be of increased diameter, and the grating placed over it to keep out leaves and other matters which might choke it up, ought to be semi-globular or conical; so that the area of the number of holes in it may exceed the area of the orifice of the conduit pipe. The object is to prevent any diminution of pressure from the body of water in the cistern, and to facilitate the flow of the water. Where the conduit pipe joins the fountain, there, of course, ought to be a cock for turning the water off and on ; and particular care must be taken that as much water may pass through the oval hole of this cock as passes through the circular hole of the pipe. In conduit pipes, all elbows, bendings, and right angles should be avoided as much as possible, since they diminish the force of the water. In very long conduit pipes, air-holes formed by soldering on upright pieces of pipe, terminating in inverted valves or suckers, should be made at convenient distances, and protected by shafts built of stone or brick, and covered with movable gratings, in order to let out the air. Where pipes ascend and descend on very irregular surfaces, the strain on the lowest parts of the pipe is always the greatest; unless care is taken to relieve this by the judicious disposition of cocks and air-holes. Without this precaution, pipes conducted over irregular surfaces will not last nearly so long as those conducted over a level."— *Encycl. of Cottage, Farm, and Villa Architecture,* page 989.

Where the reservoir is but a short distance, as from a dozen to fifty yards, all that is necessary is to lay the conduit pipes on a regular uniform slope, to secure a steady uninterrupted flow of water. Owing to the friction in the pipes, and pressure of the atmosphere, the water in the fountain will of course, in no case, rise quite as high as the level of the water in the reservoir; but it will nearly as high. For example, if the reservoir is ten feet four inches high, the water in the jet will only rise ten feet, and in like proportion for the different heights. The following table*

Height of the Reservoir.		Diameter of the Conduit pipes.		Diameters of the Orifices.		Height the water will rise to.	
Feet.	Inches.	Inches.	Lines.	Lines.	Parts.	Feet.	Inches.
5	1	0	22	4	0	5	0
10	4	0	25	5	0	10	0
15	9	2¼	0	6	0	15	0
21	4	2½	0	6½	0	20	0
33	0	3	0	7	0	30	0
45	4	4½	0	7	8	40	0
58	4	5	0	8	10	50	0
72	0	5½	0	10	12	60	0
86	4	6	0	12	14	70	0
100	0	7	0	12	15	80	0

* Switzer's *Introduction to a General System of Hydrostatics.*

shows w:th a given height of reservoirs and diameter of conduit pipes and orifices, the height to which the water will rise in the fountain.

A simple jet (Fig. 86) issuing from a circular basin of water, or a cluster of perpendicular jets (candelabra jets),

is at once the simplest and most pleasing of fountains. Such are almost the only kinds of fountains which can be introduced with propriety in simple scenes where the pre-

[Fig. 86.]

dominant objects are sylvan, not architectural.

Weeping, or *Tazza Fountains*, as they are called, are simple and highly pleasing objects, which require only a

very moderate supply of water compared with that demanded by a constant and powerful jet. The conduit pipe rises through and fills the vase, which is so formed as to

[Fig. 87. Tazza Fountain.]

overflow round its entire margin. Figure 87 represents a beautiful Grecian vase for tazza fountains. The ordinary jet and the tazza fountain may be combined in one, when the supply of water is sufficient, by carrying the conduit pipe to the level of the top of the vase, from which the water rises perpendicularly, then falls back into the vase and overflows as before.

We might enumerate and figure a great many other designs for fountains; but the connoisseur will receive more ample information on this head than we are able to afford, from the numerous French works devoted to this branch of Rural Embellishment.

A species of rustic fountain which has a good effect, is made by introducing the conduit pipe or pipes among the groups of *rockwork* alluded to, from whence (the orifice of

the pipe being concealed or disguised) the water issues
among the rocks either in the form of a cascade, a weeping fountain, or a perpendicular jet. A little basin of
water is formed at the foot or in the midst of the rockwork
and the cool moist atmosphere afforded by the trickling
streams, would offer a most congenial site for aquatic
plants, ferns, and mosses.

Fountains of a highly artificial character are happily
situated only when they are placed in the neighborhood of
buildings and architectural forms. When only a single
fountain can be maintained in a residence, the centre of
the flower-garden, or the neighborhood of the piazza or
terrace-walk, is, we think, much the most appropriate
situation for it. There the liquid element, dancing and
sparkling in the sunshine, is an agreeable feature in the
scene, as viewed from the windows of the rooms ; and the
falling watery spray diffusing coolness around is no less
delightful in the surrounding stillness of a summer evening.

After all that we have said respecting architectural and
rustic decorations of the grounds, we must admit that it
requires a great deal of good taste and judgment, to
introduce and distribute them so as to be in good keeping
with the scenery of country residences. A country residence, where the house with a few tasteful groups of
flowers and shrubs, and a pretty lawn, with clusters and
groups of luxuriant trees, are all in high keeping and
evincing high order, is far more beautiful and pleasing
than the same place, or even one of much larger extent,
where a profusion of statues, vases, and fountains, or
rockwork and rustic seats, are distributed throughout the
garden and grounds, while the latter, in themselves, show

slovenly keeping, and a crude and meagre knowledge of design in Landscape Gardening. *Unity of expression* is the maxim and guide in this department of the art, as in every other. Decorations can never be introduced with good effect, when they are at variance with the character of surrounding objects. A beautiful and highly architectural villa may, with the greatest propriety, receive the decorative accompaniments of elegant vases, sundials, or statues, should the proprietor choose to display his wealth and taste in this manner; but these decorations would be totally misapplied in the case of a plain square edifice, evincing no architectural style in itself.

In addition to this, there is great danger that a mere lover of fine vases may run into the error of assembling these objects indiscriminately in different parts of his grounds, where they have really no place, but interfere with the quiet character of surrounding nature. He may overload the grounds with an unmeaning distribution of sculpturesque or artificial forms, instead of working up those parts where art predominates in such a manner, by means of appropriate decorations, as to heighten by contrast the beauty of the whole adjacent landscape.

With regard to pavilions, summer-houses, rustic seats, and garden edifices of like character, they should, if possible, in all cases be introduced where they are manifestly appropriate or in harmony with the scene. Thus a grotto should not be formed in the side of an open bank, but in a deep shadowy recess; a classic temple or pavilion may crown a beautiful and prominent knoll, and a rustic covered seat may occupy a secluded, quiet portion of the grounds, where undisturbed meditation mav be enjoyed.   As our favorite Delille says :

> " Sachez ce qui convient ou nuit au caractère.
> Un réduit écarté, dans un lieu solitaire,
> Peint mieux la solitude encore et l'abandon.
> Montrez-vous donc fidèle à chaque expression ;
> N'allez pas au grand jour offrir un ermitage :
> Ne cachez point un temple au fond d'un bois sauvage."
>
> LES JARDINS.

Or if certain objects are unavoidably placed in situations of inimical expression, the artist should labor to alter the character of the locality.   How much this can be done by the proper choice of trees and shrubs, and the proper arrangement of plantations, those who have seen the difference in aspect of certain favorite localities of wild nature, as covered with wood, or as denuded by the axe, can well judge.   And we hope the amateur, who has made himself familiar with the habits and peculiar expressions of different trees, as pointed out in this work, will not find himself at a loss to effect such changes, by the aid of time, with ease and facility.

APPENDIX.

I.

THERE is no subject on which the professional horticulturist is more frequently consulted in America, than transplanting trees. And, as it is an essential branch of Landscape Gardening—indeed, perhaps, the most important and necessary one to be practically understood in the improvement or embellishment of new country residences—we shall offer a few remarks here, with the hope of rendering it a more easy and successful practice in the hands of amateurs.

The first and most important consideration in transplanting should be the *preservation of the roots*. By this we do not mean a certain bulk of the larger and more important ones only, but as far as possible all the numerous small fibres and rootlets so indispensably necessary in assisting the tree to recover from the shock of removal. The coarser and larger roots serve to secure the tree in its position, and convey the fluids ; but it is by means of the small fibrous roots, or the delicate and numerous *points* of these fibres called *spongioles*, that the food of plants is imbibed, and the destruction of such is manifestly in the highest degree fatal to the success of the transplanted tree. To avoid this as far as practicable, we should, in removing a tree, commence at such a distance as to include a circumference large enough to comprise the great majority of the roots. At that distance from the trunk we shall find most of the smaller roots, which should be carefully loosened

413

from the soil, with as little injury as possible; the earth should be gently and gradually removed from the larger roots, as we proceed onward from the extremity of the circle to the centre, and when we reach the nucleus of roots surrounding the trunk, and fairly undermine the whole, we shall find ourselves in possession of a tree in such a perfect condition, that even when of considerable size, we may confidently hope for a speedy recovery of its former luxuriance after being replanted.

Now to remove a tree in this manner, requires not only a considerable degree of experience, which is only to be acquired by practice, but also much *patience and perseverance* while engaged in the work. It is not a difficult task to remove, in a careless manner, four or five trees in a day, of fifteen feet in height, by the assistance of three or four men, and proper implements of removal, while one or two trees only can be removed if the roots and branches are preserved entire or nearly so. Yet in the latter case, if the work be well performed, we shall have the satisfaction of beholding the subjects, when removed, soon taking fresh root, and becoming vigorous healthy trees, with fine luxuriant heads, while three-fourths of the former will most probably perish, and the remainder struggle for several years, under the loss of so large a portion of their roots and branches, before they entirely recover, and put on the appearance of handsome trees.

When a tree is carelessly transplanted, and the roots much mutilated, the operator feels obliged to reduce the top accordingly; as experience teaches him, that although the leaves may expand, yet they will soon perish without a fresh supply of food from the roots. But when the largest portion of the roots are carefully taken up with the tree, pruning should be less resorted to, and thus the original symmetry and beauty of the head retained. When this is the case, the leaves contribute as much, by their peculiar action in elaborating the sap, towards re-establishing the tree, as the roots; and indeed the two act so reciprocally with each other, that any considerable injury to the one always affects the other. "The functions of respiration, perspiration, and digestion," says Professor Lindley, "which are the particular offices of leaves, are essential to the health of a plant; its healthiness being in proportion to the degree in which these functions are duly performed. The leaf is in reality a natural contrivance for exposing a large surface to the influence of external agents, by whose assistance the crude sap contained in the stem is altered, and rendered suitable to the particular wants of the species, and for returning into the general circulation, the fluids in their matured condition. In a word, the leaf of a plant is its lungs and stomach traversed by a system of veins."* All the pruning, therefore, that is necessary, when a tree is properly transplanted, will be comprised in paring smooth all bruises or accidental injuries, received by the roots or branches during the operation, or the removal of a few that may interfere with elegance of form in the head.

Next in importance to the requisite care in performing the operation of transplanting, is *the proper choice of individual trees to be transplanted.* In making selections for removal among our fine forest trees, it should never be forgotten that there are two distinct kinds of subjects, even of the same species of every tree, viz. those that grow among and surrounded by other trees or woods, and those which grow alone, in free open exposures, where they are acted upon by the winds, storms, and sunshine, at all times and seasons. The former class it will always be exceedingly difficult to transplant successfully even with the greatest care, while the latter may always be removed with comparatively little risk of failure.

Any one who is at all familiar with the growth of trees in woods or groves somewhat dense, is also aware of the great difference in the external appearance between such trees and those which stand singly in open spaces. In thick woods, trees are found to have tall, slender trunks, with comparatively few branches except at the top, smooth and thin bark, and they are scantily provided with roots, but especially with the small fibres so essentially necessary to insure the growth of the tree when transplanted. Those, on the other hand, which stand isolated, have short thick stems, numerous branches, thick bark, and great abundance of root and small fibres. The latter, accustomed to the full influence of the weather, to cold winds as well as open sunshine have what Sir Henry Steuart has aptly denominated the " *protecting properties*," well developed ; being robust and hardy, they are well cal-

* Theory of Horticulture.

culated to endure the violence of the removal, while trees growing in
the midst of a wood sheltered from the tempests by their fellows, and
scarcely ever receiving the sun and air freely except at their topmost
branches, are too feeble to withstand the change of situation, when removed to an open lawn, even when they are carefully transplanted.

"Of trees in open exposures," says Sir Henry, "we find that their
peculiar properties contribute, in a remarkable manner, to their health
and prosperity. In the first place, their shortness and greater girth of
stem, in contradistinction to others in the interior of woods, are ob-
viously intended to give to the former greater strength to resist the
winds, and a shorter lever to act upon the roots. Secondly, their
larger heads, with spreading branches, in consequence of the free access of light, are as plainly formed for the nourishment as well as the
balancing of so large a trunk, and also for furnishing a cover to shield
it from the elements. Thirdly, their superior thickness and induration
of bark is, in like manner, bestowed for the protection of the sap-ves-
sels, that lie immediately under it, and which, without such defence
from cold, could not perform their functions. Fourthly, their greater
number and variety of roots are for the double purpose of nourishment and strength; nourishment to support a mass of such magnitude,
and strength to contend with the fury of the blast. Such are the obvious purposes for which the unvarying characteristics of trees in open
exposures are conferred upon them. Nor are they conferred equally
and indiscriminately upon all trees so situated. They seem, by the
economy of nature, to be *peculiar adaptations* to the circumstances and
wants of each individual, *uniformly bestowed in the ratio of exposure,*
greater where that is more conspicuous, and uniformly decreasing, as it
becomes less."*

Trees in which the protecting properties are well developed are frequently to be met with on the skirts of woods ; but those standing singly
here and there, through the cultivated fields and meadows of our farm
lands, where the roots have extended themselves freely in the mellow
soil, are the finest subjects for removal into the lawn, park, or pleasure
ground.

* The Planter's Guide, p. 105.

The machine used in removing trees of moderate size is of simple
construction, consisting of a pair of strong wheels about five feet high
a stout axle, and a pole about twelve feet long. In transplanting, the
wheels and axle are brought close to the trunk of the tree, the pole is
firmly lashed to the stem, and when the soil is sufficiently removed and
loosened about the roots, the pole, with the tree attached, is drawn
down to a horizontal position by the aid of men and a pair of horses.
When the tree is thus drawn out of the hole, it is well secured and
properly balanced upon the machine, the horses are fastened in front
of the mass of roots by gearings attached to the axle, and the whole
is transported to the destined location.

In order more effectually to insure the growth of large specimens
when transplanted, a mode of *preparing beforehand* a supply of young
roots, is practised by skilful operators. This consists in removing the
top soil, partially undermining the tree, and shortening back many of
the roots; and afterwards replacing the former soil by rich mould, or
soil well manured. This is suffered to remain at least one year, and
often three or four years; the tree, stimulated by the fresh supply of
food, throws out an abundance of small fibres, which render success,
when the time for removal arrives, comparatively certain.

It may be well to remark here, that before large trees are transplanted into their final situations, the latter should be well prepared by
trenching, or *digging the soil two or three feet deep*, intermingling
throughout the whole a liberal portion of well decomposed manure, or
rich compost. To those who are in the habit of planting trees of any
size in unprepared grounds, or that merely prepared by digging *one
spit deep*, and turning in a little surface manure, it is inconceivable how
much more rapid is the growth, and how astonishingly luxuriant the appearance of trees when removed into ground properly prepared. It is
not too much to affirm, that young trees under favorable circumstances
—in soil so prepared—will advance more rapidly, and attain a larger
stature in eight years, than those planted in the ordinary way, without
deepening the soil, will in twenty—and trees of larger size in proportion; a gain of growth surely worth the trifling expense incurred in
the first instance. And the same observation will apply to all plant-

ing. A little extra labor and cost expended in *preparing the soil* will, for a long time, secure a surprising rapidity of growth.*

In the actual planting of the tree, the chief point lies in bringing every small fibre in contact with the soil, so that no hollows or interstices are left, which may produce mouldiness and decay of the roots. To avoid this, the soil must be pulverized with the spade before filling in, and one of the workmen, with his hands and a flat dibble of wood, should fill up all cavities, and lay out the small roots before covering them in their natural position. When *watering* is thought advisable (and we practise it almost invariably), it should always be done while the planting is going forward. Poured in the hole when the roots are just covered with the soil, it serves to settle the loose earth compactly

* Where expense is not so much an object as success, we cannot too deeply impress upon planters the necessity of making very deep, and very wide holes, or pits, as they are called in England. These pits should be four to five feet deep, and not less than ten to sixteen feet in diameter, and neither *round nor square*, but star-shaped, or cross-shaped, of such a form as would be produced by placing one equilateral triangle upon another, or two parallelograms across each other, so as to form a Greek cross.

   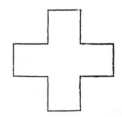

The object of departing from the square, or round form, is to introduce the growing fibres of the young trees into the *firm and poor soil, by degrees*, and not *all at once*, as in the round or square-hole manner.

When a tree is planted in the round or square pit, surrounded outside of it by poor, hard soil, it is very much in the same situation as if its roots were confined in a tub or box.

The dove-tailing, so to speak, of the prepared soil, and of the moisture it will retain, with the hard, impenetrable soil by which it is surrounded, will gradually prepare the latter for being penetrated by the roots of the trees, and prevent the sides of the pit from giving the same check to those roots, which the sides of the pot or tub do to the plant contained in it. In the preparation of these holes, the lower spot, or hard-pan, should be thrown out, and ten to twelve inches of stone substituted, for the double purpose of drainage, and retention of moisture in dry weather.—H. W. S.

around the various roots, and thus both furnishes a supply of moisture, and brings the pulverized mould in proper contact for growth. Trees well watered when planted in this way, will rarely require it afterwards; and should they do so, the better way is to remove two or three inches of the top soil, and give the lower stratum a copious supply; when the water having been absorbed, the surface should again be replaced. There is no practice more mischievous to newly moved trees, than that of pouring water, during hot weather, upon the surface of the ground above the roots. Acted upon by the sun and wind, this surface becomes baked, and but little water reaches the roots; or just sufficient, perhaps, to afford a momentary stimulus, to be followed by increased sensibility to the parching drought.

With respect to the proper seasons for transplanting, we may remark that, except in extreme northern latitude, autumn planting is generally preferred for large, hardy, deciduous trees. It may commence as soon as the leaves fall, and may be continued until winter. In planting large trees in spring, we should commence as early as possible, to give them the benefit of the April rains; if it should be deferred to a later period, the trees will be likely to suffer greatly by the hot summer sun before they are well established.

The transplanting of *evergreens* is generally considered so much more difficult than that of deciduous trees, and so many persons who have tolerable success in the latter, fail in the former, that we may perhaps be expected to point out the reason of these frequent failures.

Most of our horticultural maxims are derived from English authors and among them, that of always planting evergreens either in August or late in autumn. At both these seasons, it is nearly impossible to succeed in the temperate portions of the United States, from the different character of our climate at these seasons. The genial moisture of the English climate renders transplanting comparatively easy at all seasons, but especially in winter, while in this country, our Augusts are dry and hot, and our winters generally dry and cold. If planted in the latter part of summer, evergreens become parched in their foliage, and soon perish. If planted in autumn or early winter, the severe cold that ensues, to which the newly disturbed plant is peculiarly alive, paralyses vital action, and the tree is so much enfeebled that, when

spring arrives, it survives but a short period. The only period, there•
fore, that remains for the successful removal of evergreens here, is the
spring. When planted as early as practicable in the spring, so as to
have the full benefit of the abundant rains so beneficial to vegetation
at that season, they will almost immediately protrude new shoots, and
regain their former vigor.

Evergreens are, in their roots, much more delicate and impatient of
dryness than deciduous trees; and this should be borne in mind while
transplanting them. For this reason, experienced planters always
choose a wet or misty day for their removal; and, in dry weather, we
would always recommend the roots to be kept watered and covered
from the air by mats during transportation. When proper regard is
paid to this point, and to judicious selection of the season, evergreens
will not be found more difficult of removal than other trees.

Another mode of transplanting large evergreens, which is very successfully practised among us, is that of removing them with frozen
balls of earth in mid-winter. When skilfully performed, it is perhaps
the most complete of all modes, and is so different from the common
method, that the objection we have just made to winter planting does
not apply to this case. The trees to be removed are selected, the situations chosen, and the holes dug, while the ground is yet open in autumn.
When the ground is somewhat frozen, the operator proceeds to dig a
trench around the tree at some distance, gradually undermining it, and
leaving all the principal mass of roots embodied in the ball of earth.
The whole ball is then left to freeze pretty thoroughly (generally till
snow covers the ground), when a large sled drawn by oxen is brought
as near as possible, the ball of earth containing the tree rolled upon it,
and the whole is easily transported to the hole previously prepared,
where it is placed in the proper position, and as soon as the weather
becomes mild, the earth is properly filled in around the ball. A tree,
either evergreen or deciduous, may be transplanted in this way, so as
scarcely to show, at the return of growth, any ill effects from its
change of location.

II.

Note on the treatment of Lawns

As a lawn is the *ground-work* of a landscape garden, and as the management of a dressed grass surface is still a somewhat ill-understood subject with us, some of our readers will, perhaps, be glad to receive a very few hints on this subject.

The unrivalled beauty of the "velvet lawns" of England has passed into a proverb. This is undoubtedly owing, in some measure, to their superior care and keeping, but mainly to the highly favorable climate of that moist and sea-girt land. In a very dry climate it is nearly impossible to preserve that emerald freshness in a grass surface, that belongs only to a country of "weeping skies." During all the present season, on the Hudson, where we write, the constant succession of showers has given us, even in the heat of midsummer, a softness and verdure of lawn that can scarcely be surpassed in any climate or country.

Our climate, however, is in the middle states one of too much heat and brilliancy of sun, to allow us to keep our lawns in the best condition without considerable care. Beautifully verdant in spring and autumn, they are often liable to suffer from drought in midsummer. On sandy soils, this is especially the case, while on strong loamy soils, a considerable drought will be endured without injury to the good appearance of the grass. It therefore is a suggestion worthy of the attention of the lover of a fine lawn, who is looking about for a country residence, to carefully avoid one where the soil is *sandy*. The only remedy in such a soil is a tedious and expensive one, that of constant and plentiful topdressing with a compost of manure and heavy soil—marsh mud—swamp muck, or the like. Should it fortunately be the case (which is very rare) that the sub-stratum is loamy, deep ploughing, or trenching, by bringing up and mixing with the light surface soil some of the heavier earth from below, will speedily tend to remedy the evil.

In almost all cases where the soil is of good strength, a permanent lawn may be secured by preparing the soil deeply before finally laying it down. This may be done readily, at but little outlay, by *deep ploughing*—a good and cheap substitute for trenching—that is to say making the plough follow three times in the same furrow.   This, with manure, if necessary, will secure a depth of soil sufficient to allow the roots of plants to strike below the effects of a surface drought.

In sowing a lawn, the best mixture of grasses that we can recom· mend for this climate, is a mixture of Red-top and white Clover--two natural grasses found by almost every roadside—in the proportion of three fourths of the former, to one of the latter.

There is a common and very absurd notion current (which we have several times practically disproved), that, in order to lay down a lawn well, it is better to sow the seed along with that of some grain ; thus, starving the growth of a small plant by forcing it to grow with a larger and coarser one.   A whole year is always lost by this process— indeed more frequently two.   Many trials have convinced us that the proper mode is to sow a heavy crop of grass at once, and we advise him who desires to have speedily a handsome turf, to follow the English practice, and sow *three to four bushels of seed to the acre.*   If this is done early in the spring, he will have a lawn-like surface by mid-summer, and a fine close turf the next season.

After this, the whole beauty of a lawn depends on *frequent mowing.* Once a fortnight at the furthest, is the rule for all portions of the lawn in the neighborhood of the house, or near the principal walks.   A longer growth than this will only leave yellow and coarser stubble after mowing, instead of a soft velvet surface.   A broad-bladed English scythe (to be had at the shops of the seedsman), set nearly parallel to the surface, is the instrument for the purpose, and with it a clever mower will be able to shave within half an inch of the ground, without leaving any marks.   To free the surface from worm casts, etc., it is a common practice to roll the previous evening as much as may be mown the next day.*

---

* A very great improvement and economy in the keeping of lawns now-a-days, is in the employment of the Lawn-cutter, by which one man, with a horse-machine, will accomplish, in two or three hours, more than a dozen men can in a whole day.   The best English lawn-cutters will cut, roll, and gather the grass from *one acre, in one hour,* where it is good, close turf, and there are no trees to interfere with the action of the machine.

As the neatness of a well kept lawn depends mainly upon the manner in which it is mown, and as this again can only be well done where there are no inequalities in the ground, it follows that the surface should be kept as smooth as possible. Before sowing a lawn, too much pains cannot be taken to render its surface smooth and even. After this, in the spring, before the grass starts, it should be examined, and all little holes and irregularities filled up, and the same should be looked over at any annual top-dressing that may take place. The

When a lawn is in perfect condition, smooth, free from stones and inequalities, and is cut, as it ought to be, once a week, it is quite surprising how much gratification we derive from what used to be performed with great labor, and often with a very unsatisfactory result. There are very few places in the country where we can have complete lawns by the scythe, because, as the work must be performed early in the morning and late in the afternoon when the dew is on, it follows that a very large force, much larger than is usually kept even in our best places, must be required, to accomplish much in so short a time. In England, this is more easily done, because they turn on to the lawn at daylight, ten to thirty men, from all parts of the place, who separate after 8, or 9, A. M., to their respective and regular duties—to the garden, to the farm, to the forest. We cannot afford to do this, and as our sun is much hotter, and our dew much less time in duration than in England, it follows, that any improvement, which will allow us to cut our lawns throughout the heat of the day, is very desirable. This the mowing machine does, performing its work better when the dew is off, than on, and allowing us to mow, roll, and gather up, at the same time, and by the same means. All that remains subsequently to do, is to clip with scythe or sickle around the edges and verges, as well as near trees, or masses of shrubs, very close to which the machine should not be allowed to pass. We have found more satisfaction in the use of this machine, than in any other thing we have done since we lived in the country, and have now got our lawn into such a responsive and genial condition, that (except during May and June, when the growth of grass is more rampant, and has to be gathered), we have removed our box for catching the grass as it falls from the rollers, and permit it to fly in a little shower all over the lawn, as the cutting progresses. In this way, the lawn-top dresses itself, by returning all that it produces. By cutting and rolling once a week, this weekly cutting amounts to little more than snipping off the points of shoots half to three-quarters of an inch long, which have projected above the cutting-grade of the machine, and which are scattered in this sort of grassy shower on the lawn, decaying or disappearing in course of two to three hours, while all below the grade becomes pressed and matted by the roller into a fine and verdant sod — H. W. S.

occasional use of a heavy roller, after rain, will also greatly tend to remedy all defects of this nature.

Where a piece of land is long kept in lawn, it must have an occasional top-dressing every two or three years, if the soil is rich, or every season, if it is poor. As early as possible in the spring is the best time to apply such a top-dressing, which may be a compost of any decayed vegetable or animal matter—heavier and more abounding with marsh mud, etc., just in proportion to the natural lightness of the soil. Indeed almost every season the lawn should be looked over, all weeds taken out, and any poor or impoverished spots plentifully top-dressed, and, if necessary, sprinkled with a little fresh seed. Wood ashes, either fresh or leached, is also one of the most efficient fertilizers of a lawn.

We can already, especially in the finer places on the Hudson, and about Boston, boast of many finely kept lawns, and we hope every day, as the better class of country residences increases, to see this indispensable feature in tasteful grounds becoming better understood and more universal.

PLATE II

WODENETHE, AT FISHKILL LANDING N.Y.

RESIDENCE OF HENRY WINTHROP SARGENT

Engraved for H. W. Sargent's edition of Downing's Landscape Gardening.

Drawn by J. D. Smillie.

Engraved by R. Hinshelwood.

SUPPLEMENT

TO THE

SIXTH EDITION

OF

LANDSCAPE GARDENING:

CONTAINING

SOME REMARKS ABOUT COUNTRY PLACES, AND THE BEST
METHODS OF MAKING THEM; ALSO, AN ACCOUNT OF
THE NEWER DECIDUOUS AND EVERGREEN PLANTS,
LATELY INTRODUCED INTO CULTIVATION,
BOTH HARDY AND HALF-HARDY.

BY

HENRY WINTHROP SARGENT.

——————— " Dant utile lignum
Navigiis pinos, domibus cedros que cupressos que."
GEOR. ii. 442.

SUPPLEMENT TO LANDSCAPE GARDENING.

SECTION I.

SOME GENERAL REMARKS ON LANDSCAPE GARDENING AND COUNTRY PLACES.

Great as was the impetus given to the public mind by the first appearance of this book in 1841, and great as has been the advantage derived from its publication since, not only in assisting by certain rules as far as it is possible to apply rules to an art, but also in developing and fostering rural tastes, yet, we think, it must be conceded by observing and discriminating persons, that the style of our country places is still vastly inferior to the very marked improvement in Rural Architecture during the past ten years.

This has arisen partly from the fact that no sensible man attempts to build his own house, and the necessity of employing architects has not only developed much ability in our own professors of this art, but has also given us the additional advantage of a great deal of foreign talent and skill.

This has not been the case with Landscape Gardening. There has been no one since Mr. Downing's death who has exactly filled the niche he occupied in the public estimation. We do not mean to say that there are not at present in this country, gentlemen of taste and knowledge, and who are professional Landscape Gardeners of sufficient ability to take any place and to make it all that is desirable ; but there is no one, we think, whose judgment and opinions would have, at this moment such decided and marked influence in all matters of

rural taste, as the late Mr. Downing exercised at the
time of his death.

While, therefore, the excellence of country houses
has greatly increased, the improvement in country
places is not so evident. A great many persons are
either too indolent or too busy to give much attention
to the capabilities or wants of their places. The former
fall easily into the hands of an inferior class of nurserymen, or job-planters, and become a ready prey to the
most tasteless imposition, while the latter crowd into a
few hours a day the arrangement and adornment of
grounds which should require many months of thought
and study.

We Americans are, as a general rule, in too great
a hurry "to get through." We are apt to allow ourselves to go into the country without quite understanding what we are to do there, or how we are to live, or
whether we have true taste and capacity for country
life. Most persons are satisfied while building their
house and attempting to arrange their grounds. The
first is comparatively easy, for we have only to communicate to an architect our general wishes, and it becomes his duty to carry them out; the second is more
perplexing, simply because we do not know what we
want, or we want to have everything we have seen
that has struck us as desirable. We do not stop to
consider whether a certain style of planting or selection
of trees, harmonizes either with our house or is in
character with our grounds. We have an indefinite
idea of the pleasure certain effects gave us in other country places, and we are determined to have those effects
in our own, without any reference to propriety or good
taste, not from obstinacy, but from ignorance. We have,
to be sure, certain rules for planting, but the lazy are
too indolent, and the busy are too hurried to read or
study them. The suggestions of others are readily taken,
and the most incongruous and imperfect results necessar-

ily ensue. A willow drooping over a rustic bridge, and a pine waving its giant limbs on a rocky eminence, are each charming in its place, because in harmony with surrounding nature ; but pines and willows alternating around a house, or on a flat approach road, are most discordant and in the vilest taste, and yet we constantly meet with discrepancies in new country places, not a whit less barbarous.

A common error, and we think a very decided one, in our new places, is the anxiety to have flowers and flowering shrubs while the place is still in the rough, and before we know where to put them with propriety. A very usual employment of new grounds immediately adjacent to the house, is the most injudicious and tasteless admixture of decapitated forest trees and dahlias, with vases, evergreens, roses, altheas, and the various common plants, indiscriminately put together, a few inches, or at most a few feet apart, in the coarse weedy grass, which is the best apology for lawn which could be got up in the time—exposed to the carelessness of workmen, and the depredation of roadside cattle. We have even seen avenues—and in places too, where otherwise there are evidences of good taste—planted with alternate rows of forest trees and dahlias, with an occasional rose tree or geranium. Nothing, we conceive, can be in worse taste than this ; for though nothing can well be prettier than a rose in a rose garden properly surrounded by the most refined and ornamental shrubs, like a jewel in an appropriate setting, yet can anything be more improper or discordant than the same rose in a stubble field, or what is quite as inappropriate, in the rough and ill-kept grounds of a raw and unfinished place. Refinement must be associated with and surrounded by refinement, or it loses half its charm. We hear of and sometimes see a rough dia-mond ; but no one, we think, will pretend to say that the same diamond polished and properly set, is not infinitely more attractive.

Besides which, no flowers do well under such circum-stances; the ground is hard and rough, and the plants being placed immediately under the drip, and amidst the roots of trees, do not receive the full benefit of either sun, air, or soil, and yield the most unsatisfactory returns for the expenditure of a great deal of time and money.

Whether flowers should or should not be planted at all around a house, is a question of considerable moment, and as a general rule, we must confess, our own judgment is against it; we think the only exception is where it is desirable to retain the view from the principal windows either within the lawn, or within the immediate surroundings of the house, from the more distant prospect being flat and uninteresting, or containing objects decidedly disagreeable.

In such cases, the more the eye can be prevented from wandering to the distant points, the better, and this can be accomplished in no more pleasing way than by surrounding the house with the most dazzling flower-beds, or the most striking architectural ornaments, such as vases, sun-dials, terraces, and fountains, or distinctive and remarkable trees or plants.

Where, however, as is most often, we think, the case in this country, the place itself is of sufficient size or elevation to create a distant prospect which is agreeable, or the view beyond the boundaries presents natural features of an attractive character, such as fine mountains, lakes, or rivers, or distant peeps of pastoral country, or pretty villages, then it is not desirable to fritter these away by flowers or any objects near the house; but the arrangements of the grounds should be of the most simple character, and partake of that smooth harmonious form, most suggestive of the repose and quiet which we seem always inseparably to associate with a well-ordered country place. The trees should be so arranged, that while forming natural and graceful groups, they should act as it were as frames, through which the distant views or objects of interest on or beyond the place, seem to appear to the greatest advantage. We do not certainly wish to interdict all flowers, or banish them from the vicinity of the house; far from it. We think, on the contrary, a bed or so of roses, or a mass of the sweet-scented honeysuckle and fragrant clematis immediately under the windows of the drawing room, are most desirable, that we may enjoy their fragrance of a summer evening. We would only so arrange or place them, that they should in no way disturb the view by withdrawing the eye from something much finer beyond.

Nothing can well be prettier or in better taste than an architectural flower garden, opening from the breakfast or morning room, or perhaps on a side of the house, where the view is confined and shut in by ornamental shrubs, and which seems, by a judicious transition, to connect the house and the grounds; but we think on those sides where the views are, and especially on the entrance front, there should be nothing but the simplest and most dignified arrangements of trees and grass.

There is another, and we think a very sensible reason, why flowers and flowering shrubs should not be introduced, in profusion at least, either along the borders of the approach road, or in the immediate vicinity of the entrance front.

It is well laid down by the English Landscape Gardeners, that from the time the house is first seen on an approach, it should not be lost sight of. It being the highest architectural object on the place, no rural objects, like flowers, or any architectural features of lower art, like statues, or vases, should be permitted to divert the eye of the visitor, which they would be very apt to do, if from no other reason than the care and attention necessary to prevent driving over or against them. It is particularly objectionable, therefore, to place rows or masses of green-house plants, as is often done, on either side of the entrance, which are sure to be more or less injured by hungry horses and careless coachmen.

And finally, in this country where we have no rural sports as in England, nothing in fact for the amusement of our friends and visitors, except what is beautiful or interesting on our grounds or in our gardens, we have always thought it highly desirable not to tell our whole story from the house, but to set aside in different and distant portions of the place all our objects of interest ; a flower garden in one spot, the vegetable garden in another, an arboretum or pinetum in a third, and so make and multiply as it were, various interests in different parts—properly connected, but as widely separated as convenience or space will allow—which shall furnish to our guests excuses for a walk, and give to a small place the appearance of a large one; in other words to afford as much interest and diversion as the capacity of the grounds will allow, and prevent that ennui and fatigue, which nothing to see and nothing to do, produces not only in our visitors, but in our own families. We cannot well imagine anything more dreary than those country places where there is no motive to go out, because everything is gathered and crowded around the house and can be seen from the windows.

Although we know there is nothing produced without labor, yet it is not pleasant to be always forced to realize it. Repose is, we think, almost as essential to the highest charm of a country place as it is for our own comfort. The clink of the hammer and the sound of the anvil are all very well in their way, yet one does not desire to hear always these evidences of human toil. If therefore we surround our house with a multiplicity of objects requiring constant care and attention, we are never free from the labor of life. The highest charm of a country place is the appearance of the most refined culture and beautiful results produced without apparent effort. In fairy tales, or fairy plays upon the stage, the fascination is in the magic result produced apparently by the touch of the wand. If we are permitted to get behind the curtain and witness the hurry and vexation of the scene shifters, and the groaning, shrieking process by which to the unconscious spectators a desert suddenly becomes a paradise, we immediately realize the apples of the Dead Sea. We do not enjoy that which we see is produced through the agency of aching bones and weary limbs—and this is one reason why Nature is so attractive, because she works silently, or as a child once expressed it, " without her shoes."

In the best English places, to such an extent is this feeling carried out, that the entire machinery is kept out of sight; and flowers bloom, and lawns are shorn, and walks are swept by invisible hands, at such hours as the family is supposed not to come out.

It is told of the late Mr. Beckford, the eccentric and talented author of Vathek, that he never allowed any work to be done at Fonthill Abbey during the day ; but if he wished a walk cut, or a new plantation made, he used to say nothing in way of preparation, but merely gave orders, perhaps late in the afternoon, that the improvement or alteration should be completed and in a perfect state by the following morning at the time he came out to take his usual ride. The whole force of the place and the strength of the neighboring village were then put into requisition and employed all night. We mention this, not as an example—for there are very few of us who would or could afford to spend, as Mr. Beckford did at Fonthill, twelve or fifteen millions of dollars —but simply to show how strongly English prejudice is

against the visible connection of labor with the immediate adornment of their country homes.   Labor in its
proper place—in the forest, or garden, or harvest field—
is a necessary and appropriate feature ; but they strive
to banish it as much as possible from the repose and
quiet and simple beauty around the house, by pushing
off to more distant, and as they think, more suitable
localities, those operations with the soil which require
the constant supervision and presence of man.   It is
principally on this account, besides the other reasons
we have given, that the best examples of English places
present a simple dignified combination of trees and
lawn about the house—certainly on *two or three* sides—
while the mass of pleasure grounds and flower gardens
are usually at some distance.

If we were more willing in this country to follow such
good examples, and aim at simplicity and breadth of effect, instead of carving up our grounds about our houses
with " fragmentary pieces of misplaced ornament," our
places would not be so lamentably deficient in character
and beauty, or so frittered away into an exceedingly dis-
tasteful and artificial appearance.

Another mistake in American places is the want of a
proper termination to the ornamental grounds, or, rather,
some intelligible division between the ornamental and
practical.

We use the expression "intelligible," because we all
keep (or pretend to) under the roller and scythe, every
two or three weeks, a certain quantity of lawn, say
from one hundred feet to an acre or more, and at the
end of the last swarth starts up a hay-field, which is
mown over perhaps twice in the season ; but, in most
cases, there seems no reason why the lawn should
end and the hay-field begin just where they do, instead
of ten or one hundred feet one way or the other ; in fact
there is no good reason ; for the length and breadth of
the lawn often depends upon the horticultural zeal or

pecuniary position for the moment. If the first mowing of the season is made under the receipt of an increased or unexpected dividend, the lawn gets a swarth or two more, and a cock or two of hay is subtracted from the harvest; while the next year, under a smaller income, thrift conquers taste, and the lawn, instead of being shorn of its grass, is shorn of its fair proportions.

In order to make some appropriate boundary or division between the lawn and the park, or hay-field; in other words, between the dressed and undressed portions of the estate, great use has been made of late years of the wire fence or hurdle. By its adoption we might diminish the amount of lawn now kept under the scythe, obtaining similar results by substituting cattle—especially sheep — and increasing very much the charm of the landscape by the introduction of animated nature.

The keenest eye can hardly detect a wire fence at thirty or forty rods distance ; consequently our finest places do not really require a lawn larger than twice this breadth in diameter, provided the grass on the other side of the wire is kept equally short by sheep.

It is quite astonishing in England how very small the proportion of mown lawn is to that part which, by use of invisible wire fencing, is kept equally short and almost in as fine order, by grazing.

At Windsor Castle we doubt if the mown border or strip of grass round the park-side of the castle exceeds fifty to one hundred feet up to the wire fence, beyond which, in the park, are large masses of rhododenrons, laurels, Portugal laurels, etc., protected from thousands of deer and sheep which surround them, by invisible wire fences.

At Longleat, the magnificent seat of the Marquis of Bath—which Charles II. on his return from his exile then considered the finest place in England—there is a strip of three hundred feet of mown lawn planted with rare shrubs, between the river and one side only

of the house, and separated from six hundred acres, or
more, of grazed park by the invisible wire fence.   At
Wilton House (Lord Pembroke), Appelder-Court, Good-
wood (the Duke of Richmond's), Blenheim, Chatsworth,
Stowe, and many more of the best examples of English
places that we remember, the amount of *mown* lawn
consists really of little more than the grass borders of
walks, or the strips which divided or surrounded plantations in the gardens and shrubberies.   Three sides of
the houses are thrown open, and kept short by deer and
sheep.

Although grazing is not as profitable in this country
as in England, where the soft, mossy grass of the parks
is usually verdant and green all summer, yet much
more can be done than is.   We know many a fine
place where large expenditures have been made on
houses and grounds, where the entire effect has been
completely destroyed by the most mistaken economy
of allowing the fields which surround the house, to grow
up for hay, instead of being kept short by grazing as a
park.

In order to save a few hundred dollars of hay, the
whole effect of hundreds of thousands of dollars in
houses and grounds is completely lost.

If people will persist in this mistaken thrift, they
should, at least, plant their grazing or hay-fields in
clumps and masses of trees, appropriately and naturally
placed for park-like effects, and which would not materially interfere with the plough or the harrow, when
necessary to use them.

By surrounding these plantations with invisible wire
fences, which are quite lost against the foliage, they
could at any time, when in grass, be converted into
parks simply by the introduction of cattle and sheep.

Fig. 88.—View from Library Window at Wodenethe, looking South.

SECTION II.

HOW TO MAKE A COUNTRY PLACE.

On the Continent and in England, it is rarely that a new place is made from the beginning. The taste for country life having existed as long as England herself has existed, the whole kingdom may be said to be one universal garden; all who can, from the sovereign to the cit, live, at least some portion of the year, in the country; in fact, one's respectability is not complete, unless he is a landed proprietor. If, as we said in our preface, there are in England 20,000 country houses, each larger than the White House, at Washington, there are more than twice that number, a great deal smaller.

Places change hands, but few new places are made. This is not the case in this country. We have but few old estates, and those, whenever offered for sale, are generally so run down and desolate as to afford little attraction to the beginner of country life; besides which the universal delusion among us is that we can make a country place, cheaper than we can buy one. While we are alarmed at a sum total, we easily reconcile ourselves to progressive expenditure, until, in the end, we realize " that fools build houses and wise men live in them."

This is one great reason, we have always thought, why makers of new places so soon become discontented and discouraged, and ready to sell out at a sacrifice. A man who hesitates to give $20,000, or $100,000 for a country place, and even feels indignant at the supposition that he could be guilty of such folly, if he attempts to make his own place, generally ends by spending twice as much.

We refuse to pay $25,000 outright, and we hug ourselves with the idea that our land will cost but $6,000, and our house $8,000, and our stable $1,000, and sundries $500. But, unfortunately, these sundries are the rocks on which much rural enthusiasm is lost. It is the ice-house, and the root-house, and the gardener's-house, and the green-house, and the grape-house, with the grading, and road making, and trenching, and digging, and the labor necessary to keep these all up, that exhaust both our enthusiasm and our purse, and make us see, in the end, what we could not see in the beginning, viz : That it is always better to purchase an improved place, or one partially improved, than to begin one. For, it may be laid down as an inevitable rule, and prevent much subsequent disappointment, whenever any improvements at all are contemplated (and it is difficult, where we have no amusements or sports, to be contented without doing something), to remember one fact, that the modern accessories to a country place are at least equivalent to first cost of house and grounds—that is to say, where the improvements are in keeping with the house and place, and continued for a series of years.

There are two styles of new places most commonly, we think, attempted in this country, viz: A place without any foliage, or possibly a few stunted or unavailable trees, where all the effects are to be produced by the spade (in planting) ; and, secondly, a dense wood, where the place is to be made mostly by the axe : and we propose to illustrate these two schools by giving the history of our own residence as a specimen of the latter, and "Wellesley," the residence of H. H. Hunnewell, Esq., near Boston, as a specimen of the former We should, perhaps, mention here, that it is with much hesitation we find ourselves compelled to say so much about these two places, especially our own; but we have known them both from their commencement, with all their sins of omission and commission; and with all the motives and designs for each step taken in their improvement, and the reason why every tree was planted or cut down on either place, which is a knowledge we have of no other place, and more than all, as one was a dense wood and the other a naked field, they are better examples of the two styles than any other places we recollect, even if we had been equally familiar with others.

When we purchased our own place, in 1840, we found a house partially built in the midst of a wood, but without any view, though we were aware that we had, or ought to have, a range of mountains on one side, the Hudson River on the other, a valley on the third, and a long range of country on the fourth; but between us and these views, and all more or less around us, were thinly scattered houses, which were far from agreeable accessories to the landscape.

We felt, after studying our position, that our plan ought to be to conceal these offensive objects, by planting them out, and to open up the attractive points of river, valley, and mountain; but how to do this was the question!

The trees, like all trees grown in a forest, were tall and spindling, hiding out with their heads what they should not have concealed, and opening through their naked stems what ought to have been hid; our object therefore, was to get the branches of these trees (principally oaks and hickories) down near the ground, in order to form masses and groups, not only to hide out our boundaries and these objectionable houses, but also to produce certain effects of light and shade, as the beginning and basis of ornamental planting. We accomplished this in part by topping all the trees which had any signs

of vitality in their lower branches, as low as there was
young wood enough to carry on the circulation. Many
trees seventy feet in height, we thus reduced to thirty
and forty. This formed a thicket of background from
which we took, year by year, the weakest and most
misshapen; so that a mass, composed, eighteen years ago,
of fifty or sixty trees, seventy or seventy-five feet high,
is now reduced to twenty or thirty trees only forty
feet high, but denser, and covering much more space
than double the number of original trees. Where
necessary to obtain certain extended views, we cut boldly
and irregularly through the mass, producing, after some
years growth, the effect as represented in Fig. 88,
entitled, "View from Library Window." Where we
accomplished two distinct landscapes—the one including a charmingly wooded point called "Presqu-ile,"
the residence of Mrs. Denning, with a distant view of
Idlewild, the residence of N. P. Willis, across the
river; and the other a portion of Pollapells' island—
with a fine effect of the Dunderberg or Storm King,
as background.

But, in process of time, finding that from the irregular
shape of the house—a view of the river side of which
appears as frontispiece to this Supplement—we could, by
careful planting against the masses forming the boundaries to the view referred to (Fig. 88), not only produce
more agreeable and ornamental effects from the windows, but confine to each window one distinct and
separate view, which should be seen from that one
window and that alone—while it had also the effect of
lengthening and extending the vistas, making, as it
were, a series of cabinet pictures—we advanced an
irregular plantation of the most ornamental trees in
front of these two masses, completely masking them;
and while very much extending the view by an apparent
and, indeed, an actual elongation, it also substituted from
the windows an ornamental grouping between the house

Fig. 89.—View from Breakfast-Room Window at Wodenethe, looking West.

and the natural grouping, which is, however, omitted in this sketch.

The view from the breakfast-room window (Fig. 89), opened for the purpose of introducing a part of Newburgh and a fine wooded bank below the town, was made in the same way—the decapitated forest trees having in a few years become thick and umbrageous, made an admirable back ground for an ornamental facing of the choicest trees, both deciduous and evergreen, while these various masses, all now more or less surrounded with the rarest trees, are connected together and made to harmonize by small irregular groups and single trees, blending the different parts into one whole, but so arranged as not to injure the most striking views— ample space being left for the full development of single specimens and loose groups.

On the other side of the house—in the view entitled, "View across the park" (Fig. 90)—our intention was to attempt, with no other aid but the axe, a parklike effect by the grouping and massing of certain native oaks, without the aid of any artificial planting. This was effected by selecting the best specimens standing sufficiently near to each other for this purpose, and leaving around them a large circle of forest trees as nurses, which we thinned out from the inside, year by year, giving the permanent trees more and more light and space, until finally they stood alone, and have since continued to thrive; though if we had thinned out immediately everything about them, they would probably have perished from the too sudden removal of their accustomed shelter; but by diminishing their nurses gradually in successive years, the trees to remain, became by degrees fortified and strengthened by extended roots, and now stand as well alone as if they had been planted for this purpose.

The boundaries of the place were treated in a similar manner; the original trees reduced to half or two-thirds their height, and, when thick and bushy, faced with

ornamental plantations, as an arboretum, with collections
of trees in families, and also a portion as a pinetum—
each genus being kept by itself—and through which is a
walk making the circuit of the place ; the whole being
divided by a wire fence from the portion above described as arranged for a park, which is kept short by
cattle and sheep.

All the space necessary for vegetable and flower gardens, pinetum, arboretum, orchards, etc., was, of course,
taken entirely from the wood—the trees being cut down
and their roots grubbed up.

Having attempted to describe a place made by the
axe, out of a wood, we will now give some account of
the other and different style of country residence before
referred to, entirely by the spade and from the ground.

The whole estate at "Wellesley" consists, we believe, of two hundred acres, being an unimproved portion of an old family place of many hundred acres.

The part selected by Mr. Hunnewell for the ornamental improvement of his grounds comprises about
forty acres, originally a flat, sandy, arid plain, which,
when he took it in hand, in 1851, only seven years
since, was more or less covered with a tangled growth
of dwarf pitch pine, scrub oak, and birch, all of which
were cut down and ploughed up.

The first thing done was to trench over and thoroughly prepare with composted muck, an acre or more for a
nursery, which was planted with large quantities of
Norway spruce, white pines, balsams, Austrian pines,
Scotch firs, larch, beech, oaks, elms, maples, etc., mostly
imported from England, not over twelve to fifteen
inches high, with some few native trees of greater age,
previously prepared. The lawn was then graded, sub-
soiled, and a large portion trenched by spade, and after
being very heavily manured and enriched with compost, was for several years cultivated in order to amelior-
ate and subdue the soil; the boundaries of the place,

Fig. 90.— View across the Park, at Wodenethe, looking toward the House.

especially on the exposed part towards the public road, were then trenched over twenty to fifty feet broad, heavily composted and planted with a judicious mixture of evergreens and ornamental trees. The border, however, for many years, until the trees were fifteen to twenty feet high, and in many cases touched each other, was annually enriched and planted in potatoes, the crop being some remuneration for the expense.

The next step after deciding upon the situation of the house, was to form the avenues and plant them; the one from the Boston entrance, with alternating Pinus excelsa, and Magnolia tripetala at one end, and with large masses of rhododendrons, Kalmia latifolia, Mahonias, and other rare evergreen shrubs, as a frontage to a back ground of Norway spruces at the other; until the road reaches the Italian garden, with a view of the lake on one side, and the house and lawn on the other, when the avenue effect of the planting ceases—and groups, masses, and single specimens, and the ornamental arrangement, shown in the view, commence.

The other avenue from the Natick entrance is planted with rows of white pine and larch, now, perhaps, twenty to twenty-five feet high, and being all fine trees, the effect is already very marked.

The next step was to plant the lawn of about eight acres with the best specimens selected from the nurseries or border plantations. This has been most cleverly and successfully done, much of it in the winter with frozen balls and with the most ornamental and choicest trees; in some cases large specimens twenty to thirty feet high were brought twenty miles, but even after the clumps, masses, and single specimens on the lawn were arranged and planted, it was still annually enriched and cultivated, and the ground around each tree and mass of trees is, even to this day, kept clean to a circle following the drip of the branches.

The house. a front or entrance view of which is given

in Plate III., was then built, having among other fine
features, a hall of 54×18 feet running through it; on
one side, the fine extent of simple and dignified lawn,
and on the other side is a French parterre or architectural garden (Plate IV.) with fountains, bordered by
heavy balustrades, surmounted at intervals by vases,
with steps leading through a series of terraces to the
lake, a fine sheet of water of about a mile in extent,
having a peculiarly varied and beautiful outline. From
this French parterre, stretches off on the right the
ornamental or English pleasure-grounds, a part of the
same view, showing the summer-house very artistically rusticated, with colored glass windows, producing very curious effects of contrast by the stained
glass.

From this we pass along the lake to the Italian garden,
of which we have given a view in Plate V., and which
is the most successful, if not the only one as yet in
the country. The effect, especially by moonlight, of
the lake seen through the balustrades of the parapet,
and among the vases and statues which surmount it—
with the splashing of the fountain, and the very unique
features, at least in this country, of the formally clipped
trees and topiary work, quite lead us to suppose we
are on the lake of Como.

To Mr. Hunnewell, we believe, is due the merit of
having first attempted to clip our white pine, and the
result shows that it bears the shears quite as well as the
hemlock or yew; though in this garden are equally
successful specimens of clipped Norways, balsams, arbor
vitæ, the English maple, the beech and Scotch firs.

From the Italian garden we cross the avenue into a
wood, through which winds a walk planted on either
side with a very extensive and satisfactory pinetum,
containing all the rarest and newest conifers and evergreen shrubs, and which with the slight protection from
the winter's sun, seem to thrive exceedingly well.

PLATE 44

WELLESLEY, NEAR BOSTON

Residence of H. H. Hunnewell Esq.

Among other features of this place, and accomplished like everything else, within seven years, are various vistas through different avenues planted for this purpose—some of purple beech, others of white pine—all of which will in a few years become very interesting and effective.

If to the above we add the extensive and well-conducted vegetable and fruit gardens surrounded by most admirably kept hedges, an abundance of well trained fruit trees, peach, grape, and green-houses, and a steam engine for forcing water into a reservoir, from which distributing pipes conduct it over all the gardens, we shall, we think, conclude a description of a place almost unequalled in this country, considering the few years only it has existed.

Mr. Hunnewell's success has been attributable in the first place, to working on a plan—making no or few mistakes—having little or nothing to undo, and lastly, having the taste and ability to do everything thoroughly and well; always keeping up what has been done, so that neither tree or flower, or lawn, is ever permitted to flag.

Of the two places above described as illustrating the two schools most common in this country, we believe we shall afford consolation to many beginners of naked places by saying that our experience is extremely adverse to all attempts at converting a wood into any thing ornamental.

If two places of the same size were commenced the same day, by persons of equal taste, knowledge, and means, one a wood and the other a naked plain, at the end of ten years the naked plain would be the finer and more satisfactory.

In the first place, if one in planting, will make his holes wide and deep enough, and with judicious preparation of the soil; if instead of the ordinary three feet wide by two feet deep, our holes are prepared twelve feet wide and six feet deep, it would be easy enough to predict the result at the end of five or six years. Besides which it is a very simple matter to know the effect certain trees or certain groups of trees are going to produce by setting up a few stakes, which shall cover the same extent of ground; and it is a very easy matter to move these groups of stakes until they are rightly and properly placed beyond any question, and then to proceed with our planting. By continuing in this way with all our planting we may, as we have shown elsewhere, get every thing placed, without the possibility of error.

It is impossible to do this in a wood. We cannot carve out the views and the groups and masses, exactly as we wish, because we cannot find the trees always ready to assist us. It often happens that the finest tree is just where we should prefer to have none; and where we want density and bulk to hide unsightly objects, we have naked poles of fifty feet, with ten feet of brush up in the sky instead of where it should be, on the ground. There is no remedy in such cases but to cut down our fine tree or abandon the view it hides, and also to cut down our unavailable giants and to plant in their places. We are, in this instance, not as well off as our friend without trees, because we have to do all that he does with the additional labor of grubbing up the old stumps and renewing the soil before planting. There are, to be sure, instances as we have mentioned in our own case above, where we can make the native forest available by topping those trees which will admit it, and by planting among and in front of them; but even this, for many years, is not satisfactory. The dignity of the original trees, if any dignity is left, is much injured and frittered away by being side by side with our newly planted Norways and hemlocks of only three feet in height; while these, which, in a few years at least, would have made their mark, if no comparisons could have been instituted, will now always appear to a disadvantage in connection with the forest, besides the injury to their progress from the roots and drip of their hungry and uncouth companions.

There is, to be sure a certain class or condition of wood which chance or design has from year to year thinned out, and cattle cleared of undergrowth, resembling the oak openings of the West, which becomes after a while a sort of natural park, most desirable for country residences, but the thick, tangled, inextricable wood which will not readily admit any amelioration, but always returns for your attempted improvement, sickly and dying trees, pointing at you from every direction their weird and skeleton limbs, as if in derision and mockery at your efforts, had better be left alone in its wildness, or no attempts made to reform it.

The proper way, we have always thought, to make a country place, where there are no trees already existing, is, as we have already described as in Mr. Hunnewell's case, to dig an irregular border all round the boundary, or at least on those sides exposed to public roads or disagreeable objects, and to plant this with a judicious mixture of deciduous and evergreen trees of two or three feet high, either imported from Europe for a few dollars the hundred, or purchased from our own nurseries at wholesale prices.

We do not mean by this to be understood as recommending one of those formal belts so much employed in the time of Brown, but a picturesque boundary, with bays and recesses, and projecting curves, occasionally employing the denser and more umbrageous trees where distant and unsightly objects are to be excluded ; and again the lowest growing shrubs to admit the landscape beyond the boundaries when it is desirable to do so. This border may, the first few years, be employed as a nursery for the purpose of receiving all the trees, shrubs and plants required for the future and entire

planting and embellishing of the place, and may be
thinned out from year to year as the trees crowd each
other, or may be wanted for progressive improvement
and separate planting, until as the place advances and
the border becomes annually thinned for this purpose
it is at last reduced simply to such a number of plants,
(which must be suffered to remain), as are required to
produce the effects and objects above described.

During the first year or so, the proprietor may, at
his leisure, study the planting of his place, without
the loss of that time so precious to all good Americans,
as his trees are already growing—not in their final
place, but in his border nursery. To do this effectually and properly he must employ a quantity of stakes
or poles ten to twelve feet high, and by placing first
a stake where he thinks a tree should be planted,
and then several smaller stakes at such a distance
around it as his books or his own knowledge may in-
form him will be the extension of the tree when full
grown. By carefully observing this collection of stakes
from his point of view, which, as a general rule should
be the principal room of the house, he will at once see
whether it is in the right place, whether it is too near
the road or walk, or will injure a view. When satisfied
by many observations—and it would be well if made
from many points of view, all, however, subservient to
the principal point—that the centre stake is correctly
placed, let him substitute for it a small stake eight or
ten inches high, with the name of the tree to be planted
there legibly written on it. In the Autumn or Spring,
whichever may be the proper time for transplanting—
let the hole be dug at leisure, properly and carefully prepared, and let a tree be selected from the
border nursery on a damp or rainy day, and as properly
and carefully planted. Pursue this course with all the
single trees, groups, and masses to be planted on the
grounds, and if judiciously done the most complete

Drawn by James D. Smillie.

Engraved by James Smillie.

PL. IV.

THE FRENCH PARTERRE, WITH A PORTION OF ENGLISH GARDEN AT WELLESLEY, NEAR BOSTON.

RESIDENCE OF H. H. HUNNEWELL, ESQ.

satisfaction will be the result; because one may not only make up their own mind by studying their groups of poles, for weeks or months, even, but they can also have the advantage of criticism from intelligent visitors, and if the poles are wrong it is much easier to remove them than the trees.

If it were our object to make the most thorough place with the greatest expedition and fewest mistakes, we should plant every group, mass, and single specimen in poles, and allow them to remain when the trees were both in and out of leaf, in order to be quite certain that the planting worked equally well in all seasons, and also to study and be quite sure we were right in the harmony and selection we made of varieties for forming groups and masses.

Although the process may seem slow and tedious to new beginners, yet we are quite sure a place thus treated will, at the end of four or five years, be far more advanced and much more judiciously and successfully planted than by the more ordinary and hasty method. In the first place, there will be no mistakes—no undoing—on the contrary, the planting of the place is the making of the border : and in the second place, the trees will be better specimens, because we may at our leisure select from our border the best plants, and have them much better planted, inasmuch as when the spot for the tree is selected, the hole may be dug months, if necessary, before used—which, for spring planting, is most advantageous, by submitting the soil to the action of the frost. Whereas in the usual method, we go to a nursery and order a certain quantity of plants, and when they arrive, possibly on a disagreeable, windy day, we set about in the greatest hurry to dig holes and plant our trees, without in the least knowing the effects they are to make or mar when fully grown.

It is this careless method which produces so much bad planting and ruins so many country places. How rarely do we see trees planted at sufficient distance from each other, or from roads, or walks, or houses. One plants a pine or Norway spruce three or four feet high at about the same distance from the margin of a road. There are many approaches that we know of bordered by pines and Norway spruces, with the trees five or six feet only from the border. When these trees get a few years older they must be removed or trimmed up, and if a pine only ten or twelve years old is to be trimmed up sufficiently high to admit the passage of carriages under it, it is very easy to see how little beauty is left. If in planting avenues one would first plant stakes, they would soon discover, that to employ pines, firs, beeches, or, in fact, any tree proper for this purpose, the trees should be set back at least twenty-five to forty feet from the margin, so as to be in proper position when fully grown. In order to prevent the meagre appearance of clumps or masses, or avenues properly planted for future results, there is no objection to closer planting for immediate effect, care being taken that the latter is cut down or removed from year to year, before they crowd or injure the permanent trees. In this way with judgment and taste, a place may have the appearance of finish within a year or two ; the present group and mass producing similar effects except less light and shade, and covering the same ground as will be produced in twenty or thirty years by the two or three permanent trees, which, by that time are all that will be permitted to remain.

By this method of planting, which we recommend, we have an opportunity which is impossible in the ordinary way, of studying the character and habits of the trees, which, later in the season, we propose to substitute for our poles—to learn how they group, how they harmonize in habit, color, or growth, and we are thus enabled to produce some of those charming artistic effects by skillful combinations of color and habit, which nature so pleasingly exhibits in her own planting. Very few attempts, to our knowledge, have as yet been made, in this country, in what is called "artistic planting," that is, where reference is had to those effects attained by combination of certain colors; for instance, in order to increase the effect of a vista or opening, by planting the darker foliage nearest the eye, and the lighter at the more distant point of view, or by planting two trees in the same hole in order to produce picturesque effects in contrast to the more formal or gardenesque planting on the place. We remember to have seen at Ouchy, on the Lake of Geneva, that most graceful tree, the Weeping Silver birch, planted in the same hole with a pretty, drooping, fragile, dark-looking cedar; and the two (some twenty-five years old) had grown up together like two loving sisters, and their dark and silvery foliage and graceful arms gently entwined together, seemed to cling fondly to each other for support--the Minna and Brenda of the woods.

A selection and blending of trees with reference to their autumnal colors, is another refinement yet little practiced in this country. A group, for example, of our ash, the different maples, the liquid-amber, the sour gum, the dogwood, etc., judiciously toned down in color, from the darkest and richest to the lightest, will present a combination, which, for brilliancy and gorgeousness, would be hardly credible to those who had not witnessed the result.

In connection with this subject, we have made use of some memoranda of a visit to a place in Italy, some years since, as illustrative of artistic planting, from which, notwithstanding the advantages of climate, it is very easy to see how very far we yet fall short in this sort of perfection.

The place which we have most particularly in our mind, at present, is a bold promontory in the Lake of Como, called *Bellagio*, belonging to the Duchess of

Bologna, having a position not very unlike that of West
Point on the Hudson—supposing that the river forked
there, one arm running on each side. You stand on this
promontory and look down one lake twenty miles to Como;
and this view is similar, though finer, from the mountains being higher and more delicate, to the view down
the North River, from Kosciusko's monument; and then
on the other side, you look as it might be upon a portion
of the river running between Crow-Nest and West
Point dock, some twenty miles also down the lake to
Lecco; you then look up, as if to Newburgh, and see,
at about this distance (nine miles) the Alps, in snow-
clad majesty. The whole promontory does not, we believe, exceed five acres, rising conically perhaps six
hundred feet from the water; but the walks, which are
graveled or paved with very small pebbles, are three
or four miles in extent, most admirably managed by
means of dense plantations, tunnels, and bridges. The
promontory from the lake seems heavily wooded; and
yet everything has been done by art. The deep shade
has been produced by the most charming undergrowth
of cypress, laurel, casuaria, myrtle, and English yews.

You enter through a cavern into a glen, quite spectral
in its midnight darkness, surrounded by immense Italian
pines, and an undergrowth of yew; you are then let
out, as it were, into daylight, and into a charming peep
of one of the lakes, by the most delicate gradations of
dark to light, first going through not only the *colors* but
also the *changes of form* of the following trees : Cedars
of Lebanon, Pinus excelsa, deodars, and weeping larches,
which actually wave and dance you out into the sunlight.

After these trees, you shortly commence in the midst
of a blazing sun, among the most feathery and delicate
of the acacias, and grow cooler and darker with the
coarser varieties, and the rose acacia, all enchantingly
entangled with the Chinese wistaria, which here flowers

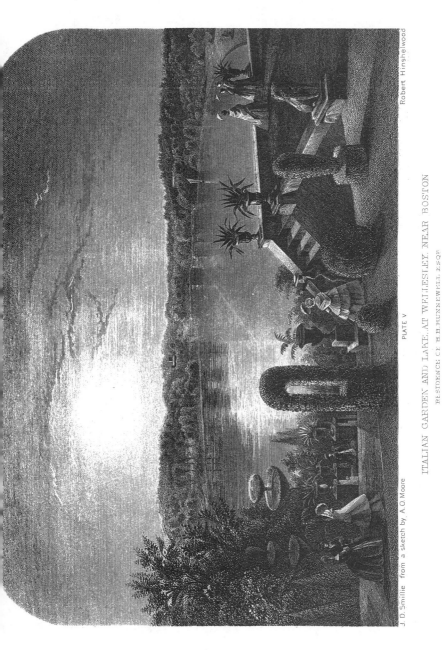

J. D. Smillie from a sketch by, A.O. Moore

Robert Hinshelwood

PLATE V

ITALIAN GARDEN AND LAKE, AT WELLESLEY, NEAR BOSTON

RESIDENCE CF H. B. HUNNEWELL ESQ?

Engraved for H.W. Sargent. edition of Downing's Landscape Gardening

all summer. After struggling through purple beeches, and some other dark foliage, you get out through a lovely grove of araucarias, Pinus excelsa, Pinus longifolia, and Abies Douglasii; from this you emerge into a little lawn, quite surrounded by high cliffs, covered with superb plantations of aloes, bananas, pepper trees, and white and scarlet horse-chestnuts, and a collection of rhododendrons, dazzling from their gorgeousness.

This lawn was devoted to magnolias of every possible variety, of which some eight or ten sorts were, when we saw them, in flower—the air being heavy with their perfume. These were in masses and as single specimens.

You left this *oasis* by the only way it seemed possible to get out—a cavern in the rocks, through which you passed, until you again entered profound darkness—gradually the light returned—at last you reached a point from which two vistas opened, one down the lake to Como, the other down the lake to Lecco; you looked at these as at a picture through a darkened tube, for the cavern was formed apparently for this purpose; these tunnels led you out to a walk bordered by natural rock, perhaps twenty feet high, covered by Lamarque and the Banksian roses in such a profusion of bloom, that the wall had the appearance of being painted white and yellow. On the other side the walk was bordered by masses of choice azalias, in every variety of color, and flowers some eight and ten feet high. Passing a charming cascade overhung with weeping beeches, waving birches, and different varieties of willows, the walk led through a maze of Judas trees (pink and white), all the varieties of double thorns, the laburnum (purple and yellow), and becoming umbrageous and mazy, with purple beeches, purple berberries, and purple filberts; finally came out again clear and bright through different varieties of heath and acacia, upon a little platform

looking up the third lake, and to the snowy Alps, and
down a perpendicular precipice of some six hundred
feet into an exquisite flower garden below, into which,
you are prevented from falling, by a parapet interlaced
with every variety of honeysuckle and clematis.

The other walk from the cavern led along a similar
wall of rock, pierced with holes, having an occasional
frame of rustic work, covered with air plants (orchids)
and parasites. This led by a grand terrace, balustraded
and statued, and commanding the three lakes to the
palace.

We have attempted to give our recollection of this
wonderful spot; not that we expect it to be a model
for anything YET to be done in America, but because it
is the only place we remember to have seen in any part
of the world which we have visited where a great
work of art has been produced in a very considerable
degree by the forms and colors of trees. The dim and
sombre effects of the caverns and tunnels have been
marvelously extended and increased by the deep, dark,
purple colors selected for this purpose, while the gay,
graceful, sparkling spray and glitter of the fairy-like
acacias, are so blended and interwoven with the sunshine that one cannot but feel, how much even nature,
grand as she always is, can some times be aided by
man. There are many bold and prominent bluffs and
promontories in this country on our beautiful and picturesque rivers and majestic lakes where much of the artistic beauty of Bellagio can be accomplished by judicious and tasteful planting, and although we have not a
climate which admits hedges of oleander and myrtle, at
least at the North, yet when we know the colors, forms
and habits of many trees which have as yet never
been employed in ornamental landscape, we shall be
surprised to find how much material we have for producing the most remarkable and the most pleasing
results.

SECTION III.

THE NEWER DECIDUOUS ORNAMENTAL TREES AND SHRUBS.

WE do not intend in this section to occupy the attention of the reader by any preliminary remarks as to the ornamental or practical value of any of the varieties we shall describe. Mr. Downing has already, to a great extent, done this in the preceding portion of the book. It remains for us simply to introduce to planters such new scions and connections of their older friends —the results, sometimes of inter-marriage between the ancient families, producing hybrids and crosses—and sometimes from the new discoveries of trees, which the increased intercourse all over the world has enabled collectors and societies to make. With this introduction we shall proceed at once to describe those trees and plants omitted in the previous edition and which our observation has induced us to believe are well worthy the attention of amateurs.

Acer. THE MAPLE.

A. Campestre, erroneously *campestris* of the Catalogues (the Common or English Field maple).—This is a beautiful, compact, round-headed tree, or rather bush, rarely exceeding twenty or twenty-five feet in height, and, if allowed to assume its natural shape, quite as broad as it is high. This tree, which is one of the most ornamental of the maples, is very rarely to be met with, though common, we believe, in our best nurseries. It is a tree, above all others of its kind, suited to small lawns, where it should stand alone, or on the outside of loose gardenesque groups, where it is accessible on all sides ; since the character

of its growth is so regular and formal (in shape of a bee-hive),
that it does not harmonize with wild or picturesque plantations,
but is peculiarly adapted to the neighborhood of the house or
to the more formal trees, like the horse-chestnut and linden·
The finest specimen we recollect to have seen, is at the late
Mr. Downing's, which is nearly fully grown ; a specimen at
Wodenethe, about fifteen feet high, and nearly as wide, is extremely beautiful.   The largest specimens in England are at
Kew, fifty years planted, twenty-six feet high ; at Milbury
Park, one hundred years planted, thirty-eight feet high.   It
should never be trimmed up ; on the contrary, if by accident
the lower limbs are injured or lost, the tree should be severely
headed back to encourage new growth from the ground.

  A. c. foliis variegatis (the Variegated maple).—A variety of
A. campestre—very much of its character and habit, though
perhaps a little looser.   This tree is extremely pretty and effective up to mid-summer, especially when placed on the boundaries of plantations, as it catches the light well ; after July, it is
apt to burn and get shabby during the dry weather.   There is
another Striped or Blotched-leaved maple, which is a variety
of the *A. pseudo-platanus*, which is still larger and less compact
than the preceding, and equally worthy of being planted by
those who fancy variegated-leaved trees.

  A. macrophyllum (the Large-leaved maple).—This superb
tree, a mere mention of which appears in a note to the previous
edition of this work, was introduced into England in 1812, and
has only within a very few years made its appearance in this
country, and we have, of course, no specimens of any size.   It
is described in its native state as varying in height from forty to
ninety feet, very graceful in form, with branches widely spreading, the wood soft, but beautifully veined ; specimens sent home
by Mr. Douglas, exhibit a grain scarcely inferior to the finest
satin wood.   Though the leaves vary much in size, yet they
are by far the largest of the maples ; this, with its hardihood
and great size and loftiness, renders it one of the noblest of its
kind, and it should invariably be planted where there is sufficient space for its development.

  A. Monspessulanum (the Montpelier maple).—This is another
of the newer maples but lately introduced here ; though of

small habit of growth, yet it is very ornamental, the leaves resembling somewhat in size and color those of *A. campestre :* the flowers are pale, and are very attractive to bees. In mild seasons, in Europe, the leaves remain on the tree until midwinter, and on this account it is much planted in France for hedges. It rarely attains a greater height than thirty to forty feet, and is readily propagated by seeds or by layers.

A. p. laciniata (Cut-leaved or eagle's claw).—A very curious low growing tree, with the lobes of its leaves jagged and somewhat resembling, as its name implies, the foot or claw of an eagle. It is one of the varieties of *A. pseudo-platanus*, and comes in well with the cut-leaved ash, beech, and other trees with this peculiar foliage.

A. p. foliis purpureis (the Purple-leaved maple).—Another sport or variety of *A. pseudo-platanus*, very peculiar and striking when the wind blows, the leaves having a fine purple underneath, and being ruffled by the breeze, presenting a curious blending of purple and pale green ; the foot-stalks to the leaves are quite distinctly pink. This tree is commonly known in the nurseries as the Purple Jersey maple, it having originated in a nursery in that island in 1828. Plants raised from seed sport so much in color that sometimes they become quite green. On this account, specimens for planting should be selected from the nursery rows while in leaf.

A. p. Tartarica (Tartarian maple) ; *A. Creticum* (Cretan Maple), Hodgkins' Seedling, with yellow blotched leaves ; *A. punctata*, with spotted leaves, and several others, are only sports or varieties of *A. pseudo-platanus*, and have not yet, to our knowledge, been planted in the United States.

Æsculus hippocastanum. THE HORSE-CHESTNUT.

Æ. h. Flore pleno (Double-flowering horse-chestnut).—A beautiful variety of *Æ. hippocastanum,* resembling it in character and foliage, but with the flowers double and very full, not unlike at a distance, a gigantic hyacinth. The tree seems perfectly hardy, and has the additional advantage of flowering when very young.

Æ. h. coccinea (Scarlet-flowering horse-chestnut).—This differs from the Rubicunda simply in color of its flower, being a deep scarlet. It is very hardy, flowers early, and is, perhaps, the most striking floral tree of the season. The specimen we have, about ten feet high, is the only one we have seen in this country, but we hardly know an ornamental tree more deserving of notice.

Æ. h. variegata (the Variegated horse-chestnut).—This is simply a variety with blotched leaves ; in fact, there are two, one mottled with white, the other with yellow; whence, the distinction of gold and silver-leaved. We do not regard either of them as particularly handsome, having more the appearance of disease than a regular blotch ; and we consequently would only recommend them for arboretums, or where one has a fancy for variegated trees.

Æ. h. laciniata (Cut-leaved horse-chestnut).—A very distinctive variety, with deeply cut leaves; in certain conditions of growth, the leaves have simply the appearance of threads. This is by far the most curious and interesting of all the cut-leaved trees, and we consider it very desirable even in small collections. It is perfectly hardy, and should be planted by itself. It is still very rare.

Æ. h. Whitleyi.—Whitley's New Scarlet is a variety of Rubicunda, as are also _Æ. Americana_, and _Æ. fol. aurea_ (Golden-leaved horse-chestnut). They can be had at our nurseries, and are well worthy the attention of planters.

The _Pavias_ are simply varieties of the horse-chestnut, with smooth fruit and leaves, and generally of lower growth, most of them are deserving of notice and one of them, _Pavia macrostachya_ (the Dwarf white-flowering horse-chestnut), is rather a shrub than tree ; but we hardly know anything more valuabe in the month of July, when covered with its long spikes or flowers, which are agreeably odoriferous.

Its habit of growth is peculiar, stoling from the root, and when standing alone, as it invariably should, making a magnificent bush, much wider than it is high. It is a native, we believe, of North America, growing most abundantly near St. Augustine in Florida, and was only introduced into England in 1820, the largest plants being at " White Knights," twenty-

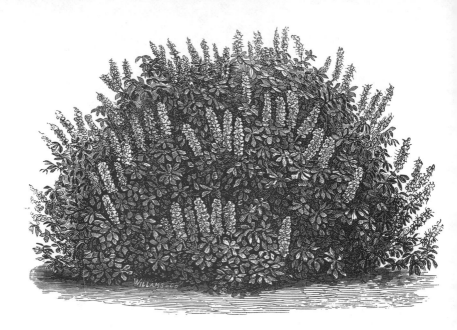

FIG. 91.—DWARF HORSE CHESTNUT, at Wodenethe. Age, 12 yrs. Height, 8 ft. Cir. 60 ft.

FIG. 92.—SCAMPSTON WEEPING ELM, at Wodenethe.
Age, 6 yrs. Height, 7 ft. Circum., 36 ft.

five years planted, fifteen feet high. At Syon House, near
London, there is a specimen, twelve feet. In this country, as
yet, it is rarely to be met with in our ornamental places,
which is the more remarkable as we do not know a shrub
which should be planted before it. It comes into bloom a
month or six weeks later than the other horse-chestnuts, and at
a period, too, when very few shrubs are in flower, and continues
a long time. Our best plant at Wodenethe—of which Fig. 91
is a sketch—twelve years old, is sixty feet in circumference
and about eight feet high, and has, at the time we write, between
three and four hundred racemes of flowers, the feathery lightness
of which, and the fine umbrageous character of the leaves render it a most striking and attractive object.

Pavia rubra (Red-flowering),—which is merely mentioned
by Mr. Downing, and which is now better known, is a shrubby
tree, seldom exceeding twenty feet, with reddish flowers sufficiently distinct to make it desirable—though *Pavia humilis
pendula* (the Weeping red *pavia*), is even more desirable and attractive. Mr. Loudon considers this one of the most beautiful
and interesting forms of *Pavia*, and recommends horse-chestnuts
of twenty to thirty years' growth to be grafted all over with it
at the points of the shoots ; care being taken afterwards, once
or twice every year, to rub off all the buds from the stock as
soon as they appear, so that the entire force of the plant may
be directed to the nourishment of the scions.

Pavia carnea pubescens (Downy leaf), from the fact of the
whole plant, including the young wood, being covered with
pubescence.

P. purpurea (Purple) ; *P. rubra atrosanguinea* (Dark red) ;
and *P. carnea superba* (Pale red), are all new varieties to be
obtained in this country, and of greater or less merit.

***

Alnus. THE ALDER.

The principle additions to this genus, since the previous
edition of this work, have been *A. cordifolia*, (Heart-shaped),
a tree of some magnitude, a native of Calabria, with
large, deep green, shining leaves, rather broad and deeply

heart-shaped, growing rapidly, and, we believe, perfectly hardy—at least, we have found it so at this place—and *A. quercifolia* (the Oak-leaved alder); although Mr. Downing places little value on the *A. glauca* (our common Swamp-alder), yet we must confess, we hardly know a more charming plant in the winter, when covered with its bright scarlet berries, especially when placed against hemlocks or other evergreens; and we are quite confident, that planted in this manner it only needs to be seen to be more generally employed.

Betula. BIRCH.

The only new varieties lately introduced of the birch are: *B. daurica* (the Daurian birch), from Asiatic Siberia, which is supposed to be only a variety of *B. alba,* not growing as tall as the common birch, nor does the trunk attain the same size, though the wood is both harder and yellower.

Betula laciniata (the Cut-leaf birch), as known in our nurseries; an exceedingly graceful, pretty tree, with a light, airy growth, inferior, however, to a still newer variety *B. laciniata pendula* (Pendulous cut-leaf), which is quite the prettiest and most feathery of the birches.

B. nana and *B. pumila* (the Dwarf and low growing birch). These two are merely shrubs, both natives of the northern portions of America, and the latter found in Sweden, Norway, and Russia; and growing only two or three feet high, merely valuable as carrying out the class in arboretums.

Castanea. CHESTNUT.

The principle additions to this genus, since the first edition are: *Castanea asplenifolia* (Cut-leaf chestnut), a very remarkable and peculiar variety, with its leaves in shreds; and *C. variegata, foliis-aureis,* and *foliis-argenteis,* (the Golden-leaved and the Silver-leaved chestnuts), both very striking and showy, especially when planted against or near evergreens, the golden variety being particularly gay. Small plants of this tree have, at Wodenethe, blossomed when only two feet high, but whether this is the habit of this variety, or accidental, we are not prepared to say.

We have also here (received some years ago from Mr. Rivers, we think), a dwarf variety, called Dwarf prolific, which has the merit of fruiting when a small shrub.

Cercis. JUDAS TREE.

The only addition to this variety, which has appeared within the past few years, is *Cercis foliis-variegatis* (the Variegated-leaved Judas) ; the leaves blotched and streaked with white, and sometimes pink and white splashes ; desirable, but at present very rare. We procured our plants, we believe, from France.

Fagus. BEECH.

There are several varieties of this tree, which have been introduced into cultivation within the last few years, well deserving of notice, and some of them very curious and interesting ; among these is, *Fagus laciniata,* called also *F. asplenifolia* and *F. incisa,* and known in the nurseries as Cut-leaved, Fernleaved and Various-leaved beech. We have all these plants under the different names, but, except the occasional sport, which the beech is peculiarly liable to, we believe them to be identical ; sometimes resembling a fern, which is the most usual, and others again with leaves very oddly cut and shredded, as it were, by insects. The Fern-leaved beech, commonly so-called, is a great favorite with us, and we hardly know a prettier or more attractive tree, or one less known or planted ; if we could plant but half a dozen trees this would certainly be one of the first. It has the close round habit of the beech with a pleasing green and glaucous color, and the most tiny and delicate foliage, the persistency of which would make it very desirable for topiary work, as it bears the shears better than any deciduous tree we know of. Its maximum height is forty to fifty feet, but we have seen no specimen in this country over twelve to fifteen feet ; its average annual growth being twelve to fifteen inches.

Fagus cristata (Crested or Curled-leaved beech), is more curious than interesting, and is what Mr. Loudon called a " monstrosity," with leaves small, almost sessile, and crowded into small tufts which occur at intervals along the branches; it never becomes a large tree.

Fagus foliis variegatis (Variegated-leaved beech).—There are two varieties of this, the Golden and Silver; the latter being the most striking.

There is also another most charming variety—*F. Cunninghamia* (the Evergreen beech), with leaves curiously small, but which does not stand our climate in this vicinity, but, which in the Southern States, we have little doubt, would be quite an acquisition to the Evergreen trees. In connection with the beech we would also mention three new varieties of *Carpinus* (Hornbeam), *C. pendula,* a pretty weeping tree, and the Golden and Silver-leaved varieties, resembling very much, though inferior to these same varieties in the beech.

Fraxinus.   ASH.

There are five or six varieties of this tree, not mentioned by Mr. Downing, that are well deserving attention; the most striking and rarest, perhaps, is *F. aucubafolia* (the Aucuba-leaved ash). The leaves blotched with yellow, like that well-known English shrub, the *Aucuba Japonica,* and to such an extent that at a little distance, a tree of some age has the appearance of this plant of extraordinary size; on the edges of plantations it catches the light so well that it works up to great advantage, and has so strong a resemblance to a tree in flower that it is constantly taken for one. The tree is yet very rare, a plant we obtained a year or two since from Messrs. Ellwanger and Barry is the only specimen we have seen.

F. aurea (Golden ash), and *F. aurea pendula* (Weeping Golden ash), are both very desirable varieties; the color of the wood of a rich golden yellow, being very striking in winter when contrasted with the snow, quite as marked as the Golden willow; on this account it would be well to plant it in sight from the windows of the house. The latter tree is, with us, quite as hardy as and a great improvement upon the old Weeping ash.

F. salicifolia (Willow-leaved ash).—This is another of those remarkable thin cut-leaved trees, of which we have specimens in the beech, horse-chestnut and even the oak. This is a most rapid and robust grower, and would, undoubtedly, be taken for a willow, by persons not very familiar with trees—and though not particularly handsome, still it is well deserving a place in all collections, where striking and curious plants are desired.

F. globosa viridis or *myrtifolia* (Myrtle-leaved ash).—A seedling, if we mistake not, of Messrs. Ellwanger and Barry, from whom we procured the plant some years ago ; is when grafted standard high, a very pretty effective little tree, with a globular head of small close, dark green foliage like the myrtle, and comes in very well, standing by itself in small pleasure grounds, or peeping out of low masses of shrubs.

F. argentea alba.—A very singular variety, with leaves entirely white, and when planted with the *aucubafolia*, the leaves of which are quite golden, producing a remarkable effect, like gigantic flowering plants. We do not know the history of this singular tree, and have only seen it at Mr. Daniel Brincker-hoff's, in this neighborhood, who has the impression he procured it some years since, from Mr. Rivers of the Sawbridgeworth nurseries in England. It differs from the varieties known in the English nurseries as *F. argentea,* from the peculiar whiteness of its foliage ; the argentea being generally streaked with green, though it may be a sport of this tree. It is apt to suffer very much in June from the insects which, apparently attracted by the white foliage at night, greedily devour the leaves, though all the other ashes standing by escape untouched.

F. lentiscifolia and *F. lentiscifolia pendula,* are both desirable trees, with neat, narrow foliage, and rapid growth. The Pendulous-branched we have found the most rapid of the ashes. The Weeping black and Gold-striped weeping, both pretty ; *F. atro-virens,* remarkable for its dark foliage ; *F. bosci,* with dark glossy foliage, and woolly shoots ; *F. juglandifolia* (Walnut-leaved) ; *F. monophylla,* single, instead of pinnate leaves ; *F.*

elonga Japonica pannosa, Nova Anglica, oxyphillas and *scolopendrifolium*, are all new varieties, for arboretums or very full collections.

MAGNOLIA.

There are several newly introduced varieties of this beautiful tree which deserve attention : among them may be mentioned, *M. Thompsoniana*, a fine distinct variety, probably a cross between *glauca* and *tripetala*, quite as hardy with us as either parent.

M. speciosa, M. gracilis, M. Alexandrina and *M. Nortbertiana.*—These four varieties so closely resemble *M. Soulangiana*, that we think they can be only seedlings, differing a little in the mingling of the white and purple, which is the color of their flowers.

M. Nortbertiana, being whiter in its flowers, may probably be a seedling or variety of *M. conspicua* ; *M. gracilis* is unquestionably only a more slender delicate variety of *M. purpurea,* having much darker flowers, especially when half expanded ; *M. Alexandrina* flowers earlier than its parent.

Another desirable variety is *M. longifolia,* which is often confounded with and sold for *M. Thompsoniana,* and is intermediate in appearance between *M. tripetala* and *M. glauca* ; the leaves are acute at both ends, longer than *Thompsoniana,* and resembling *tripetala,* but thicker, smaller, and glaucous underneath ; the flowers are very sweet but not as large as *M. Thompsoniana.*

M. galissoniere.—A plant of which we imported from France two years since, is said to be the only variety of the *M. grandiflora* which will stand our climate, and as it resists the cold of the north of France, it is not impossible it may be acclimatized here. We do not know that it has been sufficiently tested at present to be able to class it among our hardy magnolias.

Quercus.   Oak.

We have but few additions to make to this genus, and these rather of the fancy order.

Q. laciniata (Cut-leaf oak), known also as *Q. salicifolia* and *Q. filicifolia*, is a curious variety, with leaves deeply cut at the edges and laciniated.

Q. foliis variegatis (Variegated oak), both gold and silver, with leaves variegated with white or yellow and occasional streaks of red; well grown, quite showy and ornamental.

Q. purpurea (Purple oak), has the foot-stalks of the leaves and its young shoots quite distinctly tinged with purple—even the young leaves, when they first appear, are very dark, as much so as the Purple beech, and, like this tree, becoming greener as the season advances.

But of all the newer varieties recently introduced here, the *Q. pendula* (Weeping oak), is the most distinctive and remarkable. We have as yet, we believe, no trees of any size in the country. The largest tree known is at Moccas court, in Herefordshire, England, which Mr. Loudon (Arbo : Brit. vol. 3, page 1732), describes as one of the most extraordinary trees of the oak kind in existence ; the height of the trunk to the first branch is eighteen feet, total height of the trunk seventy-five feet, with branches reaching from about the middle of its height to within seven feet of the ground, and hanging down like cords ; many of these branches are thirty feet long and no thicker in any part of their length than a common wagon rope. There is another variety of Weeping oak to be found in our nurseries, and which we have had here, but the inclination of the branches is more rigid and less pendulous and graceful than the Moccas oak, and we much doubt if we have ever had this species here.

To persons curious in trees, or who are desirous of making plantations of the many dwarfs at present quite the fashion in England, we would suggest here two varieties of oak interesting for this purpose ; viz., *Quercus humilis* (the low growing oak), a native of Europe, where it never exceeds a height of three to four feet, and in the Landes near Bordeaux, not over one foot; and *Q. pumila* (an American dwarf), which seldom exceeds twenty inches.

Salix. WILLOW.

There are three or four charming varieties to add to this well known genus. Among them the newest, and perhaps the most remarkable, is the Kilmarnock Weeping, quite distinctive, with a very pendulous but close habit of growth, so much so, that the branches, at least in young trees, are quite hid out by the large glossy leaves, which, at a little distance, are not unlike the apple leaf. It seems perfectly hardy, and, with the one next mentioned, may be very appropriately planted in pleasure grounds, where the other and larger willows would be out of keeping.

S. Americana pendula, an American dwarf variety, with very slender and graceful branches, or rather shoots, which when grafted six or seven feet high, hang down like whip-cord ; this variety, we think, was first noticed by the late Mr. Downing in Rivers' nursery, and very prettily described by him as the Fountain willow, which is a much more expressive and appropriate name than the one it now goes by in the nurseries. It should always be grafted on what is called the Stock willow; if upon its own roots or worked even on itself, standard high, it becomes nothing but an awkward distorted shrub.

S. rosmarifolia (the Rosemary-leaved willow)—Is another exceedingly pretty little lawn tree, with delicate rosemary-like leaves ; this should also be worked standard high.

The Huntington willow, with large, beautiful, shining leaves, and a variety we imported from France a year or so ago, called *S. pentandra,* described there (though it has not yet realized its reputation with us), as a beautiful tree, with leaves like the laurel, are all the newer varieties proper for ornamental planting.

Sophora. THE SOPHORA.

Lin. Syst. Decandria, Monogynia.

This genus, the only hardy variety of which is deciduous, is a native of Japan, and is highly ornamental. There is not, to our knowledge, any large tree of it in this country, and from this fact, perhaps, and from its great rarity, it was classed by

Mr. Downing among the shrubs. It is in reality a large tree when grown, forty to fifty feet high, with pinnate leaves, and producing large branches of cream colored flowers in August. It is quite distinctive in winter, by the dark green bark of its young wood; and in summer by the dark blue green of its foliage. Near Paris there are some trees sixty feet high. It grows rapidly and is peculiarly adapted to the United States from one remarkable property of its foliage, which is the power it has to retain both its leaves and their color in the very hottest and driest seasons, when locusts and acacias and other pinnated-leaved *leguminaceæ* are apt to lose their foliage.

The flowers, it is said, in China make yellow dye of so superior a color, that it is reserved exclusively for the use of the Imperial family.

S. pendula (Pendulous or Weeping sophora), is more commonly met with, perhaps, than the upright sophora, though even this variety is very rare. It has long pendulous shoots; grafted near the ground it becomes a mere straggling plant, but, ten to twenty feet high, we hardly know anything more ornamental or striking; even in winter, the long slender branches of beautiful bright green render it most attractive.

There is a third variety, *variegata*, but the color of the leaf is sickly, and we do not consider it desirable, except for arboretums.

Pyrus. Mountain Ash.

A very pretty and marked addition to the varieties heretofore known, and described is *Pyrus pendula* (Weeping mountain ash), with extremely pendulous branches bending quite to the ground, and then rambling along it if not stopped; a most rapid grower, more so, we think, than the common mountain ash, and a very great bloomer.

P. nana (Dwarf mountain ash).—This is a very stunted variety of slow, close growth, but quite remarkable for the luxuriant corymbs of coral berries in the Autumn.

P. quercifolia, a distinct variety with large, hoary, oak leaves; *P. striata* (Striped-leaved), *P. vestita* (White-leaved), the young shoots and the under part of the leaves being as clearly

white as the Silver poplar. The Yellow-berried, the Large-
fruited gray, the Large-fruited red, and the Large-fruited rose,
are all deserving notice where there is ample space for planting.

***

Tilia. LIME OR LINDEN.

The only varieties of value to add to those previously enumerated in this book, are *T. laciniata* (Cut or Jagged-leaf linden), with the leaves curiously cut ; and *T. pendula alba*
(Weeping White linden), of a very pendulous habit, and the
under part of the leaf very silvery. We esteem this one of
the most, if not the most ornamental of the lindens.

***

Ulmus. ELM.

There are a good many new elms lately introduced, which
are quite remarkable in their habit, and distinctive in appearance ; among them are two Scotch varieties of weeping elms,
the *Scampston* (of which Fig. 92 is a portrait), and *Camperdown*,
both somewhat allied in appearance, though the first is the most
remarkable, having fine large foliage, and the most extraordinary droop to the branches ; so much and so regular and
formal is their inclination, that it is difficult to believe artificial
means have not been resorted to. When grafted as it should
be, fifteen to twenty feet high, the branches make a curvilinear
droop to the ground, with a growth so regular and symmetrical
as to give the whole tree the appearance of a gigantic arbor ;
regularly trained and trimmed, and by making an arched opening on one side, it can be well used for this purpose, the thick
umbrageous character of the leaves producing the most agreeable and dense shade.

The only material difference between this tree and *U. Camperdown*, is that this last is of a more open, loose foliage, and
rather less regular in the droop of the branches. They are
both, however, very fine trees and well worthy the most prominent positions in the lawn—care being taken that they shall
have ample space for their development.

U. glabra pendula is another fine variety of Weeping elm, but far inferior, we think, to the two above mentioned.

U. montana pendula, and *U. rugosa pendula*, (the Scotch weeping), and (Rough-leaved weeping), are also very desirable Weeping elms.

The Huntington elm is a rapid growing variety, with a fine large leaf.

The *U. articofolia*, (Nettle-leaved) ; *U. variegata*, (the Variegated) ; and *U. purpurea*, (the Purple), are all curious and desirable in large places ; as is also *U. adianthafolia*, a strong rugged variety with corrugated and crimped leaves very peculiar.

THE NEWER ORNAMENTAL DECIDUOUS SHRUBS.

Before enumerating the many new and beautiful shrubs which have been introduced into our gardens and pleasure grounds within ten years, we wish to say a few words respecting their employment.

We have before remarked, in another place, that the facilities afforded by railroads and steamboats are now so great, that there is a class, and a large one, of small suburban places and villa residences in the neighborhood of our large cities and rural towns, to which this kind of plant is especially valuable. In residences of a few hundred feet square to an acre or more, shrubs are much more valuable than trees, as the latter, when fully matured, become so large and cumbersome as to interfere very much with a free circulation of air, and often completely shut out all view, and are apt to make the places themselves damp and dreary. There are many of these residences where trees should never be planted, but their place should be supplied by the finer shrubs, as the Weigela, Forsythia, the Fly honeysuckle, the smaller Magnolias (*glauca, purpurea, gracilis, conspicua, soulangiana*), the Purple berberry, the Purple filbert, the Variegated syringo, the Dwarf horse-chestnut, the Fern-leaved beech, the Oak-leaved hydrangea, the Red-twigged dogwood, the Double Japan quince, the Deutzia gracilis, and the different hardy English and Belgic azaleas, among the deciduous shrubs. And among the evergreens, the English and Irish yews, the different Junipers, the different Arbor-vitæ, the Weeping cypress (*Cupressus oblonga pendula*), the eight or ten varieties of Dwarf firs, the Thuiopsis borealis, a beautiful and hardy plant from Baffin's Bay; the Hemlock, if kept clipped and bushy, the various Rhododendrons, especially the *Catawbiensis;* the Laurel-leaved holly (*Ilex laurifolia*), the American holly, and finally that most valuable of all shrubs, the Berberis mahonia. By a tasteful and judicious massing and grouping of the above plants, with occasionally a single specimen by itself alone, as the English yew, or Dwarf horse-chestnut, or Fern-leaf beech, a very pretty and ornamental effect may be produced, without shutting out the light of heaven, as is too often done by tall sparse trees, with long naked stems, producing no other sensation but a shudder at their ugliness.

In submitting the annexed list of the newer shrubs, we regret our space will not allow us to do much more than to enumerate their names ; merely premising that the most desirable are those we have already just mentioned above.

Aralia Japonica, a new variety of *A. spinosa* (Hercules' club), but much finer in foliage, and very highly esteemed in England ; hardy.

A. papyripera (the Chinese Rice-paper plant).—We have but recently imported this, and do not yet know its hardihood; it has superb leaves some three feet or more in diameter.

Ceanothus.—The *ceanothus*, of which there are several varieties, are beautiful shrubs, with white or blue clusters of flowers.

Cornus variegata (the Variegated-leaved dogwood).—A very

prettily striped leaf, and contrasting agreeably with the othei varieties.

Daphne atro purpureum.—A very marked variety of *Mezereum*, with purplish leaves.

Deutzia gracilis, and *D. scabra.*—Two very desirable shrubs introduced some six or eight years ago; the *gracilis* being perhaps, the most charming shrub at the period of its inflorescence; it has also the merit of bearing forcing well in a green-house, though perfectly hardy.

Itea Carolinia (the Carolina itea).—A charming little shrub which does best in the shade.

Leycesteria formosa (the beautiful *leycesteria*).

Ligustrum, foliis aureis, and *argenteis* (the Golden and Silver striped privet).—Very pretty and desirable, mingled with the green privet.

Forsythia viridissima.—The very green *Forsythia* is certainly one of the most desirable among the new shrubs; its flowers, a bright yellow, appear very early in the spring, succeeded by a deep, dense foliage which in winter is sub-evergreen, hanging on to the plant and retaining its color until long past Christmas. Like the magnolia, it appears to more advantage when planted against evergreens.

Persica vulgaris flore pleno alba (the Double white-flowering peach).—Beautiful, especially when planted by the Double pink.

Ribes sanguineum flore pleno, and *R. speciosum.*—Both beautiful varieties of the Flowering currant. The first a great improvement on the old *R. sanguineum,* and the last with long pendulous red flowers, like a fuschia.

Sambucus flore pleno, S. foliis aureis, S. foliis argenteis— New and striking varieties of the Black or Common elder, as yet very rare. We have found them hardy and most luxuriant growers; the Double-flowering is very striking, but the Silver and Gold-leaved are much more so. We presume they can now be procured at our nurseries, though we obtained ours from M. Leroy in France.

Spiræa callosa, S. Douglasii, S. Lindleyana, S. Nepalensis, S. prunifolia, S. Reevsii, S. r. flore pleno, are all the finest among the new Spireas; exceedingly hardy and desirable, especially *Douglasii*, *callosa*, and Double-flowering *Reevesii*. *Syringa Josikæa*, *S. Charles X.*, *S. Emodi*, are new additions to the charming family of lilacs. *Tamarix Africana*, *T. Gallica* (the African and French tamariks), are very pretty and desirable.

Weigela rosea (the Rosy weigela) is perhaps, take it all in all, the greatest acquisition to our hardy shrubs within the past ten years. We hardly know a more lovely plant or more abundant bloomer; the white and pink flowers resembling apple blossoms, almost cover the plant with a sheet of bloom.

SECTION IV.

REMARKS ABOUT HALF-HARDY PLANTS AND THE NEWER
EVERGREEN ORNAMENTAL TREES AND SHRUBS, WITH THE
METHOD OF ACCLIMATIZING AND EMPLOYING THEM.

PERHAPS in no one way has the taste for planting
more developed itself since the first appearance of
Mr. Downing's book, especially during the past four
or five years, than in the increasing predilection
for evergreens, and prevailing desire not only to plant
the better known and more common varieties, but also
those of more recent introduction.

Almost every one, even with the smallest place, now
plants not only the Norway spruce, and the Austrian
and Scotch pines, but is even desirous of trying his
hand upon deodars, cryptomerias and other varieties,
considered only as luxuries in Mr. Downing's day.

The cost of many of these plants having been reduced
from one or two guineas apiece, to fifteen or twenty
cents, the ease with which they may be imported, at
little risk, and the facility with which they live, at least
for one or two years, to say nothing of the fashion for
evergreens now-a-days, are certainly very strong temp-
tations ; but the actual beauty, great variety and
contrast in character, habit, and color, and the entire
hardihood of a great many new sorts, and the vast
addition made by this class of trees to a winter's landscape, much more frequently seen now by owners of
country places than when the first edition even of this
work appeared, all combine to make it very desirable
that some authentic information should be given, which

may be reliable as to what may and what may not be planted. We have individuals enough in this country who are willing to spend money liberally for trees if they could find out what to buy, and how and where to plant. The early edition of this work, though quite up to the time when it was published, is now singularly meagre in its chapters on Evergreens, and there are probably at this moment in this country, collections, in extent and variety (though not in size of trees), greater than was the Pinetum at Dropmore, in England, which Mr. Downing refers to, in 1841. We are quite sure there are over *ninety* varieties of evergreens, nearly all quite hardy in this middle portion of the Hudson, which are not mentioned in the first edition, and there are several distinct, beautiful, and hardy genera not even alluded to, such as the *piceas*, of which there are at present known *twelve* distinct species, all, we believe, hardy here. Mr. Downing mentions seven *abies*, and we now have in cultivation, more or less general, *twenty-three more*. We have growing in the different collections in this country, principally between Washington and Boston, twenty more pines, in addition to the fifteen he enumerates, twenty-five junipers, against *one* in the first edition ; ten new (*Thujœ*) arbor vitæ, and seven yews.

It may be objected that these are not all hardy. They may not be in one particular locality, but throughout the length and breadth of our land, we have a sufficient variety of climate for every thing, and if one cannot grow a tree on the shores of Lake Erie, one can, perhaps, in Pennsylvania or Virginia, or the Carolinas, or Florida. Besides, as we shall hope to show, a great deal more may be done in planting doubtful trees (than is done) by a judicious selection of site and soil. We further hope to show that in our best places where there is the desire and means to make large collections, that one should not discard a tree because his neighbor may have not been successful with it.

There are many reasons which may operate against the success of a tree this year, and for several years, which may disappear in time. One consideration, and that an important one, is shelter. Plant a deodar cedar in the middle of a large and high field, thoroughly and entirely exposed to every blast that blows, with the full force of a summer, and what is worse, a winter's sun, and it is hardly possible it should survive. Plant the same tree in the same place with the colder winds broken and kept off by masses of evergreens, and shielded from the pernicious effects of the early spring sun, and the chances are your tree will succeed and flourish.

Again, persons are very apt to plant their new evergreens, especially if they are rare and costly, in what are called "well prepared" holes, that is, in holes redolent, perhaps, with guano, and with the richest compost to be obtained; if the new plant is not killed immediately by over-dosing, it is at any rate so stimulated by excess of food as to make a succulent redundant growth of imperfectly ripened wood, which is sure to be killed back the first winter, and the tree become so enfeebled as to die outright the second; or the plant may have vitality enough to struggle through this surfeit and after staggering for months, or perhaps a year or so, with this indigestion, manage to work into healthy, natural, unprepared soil, and eventually become a tree. Then again, our climate is constantly changing. This, we think, is conceded by every one who has wintered in the country the past five or ten years, and trees which could not or would not stand now, may five years hence; and, lastly, a tree, like a man becomes finally more or less acclimatized — it may get knocked about somewhat at first, but eventually learns to stand up and take care of itself. The Torreya, for instance (and we have many such trees upon this place) required an immense deal of coaxing to reconcile it to to our northern and changeable climate. The first year we left it out it was protected by a double box, the interval between the sidings being filled with tan. The second year, the tree was sheathed in straw and protected besides by a single box, with a few air holes on the north ; the third year it was open at the north, but protected on the east, south, and west, by a box with three sides. The fourth year a mat was substituted for the box, and the fifth year it passed alone through the winter, the extreme tip of some of its more exuberant shoots being a little injured—the well-ripened wood being untouched—since when it survives our most severe weather without injury, and now takes its place among the really hardy evergreens. We should feel no more apprehension about its safety in our worst winters than we should about a pine or hemlock.

A curious fact connected with this tree is, that plants propagated from cuttings before it became acclimatized are still tender, while plants propagated since its hardihood became confirmed, seem quite as hardy as the parent.

We are not prepared to say that a great deal of this care was not a work of supererogation, and that the tree might have done as well with much less protection, and for half the number of winters, but we were working in the dark ; the tree was a native of Florida ; it never had been tried here, and from the climate whence it originated, we did not suppose it would stand, and felt consequently disposed to take extra pains, for which we are quite compensated by the gain of a new and most exquisite variety, and the certainty of our knowledge that all torreyas, from this plant at least, are are perfectly hardy in this latitude.

We mention this, simply as one illustration of a great many similar experiments, with results more or less successful, because we are quite sure it is within the

experience of most persons who have attempted acclimatizing plants, that success not unfrequently is the
reward, when from the habits of the plants, and the
character of the climate from which they come, a contrary result might be anticipated. We remember in
England some ten years since, seeing at Chatsworth a
plant of Weigela rosea, in a house built, if we mistake
not, expressly for it, because Sir Joseph, then Mr.
Paxton, did not think it hardy—judging probably from
the country to which it belonged; and now there is no
more common and hardier shrub, and, we may add,
more beautiful in the season, or one more generally
planted in the Northern States. Mr. Loudon very truly
observes, "That though the nature of a species cannot
be so far altered as to fit an inhabitant of a very hot
climate for a very cold one, yet that the habits of individuals admit of considerable variation, and that some
plants of warm climates are found to adapt themselves
much more readily to cold climates than others; thus
the common passion flower, according to Dr. Walker,
when first introduced into the Edinburgh Botanic
Garden, lost its leaves during the winter, but in a few
years the same plant retained the greater part of them
at that season." The same author relates that plants of
the common yew, sent from Paris to Stockholm, to
plant certain designs of Le Notre laid out there for the
King of Sweden, all died, although the yew is a native
of that country as well as France.

" Every gardener," he says, " must have observed that
the common weeds which have sprung up in pots, in
hot-beds, or in hot-houses, when these pots happen to
be set out in the open air, during winter or spring,
have their leaves killed or injured, whilst the same
species growing in the open ground are uninjured."

We have ourselves observed, that peach trees in pots,
if by chance they are left out all winter, are destroyed,
though the same tree in the ground can resist any

degree of frost. The obvious conclusion to be drawn from this is, not that peach trees are not hardy, but under certain conditions are not hardy ; which facts lead to this theory, that the habits of plants admit of a certain degree of change with regard to the climate which they will bear; that the degree in which this power exists in any plant, is only to be ascertained by experiment, by trying in the open air plants usually considered as tender, or which hitherto have been kept under glass.

Our usual method of acclimatizing a plant, is to select some very protected and shady spot, as the north side of a thicket, or what we prefer, the interior of some evergreen wood, and to prepare the holes six feet wide and three deep, with loose but poor soil, well drained with stones for the lower eight or ten inches, with barely compost enough to assist the tree through the summer. For the first two or three years in winter, a little mound of earth, eight or ten inches high, is put around the neck of the plant, to prevent the bad effects of thawing and freezing in a most sensitive part, and cedar or hemlock boughs, are placed round its branches; this covering diminishing year by year, as the tree obtains size and vigor, until it is omitted altogether. The plant, to ensure safety, is moved once or twice within this wood, each time to a more exposed situation, which has also the additional advantage (like root pruning) of checking all redundancy of growth. When it exhibits sufficient strength, it is transplanted to its final situation on the lawn—its cedar covering being renewed for a couple of winters—and, if it can be reconciled to the climate, it is now supposed to be so.

We have found it very perplexing to arrive at any thorough and satisfactory decision as to comparative hardihood of trees in different portions of the United States, from its being so difficult to reconcile the apparent discrepancies in the various returns which we have received from these places, and we are led, therefore, to these conclusions, viz : that the hardihood and success of trees depend not exclusively upon climate, and that a few degrees of latitude, north or south, are of far less importance than proper soil and situation, and that a thorough knowledge of what to do, which experience alone, after many mishaps, can teach, will often enable us to grow trees at the North and East which do not seem to succeed now at the West and the South. For instance, in the neighborhood of Natchez, within six miles of that city, and on an elevation of three hundred and twenty-six feet above the river, the Gardenia Florida, the Pittosporum, the Magnolia fuscata, the M. grandiflora, the Olea fragrans, the Myrtles in variety, the English laurel, the Laurestinus, thrive perfectly.

The Deodar cedar and Cryptomeria Japonica, never suffer except occasionally from caterpillars, and become luxuriant trees ; there being specimens of the former thirty feet high, and of the latter fifteen feet, with branches in both trees sweeping the ground. Cunninghamia Sinensis is also perfectly hardy, and has reached a height of from fifteen to eighteen feet, and yet the Abies Smithiana is reported as not *quite hardy* and sometimes injured by spring frosts, though at Newport, the Abies Smithiana is said to be the hardiest of all the spruces—more so even than the Abies excelsa (the common Norway). Again, in a report from Pennsylvania, in the neighborhood of Warrior's Mark, on the side of one of the Alleghany mountains, at an altitude above the sea of 1,020 feet, and in latitude 40° 40', and where the thermometer has indicated 23° below zero, where even the Ailanthus, Catalpa, and Paulownia are annually cut to the ground, the Cryptomeria flourishes, though browned, and the Deodar cedar survives, though making little or no progress, when the cedar of Le-

banon, the Silver cedar and the Douglas fir are killed
outright. Now at Wodenethe, we find the Silver cedar
and the Cedar of Lebanon much hardier than the
Deodar, yet at Newport the Cedar of Lebanon will not
stand, and at Philadelphia, Mr. Meehan says the Deodar
is killed on dry soil, and uninjured on wet; while at a
country place near Boston, on a slope *facing the south*,
without any protection or shelter from other trees,
Deodar cedars planted in 1853, have been browned
but slightly, though exposed to the sun all the day long.
Cedars of Lebanon planted at same time, get more
browned.

It is very evident from all this, we think, that we
cannot form any decisive opinion as to what is and what
is not truly hardy in any one portion of the country,
where we receive so many contradictory reports; but it
does not follow that a failure for one or two years,
unless very complete, should discourage us so entirely
as to prevent our trying the same plant again in other
situations and under different treatment. Because the
Indian spruce (*A. Smithiana*) suffers from spring frost
near Natchez, when the Cryptomeria and Deodar do not,
let us rather hope to acclimatize it by moving the spruce
to a higher or drier situation, where being more re-
tarded, it will either ripen off its annual growth better,
or push later in the spring. If the Indian spruce is
hardier at Newport, where the thermometer sometimes
gets very low, than the common Norway, there can be
little doubt but what it will grow near Natchez, when
properly placed. If too, the Deodar cedar, and Cedar
of Lebanon thrive near Philadelphia, in wet and low,
instead of high and dry soil, it will be very easy for
planters of these trees in that vicinity to adopt this
hint; while we, who have found the reverse of this
true, will act in accordance with our experience.

So also of the Cryptomeria—if it has been found to
withstand a cold of 23° below zero, on the Alleghany

mountains, at an elevation of 1,020 feet above the sea—where even the Ailanthus was destroyed, we cannot see why this tree may not stand in any other part of the country, at the same elevation, having no greater degree of cold, but always under the same circumstances and conditions. What these are, unfortunately, the tree only knows; possibly a frost, even as severe as this, at a great distance from the sea, may be less injurious than half the amount of frost near salt water; or the severe weather may come and go, gradually, without the great variations common in the middle States; which variation we have always believed most destructive to vegetable, as it is injurious to animal life; and finally, the conclusion we must inevitably come to is that the organism of a plant is as wonderful and mysterious as that of a man, and that, with certain general rules as to planting and treatment, we must grope in the dark until many more years of experience in different parts of the United States, enable us to know what we can and what we cannot grow. We trust, however, that some assistance may be obtained from the reports we have been enabled to procure from different parts of the country, by which planters in those localities will be able to do as well as their neighbors, if they can give their trees the same advantages.

Another reason why we proposed to give in this supplement a more complete account and list of all the evergreens, hardy and half-hardy, which have been introduced into this country of late years is (and we quote again in part from Mr. Loudon), that we think there are few scenes in an ornamental garden or pleasure-ground, of greater interest to a person having any taste or knowledge of Botany, however slight, than a collection of trees and shrubs, natives of foreign climates, which, though they would be destroyed if exposed in the winter, yet when planted (turned out), or sunk in the ground during the summer, exhibit a degree of

beauty and luxuriance which they never do or could
attain in a green-house or conservatory; and which
require in the winter simply the protection of a cool
green-house, or in most cases of a cold pit sufficiently
deep and protected to exclude the frost, and with facilities for occasionally admitting air for ventilation.
A pit of this description, well drained and dry, and
twelve or fifteen feet deep, might accommodate plants
ten or twelve feet high, which, when planted out in the
pleasure-grounds during the summer, the tub or pots
being sunk out of sight in the soil, would produce the
most extraordinary and charming effects. By an introduction and combination in our own grounds of bananas,
palms, aloes, the different arundos (a species of bamboo),
the different dracænas, the New Zealand flax (*Phor-
mium tenax*), *Bambusa metaké* (another variety of
bamboo), which we hope will prove hardy, the different
Cannas, and a mingling of the rarer evergreens, like the
Araucarias (of which *Cunninghamii* and *excelsa* are
very effective), we have, we think, produced a very
pleasing effect. These, with the Indian cedars, and
Southern and Mexican long-leaved pines, have quite
changed a portion of our grounds from an American to
a tropical and oriental landscape.

All these plants we have named, and the newer tender
evergreens which we have not as yet named, would winter safely (excepting perhaps the araucaria excelsa), in
a cold pit or cool green-house, or a dry cellar, where
there was some light and no frost. If we add to these
the great variety and number of evergreen shrubs—the
different evergreen Magnolias, the Hollies, the Laurel,
the Portugal laurel, the half-hardy Rhododendrons, all of
which are too tender for our climate, we cannot but
believe the time is not far distant when instead of
keeping green-houses for the preservation of the ordinary
green-house plants, persons of taste will build pits for
the preservation of half-hardy evergreens and ligneous

plants, which, when judiciously arranged and combined in the summer, will alter the whole character of their grounds. We have in our eye at this moment, many fine places, both on this river and in different parts of the country, where large green-houses and conservatories are kept up all winter, at a great expense, and where the plants literally " waste their fragrance on the desert air," as the families are away in cities at too great a distance to admit their flowers being sent to them.

These very places in summer present a very unattractive and meagre appearance, being planted simply with the older and less beautiful trees and shrubs—in many cases with little or no flower garden. The Camelias, Azalias, Geraniums, and other plants being stowed away out of sight, until the return of another winter, when they will again bloom for the benefit, solely, of the gardener and his friends.

Were these same houses at a consumption of one-half or one-fifth the amount of fuel and labor, devoted to the cultivation (or rather to the preservation, for they require no cultivation or attention in the winter beyond an occasional watering), of half-hardy evergreens and tender plants, the compensation and enjoyment from them in summer would be ten-fold that derived from the usual occupation of plant-houses ; and in cases where families are permanent residents of the country, let them devote a portion of their green-houses to this purpose, or have some arrangement of pits as we have above described.

We must bear in mind one fact : that as excellent models as the English are in all matters pertaining to country life, yet they use their places only in the winter, and we, as a general rule, only in the summer ; while it is, therefore, very important for them to have their grounds and green-houses adorned with those plants and shrubs which will make it most agreeable and delightful at the season when they are at home, in the winter,

yet the reverse of this is true with us. Our object
should be to make our places as gay and interesting as
possible, at those portions of the year when we live at
them. What advantage is it to plant the beautiful varie·
ties of double and single thorns, the Judas tree, the
Forsythia, or the Magnolias in those places which the
families or owners do not reach until the season of their
inflorescence is past; where one lives in the country
from June to October, the whole force should be applied to those plants, shrubs, and flowers which bloom
during these four months; and as a majority of our
country gentlemen do not get out to their places much
before June, and are apt to become very restless after
the early part of October, we think a selection of those
plants should be made most useful and attractive during
this time; and we do not know anything more effective
than the proper mingling of some of the large showy
exotics and tender evergreens we have mentioned.
Of course we do not suggest this as general, but merely
to those—and their number is now large—who have a
taste for planting the newer and more striking conifers.

In concluding this section we will merely add : that
with one or two exceptions, we have described only
those plants and shrubs which we have ourselves seen,
and which, in almost every instance, we have growing
upon our own place.   We believe that a correctness in
description, and an honest statement of the merits and
demerits of each plant, will, more than anything else,
contribute to the main end we have in view—the extension of the taste for planting the newer deciduous
and evergreen trees.

THE NEWER EVERGREEN ORNAMENTAL TREES.

Abies.   THE SPRUCE FIRS.

Abies alba nana (the Dwarf White spruce fir—or Prostrate
White spruce) is only a dwarf variety of our native White

Spruce fir, seldom growing more than a bush of three or four feet, and perfectly hardy, all over the United States.

A. a. glauca.—A very distinct and striking variety of the American White spruce, with very white, silvery leaves—originating in England, but hardy here.

A. a. minima.—Another minute English variety, being the dwarfest of all the spruces ; and we presume would be hardy in this country.

A. Brunoniana (the Indian hemlock spruce).—Classed by
Syn.   Carriere among the *Tsugas*, those kinds with
A. dumosa.   flat leaves, mostly glaucous below.

We are somewhat perplexed in making up our mind about the future condition of this charming tree, as to its availability. If it succeed at all, it will certainly require a good deal of coaxing. Our own experience has been very various. It has stood some winters well, and others, not as cold but possibly damper, seem to have destroyed it; and yet, Mr. Smith writes us from Newport, it has stood there three years. At Washington it is reported tender, as well as at Philadelphia, Flushing, and at Mr. Reids' nursery at Elizabethtown. We do not, however, see why it may not eventually prove hardy after a little acclimatization, since Dr. Hooker found it in Sikkin at an elevation of nine thousand to ten thousand feet on the side of Kunchinjinga, probably the loftiest peak in the world, where it reaches a height of seventy to eighty feet. Most persons would take it for a hemlock spruce, except that the under part of the leaves is perfectly white, forming, when moved by the wind, a beautiful blending of green and silver.

A. excelsa pygmœa—a very pretty dwarf variety of the Norway spruce, not exceeding a foot or so in height, but spreading very much. The specimens in our grounds do not seem affected by the severest winters.

A. e. monstrosa.—Another hardy variety of Norway spruce, with straggling habit, but destitute of branchlets, somewhat resembling the *araucaria imbricata* in appearance.

A. e. pendula.—Also a seedling of the Norway spruce, differing only in having its branches more drooping; hardy.

A. e. variegata.—A Variegated variety of our common Norway, pretty, distinctive, and hardy.

A. e. Clanbrasiliana (Lord Clanbrasil's variety).—Exceedingly dwarf and perfectly hardy; leaves, only half an inch long, and the mature plant not over three feet.

A. e. elegans.—A pretty Dwarf hardy variety, with slender gray foliage reaching the height of four or five feet.

A. e. diffusa, A. e. compacta, A. e. pumila, A. e. attenuata —are four Dwarf varieties of the Norway spruce, similar in growth and general appearance to those mentioned above, and very hardy. In fact, wherever the Norway spruce can be grown, these eight or ten dwarf varieties can, and when grouped with the dwarf pine, *P. strobus pumilis*, and the Dwarf Scotch fir, *P. sylvestris pumilis*, neither, of which ever exceed four or five feet, they make a very interesting and striking plantation.

A. Menziesii—(Menzies' fir) known also *A. Sitchensis*—is a tall tree, with light glaucous-colored foliage, growing sixty to seventy feet high ; a native of northern California and the island of Sitcha; quite hardy here. Our specimens, which have been out some five or six years, occasionally get scorched by the summer ; in the latitude of Philadelphia it does, likewise, very well, as also at Cincinnati, Newport, Washington, Boston, Flushing, in New Jersey, and even at Clinton, N. Y., when in shade.

A. obovata (Obovate-coned spruce), known and imported by *Syn.* us as *A. Wittmanniana*, is as yet com-
A. Schrenkiana. paratively new. Judging from the appear-
A. Ajanensis. ance of our specimens now, we should suppose it would prove hardy, which is most likely to be the case with firs coming from so high an altitude as the Altai mountains. It is also found in Siberia. It resembles the common spruce. It is quite hardy at Flushing, which is the only place we can discover where it has been tried.

A. orientalis (Eastern spruce).—A peculiar tree, with dense short foliage covering the branches on all sides, growing seventy to eighty feet high, and forming a conical-shaped head. A native of the Black Sea, on the loftiest mountains of Imeretia, in Upper Mongrelia; perfectly hardy here, and at Washington ; comparatively well at Newport, our youngest specimens here, were untouched even by the winters of 1856–7.

A. Smithiana (the Indian spruce).—This magnificent tree is found on the mountains from Bootan to Kafiristan, at an elevation of from 7,000 to 12,000 feet. It resembles somewhat in its size and habit of growth, the finest Norway spruce, though much more pendulous and graceful, and with a darker, richer foliage, especially when grown in the shade It occasionally reaches a height of 170 feet, though its usual average is 100 to 150. It is also found in China and Japan, where it is called " *Toranowo-momi* " (the Tiger's tail). Although we imported this tree some six to eight years ago, we have not as yet succeeded in raising any very fine specimens. When much exposed to the full action of the sun's rays, it becomes a dingy yellow green, and is very apt to lose its leader, and young plants are sometimes killed down to the snow-line. This is also the experience in the neighborhood of Philadelphia, Boston, and Columbus, though hardy at Cincinnati. When planted with us in the shade, however, it seems to do much better in retaining its leader, and we have little doubt it may, after some struggle, eventually be acclimatized, especially when planted in dry, gravelly, well-drained soil. At Chestnut Ilill, near Philadelphia, there are perfect specimens, eight to ten feet high, with leaders. We have no specimen at Wodenethe over six feet, though very broad in proportion. At Washington, it is returned to us as hardy and beautiful. The largest specimens in the public grounds, planted by Mr. Downing, in 1852, are five feet. At Newport, it is reported as hardier and finer than *A. excelsa* (the Common Norway), though at Messrs. Parsons,' at Flushing, Mr. Hogg's, near Yorkville, and Mr. Reid's, at Elizabethtown, the younger shoots are sometimes injured, and it does better in the shade. At Woodlawn, N. J. (Mr. Field's), the oldest specimens are seven feet high, and do not now suffer from the winter, perhaps from the redundancy of growth being slightly checked by having been moved several times. They have also borne cones, which at first were erect like the Picea's, but, afterwards pendulous like the Abies', which accounts for the confusion mentioned by Mr. Loudon, that has existed as to whether this tree was an abies or a picea.

Syn.
A. Morinda.
A. Khutrow.

A. Douglasii (the Douglas fir).—Another superb tree, respecting the hardihood of which, very much the same remarks we made about the preceding variety (*A. Smithiana*), will apply. Plants with us, in low, damp ground, suffer occasionally in color, if not in loss of leader, while those grown in the shade, or on an exposed hill-side, in poor, slaty soil, succeed admirably. This is also the case near Boston, at " Wellesley" (Mr. Hunnewell's), where trees, two years planted, are five feet high, and do admirably in the shade; while at Mr. Reid's, at Elizabethtown, it loses its leader in severe winters; and near Philadelphia, Mr. Meehan reports : " that so far it has not been satisfactory." At Washington, perfectly hardy ; at Newport, it wont stand; though at Augusta, Ga., and Cincinnati, it thrives well. The variety originates in the north-western part of North America, and along the banks of the Columbia River, where it is found in immense forests, and also on the Rocky Mountains, on the top of which, it rarely is more than a small bush, but becomes larger and more stately as it descends, until it reaches the altitude of one hundred and fifty to two hundred feet. Its foliage is very dark, and the tree generally resembles a superb balsam fir.

Syn.
Tsuga Douglasii.
Picea Douglasii.

A. Jezoensis (the Jezo fir), found in China, and the Island of Jezo, is probably hardy, though we have not heard of its being tested sufficiently to pronounce decidedly. It is quite striking. There has been a good deal of confusion in its classification, as to whether it is a spruce or Silver fir, and it would seem to be intermediate, though we believe with persistent cones. Our specimens, which are small, seem quite hardy, and are not very unlike in their general appearance, the *Torreya*, and also the *Cephalotaxus*.

Syn.
Picea Jezoensis.

ARAUCARIA.

This extraordinary and most distinguished genus of plants derives its name from Araucanos, a people of Chili, where the species known as *imbricata* greatly abounds, its seeds being used for food.

The only variety which approaches hardihood in this part of the country is the *A. imbricata*, (Chili pine), which when planted in sand and gravel on well drained soil, and in a shady wood, succeeds quite well—that is to say, we have specimens which withstood the severe winters of 1855-6-7, with no other protection than a few hemlock boughs, and came out perfectly bright and green in the spring, even with their leaders uninjured for the past three years. Both sun and wet are fatal to it, and in situations where there are no side-hills sloping to the north, it should be planted on the north of buildings, on little mounds, with at least the lower foot in the holes filled with stones for drainage. Mr. Saunders informs us that there are some fine healthy trees near Baltimore, with upright shoots. At Washington, a specimen planted, in 1852, by Mr. Downing, in the public grounds has succeeded admirably, though a little injured by the winter of 1856. It does not stand at Newport, and at Flushing, and in New Jersey succeeds only when sheltered ; so also at Cincinnati. In Augusta it is eminently successful. The other varieties, *A. Bidwili, A. Brasiliensis, A. Cunninghamii,* and *A. excelsa* (the beautiful Norfolk Island pine), are too tender for any but our extreme Southern States, though all thriving, except *excelsa,* in the open ground at Augusta, Ga. ; but for purposes of ornament to cultivated grounds in summer we know nothing more distinguished than these different varieties grown in tubs and protected in winter in a common green-house.

BIOTA.

The Chinese or Eastern arbor vitæ, so called to distinguish it from *Thuja,* the American or Western arbor vitæ.

B. orientalis, (Chinese arbor vitæ), which was but comparatively new, when this book was first published, has not proved quite as hardy or as available as was at first hoped; all our reports, from different parts of the country, speak of it in most cases as not quite hardy, at any rate doing better in protected situations. Even in New Jersey it is sometimes killed to the ground in severe winters. Our best returns are from Washington, where it is reported as very commonly planted and perfectly successful. At Woodlawn, N. J. (Mr Field's), there is a hedge of it many years planted, which suffered a great deal at first, but of late years, by severe cutting in the spring it seems to have become quite acclimatized.

B. orientalis glauca, and *B. argentea,* are new varieties, not yet, we think, introduced; the first a seedling of Messrs. Pince, of Exeter, England, of a very silvery appearance, and the latter resembling the *Aurea,* being silver instead of gold.

B. orientalis aurea, (the Golden arbor vitæ,) is a seedling of Messrs. Waterer, in England, we believe from the old *B. orientalis* (the Chinese arbor vitæ). The *B. aurea* is a pretty, dense, and beautifully compact little shrub, growing not over two or three feet high, of an exquisite delicate green in winter, and a golden color at the extremities of its branches in spring.

It is perfectly hardy with us, at Fishkill, though forty miles above us it does not stand well; but we have observed that our trees, now several years old, though untouched by the cold or sun, lose very much the compact pressed appearance so characteristic of the English plants, and its principal charm we think, on this account. In complete collections of evergreens this is one of the varieties we should recommend to be grown in pots and kept in the house during the winter, although there is no doubt of its hardihood here.

B. pendula. (Weeping arbor vitæ).—A bush or small tree,
Syn.

Thuja pendula,
Thuja filiformis.

growing ten to fifteen feet high, with very long, slender, pendulous branches; is one of the greatest acquisitions to our perfectly hardy trees. Our largest specimen, eight to ten feet, has survived our coldest winters and hottest summers for ten or twelve years, without the slightest protection. Nothing can well be prettier or more graceful than this charming little tree. We do not know why this should not be hardy in our most northern States, though, we understand, it is sometimes killed near Philadelphia; yet near Boston, and at Washington, it does as well as here. It was at one time supposed to be a hybrid between the Common Red cedar and an arbor vitæ, and to have originated in a nursery in England; but Dr. Siebold having discovered the plant wild in China, finally decided the question.

B. orientalis gracilis.—This variety, which we have received
under the latter name, *Nepalensis,* is perfectly hardy
Syn. and much more slender and graceful than the
B. Nepalensis. common Chinese. It is found in Nepaul and
Northern India. We consider it one of the most interesting of
the arbor vitæ.

B. Tartarica (Tartarian arbor vitæ).—A dense conical bush
Syn. growing ten feet high, a native of Tartary ; quite
B. pyramidalis. distinctive. Our specimen, eight feet high, has
Thuja australis. always proved perfectly hardy.

We are inclined to believe that this variety may be often
confounded with and sold for what is called the Siberian arbor
vitæ, and the place of its origin would seem to justify this ; but
we do not find, in all our authorities or in any of the English
or French catalogues, any mention of the Siberian arbor vitæ,
except as a synonym of *T. occidentalis* (the American arbor
vitæ), which, what is known in this country as Siberian, certainly is not. It is also associated with Warreana, though the
latter came from Nootka Sound, and would seem to be identical with Don's *plicata.*

Cedrus. THE CEDAR.

C. Atlantica (the Mount Atlas cedar), or better known in
Syn. this country as the Silver cedar of Lebanon, is only
C. argentea. a variety of the ordinary Cedar of Lebanon with
glaucous leaves. It is not impossible, however, but what it
may be in certain localities hardier, since it thrives perfectly at
Newport, when the common Cedar of Lebanon is cut down and
not unfrequently killed. This is also the report from Flushing.

As all the remarks, we propose to make about the Cedar of
Lebanon, apply to this tree, we shall refer our readers to the
succeeding pages.

C. deodara (the Deodar or Indian Cedar).—The anticipations
Syn. formed of this most graceful evergreen in the
Pinus deodara. first edition of this book, we truly regret to say,
have not been generally fulfilled. It grows so readily and so
rapidly, particularly in the later autumn months, that it is with

great reluctance we feel constrained to admit it is not to be de. pended upon. It is certainly the most delusive of all evergreens. We have upon this place raised specimens twelve to fifteen feet high, as perfect as could be, but which the winters of 1855–6 severely injured, and the subsequent winter finished to the snow-line. These trees are now about eight or nine feet high, with several leaders, and nearly fifty feet in circumference, mostly holding their color well so far this winter, though having been subjected to a temperature, for two days, of 15° below zero. The fault of the tree (if so charming a tree can have any fault) is its habit, like the *Cryptomeria* and *Taxodium sempervirens*, and many other of the new evergreens, of making a late autumnal growth without ripening off its wood.

The fact that the tree below the snow-line almost always appears fresh and green, proves, we think, quite satisfactorily, that some protection, and no or little sun, will go far towards establishing its hardihood. A wood, or the north side ot buildings, will accomplish this; and if to this, we add such a preparation of soil as will retard rather than stimulate the tree, so that by accomplishing an early growth it may ripen off its wood, we think we may again hope to acclimatize the Deodar, which as now grown in the Middle States, hardly amounts to more than a bush, annually increasing in amplitude, but not in height. There are portions of this country, in the neighborhood of Washington possibly, and in Southern Virginia, and about that latitude, and as far south as Augusta, Ga., where it succeeds admirably. In the extreme south it suffers from the sun in summer as much as it does here from the sun in winter. There are, however, specimens at Mr. Affleck's, near Natchez, twenty-five to thirty feet high, and feathering to the ground. At Flushing, L. I., in Ohio, in New Jersey, and near New York, it does best in some shelter ; though at "Woodlawn," near Princeton, a specimen, ten feet high, and thirty-three in circumference, stands well in the most exposed situations. When first imported, it was supposed to be *hardier* than the Cedar of Lebanon, but subsequent experience does not confirm this—at least in our case.

C. deodara viridis (the Green deodar), *C. deodara robusta* (the Robust deodar), are only varieties of the common deodar—the former being of a slenderer habit, and more vivid green, and the latter much coarser and stouter. As these two varieties are out with us for the first time this winter, we can not as yet say how hardy they may prove, and we have no returns from any other place.

We may as well, perhaps, add here, that Mr. Meehan reports, near Philadelphia, "all Deodars on wet low soils are uninjured, while those on dry are killed outright." This is the contrary of our theory and experience here certainly, but facts are better than arguments, and time alone will show whether a damp or dry soil is most congenial to this plant.

C. Lebani (Cedar of Lebanon.)—This is another variety of

Syn. the genus *Cedrus*, so distinct and remarkable
Pinus cedrus. that we regret being compelled to say it has
Cedrus Phœnicia. also fallen short of what was expected and hoped of it ; and we doubt, if, with a few exceptions, there are more specimens now in this country, or much larger, than when Mr. Downing wrote his first edition. After the specimen at Throgg's Neck (Mr. Ashe's), the next best we know of is at Woodlawn (Mr. Field's), at Princeton, N. J., where a specimen (Fig. 38) planted in 1842 is now thirty-six feet high, bearing cones, and may be considered beyond all risk ; and also some trees at Laurel Hill Cemetery, near Philadelphia, planted by Mr. J. J. Smith, the founder of that most lovely and interesting of rural cemeteries.

These trees were only slightly browned in the severe winters of 1855–6. But Mr. Field's soil is a light sandy loam, and that of Laurel Hill, a gravel or disentegrated rock, lying high above the surface of the Schuylkill, and so protected by trees as to allow even the Gordonia pubescens to flourish to the height of forty feet, strewing the ground in September with its fragrant blossoms. In both these cases, as in our own, the soil has been dry, and the tree not stimulated by a damp, rich position ; and although the winter of 1855–6 reduced, with us, a tree of fifteen feet to eight, yet other specimens, a little less exposed to the full influence of the morning sun, suffered simply a little browning of the leaves, and have since gone through an ordinary winter without any injury, leading us to the conclusion that in this latitude, the Cedar of Lebanon may be considered fairly hardy, but " slow ;" and though not growing with much rapidity, and occasionally liable to lose a little in the winter of what it has made in the summer, yet on the whole, like the tortoise in the fable, we believe it will come out first in the end, and should be much more generally planted.

At Washington, Mr. Saul writes us, it is perfectly hardy, specimens in the Capitol grounds being twelve feet high ; and at Yorkville, it is returned as hardy ; but at Flushing and at Elizabethtown its reputation is a little qualified, though supposed to become hardy as it advances. At Augusta, Ga., it is straggling and uncertain; and in Ohio, both in the neighborhood of Columbus and Cincinnati, it is very much injured by severe winters.

Cephalotaxus. The Cluster-Flowered Yews.

This fine genus, as yet very new, deriving its name (Κεφαλη —kephale—a head, and Ταξις—taxis—arrangement), from the flowers and fruit growing in close, globular heads, is likely, we think, to become a great acquisition in this country. With us it has proved quite as hardy as the Common English yew, and although like that plant, the foliage is much finer and darker in the shade, yet we have had no difficulty, for the past three years, in growing it in the sun.

The only varieties as yet known here, we think, are :

Cephalotaxus Fortuni—mas. and femina—(Fortune's Male and Female cephalotaxus), found by Mr. Fortune in the north of China, particularly in the province Yang-Sin, and also in Japan, growing from forty to fifty feet high—the foliage, not unlike that of the torreya, is longer and wider than the yew. With us the male plant seems the most hardy, the female having suffered somewhat in the winter of 1856-7.

C. drupacea—(The Plum-fruited cephalotaxus), is another fine variety which has proved hardy with us. It resembles very much the Irish yew, and also the *Taxus,* or more properly the *Podocarpus Japonica.* Mr. Carriere, in his excellent work on Conifers, makes it a synonym of the Female cephalotaxus Fortuni, but our plant certainly differs much from this, in having both darker and shorter foliage; grows about 20 feet high.

Cephalotaxus pedunculata, and *C. umbraculifera,* are the

two remaining varieties of the genus, and we think, are likely to prove as hardy as the preceding ones.

Chamœcyparis.   THE WHITE CEDAR.

Chamœcyparis sphœroida variegata—sometimes called both *Thuja* and *Cupressus variegata*—is, beyond doubt, we think, a beautiful golden variety of the White cedar, great use of which is made in England, combined with the Golden and Silver yews, and the Golden and Variegated arbor vitæ. We have had it out but one winter, but we see no reason why it should not prove hardy.

Cryptomeria.   THE JAPAN CEDAR.

Cryptomeria.—(The Japan cedar) ; from *Kruptos*, hidden, and *Meris*, a part.

C. Japonica.—This exquisite tree, deservedly called the " Queen of Evergreens," is a native of China, growing sixty to one hundred feet high. It was discovered in 1784, by Professor Thunbergh, and only introduced into England by Mr. Fortune, in 1844, where it succeeds perfectly well and is the, or certainly one of the most charming of the newer evergreens. With us, in the Southern States, it succeeds admirably ; but farther north it is apt to suffer from our severe winters. At Wodenethe we have little trouble in growing it in a wood, and we have one specimen, which we are in the habit of starving in very poor soil, and on a side hill quite exposed to the strong west winds, which has been out five years and does not even brown. This tree has a worse habit than the Deodar, of growing late into the autumn. Where this can be partially prevented, by thin, light soil, especially with some shade from a wood or buildings, we believe, as far north as Fishkill, it can be grown, though, perhaps, never to develop its full and graceful beauties. Near Philadelphia, at Chestnut Hill, it sometimes suffers, though last winter not at all ; and at Laurel Hill it has stood for several severe winters, without injury, under the shade of other trees. At Newport, it is tolerably hardy, there being specimens ten feet high. Near Boston, the roots keep alive, but no progress is made in the tree. At Washington, there is a specimen in La Fayette Square, planted by Mr. Downing in 1852, and never protected, which has reached fourteen feet, and is very beautiful. At Elizabethtown, it succeeds when sheltered. At Flushing, the extremities of the branches suffer in severe winters, and at Yorkville, near New York, it is considered hardy under favorable circumstances, as also at "Woodlawn," N. J., the residence of Mr. Field, where there are specimens twenty-nine feet in circumference, though not proportionally high. In Ohio, it is killed to the ground in severe winters. This is another of those evergreens, which grown in tubs, ten to fifteen feet high, and planted (plunged) out in summer, would produce most agreeable effects in ornamental grounds, with no care in winter beyond removing it to a cellar or cool green-house.

C. Japonica viridis, C. Japonica lobbii, C. Japonica nana.— These three are only varieties of the one above described, and we presume no more hardy, unless it be *Lobbii*, introduced from the Dutch Botanic gardens at Batavia. *C. nana*, which is a mere dwarf-bush, always seems to suffer with us more from the sun in summer than the cold in winter. We have a fourth variety, received from France, called *Pendula*, rather more slender and pendulous than *Japonica*.

CUNNINGHAMIA.

Cunninghamia.—A small tree, native of Japan and China, named after its discoverer, Mr. Cunningham. There are but two varieties, of which *C. Sinensis* or *C. lanceolata*, is the one most generally cultivated in this country. In its general character and appearance, it resembles very much *Araucaria imbricata*, with lance-like leaves, though lighter green. With us it stands generally better than the *araucaria*, and will make an admirable substitute for this tree, if it should prove hardy.

At Baltimore, we have seen a plant six or eight feet high, and apparently quite vigorous. At Newport, it is also regarded as quite hardy, and a great accession. Specimens there are six feet high, and near Natchez, fifteen to eighteen feet, nearly half its full size, and always untouched by winter. At Flushing it stands about as well as the *cryptomeria*, and will probably prove about as reliable as this tree; as yet it is comparatively new, and we have but few returns about it.

C. glauca, the remaining variety, differs only in its leaves being silvery.

Cupressus. THE TRUE CYPRESS.

This fine genus—not mentioned by Mr. Downing in the early edition of his work, and of which there are now some twenty varieties known and cultivated in England—seems peculiarly unsuited to this climate. The cypress is found indigenous in the south of Europe, China, Mexico, the East Indies, and a few varieties, erroneously classed among our cedars and junipers, in this country. There are but three varieties which may be considered as fairly hardy, and as some of these are better known under different names, we may say there is not one hardy cypress, distinctly known and recognized as such, that is cultivated in the northern and middle portion of the United States. The half-hardy varieties, such as *attenuata, excelsa, sempervirens, Goveniana, Lusitanica, torulosa,* and a few others, can probably never be cultivated, unless in pots, except at the extreme south. The only species we can rely upon here will be :

C. Nootkaensis (the Nootka Sound cypress), but better known here as *Thuiopsis Borealis*, is a tall ever-
Syn.
Thuiopsis Tchugatskoy. green tree, reaching the height of one hundred feet, with widely expanded branches, very flexible ; as it advances, the limbs are covered with small blisters, which, on being punctured, emit a fine aromatic balsam, whence is derived another synonym, *abies aromatica.* It is also found in Russia, near Lake Tschondskoe. It is but yet very new, even in England ; our specimens have been out two winters and are perfectly hardy, as it will probably prove to be in every northern part of the United States.

C. pendula.—There are three Weeping cypresses, one a synonym of *Thuja filiformis,* or *Biota filiformis* (Weeping arbor vitæ), which we have already described as very beautiful and perfectly hardy ; a second, a synonym of *C. torulosa,* a variety of which we have mentioned above as only adapted for the extreme south;* and a third, a synonym of *C. funebris.*

C. funebris (the Weeping or Funebral cypress), is another tree like the Deodar cedar and *cryptomeria,* of which much was expected, but little obtained.

It was first noticed, we believe, by Lord McCartney in his expedition to China, who described it as having the appearance as an immense evergreen Weeping willow, but it was only in-

---

* Mr. Buist thinks this may prove hardy near Philadelphia.

troduced into England, many years subsequently, by Mr. Fortune, from the celebrated tea country "Wheychou," in the north of China. It is described as attaining a height of sixty feet, with horizontal branches, sweeping upwards with its graceful curves and dropping again at the points. We observe, from our returns, it has been tried in many parts of the United States, but, so far, has only succeeded well at Augusta, Ga., where both Messrs. Berckmans and Mr. Redmond report most favorably as to its hardihood; with us it has succeeded but indifferently, though having had every advantage from poor soil and a protecting wood. Even in Washington, it is too tender to be relied on.

C. Lawsoniana (Lawson's cypress), the most beautiful of the cypresses, if not of trees, raised from seed in 1857, collected and sent to England by Mr. Murray. It grows one hundred feet high, and is found along the banks of streams and in the vallies of the mountains of Northern California, in latitude 40° to 42°.

There is one very distinctive characteristic about it, which we have observed, and by which it can readily be recognized, the drooping of the leading shoots like the Deodar. The tops of the branches hang down like an ostrich feather. It is said to resemble the *C. Nutkaensis* (*Thuiopsis Borealis*), described above, but our plants are much more slender and graceful.

We have strong hopes this charming evergreen may be acclimatized. Our trees are out for their first winter. It is also on trial at Cincinnati. It is still very rare and expensive; small plants, eight to ten inches high, costing a guinea.

Dacrydium. DACRYDIUM.

A very rare genus, found only in New Zealand and the East Indies, and so tender as hardly worth while being mentioned, except that a new variety, lately introduced into England, promises to be hardy there, and may consequently be in certain parts of the United States. This variety, *D. Franklinii* (Huon pine), is found in Van Dieman's Land, and becomes a tree of one hundred feet high, thickly covered with spray; the branches are numerous, dense, long, and very flexible in our plants (in pots) like whip-cords. We have not received any reports of this tree.

D. Cupressinum (the Cypress-like dacrydium), though not hardy, is well worthy of cultivation in pots. It is exceedingly graceful and pretty, with slender, delicate, almost thread-like, drooping shoots, thickly clothed with small, spiny leaves. A specimen we have, about eight feet high, is much admired. There are several other varieties for the conservatory.

Fitz Roya Patagonia. THE PATAGONIAN FITZ ROYA.

A large evergreen tree, found in the mountains of Patagonia growing one hundred feet high, but introduced within the past three years into England, where so far it stands well. Our specimens are out for their first winter. We have every reason to suppose this may survive our climate; since in its native country it diminishes from one hundred feet in the valleys, to only a few inches on the borders of perpetual congelation.

Glyptostrobus. THE EMBOSSED CYPRESS.

This new genus, which has been but lately introduced under this name (derived from " *Glypho*," embossed, and " *strobus*," a cone), but has been previously by some botanists regarded as a *Taxodium ;* is a native of China, where it is called the Water pine.

The only variety of this genus, apparently recognized as distinct by the English, is *G. heterophyllus*, known also as *Thuja pensilis*, and *Taxodium Japonicum ;* although Endlicher has another and very beautiful variety, which we have found perfectly hardy at Wodenethe, more so even than *G. heterophyllus*. This is the *Glyptostrobus sinensis pendulus*, which is also recognized under this name by the French arboriculturists, though in the English Pinetums, and by Gordon, in his very excellent work on Conifers, it is classed as a *Taxodium ;* and we have imported it from France as *Glyptostrobus sinensis pendulus ;* from England, as *Taxodium sinense pendulum ;* while in our nurseries, it is sold as the Weeping deciduous cypress; and we think it is generally regarded by those who have it in this country (which are very few), as identical with our Southern deciduous or Swamp cypress, and only a pendulous and more delicate variety of it; this is also the classification of the English. Under this embarrassment, we sent specimens of the three varieties to that distinguished botanist, Dr. Gray, who replied that, in his opinion, "the Genus *Glyptostrobus* will be adopted as distinct from *Taxodium*, though most resembling it;" that *Glyptostrobus s. pendulus* and *Taxodium s. pendulum* are the same thing, under different names; "while *G. heterophyllus* is the allied species, and probably not distinct."

The *Taxodium pendulum* is one of the most graceful and exquisite little trees, which will survive the rigor of our northern winters. With us, as before stated, it is untouched by the severest weather.

The resemblance to the Southern deciduous or Swamp cypress, which has led to its being confounded with this variety is chiefly in the autumn, when the leaves are expanded and spread out very much like it; but in the earlier spring months, they are twisted and compressed around the stem, having a very peculiar wavy and curled appearance.

At Newport, in New Jersey, and at Flushing, this tree is returned as hardy and very superb.

Juniperus. THE JUNIPER.

Of this large and important family of plants, *J. Virginiana*, commonly called the Red Cedar, was the only variety mentioned by Mr. Downing. The name itself is derived from the Celtic word *Juneprus*, meaning rough or rude, from the stiff character of the plants, or from *Juniores pariens*, the old and young leaves and berries being on the plant at the same time. There are some twenty-six to thirty varieties known and cultivated in Europe, of which nineteen or twenty have reached the collections in this country.

Of these, alphabetically, the first on the list is *J. Bedfordiana*, a slender variety of *J. Virginiana*, found on

the island of Barbadoes, and the Windward Islands, and
Syn.
J. Barbadensis.   erroneously cultivated by these three names,
J. Gossainthania.   by each of which we have it. We observe from our returns, that this tree, under
these three names, is also pretty generally cultivated at
the principal nurseries in this country; and while *J. Gossainthania* is generally considered perfectly hardy, and *J. Bedfordiana* nearly as much so at Newport, Washington, and
New Jersey, *J. Barbadensis* is reported as tender in the one
or two places where tried, from which, it is evident, there is
some confusion in the synonym. It is a pretty, graceful, slender
tree, with drooping branches; when fully grown, some fifty feet
high.

J. Californica (Californian juniper).—Is an extremely pretty,
delicate variety from California, with glaucous leaves, attaining
an altitude, in its native country, of forty feet. We received
this variety from Messrs. Ellwanger & Barry two years since,
and have not yet ventured it out. It is more rare in England
than here, being classed among those of which little is known.

J. Canadensis (Canadian or Common juniper).—This well
Syn.   known species in our Northern States, and the
J. depressa.   northern parts of North America, Labrador, New-
J. nana.   foundland, &c., is merely a bush, with a loose open
head, from three to five feet high. It is sometimes confounded
with the Dwarf juniper of Europe, but has a smaller and
lighter foliage, with rather more of an upright tendency; perfectly hardy.

J. Chinensis (Chinese juniper).—A very great acquisition,
Syn.   from China and Japan, perfectly hardy with us
J. Thumbergii.   in the most severe winters, and a most beautiful
variety. It is dioecious, the male plant being
distinguished with male flowers of a bright yellow color in
the spring, and very showy when fully grown, attaining a
height of fifteen to twenty feet. The female variety, known
and sold also as *J. Reevesiana*, and *J. flagelleformis*, is rather
smaller than the male; berries small, of a glaucous violet brown
when ripe. We strongly recommend these trees, especially
the male, as being perhaps, the finest of the really hardy
junipers.

J. communis (Common juniper).—This plant, which is the

Syn. ordinary juniper of Europe, is not the same as

J. Cracovia. the *J. communis*, or *Canadensis* of this country.

J. vulgaris. It is found generally on the Continent, and in
England, a loose, spreading tree or bush, of twelve to eighteen
feet high ; while on tops of mountains it becomes a straggling
shrub. There are three varieties of the common European or
English juniper, all well known, and cultivated in the United
States, viz. :

J. communis Suecica (Swedish juniper).—A native of Norway, Denmark, Sweden, and Russia, a conical, upright growing
bush, of from twelve to twenty feet, very hardy, we believe, in
every part of the country.

J. communis Hibernica (Irish juniper).—A neat, pretty,
slender variety, found on the mountains of Ireland, more
upright and delicate than the Swedish, though resembling it.
It sometimes suffers with us from the sun in midsummer, but
rarely from the cold, and this we see by our returns, is its
character generally.

J. communis compressa—which we imported some years
since, as *Hispanica*, or Spanish juniper—seems quite as hardy
with us as either of the other varieties, being compact and close
in its habit, but with a less vivid green ; it comes from the
Apennines. There is another Spanish juniper, called *J. thu-
ripera*, from the mountains of Spain, forming a dense, handsome,
pyramidal tree, tapering to a point, and growing to the height
of thirty feet, which we also find entirely hardy.

J. Japonica (Japan juniper)—is a small, hardy, bush from

Syn. the mountains of Japan, not growing over

Chinensis procumbens. one or two feet high, and distinct.

J. nana (the Dwarf juniper).—Common all over Europe,

Syn. England, Scotland ; seldom growing over one foot

J. Alpina, high, but spreading. It is so often taken for *J.*

J. Sibirica,
and eight *Canadensis* of this country, as to be constantly con-

others. founded and grown for it.

J. oblonga pendula (Weeping juniper)—unquestionably the

Syn. most attractive of the junipers ; a small tree

J. pendula vera. fifteen to twenty feet high, from the Hakone
ridge of mountains in the island of Niphon in Japan ; perfectly

FIG. 94.—THE SCALED JUNIPER, at Woodlawn, Residence of R S. Field, Esq, near Princeton, N. J.
Height, 44 feet, Circumference, 29 feet.

FIG. 93.—WEEPING JUNIPER, at Wodenethe.
Age, 10 years, Height 6 feet.

hardy with us, and the most graceful and pendulous of evergreens. Our best specimen (Fig. 93) has been planted ten years—it is nearly six feet high, though only a few inches when set out. We find it transplants badly and recovers slowly, and when necessary to be moved, should be balled in winter, or moved with greatest care. It takes several years to get under way, and often dies back from sun, but, when once started, succeeds admirably.

J. occidentalis (Western juniper).—We doubt very much if *Syn. J. excelsa.* the variety is, in this country, correct, at any rate we have no returns about it ; and if here at all it may be under its synonym of *excelsa*, with which it, and many other junipers, are frequently confounded. It is found, at an elevation of five thousand feet, on the Klamet mountains in Oregon, and also on the Rocky mountains, where it becomes an umbrella-shaped tree of forty feet, with a pretty silver bloom ; it will, no doubt prove quite hardy here.

J. oxycedrus (Prickly juniper).—This variety is reported as *Syn. J. monspeliensium.* hardy in Jersey. Our plants are out for the first winter, and we cannot, therefore, report upon them now. It is found on the Apennines, at an elevation of three thousand feet, in France, also in Spain, and Portugal. Our specimens are attractive from being more or less glaucous on both sides of their leaves ; the branches are angular and rather pendant ; it grows eight to ten feet high, and its berries are used in flavoring gin.

J. Phœnicia (Phœnician juniper).—This species, forming a bush of fifteen to twenty feet in height, of a beautiful pyramidal shape, is found on the rocks along the shores of the Mediterranean, near Nice and Calabria. We have favorable reports of its hardihood from New Jersey ; we have not tried it. There is another variety, *J. P. Lycia* (Lycian juniper), a much smaller bush than the preceding, and greener foliage, originating in the Levant, but also found, according to Prof. Pallas, in Siberia—it having been introduced in the Russian gardens as *juniperus davurica.* This is the juniper from which the gum called olibanum is collected, so much used for incense in religious ceremonies on the Continent. This, no doubt, will prove hardy in the United States

J. prostrata (Prostrate-branch juniper).—This interesting species, so well known all over the Middle and Northern States, need hardly be described; with us .t is a common road-side plant, and very much neglected in consequence. We do

Syn.
J. repens,
J. humilis,
J. sabina prostrata.

not really know a finer object than this juniper, well grown in ornamental grounds where it has ample space to develop itself There are two specimens at Mr. Field's in Princeton, truly superb, resembling immense great evergreen beds, not over two feet high, but thirty feet in circumference.

J. recurva (Weeping Indian juniper).—This is certainly a very charming variety, and we wish we could say it is perfectly hardy ; with us, heretofore, in the

Syn.
J. Nepalensis.

winter, it becomes very shabby and dingy, having much the clouded look produced by the web of the red spider ; this, however, is where it has been exposed to the winter's sun. We have now some specimens planted in a wood, and well protected, which we hope may do better.

Mr. Hogg writes us that at Yorkville, when sheltered, it may be regarded as hardy ; and this is reported also from Flushing, L. I., and in New Jersey ; at Washington it did well until in jured by the winter of 1855–6. The only unqualified return of entire success is from Augusta, Ga., where it is grown without trouble. *J. recurva densa* is the male form of this variety ; with us, the male is more dwarf, and of much closer and thicker habit. The plant itself originates in Nepaul and in Bhotan, at an elevation of eight to ten thousand feet, where it makes a small and beautiful tree ; at greater elevation it becomes a straggling bush.

J. religiosa (the Pencil or Incense juniper). We believe there is no question of the hardihood of this juniper; although no Indian conifer seems to have been more confused than this species We presume, however, that the *J. excelsa* (the Tall juniper) of our American nurseries is

Syn.
J. excelsa.
[Perhaps the tall Juniper of the American nurseries.]

not properly the *J. excelsa* of the Indian botanists, which is the true *J. religiosa*. The first is undoubtedly hardy, becoming a handsome, pyramidal tree, thirty to forty feet high ; a native of the islands in the Grecian Archipelago, Syria, Armenia, and

Georgia; the second is quite hardy with us; and we have no report from any other place. It resembles very much the Chinese Juniper, and it is often confounded with *Cupressus torulosa*. It obtains its name from its wood being burned in temples on festivals, and also from being used in cedar pencils. It is a native of Nepaul, where it rarely descends below an altitude of ten thousand feet; above an elevation of fifteen thousand feet, it degenerates into a scraggy bush; while in favorable situations, it forms a large, magnificent tree of sixty to eighty feet. It gets its name of *religiosa* from being usually employed for the Buddhist temples, and in their religious ceremonies.

J. sabina (the Common savin), a low, loose-growing bush, not, as it strikes us, particularly handsome, growing six or seven feet high, and native of the Lower Alps, Appenines, and the Altain and Taurian mountains. There is another and prettier variety, *J. s. variegatœ* (Variegated savin), with its leaves curiously striped or blotched with yellow, and intermingling with the green, making a striking contrast. We have grown these many years without any protection.

J. squamata (Scaly-leaved juniper), a large, procumbent, many branched shrub, growing four or five *Syn.* feet high, and very spreading, from the *J. dumosa Lambertina.* mountains of Nepaul and the Bhotan Alps, also in Cashmere. It seems to thrive on the loftiest mountains at elevations of eleven, twelve, and even fifteen thousand feet, forming extensive beds or masses like carpets, covering immense spaces; the foliage is a bright, vivid green, and large glossy, purplish black fruit.

The finest specimen we know in this country, and one of the most extraordinary and striking objects we ever saw among evergreens, is the *J. squamata*, at Woodlawn, N. J., Mr. Field's (Fig. 94), which was obtained from Mr. Buist, in Philadelphia, in the spring of 1851; and though only seven years planted, is now a bush of twenty-nine feet in circumference, having one leading shoot which, after ascending perpendicularly four and a half to five feet, as suddenly descends again at an acute angle to the ground, resembling somewhat an elongated ox-bow, the lower branches radiating from the stem.

and spreading in every direction with a marvellous profusion into a perfect circle. It is unquestionably hardy all over the colder portion, at least, of the United States.

Pseudo-larix kœmferi.   GOLDEN OR CHINESE LARCH.

This properly belongs to the deciduous class of trees ; though when first sent to England by Mr. Fortune,

Syn.
Abies kœmferi.
Pinus   do.

it was supposed to be a fir, and Mr. Lambert classed it among the pines. It is still very rare and very expensive; plants only two inches high costing seven dollars in England. We know of but one other specimen in this country, besides our own, which was too small to venture out this winter, though we intend doing so next. It will, no doubt, prove hardy, coming as it does from the northern provinces of China. The leaves are a beautiful bright green, when young, but before autumn assume a fine golden yellow. There being no specimens in England over a foot high, we have no further description of this tree.

Libocedrus.   INCENSE CEDAR.

This exquisite genus (for all the varieties are alike beautiful) is another of Mr. Endlicher's introductions from Chili and New Zealand. The name is derived from *libanos*, incense, and *cedrus*, the cedar. It is found upon the Andes of Chili, where it grows to the height of sixty to eighty feet, and bears so close a resemblance to the arbor vitæ, as, by many, to be classed with this tree, having the same pyramidal habit, thickly clothed with beautifully delicate, glaucous and light green imbricated leaves from its very base.

There are but four varieties, three of which have been imported, by collectors of evergreens, into this country, viz. : *Chiliensis, Doniana* and *decurrens*, of which the first and last only approach to some hope of being acclimatized.

L. Chiliensis, we have had several years. Our oldest plant survived three winters on an open lawn, protected simply by

cedar boughs, but was destroyed by the severe weather of '55–6.
At Elizabethtown, N. J., there are specimens five feet high,
and, it is reported to us, as *nearly* hardy there. At Washington,
and on Long Island it has not been sufficiently tested to be
pronounced upon. The only unqualified return of entire success is from Augusta, Ga., where it stands admirably and
becomes one of their most lovely evergreens.

L. Doniana (Don's arbor vitæ)—even more than the preceding resembles an arbor vitæ, and is more
generally known and sold as a *Thuja* than a
Libocedrus; it has the appearance of a most
exquisite fern, being of a peculiarly soft yellowish green, and
most delicate habit. There is no hope, we fear, of acclimatizing
this beautiful variety, except, perhaps, in the Southern States ;
but nothing can well be prettier or more attractive than this
and the preceding variety (*L. Chiliensis*), grown in pots or tubs.

Syn.
Thuja Doniana.

L. decurrens, the third and last variety, being more properly
an arbor vitæ, has been removed to that genus, we shall therefore describe it under its appropriate head of *Thuja*.

Picea. THE SILVER FIR.

In contradistinction to Abies, the Spruce fir is derived from
pix (pitch)—this variety producing an abundance of resin, and
having their cones *erect* and nearly cylindrical, while the cones
of the *Abies* (Spruce fir) are *pendant* and persistent for a long
time. They are found in Europe, Asia, and North America
and are, we believe, without exception perfectly hardy in the
middle and northern portions of the United States, and a very
great addition to our ornamental evergreens.

P. amabilis (the lovely Silver fir)—one of the latest additions to this tribe of plants, still rare and very
costly. There are no plants of any size in
his country. It stands well at Beach Clyffe,
the residence of Mr. Kane, at Newport, and
also at Flushing, and we presume it may prove hardy at Boston.
It is a magnificent tree in its native forests on the mountains
of Northern California, reaching an altitude of two hundred

Syn.
P. lasiocarpa.
Pinus lasiocarpa.

and fifty feet, with a naked stem of sixty feet. It was discovered by Mr. Jeffrey.

P. balsamea (the Balm of Gilead fir), has already been described in the early edition of this work, and is too well known as the common Balsam fir of the country to require further remarks.

P. balsamea longifolia, is a much finer and equally hardy variety, with longer leaves, introduced from Booth's nursery, at Hamburgh.

P. balsamea variegata—A variegated variety of our Common balsam—pretty and hardy—the new growth being yellow; though attractive in the spring, yet when the new shoots become ripened, the bright yellow becomes a little dingy, and we should hardly give it a prominent place in plantations. We have also a variety with a silvery instead of a golden variegation.

P. Bracteata (Leafy-bracted Silver fir).—This is a very rare variety as yet in this country, and will probably prove as hardy as P. Webbiana, and, like it, be apt to lose its leader. It was discovered by Douglas on the mountains of Columbia river, and afterwards in Upper California. It is a tall, slender-growing tree, one hundred and twenty feet high, straight as an arrow, and only two or three feet in diameter; sometimes only the upper third of the tree is clothed with branches.

Syn.
Abies Bracteata.

P. Cephalonica (Mount Enos fir).—This is perhaps one of the finest and most reliable of the new Silver firs. We have specimens eight and ten feet high, perfectly untouched by the remarkable winters of 1855–6, and without any advantages of position or protection.

It is called the Wild cedar by the Greeks, and was first sent home by General Napier, when Governor of Cephalonia. It has since been discovered on the different mountains of Greece, on the Sacred Apollo, on Mount Parnassus, on Mount Ætna, and also on Mount Olympus; it has, consequently, among its other merits, at least that of having early classical associations. A full grown tree is about sixty feet high.

P. Fraseri (Fraser's Silver fir).—A variety probably of our common Balsam fir, a little lighter, we think, in color; supposed to have originated in the mountains of Carolina and Pennsylvania. Neither

Syn.
Pinus Fraseri.
Abies do.

Carriere nor Gordon seem to place it anywhere else; though we have trees sent to us from Vermont, by President Wheeler, of Burlington, which he thinks identical with the southern variety; and we must confess we quite coincide with him, though they may prove some sport of our ordinary double spruce. At any rate, both varieties are as hardy as possible.

P. Fraseri Hudsonica (Hudson Bay Silver fir).—A pretty, flattish Dwarf variety of *P. Fraseri*, forming a dense close bush, never over three or four feet high, and, of course, a perfectly hardy tree, coming, as it does, from the Hudson Bay Company's territories.

P. nobilis (Noble Silver fir).—This superb variety well de-
Syn. serves its name, reaching as it does an altitude of two
Pinus nobilis. hundred feet, with regularly horizontal and spreading
Abies do. branches, and cinnamon-colored bark, forming immense forests upon the mountains of California. It was a discovery of Mr. Jeffrey, and proves unquestionably hardy wherever it has been tried. We have had it five or six years; but our trees being raised from seed, instead of being grafted, were very small (three inches only) when planted, and are not over two to three feet high now; and though fine in color and habit, do not yet show that grand characteristic which induced Mr. Downing, when in England, to describe it as the most majestic of evergreens. At Elvaston Castle, there are specimens, says Mr. Buist (in his account of his visit to that remarkable place), finer than the Araucaria excelsa (the Norfolk Island pine). It is perfectly hardy near Boston, at Flushing, New York, Baltimore, &c.; and will prove equally so in all the middle portions, at least, of the United States.

P. Nordmanniana (Nordmann's Silver fir).—Another superb
Syn. Silver fir, quite as hardy as the preceding,
Abies Nordmanniana. and as fine; indeed, we think even finer,
Pinus do. when young. We have had it at Wodenethe four or five years, and it has never suffered in our severest winters. It comes from the mountains of the Crimea, and reaches a growth of one hundred feet.

P. pectinata (Common Silver fir).—A lofty tree, growing one hundred to one hundred and fifty feet high, found all over the Alps, and also on the Apennines and Pyrenees; and yet, strange to say, it is somewhat capricious in the United States, and among our returns, we find in many places it is apt to lose its leader. This we believe, however, only takes place in young, and consequently succulent plants, which, as they advance in age, acquire a habit of solidifying, as it were, their growth, and escape injury. We have specimens fifteen to eighteen feet high, which are very perfect, and never suffer. The finest specimen we know in the country is one near Germantown, Pa. (Fig. 37.)

P. pectinata pendula (Weeping Silver fir)—Is a distinct and very rare variety of the Common Silver fir, which we had for many years—perfectly hardy, with peculiarly drooping branches. It is of French origin, we believe.

P. pectinata variegata (Variegated Silver fir)—Is very similar (though distinct) to the *P. Fraseri variegata ;* hardy.

P. pectinata nana (Dwarf Silver fir)—A pretty little shrub, quite hardy, and only growing two or three feet high.

P. grandis (Great Silver fir).—Another of the grand discoveries of Mr. Jeffrey, on Fraser's River—a superb tree, growing to the height of two hundred and eighty feet, and resembling in its character and habits the Common Silver fir, but much finer and more gigantic. Our specimens are only eight to ten inches high, and we do not know of any others in the country any or much larger; and although from its description we have every reason to suppose it will prove hardy, still we have no authority for saying so. The tree is still too young and costly (two guineas each), to make the attempt quite yet. The only report of it is from Washington, where there are plants in Mr. Corcoran's grounds, two feet high, perfectly hardy.

P. pichta (Pitch or Siberian Silver fir).—Although this tree does not become so majestic as the preceding, *Syn.* *P. Siberica.* yet it is a remarkably fine variety, and well worthy extensive cultivation. It is perfectly hardy, and has a superb luxuriant growth, which is most refreshing. It is not very unlike a very fine Balsam fir, though much denser, softer, and deeper foliage. It is found in the mountains of Siberia and Altai, and rarely exceeds twenty-five to thirty feet. There

is another variety, with longer and more glaucous leaves, called
P. longifolia.

P. Pindrow (Upright Indian Silver fir) —A fine tree, grow-
Syn.   ing from eighty to one hundred feet, and
Abies Webbiana.
Taxus Lambertiana.   found on the mountains of Bootan, at an
elevation of eleven to twelve thousand feet.   In this country,
this variety has been constantly confounded with *P. Webbiana*,
which it so closely resembles as to require the nicest scrutiny
to detect the difference.   It also, like the Webbiana, suffers
from losing its leader, and on this account, even in England, it
is recommended to be planted on the north of woods or buildings; with this protection it may be classed as tolerably
hardy.

P. Pinsapo (Pinsapo fir).—This is a *Spanish* fir, very dis-
Syn.   tinctive, and perfectly hardy everywhere, as
Abies Pinsapo.   far as tried.   Our best specimen is ten feet
Pinus   do.   high, and exceedingly fine, being as regular
and symmetrical as the Balsam fir.   Its greatest altitude
is seventy to eighty feet.   It is found in Spain, on the mountains between Ronda and Malaga ; also in Granada, and on the
highest parts of the Sierra de la Nieve—even near the summits,
where snow lies at least five months in the year.

P. Webbiana (Webb's Indian fir)—A superb tree, growing
Syn.   from seventy to eighty feet high ; discovered on
Abies spectabilis.   the Himmalayas above an elevation of ten thou-
A. densa.   sand, and Dr. Hooker found it in Sikkin at an
Pinus striata, etc.
                        elevation of thirteen thousand feet.   A beauti-
ful dye of an exquisite violet tint is extracted from the cones,
whence the name by which it is known in this country, "Webb's
Purple coned fir :" like *P. Pindrow*, it suffers in its leader, if ex-
posed, but does pretty well in a wood.

Pinus. THE PINE.

Of this, the largest and most important family of evergreens,
there are, at present, known and cultivated in England and in
collections on the Continent, about sixty varieties ; twenty-four
of which have proved hardy in the United States, or, at least,
in our portion of it on the Hudson River—and there are a few

more, besides, which may possibly become acclimatized in a
few years. Six of these have already been described by Mr.
Downing, in his early editions, leaving a gain of eighteen new
varieties—a great many for so valuable a genus, and in so short
a time as ten years.

In our Southern States, the whole sixty varieties now known
abroad, could undoubtedly be grown with entire success; we
therefore propose, in describing the twenty-four varieties which
we have ourselves tested, to give some brief mention of the
most prominent and desirable of the others, which at the North
can only be cultivated in tubs, and kept in green-houses during
the winter.

P. australis (Southern pine).—This superb tree, more commonly known as the Georgia pine, is found from
Virginia to Georgia, growing to the height of
sixty to seventy feet, with a bright green foliage,
nearly a foot long in young plants. We have great hope that
this tree may be acclimatized here. In Philadelphia, Mr.
Buist regards it as hardy ; at Elizabethtown it succeeds when
sheltered by evergreens, there being specimens there six feet
high. There is another variety, with much longer leaves, and
said to be much hardier, withstanding the coldest weather in
Germany, and coming from the northwest coast of America,
which would, no doubt, prove entirely hardy, since it was
raised, as we believe, from seed in Messrs. Booths' nurseries
at Hamburgh, where we remember we were informed peach
trees would not stand.

Syn.
P. Palustris,
P. Georgica.

P. Apulcensis (Apulco pine).—This variety, from the vallies of Mexico, is likely to prove too tender for any but our
Southern States ; it reaches a height of forty to fifty feet.

P. Ayacahnite (Ayacahnite pine).—This pretty and effective pine, with a soft, vivid foliage, has been out with us, two or
three years, in a sheltered position, and seems tolerably hardy ;
it somewhat resembles our native White pine, only is much softer
and brighter. It is from the mountains of Mexico.

P. Austriaca (Austrian pine).—This valuable tree, perfectly
hardy everywhere, is found on the mountains in
Austria, Styria, Transylvania, &c., and reaches a
height of one hundred to one hundred and twenty

Syn.
P. nigra,
P. laricio.

feet. Take it all in all, we do not know a finer or more available evergreen. It grows in any soil and has a strong, rampant, healthy look, which is positively refreshing when surrounded by its more delicate companions, the half-hardy ones It is very rapid in its progress, and has a firm, stocky growth, retaining its fine green color during our hottest summers and coldest winters. In Austria it is very much esteemed for charcoal, and the wood is said to resist the alternations of moisture and dryness better, even, than the Larch. By some, it is supposed to be only a variety of *laricio*.

P. Banksiana (Sir Joseph Banks' pine)—Is a stunted, scrubby, straggling bush, from five to ten feet high; in good soil it reaches, sometimes, fifteen feet. It is found in the most northern parts of North America, in Maine, Nova Scotia, Labrador, &c., and is only valuable to complete a collection.

Syn.
P. Hudsonica.

P. Beardsleyi.—We are inclined to think both these trees are identical, and are synonymous with *P. ponderosa*, though they are sold as distinct in the English nurseries, and in ours also. They belong to what are called the "Long-leaved Californians," such as Benthamiana, Ponderosa, Macrocarpa, &c., and when young, they resemble each other so closely that we must confess we are puzzled to tell them apart, and are not surprised at the confusion. Carriere, in his Histoire Général des Coniferes, makes *Beardsleyi* a distinct variety, but does not describe it, merely saying, it was introduced in seed in 1855, from North America ; but Gordon, who seems the more thorough as well as the latest writer, regards them as synonyms of Ponderosa. In the absence of any more light, or until the trees get larger, so as to show the difference, if it exists, we shall adopt this classification, and refer our readers to our subsequent description of Ponderosa, for what may prove, presently, to answer for these trees.

Syn.
P. Craigeana.

P. Benthamiana (Bentham's pine).—This superb tree, said to be the grandest of the "Long-leaved Californians," was found by Mr. Hartweg, on the mountains of Vera Cruz, where he discovered specimens two hundred to two hundred and twenty feet high, with stems

Syn.
P. Sinclairi.

twenty-eight feet in circumference. It seems peculiarly a mountain pine, flourishing above the region of P. Sabiniana, and in the greatest abundance, near Monterey, and on the mountains above Bear Creek. The timber is said to be the most valuable of the pines, though at five dollars apiece for small plants eight to twelve inches high, we are not likely to test this excellence for some years. It proves very hardy at Wodenethe. Our specimens, but slightly protected, have stood for three years without injury.

It is also hardy at " Wellesley," near Boston, the residence of Mr. Hunnewell. In the public grounds at Washington, there are fine specimens three and four feet high. At Yorkville, it is hardy, though the plants being very small, are often under the snow. At Flushing, on the contrary, it is returned "not hardy," and it may belong to those pines which do not flourish near the sea. Being still very rare and costly, it has not yet been much planted.

P. Brutia (Calabrian Cluster pine).—A fine lofty tree of sixty to seventy feet, and bright green foliage, with spreading head, found in Calabria, and closely resembling *P. Halepensis* (the Aleppo pine). It is not unlike, in its general appearance, some of the numerous varieties of Maritima; it proves perfectly hardy with us, having been out several winters.

Syn.
P. conglomerata.

P. Canariensis (Canary Island pine).—A charming, graceful, slender pine, with long pendulous leaves, growing seventy to eighty feet, in its own country, but too tender for any thing but pot-culture here, though it might do at the extreme South.

P. Cembra (Swiss Stone pine).—All travellers who have crossed Mount Cenis and the Tyrol, must have been struck with the vast forests of this tree, which abound in those stupendous regions. It is the pine of the Alps ; and as such must prove hardy anywhere at the North. It grows about fifty feet high, but very slowly, though always forming a pretty, compact tree. There are many synonyms, and two varieties; the Siberian Stone pine, with shorter, denser, and greener leaves, and the Dwarf Cembran pine, found on the rocks of the Ural Mountains. The seeds of all three of these varieties are eatable.

Syn.
P. Helvetica.
P. montana, &c.

P. Devoniana (Duke of Devonshire pine)—A fine, delicate, pendulous tree, with a charming green foliage, re-
Syn.
P. Blanco. sembling very much our *P. palustris* — called also, *Pino real*, or Royal pine, from its majestic character. It is from Mexico, growing 80 feet high—tolerably hardy in England, and perhaps in our Southern States, but too tender for us at the North, except for pot-culture.

P. excelsa (Lofty Bhotan pine).—We hardly know what to say of this splendid tree, called by Mr.
Syn.
P. pendula. Downing, that "affectedly pretty pine." It is
P. Nepalensis. universally returned to us as hardy, from all
&c., &c. parts of the country, though sometimes suffer-
ing from sun in summer. Near Boston, this is the case, and at Natchez, where plants have to be shaded from the summer sun. Mr. Barry writes us from Rochester, it is hardy there, but will not make an old tree. Our own trees at Wodenethe, which perhaps are some of the oldest in the country, being, or rather having been, sixteen and eighteen feet high, certainly suffer from sun and not cold. The winter of '55 and '56, which destroyed some and damaged many other white pines here, and even road-side cedars, produced no effect upon this tree, which was entirely unprotected and uninjured; and yet often in midsummer, it will become ruptured in its leading shoots, and die back. This may be on the principle of the frozen sap-blast in fruit trees, where the damage done in winter, does not develope the injury before the succeeding summer; but we are more inclined to believe, that the tree, if planted in rich holes, over-grows, and a sort of apoplexy supervenes. We form this theory, from observing that, where a great redundancy of growth has taken place, and the leading shoot is three or four feet long and extremely succulent, this rupture is most often the result, when the sun being hot, activity of circulation is excessive; when, however, the exuberance of growth is checked by poor, thin soil, the tree grows enough, and seems to mature its wood as it advances through the summer—at any rate sufficient to withstand what might be called determination of sap to the head; so that in future we shall always plant Excelsas in poor soil. The variety itself is found in Nepaul, in the mountains, and in Bhotan, above the region of the Deodar. It reaches a

height of one hundred and fifty feet. It is sometimes called the Himalayan Weeping fir. Take it all in all, it has been the greatest favorite, and the most successful of all the new conifers—having a charmingly graceful habit, and soft, pretty glaucous foliage.

P. filifolia (Thread-leaved pine).—Certainly this and *P. patula* are the most delicate and graceful of pines,
Syn.
P. Skinneri. exquisite for pot-culture, but too tender for any portion of this country, except the extreme South. It is a native of Guatemala, growing there to the height of forty to sixty feet, and resembling very much our Georgia pine (*P. palustris*), with its long, beautiful, thready leaves, twelve to fourteen inches in length.

P. flexilis (Contorted-branched pine).—This curious tree was found by Mr. Jeffery, at an elevation of nine thousand feet, and even fourteen thousand, in the neighborhood of Fraser's river, where it makes a small tree of forty feet high, with a peculiarly flattened head; and on the highest portion of the mountain, where it degenerates into a shrub of only three feet high, it becomes so compact that a person may walk on the top of it. It has not been introduced here yet, and hardly into England; but from its being found so near the snow-line, we should suppose it might prove hardy.

P. Fremontiana (Colonel Fremont's pine).—This pine was
Syn.
P. monophylla. discovered by Col. Fremont, during his exploring expedition, when crossing the Sierra Nevada,
P. Llaveana. growing on both sides, extending over the top of that great, snowy chain. It does not reach a size of over twenty feet, is very spreading in its habits, and will probably prove perfectly hardy in this country, since Col. Fremont often found the thermometer at two degrees below zero, at night, and four feet of snow where the tree grew. The seeds are eatable, and are quite an article of commerce with the Indians, in the season, under name of Nut pine.

P. Gerardiana (Gerard's pine).—A slow-growing but vigorous variety from the mountain of Kunawar, in
Syn.
P. Neoza. India, reaching the height of fifty feet, and
P. Aucklandii. forming a close, compact head; the leaves of
P. Chilghosa. these are stiff, and of a bluish green. We had this

twelve years ago as (if we are not mistaken) "The Short-leaved Weymouth," which we never thought correct, but there was so little to distinguish it from an ordinary pine that we replaced it by something more valuable. It was perfectly hardy.

P. Halepensis (Aleppo, or Jerusalem pine).—This variety resembles the Brutia (which we have already described) so much as to be often sold for it. We cannot quite, as yet, make up our mind whether it will stand our climate here, or not. It does very well in a wood, and a specimen more exposed, does equally well, if it is true ; but the resemblance to Brutia is so great that it may be this variety; Maritima is often confounded with it. Messrs. Hovey, in Boston, report it as hardy and fine there ; but their plants, like ours, may prove Brutias, or something else. It is found on the east and west sides of the Apennines, and in Sicily, among the rocks in Lybia, and in Greece, growing to be a tree of thirty feet.

Syn
P. Hierosolymitana.
P genuensis.

P. Hartwegii (Hartweg's pine).—This is a fine variety that we remember to have struck us very forcibly ten years ago, in England (when very small), from the fine, dense color of the foliage. It is one of the Mexican pines, forty to fifty feet high, and beginning on the mountains at ten thousand feet elevation, where the Picea religiosa ceases. We have tried it for several years with but indifferent success, and have abandoned it as too tender for any climate north of Virginia. It is too coarse for pots.

Syn.
P. resinosa.
P. Standishi.

P. inops (The New Jersey pine).— This variety, too well known to need description, is found from Carolina to the Hudson River, but does, we think, extend beyond it. It has a spreading top, and is thirty to forty feet high, and, of course, must be planted in collections, though hardly otherwise would be selected by the amateur.

Syn.
P. variabilis.

P. insignis (the Remarkable pine).—We regret that this certainly most beautiful pine will not resist our winters, even in a wood ; though it will, no doubt, do well and prove a very great acquisition in our Southern States. It is so attractive in its appearance, that it was one of the earliest of the new conifers tried here, but without any success. It is

Syn.
P. Californica, *of Loisel.*
P. minteragensis.

found in many portions of California, growing to the height of eighty to one hundred feet.

P. Jeffreyi (Jeffrey's pine).—We doubt if this has been tried at all in this country yet. Our own plants are extremely small, and not yet out. It is a majestic tree, one hundred and fifty feet high, from Northern California.

P. Lambertiana (Lambert's pine).—This superb variety, reaching an altitude of one hundred and fifty to two hundred feet, and twenty to sixty feet in girth near the ground, is from the northern parts of California; and is, without doubt, perfectly hardy in this latitude. Our plants have escaped injury the severe winters of '55 and '56. Our reports from Boston, Flushing, New Jersey, and Washington all coincide as to its hardihood; so that we may place this among the "*safe trees.*" Its resemblance to the *Pinus strobus* (White pine) has been stated as an objection, but it might resemble a worse tree ; besides, we do not think this is quite so. To us it is very distinctive ; and it has long been a great favorite with us for its fine, deep green, and vigorous, healthy habit. It has this merit, to say the least, even if its character is not as marked as many of the less robust pines.

P. laricio (the Corsican pine).—This tree with many synonyms, is a native, as its name implies, of Corsica, though found also in Europe, Greece, and Spain; and is the great tree upon Mount Ætna, growing rapidly to a height of eighty to one hundred and thirty feet. It is quite as hardy as Lambertiana, or Austriaca, all over the country, having somewhat the robust habit of the latter, only a less vivid green. Some of our specimens of this variety made leading shoots last year of five feet.

Syn.
P. maritima.
P. Corsicana pyramidalis, &c.

P. l. Calabrica (the Calabrian pine), *P. l. Caramanica* (the Caramanian pine), *P. l. pygmœa* (the Dwarf Corsican), and *P. l. contorta* (the Twisted Corsican), are only varieties.

P. leiophylla (the Smooth-leaved Mexican pine).—A large tree, with an irregular open head, vertical branches, and drooping foliage, growing sixty to one hundred feet high ; from the mountains of Angangueo, in Mexico, and is called by the natives "Ocote Chino," from its abundance of resin, and being used for torches and candles. The wood is so hard, as to resist the plane. The tree is too tender for the Middle States, but would doubtless succeed south of Virginia.

P. Lindleyana (Dr. Lindley's pine).—This variety, often confounded with Montezumæ, and as such, imported *Syn.* by us some year or so ago, is really quite dis-*P. Montezumæ.* tinct, and is a robust, bushy looking tree of forty feet; found near the " Sumate," on the mountains of Mexico. It will, no doubt, prove hardy, coming from so high an elevation. We do not know that it has as yet been tried, nor do we think it very desirable, except in very full collections.

P. longifolia (the Long-leaved pine).—This is one of the class of *exquisite* pines, of which *P. filifolia*, *Syn.* *P. serenagensis.* patula, *Canariensis*, and even *Australis* are also representatives. They are all, except Australis (Palustris), too tender even for the climate of Great Britain, and will not of course do at all here, except in Georgia, the Carolinas, and our Southern States, where no greater addition to ornamental plantations can be made; they are charming for pot-culture with us, which is the only way they grow them in England generally. The timber of Longifolia is excellent, and full of resin, which is another recommendation for the South. The foliage is of an exquisite light green, and the leaves, twelve to fourteen inches long, delicate and thready.

It comes from the lower ranges of the Himmalayan mountains, from Bootan to Affghan, growing forty to one hundred feet high, with a peculiar spiral arrangement of bark and fibre, like a cork-screw.

The chips are used in India for candles, and are called "Chamsing" (night lights). According to Dr. Hooker, ink is made in Sikkin from the charcoal of the burnt leaves mixed with water. It is also remarkable for its fragrance.

P. macrocarpa (Dr. Coulter's pine).—This is a grand tree, which we have had several years under each of *Syn.* *P. Coulteri.* the above names; though now we believe culti-*P. Sabiniana.* vators have settled down upon *macrocarpa* and *P. macrocarpa.* *Coulteri*, as the proper ones. Our best specimens would have been eight to ten feet high, having worked through the winters of '55 and '56, with very trifling injury, when, unfortunately, all the terminal buds were eaten off by sheep; and though the trees might have stood climate alone, yet they were unable to resist both climate and sheep, and they consequently perished.　It has rugged, stiff leaves, ten or twelve inches long, and becomes a very striking tree, eighty to one hundred feet high; from the mountains of Santa Lucia, in California, at an elevation of three or four thousand feet.

P. macrophylla (the Long-leaved Mexican).—An uncom-

Syn.　monly fine variety, which we lost in the winter of

P. Leroyi.　1855, in a very exposed situation, though we are not prepared to say it would have stood better in a protected one.　It is a very striking tree, from one of the highest mountains of Mexico, growing twenty to thirty feet high, with a fine, ample foliage, fifteen inches long.　It is almost too stout and coarse for pot-culture, but would be very ornamental at the South, where it would grow perfectly well.

P. maritima (the Maritime pine).—This tree, so called and so sold in our nurseries, is simply a nurseryman's name, there really being no such tree.　It is very curious, but nevertheless true, that the greatest confusion prevails, both in the English and French nurseries, about this variety.　In England, it is confounded often with P. pinaster, Halepensis, and Laricio; and in France, with Pallasiana, Pithyusa (Halepensis), Laricio, and Pyrenaica, and made synonymous with each; and in this country, it seems to represent any thing which is unknown.

The specimens we have seen in our neighborhood as Maritima, are probably Calabrica—a sub-variety of Laricio—and, we think, most Maritimas in our nurseries are Laricio or Pinaster. Representing, as it does, so many different trees, it is difficult to get any reputation about it which is to be depended on.　In Boston, it is returned to us as *tender*, from which we assume that the variety there may be Pinaster, which is sometimes tender here; while at Rochester, it is reported hardy, and may be Calabrica, or one of the hardy synonyms.　At Washington, the variety known as Maritima does well, and also at Elizabethtown; but what these trees really are at these two places, we have no means of knowing, except that they are *not* Maritimas.

FIG. 96.—TORREYA TAXIFOLIA, at Wodenethe. Age, 6 years. Height, 8 feet. Circumference, 20 feet.

FIG. 95.—PINUS PATULA, at Wodenethe. Height, 5 feet. Two years planted.

P. mitis (Yellow pine).—This well-known variety, so com-

Syn.   mon once in many portions of the United States, re-

P. variabilis.   quires no description.   It has been singularly con-
P. tæda.

P. roylei.   founded with many other varieties, and has only

P. lutea.   recently been distributed by the East India Company, as a new species, under the name of P. roylei, which
farther experience shows clearly was the common American
yellow pine.

P. monticola (the Mountain pine).—We have had this tree

P. Lambertiana.   out for several years.   It is quite as hardy as

P. brevifolia.   our White pine, and so closely resembling it as
hardly to pass as distinct.   It grows as tall as the White pine,
but has a denser head, and shorter and more glaucous foliage—
found on Trinity Mountain, in Northern California.

P. Montezuma (Montezuma Mexican pine). — This fine
variety has stood out with us several winters, though somewhat
protected.   It is found on the mountains of Mexico, at an
elevation of eleven thousand feet, growing forty to sixty feet
high, with a spreading head.   This does not appear as yet to
be in any of the American collections besides our own.

P. Mugho (the Mugan pine).—A small tree, thirty feet high,

P. sylvestris Mugho.   from the Alps, perfectly hardy everywhere,

P. Mughus.   but not very attractive.   There are four
varieties, all small, and Mugho nana (Knee pine), not more
than three feet high.

P. nivea (the Snow pine)—Is only a variety of our common
White pine (*P. strobus*), with the under part of the leaves,
silvery—quite as hardy as its parent.

P. palustris.—We have already described as Australis.

P. patula (the Wide-spreading Mexican pine).—Of all the
pines which we have ever seen, this is beyond measure the
most graceful and charming, not only in its growth and habit,—
a representation of which is given in Fig. 95—but in the
nature, softness, and color of its leaves.   It resembles a
beautiful, delicate green fountain of spun glass, and has a parti-
color, like shot-silk, which catches the sunlight almost like a
kaleidoscope.   The leaves resemble the silk of maize, being
as soft and delicate, and not unlike it in color.   Although
found in the colder regions of Mexico, on the Real del Monte

mountains, it has not the appearance of being hardy, and we have not yet attempted to acclimatize it—having but two plants, which are quite beautiful enough for pot-culture to satisfy anybody. It would unquestionably grow at the South. We have no reports about it, and know but one other specimen in the country, which is at Wellesley, near Boston, grown, like ours, in a pot. There are two other varieties, *P. patula stricta* (more erect), and *P. patula macrocarpa* (much larger and taller); neither, we think, in this country.

P. pinaster (Star or Cluster pine.)—This fine tree, which, when first introduced, and before thoroughly tested, promised to be the most artistic of pines (at least of available pines)—doing for our landscape what *P. pinea* (the Stone pine) did for Claude in the Italian Landscape—has, in our latitude, proved itself a little questionable.

Syn.
P. Nepalensis.
P. maritima.
P. Japonica,
and
seven others.

It will certainly stand uninjured our ordinary winters; but such uncommon ones as those of 1855-6, when, with us, the mercury sank to twenty degrees below zero, destroyed, at Wodenethe, specimens eighteen and twenty feet high, and this seems the experience of our returns.

It is a most admirable tree for planting near the sea-shore, where it thrives wherever the climate will permit, and is to be found all along the Cornish road, bordering the Mediterranean, in Spain, Portugal, Greece, Turkey, Japan, New Holland. From the facility with which it flourishes near the sea, it received its synonym of *maritima*. No doubt *P. pinaster Hamiltonii, Lemoniana, minor variegata*, are varieties.

P. ponderosa (the Heavy-wooded pine.)—The *hardiest*, we should say, of all pines, not excepting our native White pine, and the *fastest* grower. We have a specimen, sixteen to eighteen feet high, raised from seed in less than seven years. This variety is gigantic in every sense of the word; the new shoots are two or three times as thick as those of our White pine, and same with the buds. The annual leading shoots exceed a yard. It is from the Northwest coast of America and California, where it grows one hundred feet high. Although a strik-

Syn.
P. Craigeana.
P. Beardsleyi.

ing, it is not a handsome tree, the interval between the tiers of branches being so wide and the foliage so coarse and sparse, as to give it a thin and naked look ; besides which, it has an ugly habit of working the crown of the root out of ground, so as to give the tree the appearance of insecurity. Our tree, though eighteen feet high, and grown from seed where it stands, still requires, or seems to require, support. It is, of course, hardy all over the United States—at least, we doubt if any cold will affect it, though it might suffer from sun in the extreme South.

P. Pallasiana Taurica (Taurian pine.)—A large tree, seventy to eighty feet high, found as yet only in the Crimea and along the coast of the Black Sea. We have specimens which have been out several years without protection ; perfectly hardy, though not very distinctive, as it resembles exceedingly our White pine.

P. pumilis (the Mountain pine.)—A remarkably stiff, ungraceful dwarf, resembling the Scotch fir—in some favorable situations, becoming a tree thirty feet high, but generally only a low, straggling, slow-growing bush. It is very common on the Alps and the Carpathian Mountains ; perfectly hardy.

Syn.
P. Tartarian, &c.

P. pinea (Italian Stone pine).—No one, we think, who has ever been to Rome, will have forgotten the Colonna pine, which, together with St. Peter's, divided one's enthusiasm, at the first sight of the eternal city. This superb object, rising abruptly from the midst of the Colonna gardens, is so much associated in our early recollections, with all views of Rome, that now it is gone,* it would really seem as if we had lost an old friend. It is the great tree of Claude, and all the old masters, and no Italian garden would seem quite perfect without it. It is generally, we think, too tender for this climate, though suited well to the South. We have tried many times to acclimatize it ; but though it may struggle on for a few years, yet it never would form, probably, the picturesque tree, so valuable for the composition of certain landscape effects.

Syn.
P. Latina.
P. domestica.
P. arctica, &c.

* Blown down in 1851.

P. Pyrenaica (Pyrenean pine).—A very hardy, robust

variety from the Pyrenees, perfectly hardy with us, having survived several winters; but, like P. nivea and P. Pallasiana, too much resembling our native White pine to be very distinctive.

P. radiata (Radiated-cone pine).—This tree, from Upper California, is one of Dr. Coulter's introductions, closely resembling the P. insignis; but, being a little denser and stouter, may prove hardier. It seems to thrive near the sea-shore; the specimen found by Dr. Coulter being one hundred feet high, with a straight stem, feathered to the ground. The wood is much used at Monterey for boat-building. Not to our knowledge introduced here yet.

P. rigida (Stiff-leaved pine).—Another of our "Native

Americans," extending throughout the whole of the United States, as far north as Brunswick, in Maine. Not desirable, except to complete collections.

P. resinosa (Red pine).—An American tree, principally

found in Canada and Nova Scotia; not very unlike the Corsican. It abounds in resin, and is esteemed for its strength and durability.

P. Sabiniana (Sabine's pine).—This majestic tree—from the Cordilleras of Mexico, where it grows to the height of one hundred and fifty feet—is very distinctive, and, we believe, will prove hardy. Our trees have been out since the severe winters of 1855-'56, and stand in a protected place thus far very well. The tone of the foliage is peculiarly soft and pleasing, being of a light glaucous color.

P. strobus (White or Weymouth pine).—A description of this well-known tree will be found in the first part of the book, under Mr. Downing's section on evergreen trees.

P. sylvestris (Scotch fir).—This valuable variety is also too well known to require description or even mention, beyond the fact that, take it all in all, it is perhaps the most important of all foreign pines. It is perfectly hardy everywhere in this country, and in Europe, where it is cultivated under twenty different names. It is not a beautiful tree, though it assumes,

with age, a good many picturesque forms. It is very cheap—
plants, two or three feet high, can be imported from the English nurseries, at three or four dollars the hundred—and very
valuable as a hack tree for planting out disagreeable objects
and making screens. There are a good many varieties ; among
them are, Variegata, which is with us as hardy as Sylvestris,
having a golden stripe or blotch on the leaves ; Pygmea, a
dwarf, of two feet or so; Argentea, a silver-leaved variety.

P. tæda (Loblolly pine).—Another of our native trees,
Syn. found from Florida to Virginia, forming a tree
P. Virginiana. of eighty feet high, with a spreading head. This
P. Pennifolia. is also called the Frankincense pine, and is dis-
tinguished by its delightful aroma.

P. tuberculata (Tuberculated-cone pine).—We have but
Syn. lately had this variety, and by its synonymous
P. Californica. name (*Californica*). It was discovered by Dr.
Coulter, immediately on the beach, near Monterey, and afterwards was found on the Santa Cruz mountains, by Mr. Hartweg. Mr. Jeffrey, also, found it on an elevation of five thousand feet. It is said to be slow-growing, reaching a height of
forty feet. Our specimens, so far, resemble P. Sabiniana. We
have no reports about it, and never saw any other specimens
except our own.

PODOCARPUS.

This comparatively rare genus obtains its name from two
Greek words, πους, a foot, and Καρπος, a fruit; and is found in
Asia, Africa and America, and may be anglicised into the
Fruit foot-stalked yew, from which it seems only slightly differing, many varieties being sold as *Taxus* (Yew), instead of
Podocarpus. There are about ninety varieties introduced into
the collections on the Continent and in England; a great many
of these are very tender, even abroad, and we do not, as yet,
find more than four which promise at all well for this country.

Of these, *P. Japonica* (Japan podocarpus), seems the best
known as yet, and the hardiest. It is a small tree, from Japan,
where it abounds, and is not very unlike Taxus Hibernica (the
Irish yew), only with a broader and, perhaps, flatter leaf; our

specimens have been through two winters without any injury
—it is certainly with us quite as hardy as the Irish yew. It
is reported to us as hardy at Flushing and at two different
places in Georgia, but being new and costly it has not as yet
been tried anywhere else.

    P. Andina (The Andes podocarpus).—Another pretty, small
Syn.   tree, ten to twenty feet high, from the Alpine
P. Taxus spicata. regions of South Chili, with a broader and
more leathery leaf than the preceding variety; our specimen
is out, for first time, this winter, and we have but one return
about it, which is from Augusta, and is satisfactory.

    P. coriacea (Leathery-leaved podocarpus). — This variety
Syn.   comes from the Blue Mountains of Jamaica,
Taxus lancifolia. and also the Antilles, growing fifty feet high.
We have more doubt about this than the two above, and we
have but one return, from Flushing, L. I., where it is marked
" hardy."

    P. taxifolia (Yew-leaved podocarpus).—There is no question
Syn.   we think, of the hardihood of this variety
Taxus montana. We have had it out three years without
Torreya Humboldii. injury. It resembles still more the Irish
yew, than P. Japonica. It comes from the mountains of Peru,
at an elevation of eight thousand feet, where it is a tree of
sixty feet. We have no returns.

    There is one other variety, not yet received into this country,
to our knowledge, which promises better than any of the above,
viz. : *Podocarpus Nubigena*, which is described as one of the
finest, as it is unquestionably one of the hardiest and most distinct, of all the conifers introduced within a few years. It is a
native of Patagonia and is found also on the Andes, near the
Araucaria imbricata, which tree it much resembles—the
branches being produced at regular distances like it.

—————

    Saxe Gothœa conspicua. PRINCE ALBERT'S YEW.
        Syn. Taxus Patagonica.

    A genus by itself, and this the only species ; a small bush or
tree found on the mountains of Patagonia, growing thirty feet
high, with very much the habit and appearance of the common

yew, but not so fine a color. We have no report about it in this country, and presume it will, at the North, at least, have to be grown in tubs, though we have a specimen out this winter.

Sequoia sempervirens.   CALIFORNIA RED WOOD.

Better known here as *Taxodium sempervirens.* Found in the northwest part of North America, forming a majestic tree two hundred to three hundred feet high, and often confounded with Washingtonia gigantea, quite a different thing ; the foliage of the Sequoia being flat, two-rowed, and dark green, while that of Washingtonia is needle-shaped, spirally alternate, and on the branchlets very close and regularly imbricated like an Arbor vitæ, besides being a light or yellowish green. The two varieties are probably the most gigantic evergreens in the world. There is a slab of the wood of the Sequoia at St. Petersburgh, measuring fifteen feet in diameter, and having one thousand and eight annual rings to mark its age.

We have tried it many winters, but with hardly any success. It grows too rapidly and too late in the autumn to ripen off its wood, and almost always with us gets killed back to the snow-line, though generally shooting up again the next spring to meet a similar fate the succeeding winter. We have no returns about this tree other than tender, except from Washington, where a specimen, six feet high, planted by Mr. Downing, in 1852, is growing beautifully though slightly injured in '55–6. There is no reason why, in our Southern States, it should not succeed perfectly.

Taxodium distichum.   DECIDUOUS CYPRESS.

Syn. Cupressus Virginiana, &c., &c.

Though not an evergreen, yet this valuable genus is closely allied to coniferous trees, and is well known by all planters as the Southern or Swamp cypress, found along the banks of rivers and swamps in vast quantities ; in Georgia, Carolina, Florida, and all the Southern States, it reaches the height of one hundred and twenty feet.   It is perfectly hardy at the

528   LANDSCAPE GARDENING.

North. The varieties, *fastigiatum*, *pedulum*, *nutans*, &c., are
described under the head of *Glyptostrobus*.

Taxus. THE YEW.

Great additions have been made to this class of ever-
greens, since the first edition of this book, where only three
foreign and one American varieties are mentioned, viz. :
T. baccata (the Common English), *T. fastigiata* (the
Upright yew), and the *T. fructo-flava* (Yellow-berried).
Among the new ones which we have found hardy, are :

T. adpressa (Flattened or Creeping yew).—An exceedingly
Syn. dark, striking bush, never, we believe, ex-
Cephalotaxus adpressa, ceeding three feet high, but spreading
T. brevifolia. horizontally ; with very minute close
leaflets and pretty bright red berries, very desirable ; like all
the yews, doing better in the shade.

T. argentea and *T. aurea* (Silver and Golden yew).—These
two are very beautiful and desirable varieties of the Common
yew ; the first having silvery white-striped leaves, and the
second golden. They seem perfectly hardy here. We
have some Golden yews grafted standard high on the Green
yew, which produces a very pleasing contrast. They are more
commonly known in the English nurseries as *Taxus elegans* and
Taxus elegantissima.

T. Dovaston (Dovaston's yew).—A singular Weeping
Syn. variety of common English yew, found some years
T. pendula, ago, if we remember aright, in the yard of a cob-
T. horizontalis. bler near Shrewsbury ; described as pendulous as
a birch or weeping willow ; quite hardy with us, and well
worth cultivating.

T. erecta (the Erect yew)—A slender variety of the com-
Syn. mon English yew, with smaller foliage, and
T. pyramidalis, more erect habit of growth ; sometimes called
T. stricta. Fulham yew. It is thought by some cultivators in this country to be hardier than the common English yew,
though the latter with us, especially after a year or so,
succeeds perfectly well, though possibly a little browned in
very severe winters.

THE NEWER EVERGREEN ORNAMENTAL TREES.

T. ericoides (the Heath-like yew).—A very pretty, slender
Syn.   variety, with very minute foliage, quite dis-
T. microphylla.   tinctive and hardy here, and at Newport.

T. Hibernica (the Irish yew).—The same as *Fastigiata*, a very
striking pyramidal tree, resembling in its close compact habit,
the Lombardy poplar. There are specimens in England twen-
ty-one feet high, though usually twelve to fifteen feet seems its
common height; it is also known as the Florence Court yew.
It is quite hardy generally, though sometimes a little browned
by severe winters. This is a most admirable variety for pot-
culture.

T. nana (Dwarf yew).—A very dwarf, hardy variety, never
Syn.   exceeding two or three feet, but very spreading,
T. Foxii.   like the Prostrate juniper.

T. variegata (Variegated yew).—A handsome variety, differing a little from the Golden yew, and sometimes sold as *T. elegans*; hardy here.

Thuiopsis.   BROAD-LEAVED ARBOR VITÆ.

Name derived from *Thuia*, arbor vitæ, and *opsis*, like. There
is but one variety of this new genus recognized in Gordon's
Pinetum, viz., *Thuiopsis dolabrata*. The remaining variety,
known in this country as *Thuiopsis borealis*, is classed by Mr.
Gordon among the *Cupressi*, and has already been described by
us as a most valuable and hardy tree, known as *Cupressus
Nootkaensis*. We think, ourselves, it would be better to adopt
the nurserymen's name, *Thuiopsis Borealis*, by which it is generally invoiced.

Thuja.   THE ARBOR VITÆ.

So many of this family have been already described under
the head of *Biota*, and Mr. Downing having said all that was
necessary upon the common American arbor vitæ (*Thuja occidentalis*), but few distinctive Thujas remain for us to mention.

Thuja gigantea (Gigantic arbor vitæ).—If this succeeds in
Syn.   the United States—and there is every
T. Craigiana.   reason to be satisfied with its success
T. Libocedrus decurrens.   thus far—it will unquestionably be the

noblest addition this genus ever received. Accustomed as we are to regard the Arbor vitæ as a small bush, principally available for hedging or single specimens, ten to twenty feet high, for small villa-gardens and village-yards, we shall find it difficult to realize that we are to have an arbor vitæ reaching to the dignity of a majestic tree, one hundred and forty feet upright, with a fine umbrella-shaped top and picturesque head. This is another of the giants from the Columbia river and Nootka sound. Mr. Jeffrey discovered it along the banks of Scott's river, and sent it home to England as *Thuja Craigiana*. Mr. Nuttall, in his Rocky Mountain expedition, also discovered it, and gave it the name of *Thu. gigantea;* and finally, Dr. Torrey has classed it as a *Libocedrus,* and distinguished it as *decurrens*. It has since again been discovered in California, in 1853, by M. Borusier de la Rivière.

It has been discovered so many times, by different people, and received different names, that a good deal of confusion exists about it, and it is often confounded with another *Thu. gigantea*—so named by Sir William Hooker, in his American Flora—but which, though coming from California, is a more slender tree, not over fifty feet, and is beyond doubt, the true *Thu. Menziesii,* which is also sometimes called *Thu. plicata,* and very much resembling the American arbor vitæ. In fact, it would seem as if there often existed among Arbor vitæs botanical rather than physical differences, which often, as in this case, and that of the Siberian Arbor vitæ, produces great perplexity.

As these two giganteas are completely mixed up, we will describe them separately, with the hope of throwing some light upon their difference.

The *real Thu. gigantea* has its branches rather *erect,* long, slender, and spreading laterally, with numerous smaller ones ; branchlets, short, flattened, channeled along the sides ; leaves, awl-shaped, lanceolate, *loosely* imbricated in *four rows,* the outer pair being the longest, and folded partially over the inner pair on both sides, giving the young shoots a trident-like appearance.

The *Thu. Menziesii,* on the contrary, has its branches *spreading,* flat, more or less horizontal, slender, and of a deep brown

color, alternately two *round*, and nearly all the inner side quite
straight ; leaves in alternately opposite pairs, *closely* imbricated,
those on the branchlets being much shorter, more rounded, and
furnished with a short spiny point ; besides which, one forms a
tree of one hundred and forty, while the other (*Thu. Menziesii*)
only attains an altitude of forty feet.

We are not yet able to say what either of these trees will
do in this country. The real *gigantea* is said to be hardy, and
the false not. At Elizabethtown, N. J., Mr. Reid writes us,
" The true one grows rapidly, and will no doubt prove hardy."
At Augusta it stands perfectly well. At Flushing, not quite
hardy. These are the only reports we have, and our own plants
are out for the first time.

Thu. macrocarpa.—This is a variety we received, if we mistake not, several years since, from Messrs. Ellwanger & Barry,
of Rochester, and about which we can find no mention in any
of the books, nor does it seem to exist in any of the foreign
Pinetums, or in any nurserymen or collectors' catalogues. It
resembles so much the *Thu. gigantea,* that we are inclined
to think it is this variety under a different name. We have
never tried it out, as we could not find anything of its character or habits under this name.

Thu. variegata (Variegated arbor vitæ).—Only a golden-
striped variety of our common arbor vitæ, but pretty and distinctive, and perfectly hardy.

Thu. aurea Americana (American Golden arbor vitæ).—Is
an exceedingly pretty and well-marked seedling, found accidentally in a nursery row by our neighbor, Mr. Daniel Brinck-
enhoff, and named by us as above. The new growth is very
distinctly yellow, and the old foilage, which is a bright clear
green, tones off so gradually and delicately into the golden
hue of the new, as to produce a most pleasing little tree, and
perfectly hardy.

Thu. Hoveyi (Hovey's arbor vitæ).—Another American
seedling not yet introduced, but which is described to us by
Messrs. Hovey (in whose nursery, near Boston, it was found)
as a seedling of Occidentalis, as hardy as an oak, having never
lost a limb in the severe winters of '55 and '56. Very nearly of
the same habit as Aurea, compact and upright branches ; leaves

as fine as Aurea, making a most superb tree. It holds its color
even better than Thu. Siberica, while it is a lively, soft green,
brighter than Aurea, and not as sombre as Siberica. It is now,
even in midwinter, as green as most arbor vitæs are in summer.
Messrs. Hovey have two other seedlings, not as distinct or
fine as the above.

Thu. plicata (Nootka Sound arbor vitæ).—These two plants

Syn.

Thu. Warreana.
Thu. compacta.
Thu. robusta.

plicata and *Warreana*, though often sold by separate names, are, beyond question, identical;
this is the conclusion both of the English and
French authorities; although there is another
plicata, a synonym of *Thu. Menziesii* in the English collections,
and another Warreana in some of the French collections, as
among "les variétiés horticoles," but only another name for
Thu. occidentalis. The *true* plicata and *true* Warreana are one
and the same thing.

The Nootka Sound arbor vitæ is found on the western shores
of North America, at Nootka Sound, quite hardy, everywhere,
and differing from the common American arbor vitæ, in having
its branches shorter, more compact, stouter, and densely covered
with small, flattened leaves, bluntly pointed, and with a plaited
and jointed appearance.

We have already alluded, under the head of Biota, to the difficulty in recognizing the origin of B. Siberica, which is sometimes confounded with Tatarica, but more generally with Warreana. This latter (Warreana) was named from Mr. Ware, a
nurseryman at Coventry, in England, and Mr. Loudon considered it as a distinct variety; but it seems now to be referred
back again to Thu. occidentalis; and Siberica adopted as its
name without any botanical authority, and simply as a nursery distinction; and we presume, consequently, that all plants
grown in this country, as the Siberian arbor vitæ, are Warreana, or its synonym, plicata.

———

Torreya. THE TORREYA.

Vulgarly, the Stinking Yew.—Small evergreen trees, found
in North America, China and Japan, emitting, when bruised,

a strong, disagreeble smell, and named after Dr. Torrey, the celebrated American botanist.

T. grandis (The Grand Torreya).—Discovered by Fortune in northern part of China, as a large tree with a spreading head, but so resembling a Cephalotaxus (which most of the others do) as to render it uncertain whether it may not yet prove one. It is considered very desirable whatever it may be, but just introduced into England and not yet, to our knowledge, here.

T. myristica (Californian nutmeg).—A small, bushy tree, twenty to forty feet high, with spreading horizontal branches, found on the Sierra Nevada, in California ; quite hardy in England and likely to prove so here. Our specimens are out for first winter, and we have no returns. Like all the Torreyas, emitting a most disagreeable odor when bruised or burnt, and called by emigrants the Stinking yew or California nutmeg.

T. nucifera (Nut-bearing Torreya).—This is out with us at Wodenethe, for the first winter, and we have no returns about it. It is another small tree, twenty to thirty feet high, found on the mountains of Niphon and Sikok, in Japan, where an oil is made from the kernel of the nuts, used there for culinary purposes. The nut itself, and the leaves and branches, have the distinguishing characteristic of all the Torreyas—a disagreeable odor.

T. taxifolia (Yew-leaved Torreya.)—This is one of our *Syn.*   greatest accessions in the Middle States—be-
Taxus montana.   ing now perfectly hardy with us, as already described in our introductory chapter on evergreens, and very distinctive.

It is a handsome pyramidal tree, with numerous spreading branches, growing from forty to fifty feet high, found in the middle and northern parts of Florida, where it is commonly known by the inhabitants as Stinking cedar and Wild nutmeg.

Our best specimen (fig. 96), is about eight feet high, very dense, showing nothing but foliage, like a thrifty arbor vitæ, and remarkable, particularly in winter, for the star-like appearance of the extreme tips of its young shoots.

We have returns of this tree from Elizabethtown, N. J., Dobb's Ferry, Yorkville, Flushing and Newport, in all of which places it succeeds well, and is considered hardy, except at the last place where it is reported tender.

* * *

Washingtonia gigantea. THE MAMMOTH TREE.

This truly most magnificent of all trees—deciduous or ever-

Syn.
Wellingtonia gigantea.
Sequoia gigantea.

green—was discovered in a valley at the source of one of the tributaries of the Cala-
veras, California. Within an area of fifty acres only, ninety two trees of this species were found standing, beyond doubt the most stupendous vegetable products on earth.

They were first discovered in 1850, by some hunters, whose accounts were considered fabulous until confirmed by actual measurement. The largest tree was one called the "Father of the Forest," four hundred and fifty feet high, one hundred and twelve feet in circumference. The next largest the "Mother of the Forest," three hundred and twenty-seven feet high, and ninety feet in circumference.

Three trees, growing together, called the "Three Graces," are each three hundred feet high, ninety feet in circumference. There is another which has fallen, and through which a man on horseback may ride seventy-five feet, and twelve feet in the clear. These trees may be truly termed the "Lions of California," and in such estimation are they held, that it has been found sufficiently remunerative to erect a hotel and run a line of stages to Sacramento city and Sonora, for the accommodation of visitors to these great natural curiosities.

The botanical discovery of this genus was, however, probably made by the unfortunate Douglas, in 1831, when he writes to Mr. Hooker : "The splendor of the Californian vegetation consists of a species of Taxodium which gives to the mountains an especial beauty, which I may almost call terrible."

This wonderful tree, which closely resembles, in our plants, the Weeping arbor vitæ (*Thuja filiformis*), in its imbricated leaves, of a more delicate color than the arbor vitæ, being of a pleasing light green, is, we are happy to say, promising to be hardy in the United States.

Our own plants have only been out one year, but seem to succeed perfectly well. We have returns from a good many parts of the country where it has not been left out all winter, and also from Mr. Reid, at Elizabethtown, where it was, and who has a specimen four to five feet, perfectly hardy. He thinks, in time, it may prove as common as a Norway spruce, being very rapid in its growth. At Woodlawn, N. J., it stands well, the largest specimen being four to five feet. At Rochester, it is hardy, and also at Augusta.

Widdringtonia. The African Cypress.

A new, distinct variety of cypress, found at Cape of Good Hope, and Madagascar, and named after Capt. Widdrington, and a variety of which, erroneously called *Widdringtonia ericoides*, has been imported into this country, and is cultivated with some success, doing very well here in the shade, and also at Washington and Augusta. We hardly know why it comes out to us as a Widdringtonia. In the English collection it is called *Retinispora ericoides*, and in the French, *Chamæsyparis ericoides* ; but, by whatever name it is called, it is a pretty heath-like little shrub, resembling somewhat the Irish juniper. It is cultivated in Japan (its native country), in pots, and called "Nezu,"—(Dwarf.)

EVERGREEN ORNAMENTAL SHRUBS.

But very little progress has been made in the planting of evergreen shrubs. As great as has been the advance in trees, especially the coniferous, there has been nothing to correspond with it in the introduction of evergreen shrubs. With the exception of a few varieties of the Berberries—like Japonica, Bealii, Intermedia, &c., we do not remember any thing available for this

climate now, which was not well known when Mr.
Downing wrote.

There are, perhaps, a few things, untried ten years
ago, which have been tested the past three or four
years, and not "found wanting;" such as some of the
smaller English shrubs, like the Andromeda—especially
Floribunda—the Cotoneaster, of which Buxifolia, with
us, proves the hardiest, though Microphylla and Margi-
nata, both do well *in the shade*. And here let us remark,
once for all, that no evergreen shrubs do at all well in
this country, in the sun. Every thing, from the yew
down to the creeping periwinkle, succeeds *well*, only
in shade.

If it is impossible or inconvenient, to have these
shrubs otherwise than exposed in open lawns, we should
recommend only the employment of certain varieties,
like the Rhododendrons, Catawbiensis, Kalmia latifolia,
Mahonia aquifolium, and Ilex laurifolia.

These four shrubs seem to stand any amount of heat
and cold. Our thermometer, while we now write, indicates *sixteen below Zero ;* and last summer they passed
through a fiery ordeal of 95° to 100° : and this they
have done for many years, with no other ill effect than
that the very hot weather changes that fine, deep,
dense color they universally have in the shade, into a
yellowish green, but they survive and grow and flourish
and bloom, though certainly less fine than when planted
on the north of buildings or woods.

Take it all in all, we consider the Mahonia (sometimes called Berberris mahonia), the most valuable
of all shrubs, deciduous or evergreen.

If there is any exception to our remarks above, about
the necessity of growing evergreen shrubs in the
shade, we should make it in favor of this variety.
It may be imported very cheap. Messrs. Waterer &
Godfrey, Knaphill Nursery, Woking, near London, offer
plants, one foot high, at eighty shillings sterling, per

thousand, and in same proportion for smaller quantities. It is perfectly hardy—a most rapid grower—has a very attractive, yellow flower early in spring, succeeded by fine purplish berries in autumn, which, in England, are used for preserves by the agricultural classes, very much, as in New England, the common Berberry is used for same purpose. It is evergreen, or if not entirely so, it has what is even better, a most superb rich, brown tone, mingled with the most gorgeous scarlet and crimson, like our highest autumnal coloring, and the leaves covered with a brilliant lustre-like varnish. We believe it does not grow over five or six feet high, and we find the plant is much improved by keeping it back by occasional clipping, as it sometimes has a tendency to straggle. It should be always planted in beds or masses, by itself.

The Rhododendron is too well known to require description. Although the R. Ponticum and many of the hardy hybrids like Nero, Atrosanguineum, Ferrugineum, and a few others are quite satisfactory in the protection of a wood, yet the only truly reliable ones in exposed situations, are the English varieties of the Catawbiensis, of which Messrs. Waterer & Godfrey (and we presume they can also be procured now at our nurseries) offer thirty varieties in color, all hardy here, one and a half to two feet high, mostly with flower buds, at fifty shillings sterling, per hundred, for plants *not* named, and ten pounds per hundred (about fifty cents each) for named varieties.

It is perhaps well to say here that Rhododendrons, Azaleas, and most of these evergreen shrubs, do well enough in ordinary garden soil, but are much improved in color and habit, by a soil prepared equally of peat, leaf soil, and sand or sandy loam. There is no more superb plant cultivated than the Rhododendron, and we earnestly recommend the adoption in pots (to be kept in the green-house during winter) of the varieties below mentioned,* too tender to be entirely exposed all the year.

The *Ilex laurifolia* (Laurel-leaved holly), strikes us, after the Mahonia, as the next most valuable evergreen shrub, even more so here than our native Kalmia, which is very apt to suffer from our hot August weather. We have grown this Ilex many years, both in a wood and in the most open situation, and apparently with equal success; though we presume in certain seasons, with great alternations of heat and cold, those exposed would be apt to scorch. It has a leaf of a color and habit like the Camelia, and even finer ; and, if we regard foliage alone without flower (though even this is pretty), we should say we had no finer plant upon this place. It is an exceedingly great favorite of ours, and strange to say, we have never seen it elsewhere.

The *Kalmia latifolia* (the Broad-leaved Kalmia), or American Sheep-laurel, as it is commonly called, is another very desirable shrub, as well as its varieties— *K. angustifolia* (Narrow-leaved Kalmia) ; *K. myrtifolia* (Myrtle-leaved) ; *K. carnea* (Red-flowering Kalmia), &c. It is somewhat difficult to move, and although the mountains in our neighborhood abound with them, we have found it less expensive to import plants from England, raised from seed, at fifteen cents apiece, than to transplant the native habitats of the mountains, with their long straggling roots. Though it will grow in the sun, yet in the shade it becomes a different plant.

The above, with the different Yews, Arbor vitæs, creeping and low-growing Junipers, &c., are the only dependable evergreen shrubs that we can at this

* *Atro sanguineum* (Superb Deep maroon); *Archimedes* (Superb Rose de Chine); *Angiola* (Superb Cherry pink); *Brayamum ; Currcanum* (Superb Truss lilac rose); *Chancellor ; Fastuosum* (Magnificent Truss lilac); *Giganteum; Hannibal ; Henry Drummond ; Luxidum ; Rubrum Maculatum , Nero ; Ne Plus Ultra* (Fine lilac); *Poussin ; Reedianum* (Small Truss rose-pink, but fine); *Sir Isaac Newton ; Vandyck ; Victoria* (Superb Deep lilac); *Cleopatra ; Invictum ; Proserpine ; Speciosum.*

moment recommend for general planting in exposed sunny situations.

For amateurs, who have the advantage of a wood, or a long line of high fence, upon the northern side of which they may have a shaded border, there are several other things we would suggest : such as the hardy Heaths, the hardy *Belgic azalias*, costing in England £10 per hundred (fifty cents apiece), for named vari· eties, in twenty different colors : the different Andromedas, the Rhodora Canadensis, the various Gaultherias, the Ledums, the pretty family of Menziesias, the Epigæa, the different varieties of Box, the green and the variegated Euonymous.

The Ilex Scottica is represented to us as quite as fine and as hardy as Ilex laurifolia, though we have not yet tried it.

In those parts of the country, too cold to grow the English ivy, we would suggest large circular beds, in appropriate parts of the pleasure-grounds, to be planted in ivy ; and which, while permitted to fill the bed, should be kept within it by clipping. Beds in this way filled (the ground being well covered in) with the different varieties of the Gold-striped, the Silver-striped, and the Dark Giant, are very effective and striking, and when not protected by snow in winter, can readily be so by a few cedar or hemlock boughs thrown over them.

NOTE.—As this work is passing through the press, we have received a twig, perfectly green and fresh, of an Abies Douglasii, from a tree at Cazenovia, New York, planted in 1853, when only eighteen inches high, and that has now reached the altitude of eight feet, making annual shoots of fifteen to twenty inches, withstanding a temperature in 1855–6–7, of 25° to 28° *below* zero, without the slightest protection or the least injury ; while the A. Menziesii is immediately destroyed, and the Silver fir raised with difficulty, and where neither the Cedar of Lebanon, the Pinus excelsa, or Picea pinsapo, succeed at all.

The tree from which the specimen was sent us, is growing in a retentive loam, rarely suffering from drought, but planted on an open lawn, entirely exposed on every side.

This seems conclusive evidence that *cold* at least, does not injure the Douglas fir, and that it may be classed "Perfectly hardy" in a climate usually considered the most severe, or one of the most severe, in the State of New York.

TABULAR VIEW showing the comparative hardihood of the new Evergreens in the United States.

Note.—(*) Suffers from sun; (h) Hardy; (t) Tender; (o) Has stood out 3 years; (p) Perfectly; (t) Loses its Leader.

	Fishkill.	Boston.	Newport.	Philadel'a.	Wash'ton.	New-York.	Clinton, N. Y.	Natchez.	New Jersey.	Flushing, L. I.	Augusta, Ga.	Columbus, Ohio.	Cincinnati, Ohio.	Rochester.
ABIES.														
Alba,	Hardy	Hardy	Hardy	Hardy	Hardy		Hardy		Hardy	Hardy		Hardy	Hardy	Hardy
Amabilis,	do	do	do		do				Hardy	do				do
Fraseri,	do	Hardy		do	do					do				
Longifolia,														
Brunoniana,	Tender	Hardy	Hardy o	Hardy	Tender				Tender	Tender			Tender	
Cephalonica,	Hardy	do	do	do	10 ft. high	Hardy			Hardy	Very h				do
Clanbrasilliana,	do		do		Hardy				do	do				do
Densa,	do													
Douglasii,	In shade h	In shade h	Tender	Not h	not quite h		Hardy	Hardy	Loses t	Hardy	Hardy		Hardy	
Taxifolia,	Hardy	Hardy	Hardy	Hardy	Hardy	Hardy		Hardy	Hardy	do			Hardy	do
Excelsa,	do	Hardy	Hardy	Hardy	Hardy		Hardy		Hardy	do	do	Fine	Hardy	do
Elegans,	do	do		do	do					do				
Foliis Variegata,	do	do		do	do					do				
Monstrosa,	do	do									Suffers*			
Nigra,	do	Fine		Hardy	Hardy	Hardy	Hardy		Hardy	do		Stand well		
Pendula,		Hardy	Hardy		Hardy					do				do
Pygmaea,	do			do										
Stricta,														
Grandis,	do	do	Hardy	do	Hardy									do
Hudsonia,	do			Hardy	Hardy									
Jezoensis,	Possibly h			Hardy		Untried			Tender	Untried				
Kaemferi,	do									Hardy				
Lasiocarpa,	Hardy	Hardy		Hardy	Hardy				Hardy	Hardy				
Menziesii,	Hardy	Fine	Hardy	Hardy	Hardy	Hardy	In shade h			Fine			Hardy	Hardy
Nobilis,	Hardy	Hardy	Hardy	Hardy	Hardy	Hardy			Hardy	do			do	Hardy
Nordmanniana,	do	do	do	do	do	do				do			Succeeds	
Orientalis,	do	do	do	do	do	Loses t	Tender		In shade h	do			Hardy	do
Smithiana, Syn. of Morinda,	In shade h	In shade h	Very h	Loses i	do	Loses i	Tender	Suffers		do				Tender
Taxifolia,	in shade h		Hardy	Hardy	do	Not h			Loses i	Loses t				Tender
Webbiana,	in shade h			Tender	do		Loses t		Hardy					Loses t
Whittmanniana,	Prob'bly h					Not h	Not h							
ARAUCARIA.														
Cunninghamia,	In pots t			Tender				Tender		In pots t	Hardy	Tender		
Brasiliensis,	do							do		do	Fine h	do		
Excelsa,	do		Tender					do	Nearly h	do	Tender	do		
Imbricata,	In shade h				Pretty h	Not h				In shade h	Hardy	do	Pretty well	
BIOTA.														
Japonica,	Pretty h	Injured	Pretty h	Gener'ly h	Hardy	Hardy			Killed	Hardy	Very well	Pr'tty well		
Orientalis,	Hardy	Very well	Hardy	do	do	do				do				Hardy
Argentea,	do		Perfectly h	Tender	do	do								
Aurea,	Hardy	Hardy		Hardy	Hardy				Hardy		Fine			
Gracilis,		Hardy		do	do									
Glauca,				do	do									
Variegata,	Hardy			do	do					Untried				do

	1	2	3	4	5	6	7	8	9	10	11	12	13	14
Pendula,	Hardy	Very h		Well	Hardy		Hardy		Nearly h	Hardy		Well		do
Tatarica,	do			do	do				do	do		do		do
CEDRUS.														
Africana,	Hardy	Slightly tender	Hardy and fine Suffers*	Stands well	Hardy in dry soil	Suffers in sun		p h 30 ft.	Hardy In shade	Very hardy	Well and Very fine			Hardy
Argentea,	In shade h	do		do					do	Injured				Nearly h
Deodara,	do	do		Hardier	Hardier					Stronger				
Do. Robusta,	do	do												
Do. Viridis,	Hardy	do	Tender	Tender	Perfe'tly h	Hardy	Too tender		h when advanced	In some localities h	} Well	Promising	Tender	
Libanis,								Hardy }						
CEPHALOTAXUS.														
Adpressa,	Hardy			Hardy		Hardy			Hardy					
Drupacea,	do	Hardy							do	Very well				
Fortunii, Mas. and Fem.,	do	Hardy		do	Tender				do					
Pedunculata,								Probably h	More t					
CHAMÆCYPARIS.														
Sphæroida,	Hardy					Hardy				Hardy				
Variegata,	do			Tender										
Thurifera,											Very well			
CRYPTOMERIA.														
Japonica,	In shade h	Slightly t	Toler'bly h	Tolerably	14 feet h	Shelter'd h		15 feet h	Shelter'd h	Injured	Very well	Tender		Uncertain
Pendula,	In pots t	do		do		do			do		do	do		
Nana,	In shade h	do		do		do			do	Hardy	do			
Lobbii,	In pots	do		do										
Viridis,	do	do		do										
CUNNINGHAMIA.														
Sinensis,	Hardy		Quite Hardy	Does Pr'tly well				Hardy		Injured by sun		Tender		
Lanceolata, }	in shade							15 feet						
Glauca, }														
CUPRESSUS.														
Excelsa,	In pots t		Tender	Hardy	Tender	Hardy				Tender	Very well	Tender	Tender	
Funebris,	do			Not hardy	Tender	Not hardy			Too tender	do	do		On trial	
Goveniana,	On trial		Tender	do		do			do	do				
Lawsoniana,	In pots				16 feet	do			do	do				
Lusitanica,					Destroyed									
Macrocarpa,	Hardy			Hardy		Hardy				Tender				
Nana,	do			Does well	Hardy	do				do				
Pendula,	do			Tender	Hardy					do				
Oblonga Pendula,	In pots t		Tender	do	do									
Sempervirens,	Hardy			Hardy						Hardy				
Variegata,	In pots			Generl'y *										
Torulosa,	do													
Tourneforti,	do					Hardy								
Whitleyana,								Hardy						

NOTE.—(*) Suffers from sun; (h) Hardy; (o) Has stood out 3 years; (p) Perfectly; (t) Tender; (t) Loses its leader.

541

TABULAR VIEW showing the comparative hardihood of the new Evergreens in the United States.

NOTE.—(*) Suffers from sun; (h) Hardy; (t) Tender; (d) Doubtful; (p) Perfectly; (l) Loses its Leader.

	Fishkill.	Boston.	Newport.	Philadel'a.	Wash'ton.	New-York.	Natchez.	Clinton, N.Y.	New Jersey.	Flushing, L.I.	Augusta, Ga.	Columbus, Ohio.	Cincinnati, Ohio.	Rochester.
DACRIDIUM.														
Franklinii,	In pots d								Tender	In pots d				
Cupressinum,	do d								do	do d				
FITZ ROYA.														
Patagonica,	Doubtful			Suffers *					Tender	Untried	Very well			
GLYPTOSTROBUS.														
Heterophyllus,	Hardy		Perfe'tly h						Rather t	Hardy				
Pendulus,	do								Hardy	Superb h				
JUNIPERUS.														
Bedfordiana, } Synonyms, Barbadensis, }	Hardy		Perfectly Hardy		Hardy	Hardy			Hardy			Tender		
Californica,	Doubtful													
Canadensis,	Hardy	Hardy	do	Hardy	do	do	Hardy		do	Uncertain	Well	Succeeds	Hardy	Hardy
Chinensis, Femina and Mas.,	Hardy	do		Hardy					do	Hardy	Very new	do	do	do
Communis,	do			do	do	do	Protec'n h		do	do	Hardy			do
Ericoides,	do			Does well					do	do	do			
Hibernica,	do		do	Hardy	Hardy		Hardy		do	do	do	do	do	do
Suecica,	do				14 feet h				do	do	Too new			
Gossainthanea,	do								do	do				
Hispanica,	do								do	do				
Japonica,	do								do	do				
Macrocarpa,	do								do					
Mexicana,														
Nana,	do								Beautiful h	do	Very well			Hardy
Oblonga Pendula,	do	do	Gener'ly h	Hardy	Hardy	Hardy				do	Very well	do		do
Occidentalis,	do	do		do					do	do	Hardy			
Oxycedrus,	In pots d									do	do			
Phoenicia,	Hardy			Hardy					do	do				
Prostrata,	do	do		do					Hardy	do	Tol'ly well	do	do	do
Recurva,	In pots d		Hardy	Protec'd h	Rather t	In shade h		Hardy	Not hardy		Well			
Religiosa,				Hardy						do				
Sabina,	Hardy			Hardy	Hardy				Very h					do
Squamata,	do													
Taxifolia,	Hardy													
Variegata,	Hardy										Hardy	Cultivated		
LARIX.														
Pendula,	Hardy	Hardy	Hardy	Hardy	Hardy			Hardy	Hardy	Hardy	Hardy	do	Hardy	Hardy
Kaempferi,	Prob'bly h	In pots d								do	do			
Griffithiana,	In pots d													
LIBOCEDRUS.														
Chilensis,	In pots t			Tender	Not tested				Nearly h	Untried	Very well			

542

	Prob'bly h	Hardy	Untied	Hardy	Fine h	Hardy	Nearly h	Not quite h	Very fine	Very t	Hardy	Hardy
Decurrens,												
PICEA.												
Amabilis,	Hardy	Hardy					Hardy	Hardy				Hardy
Bracteata,	do						Hardy	do				do
Grandis,	do	do					Hardy	do			do	do
Nobilis,	do	do					Hardy	do			do	do
Nordmanniana,	do	do				Not h	Hardy	do				do
Pectinata,	do	do	Little t				Hardy	do	Suffers*	Suffers*	do	do
P. Pendula,	do	Little t	100 feet h				Hardy	do	Suffers*			do
Pichta,		Hardy	Hardy	Seems h			Hardy	do	Succeeds	Succeeds		
Pindrow,	Gener'ly t	Hardy	do			Hardy	Hardy	Little t		do	do	do
Pinsapo,	Hardy	do	do			do	Hardy	Hardy		do	do	do
Webbiana,	Gener'ly h	Not quite h					Hardy	Little t		Loses i	do	Loses i
PINUS.												
Australis,	In pots d	Prob'bly h	6 feet h		Fine h		Hardy	Hardy	Native			
Apulcensis,	Hardy	Hardy	Hardy				Hardy	Hardy	Straggling	Fine	Hardy	Hardy
Austriaca,	do	do					do	do			do	do
Ayacahuite,	do	do					do					
Banksiana,	do	do					do					
Beardsleyi,	do	do					Hardy					
Benthamiana,			do				Not hardy	Not hardy	Too new	Too new		
Boothiana,	do	do										
Bonapartea,												
Brutia,	do											
Bungeana,	In pots t	do					Hardy	Hardy			Hardy	Hardy
Canariensis,	Hardy	Hardy					Hardy	Hardy				
Cembra,	do	Hardy					Hardy	Hardy			Hardy	Hardy
Craigeana,	In pots d	do										
Devoniana,	Hardy	Hardy					Hardy	Hardy			Hardy	Hardy
Engelmanniana,			Does well				Hardy	Hardy			Hardy	Hardy
Excelsa,	Hardy	Hardy	Half hardy				Hardy	Hardy	Very well	Succeeds	Hardy	Hardy
Filifolia,	In pots t	Hardy					15 ft. high	Hardy				
Flexilis,	Hardy	Hardy					Hardy					
Fremontiana,												
Hartwegii,	Tender	Tender							Too new	Too new		
Halepensis,	Shaded h	Doubtful					Hardy					Hardy
Inops,	Hardy	Hardy					Tender	Tender			Tender	
Insignis,	In pots t	Hardy	Too tender				Tender	Tender	Too new	Succeeds	Tender	Hardy
Jeffreyi,	Hardy	Hardy	Hardy				Hardy	Hardy				
Lamberdiana,	do	Hardy					Hardy	Hardy				
Laricio,	do		Hardy			Hardy	Hardy	do			Hardy	do
Leiophylla,	Hardy		do					do	Promising	Promising		do
Lindleyana,	In pots t	Hardy										
Longifolia,	Hardy	Hardy										
Macrocarpa,	do	do										
Macrophylla,	do	do										
Maritima,		Tender	Shelter'd h				15 ft high h				Hardy	Hardy
Mitis,	do	Hardy	Hardy	Hardy	Hardy	Hardy	Hardy	Hardy	Hardy	Hardy	Hardy	Hardy
Monstrosa,	do								Cultivated			do
Montezuma,	do								Cultivated			do

NOTE.—(*) Suffers in the sun; (h) Hardy; (t) Tender; (d) Doubtful; (p) Perfectly; (t) Loses its leader.

TABULAR VIEW showing the comparative hardihood of the new Evergreens in the United States.

NOTE.—(*) Suffers from sun; (h) Hardy; (t) Tender; (o) Has stood out 3 years; (p) Perfectly; (t) Loses its Leader.

	Fishkill.	Boston.	Newport.	Philadel'a.	Wash'ton.	New-York.	Clinton, N.Y.	Natchez.	New Jersey.	Flushing, L.I.	Augusta, Ga.	Columbus, Ohio.	Cincinnati, Ohio.	Rochester.
PINUS.														
Montecata,	Hardy	Hardy	Hardy					Hardy		Hardy				Hardy
Mugho,	do			Untried										
Nivea,	do	do												
Pallasiana,	Possibly h							Hardy						
Palustris,	In pots t			Hardy				Hardy	In shade h		Native			
Patula,	Hardy	In pots t												
Pendula,	In pots d													
Picea,	Hardy													
Pinaster,	do		Toler'bly h	Stand well										
Sabiniana,	do	Hardy		Hardy	Hardy	Hardy			Hardy	do				do
Ponderosa,	do	do		Hardy	do	do			do	do		Promising	do	do
Pumilio,	do	do		do						do		Cultivated	do	do
Pyrenaica,				do									do	
Radiata,	do													
Rigida,	do	Hardy	Hardy	do			Hardy	Hardy	do	do	Well	Well	do	do
Strobus,	do	do	do	do	do	do			do	do	do	do	do	do
Sylvestris,	do	do		do	do	do			do				do	do
Do. Variegata,	do								do					
Do. Pygmaea,	do								do					
Do. Nana,									do	do				
Do. Argentea,														
Tœda,														
Tuberculata,						Hardy		Fragrant		Tender				
PODOCARPUS.														
Angina,	In pots									Hardy	Very well			
Coriacea,	do		Hardy							do	do			
Japonica,			do							do				
Taxifolia,	Hardy									do				
SALISBURIA.														
Adianthefolia,	Hardy	Hardy	Hardy	Hardy.	Hardy	Slightly t	Hardy		Hardy	do	do			Hardy
SAXE-GOTHAEA.														
Conspicua,	Untried; In pots								Untried	Untried	Too new			
SEQUOIA.														
Sempervirens,	In pots t			Not hardy	Injured		Tender		Tender	Tender		Very t		
TAXODIUM.														
Sempervirens,	In pots t	Hardy	Tender		do	Hardy	do		Hardy	do	Very well	do		
Distichum,	Hardy	do	Hardy	Hardy	Hardy	Hardy	Hardy		do	Hardy	Native	Deep soil h		do
Fastgiatum,	do								do	do				
Nutans,	do	do							do					
Pendulum,	do													

TAXUS.

Species													
Adpressa,	do		Perfe'tly h	Hardy	Hardy	Half h		Hardy	Hardy	Well	Succeeds			Nearly h
Baccata,	do	Hardy	Toler'bly h	Hardy	Hardy	Hardy		do	do	Tolerably	Suffers*			Hardly
Argentea,	Pretty h		do	do	Hardy	Hardy		do	do		Cultivated	Hardy		do
Aurea,	Very h		do	do	Hardy			do	do		Hardy	do		
Canadensis,	Hardy	Hardy	do	Pretty h	Hardy	Hardy		do	do	Suffers*	Hardy	do		
Dovastonii,	do		Hardy	Hardy	do			do	do	do			
Erecta,	do				do		do	do	do			
Ericoides,	do	do	Hardy	Hardy	Pretty h				Very well	Very h	not quite h			Nearly h
Fastigiata, } Syn.,	Pretty h	not quite h	do	do	Hardy	Pretty h	Tender	In shade h	In shade h	Not h	Well	Succeeds*	do	Nearly h
Hibernica, } Syn.,					Hardy }	Injured		do	do	do				h and fine
Nana,	Hardy					Noi h		Suffers*	In shade h	Suffers*				
Variegata,	Pretty h									Tender				
Harringtonii,														

THUIOPSIS.

Dolabrata,	Very h	Fine						Hardy	Hardy	Hardy			
Borealis,													

THUJA.

Doniana,	In pots t		Hardy	Hardy	Hardy	Hardy			In pots d		Well	Cultivated	Hardy	
Filiformis,	Hardy		do	do	do			Hardy	Hardy		Very well	Very well	Hardy	Hardly
Occidentalis,	do							do	do		Suffers*	do		
Variegata,	Probably h			do	Hardy			Nearly h	do	Nearly h	Very well	Cultivated		
Decurrens,									do	do				
Macrocarpa,	In pots d			do	do			Hardy	do	Hardy				
Gigantica,								do	do				
Compacta,	Hardy			do	do				do	do	Well	Succeeds	Hardy	Hardy
Tatarica,	do			do	do				do	do	Very well	do	do	
Pendula,													
Plicata, } Syn.,	do	Hardy	do	do	Hardy	Hardy		do	do	do	Well	do	do	do
Siberica, } Syn.,													
Warreana, } Syn.,													

TORREYA.

Grandis,										Untried			
Myristica,	In pots									do			
Nucifera,	Hardy		Tender	Hardy	Hardy			Hardy	Hardy	Hardy			
Taxifolia,												

WASHINGTONIA.

Gigantica,	Prob'bly h	Hardy	Hardy	Hardy				Hardy	Untried	Untried	Well	Cultivated		Hardy

WIDRINGTONIA.

Ericoides,	Pretty h				Hardy						Browned			

NOTE.—(*) Suffers from sun; (h) Hardy; (t) Tender; (p) Perfectly; (l) Loses its leader.

A Report from Mr. Edwards, Secretary of the Illinois State Agricultural Society, on the hardihood of certain evergreens in his State, arrived too late to be incorporated in this Tabular View, but may be found on page 559.

SECTION V.

HISTORICAL NOTICES.

It is with great reluctance that we undertake this portion of our task, from a consciousness of our entire inability to do justice to the many fine places which exist all over the United States, and which require a greater knowledge than we have of them, as well as more space and time than is allowed us, for the remainder of this supplement.

With Mr. Downing, in his first edition, this labor was comparatively a light one, as, twelve or fifteen years ago, there were only a few marked places in the neighborhood of our large cities, and upon the banks of the Hudson river and Long Island sound, which were so distinguished and prominent as to be easily described; of this class were Col. Perkins' and Mr. Lyman's near Boston; the Manor of Livingston, Montgomery place and Hyde Park, upon the Hudson; the Bartram garden, Stenton, Woodlawn, etc., near Philadelphia; and a few others. Since this period, however, the taste for country life has advanced so rapidly, that, in and about these very neighborhoods, there are, at present, scores of country houses, many of them of the finest and most expensive character, but all partaking more or less of similar disposition and style of grounds, and a similar fashion of planting.

We have already said, in the introduction to this supplement, that since Mr. Downing's time, though the style of country houses had vastly improved, yet an equal improvement was not so evident in Landscape Gardening. This we attributed to the fact that, while an Architect was employed to build the house, no professional artist was employed to arrange the grounds, and great errors and mistakes constantly occurred—in many cases so gross, as to destroy the entire effect of what would be otherwise a very fine and attractive place.

Although there has been great expenditure of money in country houses and costly glass-buildings, during the past ten years, yet, in a great many cases, very inferior arrangement and planting have been exhibited in the grounds. Landscape Gardening is just as much a picture, though a living one, made by trees, as a painted landscape is made by the pencil or brush; both require long years of study, artistic perceptions, and a knowledge of how to handle the tools. It would be quite as unreasonable, we think, to expect one of our merchants or lawyers, in active business, to make a landscape, as to paint one. How can a person who has passed his life in the whirl and excitement of active business, or professional occupations, be suddenly transferred to the country and be expected to make a garden? It would be just as absurd as to expect that a gardener can be transferred to the counting-room, and become, the next day, a merchant. It is quite as necessary in the one case as in the other to be educated up to whatever you are to succeed in.

It requires more and different qualities to make a country-place than are required for any other profession. For while industry, knowledge, prudence, sagacity, are generally all that are necessary for a merchant, or lawyer, or doctor, the Landscape Gardener must have not only these but also *taste*—a knowledge of the beautiful, and a perception of the harmony of form and color; in other words, he must be an artist.

The fashion of living in the country has not existed long enough (though rapidly increasing) for this knowledge or taste to have been very widely extended; for every good

place there are a great many bad ones, and we cannot but
think that our country residences would be much more
agreeable, if artists were allowed to arrange the places—
at least, to make suggestions, just as artists are allowed
to build the houses, or, at any rate, help build them.
The necessary result then, as we have previously
observed, is that a person going into the country
to live, makes his own place from his neighbor's suggestions, or from ideas derived from his neighbor's
place—which may be very faulty or of an entirely different character from his own—with the aid, perhaps, of
his gardener and a suggestive nurseryman. A great
many places are manufactured from these three sources ;
and the general character of them all is so much alike,
that there is little or no distinction between half a dozen
in the same neighborhood, though a competent Landscape Gardener might have developed many different
beauties in each.

In the absence, therefore (from having been already
mentioned in the first part of this book), of any of those
very marked and distinguished residences which have
received the stamp of years, where trees have grown
into studies, and the places themselves have become
schools for the lovers of art, we trust we shall
not be thought invidious if we confine ourselves
to a brief mention of a few of the prominent places
which have come under our notice — being quite
aware that they are well deserving of much more than
we have an opportunity to say. We were in hopes
with many of these to have given illustrations, but here
again time failed us ; even the one or two we succeeded
in procuring were too late for the engraver.

We are quite aware we shall be forced to omit a
great many in more remote parts of the country, which
we have not yet had the pleasure of seeing, and this
makes us the more regret that our limits and our time
will allow us to do so little.

The neighborhood of Boston was so thoroughly described in the first portion of the present volume, that but little is left us to add to this account. The same places, more or less, which were prominent then, are quite as distinctive now.

Mr. Lee's lawn, as yet, has no rival, unless perhaps that of Mr. Mudge, at Swamscot, near Lynn. Wellesley, the residence of Mr. Hunnewell, we have already described; and though there are a great many other fine houses, the places themselves are yet comparatively newly planted.

Kenwood, the residence of Mr. Peabody, near Salem, has a great deal of quiet pastoral beauty, and much artistic effect is shown in the arrangement of the house and grounds.

Linmere, the residence of R. S. Fay, Esq., has great capabilities, not yet taken advantage of. There is here a very valuable collection of rare deciduous and evergreen trees, which, if properly thinned out and planted, would be very effective. The place itself is a fine estate of some five hundred acres or more, mostly surrounding a lake, and very much resembling Scotch scenery.

The house and grounds of the late John E. Thayer, Esq., including a vast extent of glass, are perhaps the most expensive in the neighborhood of Boston.

The residence of Mr. J. L. Gardener has a pretty sloping lawn, and an attractive flower garden, with many fine Norways and other trees.

The difficulty of procuring suitable residences in the city, has forced many persons into the country, and the consequent high prices have prevented the occupation of much land by any single individual.

The new residences are, consequently, surburban, but very complete in all the outer accessaries of country life—stables, green and fruit-houses, and very substantial and handsome walls.

Within a few years, there has been very visible im·
provement in the style and character of the marine
residences in the neighborhood of Boston.

At Lynn, and on what is called the Beverley shore,
are the marine villas of Mr. Prescott, Mr. Curtis, Mr.
Lawrence, Mr. Jasigi, Mr. J. D. Bates, Mr. Loring, and
the late Mr. Dexter—all more or less distinguished
by the excellence of their houses, and with most
charming views.

Newport, having become, of late years, a very
desirable place of residence for people of fortune,
abounds, like the neighborhood of Boston, in very tasteful and agreeable villas and cottages, with prettily
arranged and well kept grounds, the most successful
of which, taking grounds with house, is *Beachclyffe*, the
residence of Delancy Kane, Esq. Mr. Kane's house, a
very fine one, is in the style of the French chateaux,
with extensive views both inland and seaward, and his
lawn is quite as successful as any we know in this
country. The place is about twenty acres, and very
charmingly planted with a great variety of the most
valuable trees. We think the growth of certain varieties unsurpassed in any place we have ever seen;
and there is a luxuriance of habit and depth of color in
the masses which form his boundary plantations, which
is truly remarkable.

Mr. Kane had a great advantage over many of his
Newport neighbors, in finding quite a number of well-
grown horse-chestnuts, and other ornamental trees,
which he has contrived to work, with much good taste,
into his own plantations. The gate-lodge here is quite
a little gem in its way.

Malbone Place.--The residence of Mr. J. Prescott
Hall is a fine house of red or rather brown freestone,
commanding an extensive view of Narragansett bay, and
surrounded by some most extraordinary Red cedars, of
great antiquity, but with their heads, so flattened and

distorted by the winds as to produce the closest resemblance to that peculiar horizontal growth which characterizes the Cedar of Lebanon.

Mr. Hall's farm is, we believe, a fine one, and he has great command of water from a hydraulic ram, in the driest seasons, sufficient to irrigate his entire garden. The celebrated Buffum pear originated on this place, and is still very prolific.

Mr. Wetmore's residence, built of Fall River granite, is the largest and most expensive house at Newport, with a very successful lodge, and a fine extent of glass, containing a vinery, and a very handsome octagonal conservatory. The view of the sea from this place is very impressive.

Mr. Parish has a fine place in the neighborhood of Mr. Wetmore. The house, of brick and stone trimmings, is a very striking one, and the lawn admirably kept to the water's edge. Adjoining this is the estate of Mr. Cadwallader, where at present there is no house. We believe great and extensive improvements are contemplated in this place; it is still in an unfinished state.

The residence of Mr. King is a handsome brick house, in the Italian style, surrounded by some fifteen acres, with some remarkably fine specimens of Pinus cembra, twelve to fifteen feet high; also some fine Junipers and Purple beeches.

Mr. Calvert's grounds, near the town, contain some fine trees grouped with much taste.

Among other residences of more or less merit, are those of Messrs. Russell, Lyman, Hoppin, Van Rensselaer, Wright, Mason, and Mr. Morgan Gibbes.

Notwithstanding the difficulty which is always supposed to exist, in producing any effect by trees so immediately in the neighborhood of the sea, yet experience shows that, at Newport, at least, much is and has been done by judicious planting. Mr. Kane informs us, and

in this, we believe, Mr. Smith, who is the great autho·
rity at Newport on trees, coincides, that in making an
evergreen screen from the sea, the Scotch and Austrian
pines should be placed outside, Siberian (*Thuja Warreana*) Arbor vitæ, and Pinus cembra next, with perhaps the Common Red cedar; and among deciduous
trees, nothing succeeds better than *Acer pseudo-platanus* and *Platanus orientalis* (the Eastern plane).

Upon the Hudson, the most marked place which has
been created since the first edition of this book, is *Rockwood*, the residence of Edwin Bartlett, Esq., near Tarrytown. The house (Fig. 97), is truly a princely mansion,
with a façade of nearly or quite one hundred and fifty feet,
and with its internal arrangements and decorations, we
should say, quite the most complete establishment in
the United States. The estate itself consists of several
hundred acres, very cleverly planted with park-like
effect; and the approach, which is quite a long one, so
judiciously managed, that it conveys the idea of a very
large place, and gives a stranger the most agreeable
impression of the house, at the first appearance, when
emerging from a ravine or passage between two rocky
eminences.

The views from the house and the plateau or terrace
around it, are very superb, and unrivalled, we think,
upon the Hudson River.

Very extensive green-houses and conservatories have
been erected under the supervision of Mr. Luchars, a
builder of great experience; and we do not see why,
in a few years, with the taste and liberality of expenditure on the part of the proprietor, Rockwood will not
be the, or certainly one of the most distinguished
country-seats in America.

With regard to Hyde Park (Mr. Langdon's), Ellerslie
(Mr. Kelly's), Montgomery Place (Mrs. Livingston's),
and Annandale (late Blithewood), Mr. Bard's, which we
have always considered the four great places in this

Fig. 97.—Rockwood, Residence of Edwin Bartlett, Esq., near Tarrytown, N. Y.

country, we can only refer our readers to Mr. Downing's remarks about them in the first portion of this volume. While the hand of time has even still more mellowed their beauties by those touches and effects which Nature alone can produce with years, yet even here the hand of man has not been idle.

At Annandale and Hyde Park, extensive ranges of glass have replaced the old ones of previous owners,* while at Montgomery Place and Ellerslie the most showy and superb conservatories and green-houses have been erected.

At Montgomery Place also, there has been planted within the past ten years, the most complete and satisfactory arboretum in the United States. Neither pains or expense have been spared in obtaining the most entire and thorough collection, or in the peculiar and appropriate preparation of soil for the reception of the different varieties.

In the neighborhood of Rhinebeck, is " Wyndclyffe," the residence of Miss Jones, a very successful and distinctive house, with much the appearance of some of the smaller Scotch castles. This place is still quite new, but the situation is one of great beauty, upon a bold, projecting point of land, in admirable harmony with the style of the house, and with the most extensive and superb views.

Immediately above Hyde Park, is the fine house of Mr. Curtis, one of the most expensive and costly upon the Hudson, possessing very much the same extended views of river and mountain as at Hyde Park.

Roseneath—the residence of C. M. Wolcott, Esq., in our own immediate neighborhood, is the creation of the past few years, and we are very much indebted to it for a great many advantages to our own place, which

---

* At Hyde Park, a very graceful and elegant house of the composite order, designed and built by Platt, of New York, and with a façade of one hundred and fifty feet, has within a few years, replaced the hospitable old mansion of the late Dr. Hosack.

we should not otherwise possess. By the employment of wire fences, and some careful planting out of the houses in both places, a great deal of what Nature has done for each, has been appropriated by both. We know of no other place where such successful masses of Rhododendrons, Azalias, and Mahonias are grown as here, being on the north side of the house, and getting but little or no sun. The graperies, green-house, and gardens, are extensive, and admirably kept. By means of a steam-engine, water can at any moment be forced into the mansion and an outside reservoir, from which it can be distributed over the gardens. In the comparatively small space of sixteen acres, Mr. Wolcott has every attribute of a well-kept country place—several lawns, each distinct from the other, with separate and lovely views ; an English flower-garden, a most successful vegetable-garden, green-house, grapery, and forcing-house, the most charming views, and no apparent boundary but river and mountain.

Idlewild—the residence of N. P. Willis, Esq., across the Hudson, some four miles below Newburgh, is a piece of Nature's Landscape Gardening, where the hand of man should not, and, from the good taste of the owner, has not been allowed to appear, except in the necessary buildings. In a work like this, for the purpose of showing the progress of Landscape Gardening, this place should, properly, not be mentioned ; and we refer to it, simply to show how delicate and refined that taste must be which, appreciating all that Nature has done with so much prodigality of beauty, as at "Idlewild," has the courage to let her alone.

In the neighborhood of Philadelphia, there are a great many fine places ; among them is *Medary*, the residence of Harry Ingersoll, Esq. A tasteful and substantial house, built by Notman, we believe, with pleasure-grounds of very considerable extent, and of a pretty, graceful character, softly undulating, and well planted. The landscape and the character of the country in the neighborhood of Medary, though deficient in the bolder outlines of many of our more northern places, yet has, what we confess is a great attraction to us, the quiet sylvan beauty of English scenery—that pastoral look, which seems to suggest the presence of animated nature ; and Mr. Ingersoll has, with great good taste, we think, taken advantage of this hint, by the introduction of fine cattle, which harmonize most pleasingly with the character of the place. There is here a pretty flower-garden, plant-cabinet, green-house, vinery, and some new peach and orchard-houses.

Brookwood—the residence of Charles Henry Fisher, Esq.—a very extensive and complete establishment, with a great amount of glass, most charming views, and a great deal of well-kept, ornamental ground, will, in a few years, be one of the most striking places near Philadelphia.

Alverthorpe—the residence of J. Francis Fisher, Esq., is another superb place, where a vast deal has been accomplished, both with house and grounds. The park-like view from the front is extensive and exceedingly striking. An effective architectural appearance is produced in connecting the mansion and green-houses by a sort of cloister, or gallery. The collection of trees and shrubs at this place is also large and very choice.

Fern Hill—nearer town, is the residence of J. Pratt McKean, Esq., and is another of those remarkably fine and imposing houses which have been erected in the neighborhood of Philadelphia within a few years. Here, also, are fine ranges of glass, and extensive and interesting views, and a great work in process of being accomplished.

There are many other places near Philadelphia (and we think the vicinity of no other city abounds in so many costly country residences) which we shall be compelled

to pass over, from want of time and space, simply with
their names : such as the fine and expensive house of
Col. Eastwick, on the old Bartram garden ; *Woodfield*,
the fine residence of Mr. Swift ; *Devonshire*, the seat of
Mr. Blight, remarkable for its evergreens ; and *Champ-
lost*, the most charming old country residence of Charles
P. Fox, Esq.

In the vicinity of Princeton, N. J., are some fine residences. The most interesting one to us is *Woodlawn*,
belonging to Richard S. Field, Esq, and which we have
alluded to so often in course of this supplement, that
we have no right, perhaps, to say anything more. The
house is a very fine one, and the place most successful
in certain varieties of evergreens.

There is here a Cedar of Lebanon (Fig. 38) larger
than any other in the country, except Mr. Ashe's at
Throgg's Neck ; a Juniperus squamata, unsurpassed in
any collection, and Siberian arbor vitæ (as they are
called) though probably the Thuja Warreana, and many
other evergreens of matchless size and beauty.

Near Wilmington, Del., is the fine place of Mr. Ship-
ly ; and in the neighborhood of Baltimore, is *Farm-
lands*, the noble estate of G. W. Lurman, Esq., comprising nearly six hundred acres, a large portion of
which is cultivated for agricultural purposes, with very
remunerating success. The mansion, without any architectural pretension, is one of great comfort and extent,
commanding varied views over a fine rolling country to
the city, and adjacent Chesapeake ; a well designed walk
leads from the lawn, shaded by majestic oaks, with a
few fine and effective cedars, to a pretty valley, bordered
by masses and clumps of Rhododendrons, Hollies, Azalias,
and other rare and valuable shrubs and trees ; the whole
terminating in a brilliant French parterre, surmounted
on a terrace by an extensive green-house, in the rear of
which, a gardener's house, a double curvilinear vinery,
a frame-yard with several hundred feet of brick pits, a

well concealed vegetable and fruit garden, complete the modern appliances of a fine country seat.

Hampton, the residence of John Ridgley, Esq., is situated about nine miles north of Baltimore, and belongs more properly to the early edition of this work, than to this supplement, which is intended simply to describe what has been done within ten years. It has been truly said of *Hampton* that it expresses more grandeur than any other place in America. It belongs to the stately order of places almost unknown here at the North, situated as it is in the midst of a domain of six thousand acres. The façade of the house is one hundred and eighty feet in length, with offices attached, erected soon after the Revolution, in 1783.

The entrance hall, of great width and dignity, passes the visitor to the south front, where is a terraced garden of great antiquity, with clipped cedar hedges of most venerable appearance. The formal terraces of exquisitely kept grass, the long rows of superb lemon and orange trees, with the adjacent orangerie and the foreign air of the house, quite disturb ones ideas of republican America.

Clifton Park, near Baltimore, the residence of John Hopkins, Esq., is unquestionably one of the most elaborate places in this country. We remember no other, where in addition to a fine and costly house, there is so large a range of glass, with such diversified and extensive grounds; the varieties of trees, shrubs, walks, lawns, large pieces of ornamental water, containing numerous islands planted with masses of rhododendrons and evergreen shrubs, and connected by appropriate and tasteful bridges, are all, certainly, much in advance of any other place we know.

Lyndhurst, the country seat of Reverdy Johnson, Esq., has a new and very striking house, with a most extended and superb view.

Carroll Manor is another fine old place, like Hampton,

with a turf unbroken for nearly two hundred years, and of the softness and thickness of velvet. *Mondawmin*, the residence of Mr. Brown, is a very attractive place, prettily laid out and planted.

In concluding our remarks on what has been done the past ten years, in various parts of the United States, as illustrating the progress in country life, we insert a short account of the state of Landscape Gardening in Ohio, extracted from a letter of Robert Buchanan, Esq., a well known enthusiast in rural matters, whose tastefully arranged grounds should, undoubtedly, have a place in the list of beautiful residences in the picturesque environs of Cincinnati.

"Landscape Gardening, according to the modern taste in that beautiful art, is of but recent introduction into the West. Previous to the publication of Mr. Downing's valuable book on that subject, the improvements of public and private grounds were made under the direction of the proprietors, or of some gardener who had strayed out to this new country to better his fortune. There was no system—nothing to copy after; and although all were desirous to improve in good taste, they had no guide, until Mr. Downing's work appeared, and that was at once adopted as the text-book. Since that period, the magic wand of the enchanter has passed over the country, and in the vicinity of our cities and towns has transformed the barren hills and vales of their environs into tasteful suburban villas, through the skill of the Landscape Gardener.

"No public or private grounds with any pretensions to elegance, are now undertaken to be improved, without the supervision of a competent master of this art; for no one wishes to have it said, that his improvements were in bad taste.

"In the vicinity of Cincinnati, on the beautiful hills surrounding the city, many fine specimens of well-improved country seats are to be found. Among others, may be mentioned those of R. B. Bowler, Wm. Resor, W. B. Smith, Griffin Taylor, Thos. Sherlock, S. J. Kellogg, and Henry Probasco, of Clifton; W. W. Scarborough, and his neighbors of East Walnut Hills; Miles Greenwood, and others, of Avondale; several on College Hill, in the neighborhood of Farmers' College; and Jacob Hoffner, of Cumminsville, in the valley below.

"In the West, of late years, the establishment of Rural Cemeteries in the vicinity of towns and cities has been introduced with commendable zeal, and with a refining influence on those interested, as well as on the public at large. Among the most prominent of these improvements may be named 'Spring Grove Cemetery,' near Cincinnati; 'Alleghany Cemetery,' near Pittsburgh; 'Bell Fountain,' of St. Louis; 'Cave Hill,' of Louisville; and those of Lexington, Frankfort, Dayton, Columbus, and Cleveland; many of them presenting good specimens of the art of and taste in modern Landscape Gardening.

"The environs of these last-named cities are also adorned with many elegant country residences, too numerous to mention here; but the country seats of John H. Shoenberger, of Pittsburgh; Dr. C. W. Short, of Louisville; and Col. John O'Fallon, of St. Louis, may be given as examples. The latter, for extent and beauty, is excelled by none in the West."

In connection with Landscape Gardening at the West, we feel the importance of impressing upon all planters the great advantage, and even necessity of thick belts and screens of evergreens on the prairies, to shelter orchards, buildings, and stock-yards from the severity of the winter winds.

Mr. Edwards, the Secretary of the Illinois State Horticultural Society, writes us, that in this State, especially in the neighborhood of Lamoille, Bureau County, the following evergreens do well : the White, Gray (Banksiana), Austrian, Cembran, and Scotch pines ; the Red, Black, White, and Norway hemlock spruces ; also, the Red cedar, the Savin, the Swedish and Irish junipers, the Balsam fir, the American and Siberian Arbor vitæ ; that the Pine and Juniper are peculiarly adapted to the high, dry prairies—the Arbor vitæ and Spruce to moist localities ; and that the following varieties have been tried, but *all need protection* in the winter: Araucaria imbricata, Cedar of Lebanon, Pinus excelsa, Pinus maritima, Deodar cedar ; Douglas, Menzies, and Pinsapo spruces ; English and Irish yews, English Silver fir, Chinese and Golden arbor vitæ ; the Tree box, and even the Dwarf box, for edging.

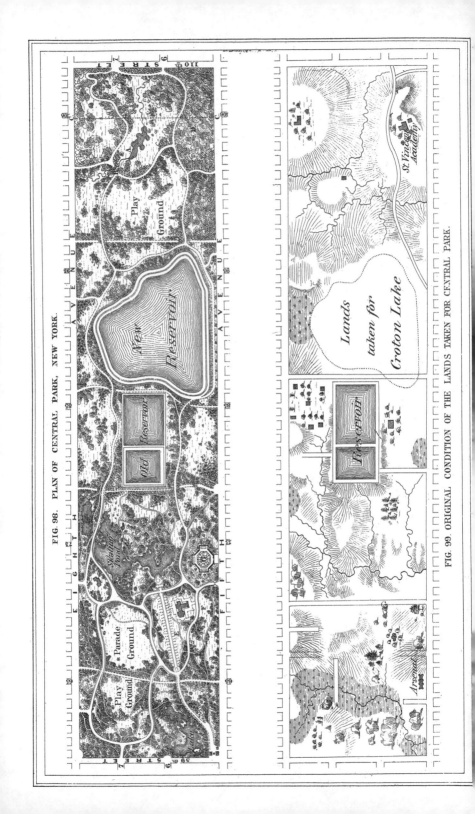

FIG. 98. PLAN OF CENTRAL PARK, NEW YORK.

FIG. 99. ORIGINAL CONDITION OF THE LANDS TAKEN FOR CENTRAL PARK.

SECTION VI.

HISTORICAL NOTICES CONTINUED.

NOT very many years have passed, since from the crowded and confined state of our public Burial Grounds within our large cities, the question of extramural interments excited great and earnest consideration, and eventually led to the establishment of Rural Cemeteries.

The first one of any importance, was that at Laurel Hill, near Philadelphia, a most successful enterprise, mainly due to the taste and perseverance of Mr. John Jay Smith, of that city. This was followed by the one at New Haven; Mount Auburn, near Boston; Greenwood, at New York; Spring Grove, near Cincinnati; two near Baltimore, &c., until there is hardly a city or town of any size in the Union which does not possess its Rural Cemetery.

This was one of those grand improvements in civilization, the importance and necessity of which was so apparent, that it has since been universally adopted, and may be fairly considered now one of our institutions.

Another, and the next great step onward which is now exciting much attention throughout the land, is the establishment of Parks, which may be classified as Public Parks, for the enjoyment of the People of our Cities and larger Towns, as the Central Park in New York, and Hunting Course Park, near Philadelphia; semi-Public Parks, owned and enjoyed by the persons who live around them; and lastly, the Parks, or Ornamental Grounds, attached to our Public Buildings,

Colleges, &c. As illustration, we will give from each
class one example, selecting such as we happen to be
the most familiar with.

The *Central Park*, in New York, being the most
important work of the kind that has been undertaken in
America, some slight reference to its plan and general
intention will be appropriate here, the more especially,
as the editorial articles that appeared in the "Horticulturist," urging its necessity, and setting forth its
advantages, unquestionably exercised an important influence in favor of the project.

The ground set aside for the purpose, consisting of
about 750 acres (represented by the small diagram, Fig.
99), was appropriated by an Act of Legislature, in the
course of the year following Mr. Downing's death. It
was not, however, till the close of 1857, that the actual
purchase of the land was completed. Premiums for designs were at this time offered by the Commissioners
intrusted with the conduct of the enterprise, and early
in June, 1858, the plan (Fig. 98), submitted by Fred.
Law Olmsted, and Calvert Vaux, was adopted by the
Board. The work was at once actively commenced,
under the guidance of the designers, and has since been
steadily pressed forward by the Commission—a force of
over 2,000 men being employed during the most favorable part of the season.

From the published description of the design, and
such other data as have been furnished us, it appears
that the Park is two and-a-half miles long and half a
mile wide. It is divided into two distinct parts by the
old and new Reservoirs—the former a quadrangular
basin of mason-work; the latter, of an irregular curved
outline, with an earth embankment to retain the water.
These two artificial structures occupy a considerable
space, and when complete, will have appropriated
about 150 acres of ground out of the middle of the site;

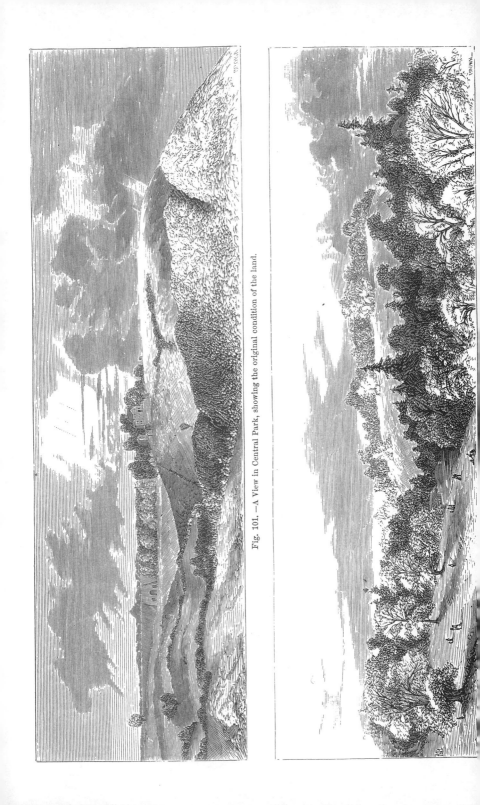

Fig. 101. —A View in Central Park, showing the original condition of the land.

narrow spaces being left on either side, that at certain points become mere connecting links between the upper and lower portions of the Park.

The horizon lines of the upper Park, between the New Reservoir and 106th street, are bold and sweeping, and the slopes have considerable breadth and amplitude in almost every direction in which they may be viewed. This character is, perhaps, taken altogether, the best that can be desired for a park ; and but little alteration of surface is, therefore, needed.

A ravine of considerable extent runs through this section of the Park, in which a small lake (A) may readily be formed, a view of which is given in Fig. 102; and west of this point (B), where the road meets the dip of the two most important hills, a stone bridge is proposed to be erected, so that the main circuit-drive may include in its course a view of all the principal features of interest in the upper Park. The land, for some distance to the north of the boundary line (CC), provided by the Act of the Legislature, should have been included in the original grant, as it commands extensive views that are not obtained within the present limits, and consists of a series of bold and picturesque rocky bluffs, terminating abruptly at 110th street, which offer the only natural boundary to the Park property. The advisability of making this alteration in the line is now evident to all who visit the locality ; and the attention of the city authorities has been, for some time past, drawn to the subject. It is, therefore, quite possible that the northern boundary may soon be advanced to 110th street. This will add about sixty acres to the area of the Park.

On the easterly side of the upper Park it is proposed to plant an American Arboretum (D), so that every one who wishes to do so may become acquainted with the trees and shrubs that will flourish in the open air, in the northern and central parts of our country.

It is not intended to be arranged formally, but so that
it may present all the most beautiful features of lawn
and woodland landscape, preserving, at the same time,
the natural order of families, as far as practicable. In
the event of the extension of the Park to 110th street
being made, the space occupied by the Arboretum
might be considerably enlarged.

The lower Park, between 59th street, and the New
Reservoir, is far more heterogeneous in its character,
and requires a much more varied treatment. Its most
prominent and characteristic feature is the long, rocky
hill-side immediately south of the Old Reservoir ; and
this has been accepted as the central point of landscape
attraction, to which the other ornamental arrangements
of the plan are to be made more or less subservient. A
skating-pond, or lake, of varied outline, and containing
about fifteen acres, surrounds a considerable portion of
the base of this hill, and, in a measure, separates it from
the rest of the lower Park. Expanses of lawn are prepared on the table-land forming the summit of the hill,
and the side is converted into a ramble, with a labyrin-
thine arrangement of foot-paths, leading the visitor
among groves and shrubbery, rivulets, rocks, and glens,
to the prominent points of view that are obtained in this
part of the grounds.

A cavernous passage formed by large, overhanging
rocks has been discovered, and excavated during the
summer, and is an interesting incident heightening the
naturally picturesque character of the ramble.

The Promenade (*E*) is the feature next in importance in
the lower Park. It consists of a broad level walk between double rows of elms. The boundaries are to be
on all sides irregularly planted, so that its formality will
scarcely be perceived, except within itself. Its northern
extremity is finished architecturally, and, as suggested
by the original outline of the surface, is elevated about
twenty feet above the ground immediately to the north,

Fig. 103.—View of Water Terrace in Central Park.

overlooking the hill-side occupied by the ramble, and being connected with the intervening lake by a Water Terrace (see Fig. 103), with which it communicates by flights of stone steps, and also through a spacious corridor passing under one of the carriage-drives.

To the west of the promenade a tract of about twenty-five acres, of nearly level ground, has been prepared, by the removal of rocks and other obstructions, which is intended to be used as a parade-ground.

On the east of the promenade (E), and partially separated from it by an intervening ridge and plateau, is a stretch of pleasantly undulating ground (F), intended to be carefully cultivated and planted with fine shade trees. To the southwest of the promenade is the play-ground, containing now about fourteen acres of levelled surface, overlooked by picturesque rocks that offer ample opportunity for spectators to view the games.

The southern extremity or entrance to the promenade is approached by roads and foot-paths leading from the different gates at the lower end of the Park, and offers a point of concentration and divergence both for pedestrians and those driving. Commencing at this point, a short circuit or *vis-a-vis* drive of a mile is provided around the parade and play-grounds, with branches connecting it with the longer circuit-drive that passes through the whole length of the upper and lower Parks.

Between the Fifth and Sixth Avenue entrances, near the southern boundary of the Park, another lake of about six acres is provided in low ground that is suggestive of such an arrangement.

Around the New Reservoir it is intended to construct a course for riding, and connecting with it, a bridle road is arranged, that commences with the principal entrance gates, and winds through the Park, passing under the roads and foot-paths by bridges, one of which is shown in Fig. 100.

Fig. 100.

Along the westerly side of the Park, for a distance
of nearly two miles, there will be a winter-drive, protected by hardy evergreens; and on the easterly side of
the lake, a Geometric flower-garden (*G*) of considerable
size is proposed, as will be seen on the diagram of plan.
Fig. 99.

In adapting to its present purpose the site selected
for the Park, its situation in the probable future heart
of the city had to be considered, and transverse roads
between the east and west sides of the city were, of
course, demanded. The Park being two and-a-half miles
in length, it was also evident that these transverse roads
would, at no very distant time, become crowded thoroughfares, having nothing in common with the Park
proper, but every way at variance with the agreeable
sentiments it should inspire. Eight times in a single
circuit of the Park, they would oblige a pleasure-drive or

stroll, to encounter a turbid stream of traffic. Each of these roads has, therefore, been so located and arranged on the adopted plan, that it may be carried through the Park on a grade that will allow the pleasure-drives to pass entirely over it at the necessary points of intersection, without any obvious elevation or divergence from their routes. Short tunnels are preferred for this purpose to ordinary bridges, so that the spaces at the sides of the pleasure-drive may be thickly planted, and the view of the city-street below shut out from view. To illustrate still further the treatment of the grounds, we have selected two of the more important points of view (Figs. 101 and 102, 103 and 104), showing the original condition of the land, and the improvements which are contemplated.

In regard to the second description of Parks, we would first remark, that in the United States, the most numerous class from whom the art of Landscape Gardening will receive attention, is composed of persons of moderate means. They are mostly merchants or professional men, who seek a refuge from the confined and unwholesome air of the city, or whose taste leads them to find agreeable recreation in the cultivation and adornment of a country residence; who still maintain their business, or social connection with the adjacent city or town, but whose time and means which can be appropriated to their " place," are more or less limited.

We have, indeed, a rapidly increasing number of men of fortune, whose estates are large enough, and whose means and liberality are adequate for the production of the highest results of the art; but our best efforts must fall far short of the grand effects attainable under the English system of proprietorship, and the great majority of the practical exponents of American Gardening, will always be cultivators of few acres, whose taste, if correctly formed, will lead them to attempt only modest results.

There are many practical difficulties, which every
one must find, who essays to make such country or suburban residences. If the selection of a site is to be
made, the proximity of nuisances, or the danger that
an advancing population from the neighboring city will
soon supply them, renders the task one of much perplexity. The limits of your place, plant as you may,
can not always be concealed, without shutting out the
distant prospect; and all breadth of effect, and grace
of outline, is destroyed by the effort to secure yourself
from present or anticipated annoyances. High boundary
fences, and a separate gate-lodge for each place, seem
necessary for protection from marauders—while the
idea of even a respectable drive over your own ground,
secure from the disagreeable objects of the public highway, is rarely entertained. These difficulties, and many
others, the enthusiastic lover of a country life will
bravely meet, and patiently endure, when they are
insurmountable; but the attempt to overcome them
has been made with apparent success, by the project
before mentioned, of a semi-public, or, as it is, we
believe, called a *Neighborhood Park*. The general
plan on which such an enterprise can be based, may
perhaps, be best elucidated by the history and description of *Llewellyn Park*,* at Orange, New Jersey, in
illustration of which, the engraving on steel (Plate VI.),
presents a view of the entrance. A Plan of the same
is also given in Fig. 105, and the upper and north-
western part of the Park is shown in Fig. 106, the
figures being further explained by the Table of References, page 573.

The site selected for this Park is on the eastern slope
of the Orange mountain, which here forms an inclined

---

* The origin and execution of this valuable scheme, is attributable to
Mr. L. S. Haskell, a merchant of New York, who has enthusiastically devoted
the past three years to the development of this, his favorite idea.

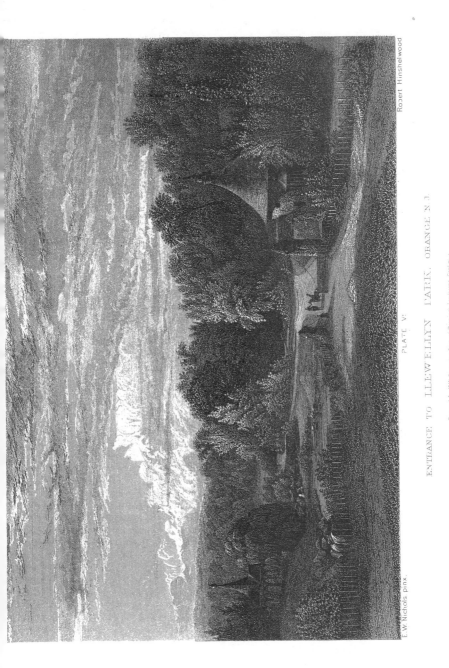

E.W. Nichols. pinx

Robert Hinshelwood

PLATE V.

ENTRANCE TO LLEWELLYN PARK. ORANGE N.J.

Engraved for H.W. Sargent's edition of Downing's Landscape Gardening.

plane, starting from an elevated plateau, on which is the village of Orange, and ascending westerly, at a moderate grade, for about a mile, until surmounted by a rocky cliff of "Trap," which forms the crest of the mountain. The location gives accessibility to New York, by railroad, and to the pleasant village at the base of the mountain. The view from the grounds comprehends the entire area, extending to the city of New York, with a peep of the ocean through the Narrows, on the east; the Highlands of the Hudson on the north; and the receding blue of the New Jersey plains in the south; with the intervening cities, villages, forests, and farms. The tract of land procured for the enterprise, consisted of some 350 acres, mostly of half-cultivated or deserted farms—partly forests of oak, hickory, chestnuts, cedar, and pines.

It will usually be found, as in this case, that the most suitable land for such a project is—from the desirable irregularities of surface, the profusion of rocks and ravines, and its elevated position—the least useful for the agriculturist. That portion of the grounds selected for the Park proper is centrally situated, as regards the whole tract, and in form it is irregular, following the natural indications of the surface—being traversed by a finely wooded ravine, through which flows a brook, affording material for ornamental water and cascades, which have been tastefully made throughout its course. It comprises nearly sixty acres—its greatest length measuring one mile—the entire tract being encompassed by a road which gives access to the surrounding residences; and the other drives made for the convenience of those sites not immediately contiguous to the Park, increase the extent of carriage roads to an aggregate of five miles. The walks, measuring about the same length, lead from the entrance, to the summit of the cliff, and to other interesting parts of the grounds; while at suitable points are kiosks, seats, and bridges, constructed in rustic-work, to be in keeping with the natural character of the surrounding forests. The entrance from the public road is protected by a gate-lodge, and is set back from the highway two hundred and fifty feet; a liberal space here rendering the change from the road to the cultivated grounds of the park less abrupt, and expressing the idea of hospitality. The main avenue from the entrance soon leads the visitor into the ravine, while on either hand diverge the other roads; following Glen Avenue, we emerge from the ravine, by a picturesque turn up the precipitous bank. The somewhat labyrinthian drives which now offer themselves, lead in graceful curves throughout the estate, the unity of which is not marred by interior fences; for though the proprietors are not restricted in this respect by any rule, they have, by common consent, thus far avoided the erection of any barriers, excepting those necessary to enclose the whole tract. The Park itself and all the private places, seem like one large estate, enlivened by the dwellings and embellishments which, at intervals, are seen throughout the vistas of the forest. After making the detour of these grounds, the drive may be continued to other interesting places in the neighborhood, among which is "Eagle Rock," a bold projecting portion of the cliff, commanding a wider scope of the horizon, and more nearly a birds-eye view of the landscape. Around this central tract, especially termed "the Park," the remainder of the property is divided into about fifty villa sites, of from three to ten acres each, the proprietors of which have a joint interest in and common access to the Park, but who possess the sole and unrestricted right to the lot which they may have selected. The fund for the purchase and embellishment of the Park is derived from an assessment on the surrounding sites, of one hundred dollars per acre; and for the maintenance of the Park, and future improvements, an annual assessment is made

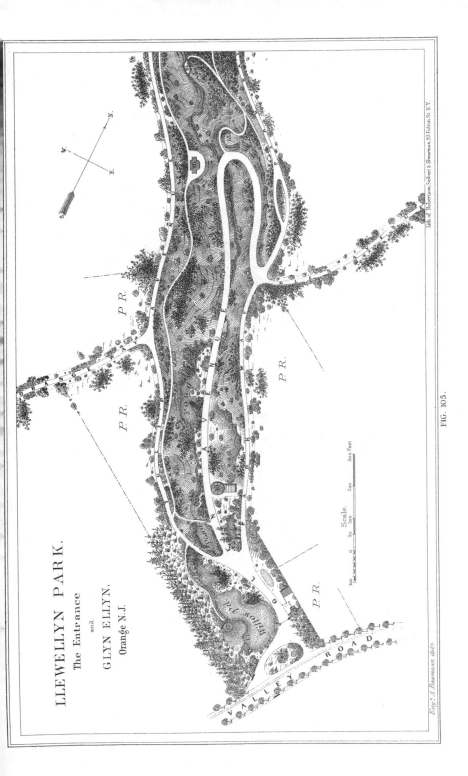

LLEWELLYN PARK.

The Entrance

and

GLYN ELLYN.

Orange N.J.

Scale.

FIG. 105.

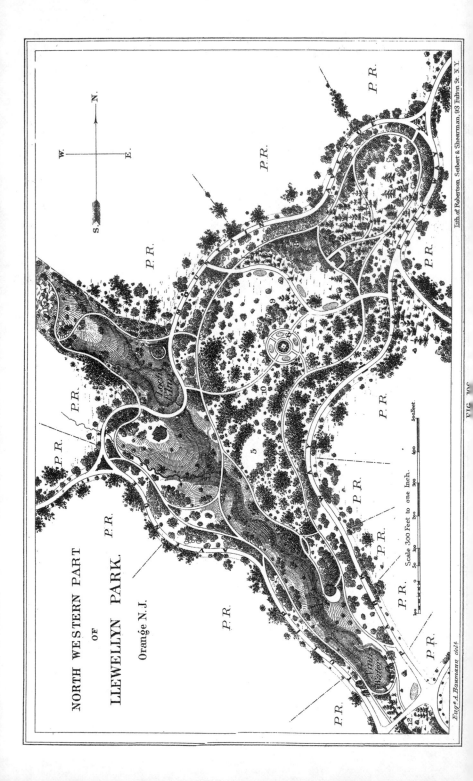

NORTH WESTERN PART
OF
LLEWELLYN PARK.

Orange N.J.

Scale 300 Feet to one Inch.

Eng.d A.Bauman del.t

Lith. of Robertson, Seibert & Shearman, 93 Fulton St. N.Y.

FIG. 705.

by the proprietors, not to exceed ten dollars per acre. The fee of the Park is in three trustees and their successors, and its care and embellishment is entrusted to a "Committee of Management," who are elected annually by the lot owners.

Some of the advantages which are aimed at, in what may be termed the social park, may be thus stated :

1. The securing a neighborhood free from nuisances and an inferior class of buildings.

2. The rural character of the grounds is preserved, instead of assuming the rectangular forms of a village, which are a repetition of city lots on an inferior scale.

3. The different places can be laid out with mutual reference to each other, so that the subdivisions are not apparent in a way detrimental to the general effect.

4. A fine entrance and approach road can be secured, even where the private grounds are small, and the amount appropriated to these embellishments limited.

5. The Park affords extensive drives and walks for the exclusive use of the proprietors, with a variety in the ornamental grounds unattainable on places of ordinary magnitude.

To illustrate the general mode of treatment of the private grounds adjoining the Park, we give, in Figs. 107 and 108, plans of one of the sites of five acres. It is situated on a gentle knoll, and the house, which is in the Tuscan manner, occupies the summit, and commands fine distant views in all directions. The place is laid out in the natural style, by that very clever Landscape Gardener, Mr. Bauman, and an appropriate connection between the house and the surrounding grounds is maintained by an artificial terrace, fifteen feet wide at the top, and ornamented with vases, etc.

The plans may serve, also, to show the method of grouping the trees—their positions, and the varieties used, being given in the Table of References, page 573.

Another phase of improvement in our rural taste is the increasing care and attention bestowed upon the

grounds attached to our colleges, hospitals, and other
public buildings.

Mr. Downing, we think, did much to develop this in
the taste he displayed in the arrangement of the grounds
attached to the Smithsonian Institute and La Fayette
Square, in Washington. We are rapidly passing from the
straight, formal walks, and the rectangular plantations
of the past, into the more harmonious and pleasing
arrangements of the modern school. Clinton Park and
Botanic Garden, which contains within its limits Hamilton College, at Clinton, N. Y., is a very successful illustration of this improvement. Fifteen or twenty acres
have been enclosed within the College Park, and entirely laid out in the most skillful and artistic manner.
Broad and extensive lawns are divided by graceful
walks throughout the whole extent; trees and shrubs,
of every description flourishing in this climate, have been
planted in groups, masses, or as single specimens.

A section of the ground will be used as a Botanic
Garden, in which trees, shrubs, and flowers will be
arranged according to their several families.

The humanizing influence of harmonious and beautiful surroundings upon every one, is beyond all question;
and it was truly said by the Rev. Mr. Gridley, to whose
taste and energy much of the success of the Clinton
Park is due, that "it is no vain thing to suppose that
the minds and hearts of students will be benefited by
daily walks through such grounds, and in view of such
a varied and wide-spread landscape: these peaceful
shades and sunny slopes and laughing streams—this
hum of cheerful industry—the music of distant church
bells, and the glimpses and echoes here caught of the
great thoroughfares of business and travel that mark
the great world without—these skies, ever changing and
ever beautiful, and the seasons rolling through them—
what mind can be brought into the midst of such scenes
without deriving from them essential profit?"

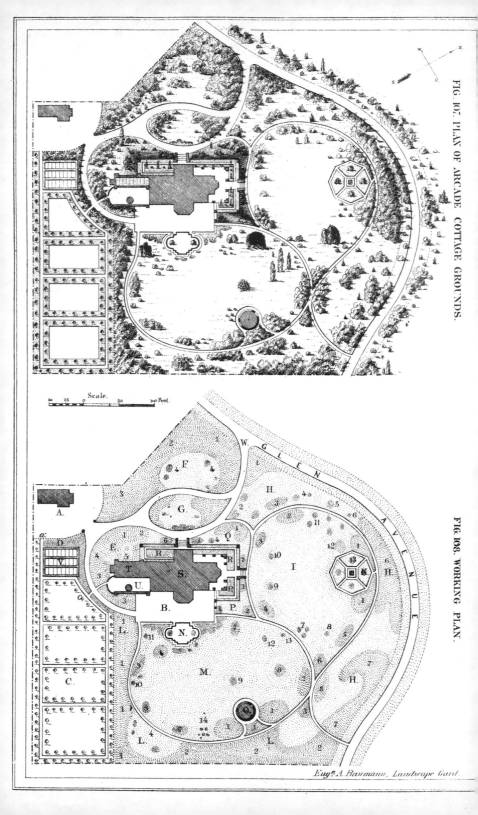

FIG. 107. PLAN OF ARCADE COTTAGE GROUNDS.

FIG. 108. WORKING PLAN.

Scale.

50   25   0   50   100 Feet.

GLEN AVENUE

Eugᵉ A. Baumann, Landscape Gard.

REFERENCES.

EXPLANATION OF REFERENCES FOR FIGURES 105 & 106.

No. 1. Lyceum.
" 2. The Wigwam.
" 3. Summer-house.
" 4.   "   "
" 5. Children's Play-ground.
" 6. Social Circle.
" 7. The Evergreens.
" 8. The Hickories.
" 9. The Chestnuts.
" 10. The Oaks.
" 11. The Rocks.

No. 12. Stone Bridge on Oak Bend.
" 13. The Cascade.
" 14. Gate-lodge.
" 15. Conservatory and Propagating house.
" 16. Prospect Tower.
" 17. The Kiosk.
" 18. Rockwork.
" 19. Ravine Spring.
P. R. Private Residences.

TABLE OF REFERENCES FOR FIGURES 107 & 108.

S. The House.
T. The Conservatory.
R. Grass Terrace.
B. Gravelled Terrace.
W. Approach.
N. Fountain and Jet d'eau, surrounded with beds of flowers.
O. Kiosk, from which is the best view of the house.
K. Rosery, in the centre of which is a suitable place for a statue or vase.
A. Coach-house and Stable.
C. Kitchen-garden, separated from the lawn by a belt of trees, D L L.
E 1. Sugar Maple.
   2. Silver "
   3. Norway "
   4. Lombardy Poplar.
   5. Screen of American Arbor Vitæ.
   6. Group of Rhododendrons.

F 1. Group of White Pines.
   2. Lofty growing trees, near the boundary, Oaks, Maples, and Tulips.
   3. Chinese double-flowering Apple, Kentucky Coffee tree, and Kölreuteria.

H 1, 6, & 7. A large group of trees, both Evergreen and Deciduous, planted on the outskirts of the place.
   2. Acacia Bensoniana.
   3. Group of Euonymus (purple-leaved).
   4. Austrian Pine and Pinus excelsa.
   5. European Weeping Ash.

I 1. Group of low evergreen trees, Yew & Arbor Vitæ.
   2. Group of Mountain Laurels.
   3.   "   of Mahonias.
   4.   "   of Bohemian Olives.

5. Thuja Warreana.
6. Syringa Chinensis.
7. Group of Lindens.
8. A Weeping Willow.
9. Red Flowering Horse-chestnut.
10. Double-white   "   "
11. Hemlock, European Silver Fir, Irish Juniper, and Picea Webbiana, planted singly.
12. Pyrus Japonica.

M 1. Groups of Evergreen Trees.
   2. Syringa grandiflora, Forsythia Viridissima and Kerria Japonica.
   3. Berberis purpurea, Amygdalus pumila, Calicanthus lævigatus, and Deutzia gracilis.
   4. Double-flowering Cherry.
   5. Three single American Silver Firs.
   6. Juniperus communis.
   7. American Weeping Willow.
   8. Magnolia tripetala.
   9. Magnolia Soulangiana.
   10. Deciduous Cypress and Ginko.
   11. Purple-leaved Beech.
   12. Paulownia imperialis.
   13. Judas Tree and Amer. Nettle Tree.
   14. Spireas.

P 1. Group of six Mahonias.
   2.   "   of Rhododendrons.
   3.   "   of Kalmias and Epigea repens.

Q 1. Group of Roses, Spireas, and Weigolias.
   2. Azalias.
   3. Rhododendrons.
   4. Magnolia purpurea.

U Yard and Well.

GENERAL INDEX.

A CATALOG OF SELECTED
DOVER BOOKS
IN ALL FIELDS OF INTEREST

A CATALOG OF SELECTED DOVER BOOKS IN ALL FIELDS OF INTEREST

DRAWINGS OF REMBRANDT, edited by Seymour Slive. Updated Lippmann, Hofstede de Groot edition, with definitive scholarly apparatus. All portraits, biblical sketches, landscapes, nudes. Oriental figures, classical studies, together with selection of work by followers. 550 illustrations. Total of 630pp. 9⅛ × 12¼.
21485-0, 21486-9 Pa., Two-vol. set $29.90

GHOST AND HORROR STORIES OF AMBROSE BIERCE, Ambrose Bierce. 24 tales vividly imagined, strangely prophetic, and decades ahead of their time in technical skill: "The Damned Thing," "An Inhabitant of Carcosa," "The Eyes of the Panther," "Moxon's Master," and 20 more. 199pp. 5⅜ × 8½. 20767-6 Pa. $3.95

ETHICAL WRITINGS OF MAIMONIDES, Maimonides. Most significant ethical works of great medieval sage, newly translated for utmost precision, readability. Laws Concerning Character Traits, Eight Chapters, more. 192pp. 5⅜ × 8½.
24522-5 Pa. $4.50

THE EXPLORATION OF THE COLORADO RIVER AND ITS CANYONS, J. W. Powell. Full text of Powell's 1,000-mile expedition down the fabled Colorado in 1869. Superb account of terrain, geology, vegetation, Indians, famine, mutiny, treacherous rapids, mighty canyons, during exploration of last unknown part of continental U.S. 400pp. 5⅜ × 8½. 20094-9 Pa. $7.95

HISTORY OF PHILOSOPHY, Julián Marías. Clearest one-volume history on the market. Every major philosopher and dozens of others, to Existentialism and later. 505pp. 5⅜ × 8½. 21739-6 Pa. $9.95

ALL ABOUT LIGHTNING, Martin A. Uman. Highly readable non-technical survey of nature and causes of lightning, thunderstorms, ball lightning, St. Elmo's Fire, much more. Illustrated. 192pp. 5⅜ × 8½. 25237-X Pa. $5.95

SAILING ALONE AROUND THE WORLD, Captain Joshua Slocum. First man to sail around the world, alone, in small boat. One of great feats of seamanship told in delightful manner. 67 illustrations. 294pp. 5⅜ × 8½. 20326-3 Pa. $4.95

LETTERS AND NOTES ON THE MANNERS, CUSTOMS AND CONDITIONS OF THE NORTH AMERICAN INDIANS, George Catlin. Classic account of life among Plains Indians: ceremonies, hunt, warfare, etc. 312 plates. 572pp. of text. 6⅛ × 9¼. 22118-0, 22119-9, Pa. Two-vol. set $17.90

ALASKA: The Harriman Expedition, 1899, John Burroughs, John Muir, et al. Informative, engrossing accounts of two-month, 9,000-mile expedition. Native peoples, wildlife, forests, geography, salmon industry, glaciers, more. Profusely illustrated. 240 black-and-white line drawings. 124 black-and-white photographs. 3 maps. Index. 576pp. 5⅜ × 8½. 25109-8 Pa. $11.95

CATALOG OF DOVER BOOKS

ILLUSTRATED GUIDE TO SHAKER FURNITURE, Robert Meader. All furniture and appurtenances, with much on unknown local styles. 235 photos. 146pp. 9 × 12.   22819-3 Pa. $8.95

WHALE SHIPS AND WHALING: A Pictorial Survey, George Francis Dow. Over 200 vintage engravings, drawings, photographs of barks, brigs, cutters, other vessels. Also harpoons, lances, whaling guns, many other artifacts. Comprehensive text by foremost authority. 207 black-and-white illustrations. 288pp. 6 × 9.
24808-9 Pa. $8.95

THE BERTRAMS, Anthony Trollope. Powerful portrayal of blind self-will and thwarted ambition includes one of Trollope's most heartrending love stories. 497pp. 5⅜ × 8½.   25119-5 Pa. $9.95

ADVENTURES WITH A HAND LENS, Richard Headstrom. Clearly written guide to observing and studying flowers and grasses, fish scales, moth and insect wings, egg cases, buds, feathers, seeds, leaf scars, moss, molds, ferns, common crystals, etc.—all with an ordinary, inexpensive magnifying glass. 209 exact line drawings aid in your discoveries. 220pp. 5⅜ × 8½.   23330-8 Pa. $4.95

RODIN ON ART AND ARTISTS, Auguste Rodin. Great sculptor's candid, wide-ranging comments on meaning of art; great artists; relation of sculpture to poetry, painting, music; philosophy of life, more. 76 superb black-and-white illustrations of Rodin's sculpture, drawings and prints. 119pp. 8⅜ × 11¼.   24487-3 Pa. $7.95

FIFTY CLASSIC FRENCH FILMS, 1912–1982: A Pictorial Record, Anthony Slide. Memorable stills from Grand Illusion, Beauty and the Beast, Hiroshima, Mon Amour, many more. Credits, plot synopses, reviews, etc. 160pp. 8¼ × 11.
25256-6 Pa. $11.95

THE PRINCIPLES OF PSYCHOLOGY, William James. Famous long course complete, unabridged. Stream of thought, time perception, memory, experimental methods; great work decades ahead of its time. 94 figures. 1,391pp. 5⅜ × 8½.
20381-6, 20382-4 Pa., Two-vol. set $23.90

BODIES IN A BOOKSHOP, R. T. Campbell. Challenging mystery of blackmail and murder with ingenious plot and superbly drawn characters. In the best tradition of British suspense fiction. 192pp. 5⅜ × 8½.   24720-1 Pa. $3.95

CALLAS: PORTRAIT OF A PRIMA DONNA, George Jellinek. Renowned commentator on the musical scene chronicles incredible career and life of the most controversial, fascinating, influential operatic personality of our time. 64 black-and-white photographs. 416pp. 5⅜ × 8¼.   25047-4 Pa. $8.95

GEOMETRY, RELATIVITY AND THE FOURTH DIMENSION, Rudolph Rucker. Exposition of fourth dimension, concepts of relativity as Flatland characters continue adventures. Popular, easily followed yet accurate, profound. 141 illustrations. 133pp. 5⅜ × 8½.   23400-2 Pa. $4.95

HOUSEHOLD STORIES BY THE BROTHERS GRIMM, with pictures by Walter Crane. 53 classic stories—Rumpelstiltskin, Rapunzel, Hansel and Gretel, the Fisherman and his Wife, Snow White, Tom Thumb, Sleeping Beauty, Cinderella, and so much more—lavishly illustrated with original 19th century drawings. 114 illustrations. x + 269pp. 5⅜ × 8½.   21080-4 Pa. $4.95

CATALOG OF DOVER BOOKS

THE BLUE FAIRY BOOK, Andrew Lang. The first, most famous collection, with many familiar tales: Little Red Riding Hood, Aladdin and the Wonderful Lamp, Puss in Boots, Sleeping Beauty, Hansel and Gretel, Rumpelstiltskin; 37 in all. 138 illustrations. 390pp. 5⅜ × 8½. 21437-0 Pa. $6.95

THE STORY OF THE CHAMPIONS OF THE ROUND TABLE, Howard Pyle. Sir Launcelot, Sir Tristram and Sir Percival in spirited adventures of love and triumph retold in Pyle's inimitable style. 50 drawings, 31 full-page. xviii + 329pp. 6½ × 9¼. 21883-X Pa. $7.95

AUDUBON AND HIS JOURNALS, Maria Audubon. Unmatched two-volume portrait of the great artist, naturalist and author contains his journals, an excellent biography by his granddaughter, expert annotations by the noted ornithologist, Dr. Elliott Coues, and 37 superb illustrations. Total of 1,200pp. 5⅜ × 8.
Vol. I 25143-8 Pa. $8.95
Vol. II 25144-6 Pa. $8.95

GREAT DINOSAUR HUNTERS AND THEIR DISCOVERIES, Edwin H. Colbert. Fascinating, lavishly illustrated chronicle of dinosaur research, 1820's to 1960. Achievements of Cope, Marsh, Brown, Buckland, Mantell, Huxley, many others. 384pp. 5¼ × 8¼. 24701-5 Pa. $7.95

THE TASTEMAKERS, Russell Lynes. Informal, illustrated social history of American taste 1850's–1950's. First popularized categories Highbrow, Lowbrow, Middlebrow. 129 illustrations. New (1979) afterword. 384pp. 6 × 9.
23993-4 Pa. $8.95

DOUBLE CROSS PURPOSES, Ronald A. Knox. A treasure hunt in the Scottish Highlands, an old map, unidentified corpse, surprise discoveries keep reader guessing in this cleverly intricate tale of financial skullduggery. 2 black-and-white maps. 320pp. 5⅜ × 8½. (Available in U.S. only) 25032-6 Pa. $6.95

AUTHENTIC VICTORIAN DECORATION AND ORNAMENTATION IN FULL COLOR: 46 Plates from "Studies in Design," Christopher Dresser. Superb full-color lithographs reproduced from rare original portfolio of a major Victorian designer. 48pp. 9¼ × 12¼. 25083-0 Pa. $7.95

PRIMITIVE ART, Franz Boas. Remains the best text ever prepared on subject, thoroughly discussing Indian, African, Asian, Australian, and, especially, Northern American primitive art. Over 950 illustrations show ceramics, masks, totem poles, weapons, textiles, paintings, much more. 376pp. 5⅜ × 8. 20025-6 Pa. $7.95

SIDELIGHTS ON RELATIVITY, Albert Einstein. Unabridged republication of two lectures delivered by the great physicist in 1920–21. *Ether and Relativity* and *Geometry and Experience*. Elegant ideas in non-mathematical form, accessible to intelligent layman. vi + 56pp. 5⅜ × 8½. 24511-X Pa. $2.95

THE WIT AND HUMOR OF OSCAR WILDE, edited by Alvin Redman. More than 1,000 ripostes, paradoxes, wisecracks: Work is the curse of the drinking classes, I can resist everything except temptation, etc. 258pp. 5⅜ × 8½. 20602-5 Pa. $4.95

ADVENTURES WITH A MICROSCOPE, Richard Headstrom. 59 adventures with clothing fibers, protozoa, ferns and lichens, roots and leaves, much more. 142 illustrations. 232pp. 5⅜ × 8½. 23471-1 Pa. $3.95

A CONCISE HISTORY OF PHOTOGRAPHY: Third Revised Edition, Helmut Gernsheim. Best one-volume history—camera obscura, photochemistry, daguerreotypes, evolution of cameras, film, more. Also artistic aspects—landscape, portraits, fine art, etc. 281 black-and-white photographs. 26 in color. 176pp. 8⅜ × 11¼. 25128-4 Pa. $13.95

THE DORÉ BIBLE ILLUSTRATIONS, Gustave Doré. 241 detailed plates from the Bible: the Creation scenes, Adam and Eve, Flood, Babylon, battle sequences, life of Jesus, etc. Each plate is accompanied by the verses from the King James version of the Bible. 241pp. 9 × 12. 23004-X Pa. $9.95

HUGGER-MUGGER IN THE LOUVRE, Elliot Paul. Second Homer Evans mystery-comedy. Theft at the Louvre involves sleuth in hilarious, madcap caper. "A knockout."—Books. 336pp. 5⅜ × 8½. 25185-3 Pa. $5.95

FLATLAND, E. A. Abbott. Intriguing and enormously popular science-fiction classic explores the complexities of trying to survive as a two-dimensional being in a three-dimensional world. Amusingly illustrated by the author. 16 illustrations. 103pp. 5⅜ × 8½. 20001-9 Pa. $2.50

THE HISTORY OF THE LEWIS AND CLARK EXPEDITION, Meriwether Lewis and William Clark, edited by Elliott Coues. Classic edition of Lewis and Clark's day-by-day journals that later became the basis for U.S. claims to Oregon and the West. Accurate and invaluable geographical, botanical, biological, meteorological and anthropological material. Total of 1,508pp. 5⅜ × 8½.
21268-8, 21269-6, 21270-X Pa. Three-vol. set $26.85

LANGUAGE, TRUTH AND LOGIC, Alfred J. Ayer. Famous, clear introduction to Vienna, Cambridge schools of Logical Positivism. Role of philosophy, elimination of metaphysics, nature of analysis, etc. 160pp. 5⅜ × 8½. (Available in U.S. and Canada only) 20010-8 Pa. $3.95

MATHEMATICS FOR THE NONMATHEMATICIAN, Morris Kline. Detailed, college-level treatment of mathematics in cultural and historical context, with numerous exercises. For liberal arts students. Preface. Recommended Reading Lists. Tables. Index. Numerous black-and-white figures. xvi + 641pp. 5⅜ × 8½.
24823-2 Pa. $11.95

HANDBOOK OF PICTORIAL SYMBOLS, Rudolph Modley. 3,250 signs and symbols, many systems in full; official or heavy commercial use. Arranged by subject. Most in Pictorial Archive series. 143pp. 8⅛ × 11. 23357-X Pa. $6.95

INCIDENTS OF TRAVEL IN YUCATAN, John L. Stephens. Classic (1843) exploration of jungles of Yucatan, looking for evidences of Maya civilization. Travel adventures, Mexican and Indian culture, etc. Total of 669pp. 5⅜ × 8½.
20926-1, 20927-X Pa., Two-vol. set $11.90

CATALOG OF DOVER BOOKS

DEGAS: An Intimate Portrait, Ambroise Vollard. Charming, anecdotal memoir by famous art dealer of one of the greatest 19th-century French painters. 14 black-and-white illustrations. Introduction by Harold L. Van Doren. 96pp. 5⅜ × 8½.
25131-4 Pa. $4.95

PERSONAL NARRATIVE OF A PILGRIMAGE TO ALMANDINAH AND MECCAH, Richard Burton. Great travel classic by remarkably colorful personality. Burton, disguised as a Moroccan, visited sacred shrines of Islam, narrowly escaping death. 47 illustrations. 959pp. 5⅜ × 8½. 21217-3, 21218-1 Pa., Two-vol. set $19.90

PHRASE AND WORD ORIGINS, A. H. Holt. Entertaining, reliable, modern study of more than 1,200 colorful words, phrases, origins and histories. Much unexpected information. 254pp. 5⅜ × 8½. 20758-7 Pa. $5.95

THE RED THUMB MARK, R. Austin Freeman. In this first Dr. Thorndyke case, the great scientific detective draws fascinating conclusions from the nature of a single fingerprint. Exciting story, authentic science. 320pp. 5⅜ × 8½. (Available in U.S. only) 25210-8 Pa. $6.95

AN EGYPTIAN HIEROGLYPHIC DICTIONARY, E. A. Wallis Budge. Monumental work containing about 25,000 words or terms that occur in texts ranging from 3000 B.C. to 600 A.D. Each entry consists of a transliteration of the word, the word in hieroglyphs, and the meaning in English. 1,314pp. 6⅜ × 10.
23615-3, 23616-1 Pa., Two-vol. set $31.90

THE COMPLEAT STRATEGYST: Being a Primer on the Theory of Games of Strategy, J. D. Williams. Highly entertaining classic describes, with many illustrated examples, how to select best strategies in conflict situations. Prefaces. Appendices. xvi + 268pp. 5⅜ × 8½. 25101-2 Pa. $5.95

THE ROAD TO OZ, L. Frank Baum. Dorothy meets the Shaggy Man, little Button-Bright and the Rainbow's beautiful daughter in this delightful trip to the magical Land of Oz. 272pp. 5⅜ × 8. 25208-6 Pa. $5.95

POINT AND LINE TO PLANE, Wassily Kandinsky. Seminal exposition of role of point, line, other elements in non-objective painting. Essential to understanding 20th-century art. 127 illustrations. 192pp. 6½ × 9¼. 23808-3 Pa. $5.95

LADY ANNA, Anthony Trollope. Moving chronicle of Countess Lovel's bitter struggle to win for herself and daughter Anna their rightful rank and fortune—perhaps at cost of sanity itself. 384pp. 5⅜ × 8½. 24669-8 Pa. $8.95

EGYPTIAN MAGIC, E. A. Wallis Budge. Sums up all that is known about magic in Ancient Egypt: the role of magic in controlling the gods, powerful amulets that warded off evil spirits, scarabs of immortality, use of wax images, formulas and spells, the secret name, much more. 253pp. 5⅜ × 8½. 22681-6 Pa. $4.50

THE DANCE OF SIVA, Ananda Coomaraswamy. Preeminent authority unfolds the vast metaphysic of India: the revelation of her art, conception of the universe, social organization, etc. 27 reproductions of art masterpieces. 192pp. 5⅜ × 8½.
24817-8 Pa. $5.95

CATALOG OF DOVER BOOKS

AMERICAN CLIPPER SHIPS: 1833–1858, Octavius T. Howe & Frederick C. Matthews. Fully-illustrated, encyclopedic review of 352 clipper ships from the period of America's greatest maritime supremacy. Introduction. 109 halftones. 5 black-and-white line illustrations. Index. Total of 928pp. 5⅜ × 8½.
25115-2, 25116-0 Pa., Two-vol. set $17.90

TOWARDS A NEW ARCHITECTURE, Le Corbusier. Pioneering manifesto by great architect, near legendary founder of "International School." Technical and aesthetic theories, views on industry, economics, relation of form to function, "mass-production spirit," much more. Profusely illustrated. Unabridged translation of 13th French edition. Introduction by Frederick Etchells. 320pp. 6⅛ × 9¼.
(Available in U.S. only) 25023-7 Pa. $8.95

THE BOOK OF KELLS, edited by Blanche Cirker. Inexpensive collection of 32 full-color, full-page plates from the greatest illuminated manuscript of the Middle Ages, painstakingly reproduced from rare facsimile edition. Publisher's Note. Captions. 32pp. 9⅜ × 12¼. 24345-1 Pa. $4.95

BEST SCIENCE FICTION STORIES OF H. G. WELLS, H. G. Wells. Full novel *The Invisible Man,* plus 17 short stories: "The Crystal Egg," "Aepyornis Island," "The Strange Orchid," etc. 303pp. 5⅜ × 8½. (Available in U.S. only)
21531-8 Pa. $6.95

AMERICAN SAILING SHIPS: Their Plans and History, Charles G. Davis. Photos, construction details of schooners, frigates, clippers, other sailcraft of 18th to early 20th centuries—plus entertaining discourse on design, rigging, nautical lore, much more. 137 black-and-white illustrations. 240pp. 6⅛ × 9¼.
24658-2 Pa. $6.95

ENTERTAINING MATHEMATICAL PUZZLES, Martin Gardner. Selection of author's favorite conundrums involving arithmetic, money, speed, etc., with lively commentary. Complete solutions. 112pp. 5⅜ × 8½. 25211-6 Pa. $2.95

THE WILL TO BELIEVE, HUMAN IMMORTALITY, William James. Two books bound together. Effect of irrational on logical, and arguments for human immortality. 402pp. 5⅜ × 8½. 20291-7 Pa. $7.95

THE HAUNTED MONASTERY and THE CHINESE MAZE MURDERS, Robert Van Gulik. 2 full novels by Van Gulik continue adventures of Judge Dee and his companions. An evil Taoist monastery, seemingly supernatural events; overgrown topiary maze that hides strange crimes. Set in 7th-century China. 27 illustrations. 328pp. 5⅜ × 8½. 23502-5 Pa. $6.95

CELEBRATED CASES OF JUDGE DEE (DEE GOONG AN), translated by Robert Van Gulik. Authentic 18th-century Chinese detective novel; Dee and associates solve three interlocked cases. Led to Van Gulik's own stories with same characters. Extensive introduction. 9 illustrations. 237pp. 5⅜ × 8½.
23337-5 Pa. $4.95

Prices subject to change without notice.
Available at your book dealer or write for free catalog to Dept. GI, Dover Publications, Inc., 31 East 2nd St., Mineola, N.Y. 11501. Dover publishes more than 175 books each year on science, elementary and advanced mathematics, biology, music, art, literary history, social sciences and other areas.